People Building Peace
35 Inspiring Stories from Around the World

People Building Peace

35 Inspiring Stories from Around the World

A publication of the European Centre for Conflict Prevention, in cooperation with the International Fellowship of Reconciliation (IFOR) and the Coexistence Initiative of State of the World Forum.

Financially supported by the **Swedish International Development Cooperation Agency** (Sida) and **The Abraham Fund**.

1999
European Centre for Conflict Prevention
P.O. Box 14069
3508 SC Utrecht
The Netherlands

e-mail: euconflict@euconflict.org
website: www.euconflict.org

© 1999, European Centre for Conflict Prevention

ISBN 90 57 27 029 3

Editing and Production Bureau M&O, Amsterdam
Set and designed by Karel Meijer
Cover-photography by Henny van der Graaf (Flame of Peace, Mali), Hague Appeal for Peace
(Archbishop Desmond Tutu) and City Montessori School, India (school class)

Contents

Acknowledgements

It took seven months and the dedication of a large number of individuals to produce 'People Building Peace'. We take the opportunity here to extend our sincere thanks to all the committed, hard-working people who made this publication possible.

Three organisations cooperated in this project, IFOR (International Fellowship of Reconciliation), the Coexistence Initiative of State of the World Forum and the European Centre for Conflict Prevention, who coordinated the project. We thank Kumar Rupesinghe director of the Coexistence Initiative, Anke Kooke, secretary-general of IFOR, David Grant, Jan Schaake and Shelley Anderson of IFOR, for their cooperation.

The ideas for the project were given a boost at the State of the World Forum in November 1998 in San Francisco, where it was discussed at the workshop on 'Coexistence and Communitybuilding', co-moderated by Susan Collin Marks and Kumar Rupesinghe.

Several participants at that Coexistence workshop expressed their willingness to contribute to this book: Alan Slifka, Prof. Mari Fitzduff, Prof. Hizkias Assefa, Georges Berthoin, Edy Kaufman and Peter Gastrow. Other valuable contributions came from Prof. John Paul Lederach, Michelle Parlevliet, Louise Diamond, Prof. Manuel Hassassian, Prof. Benjamin Yanoov, Marigold Bentley, Jordana Friedman and Nick Killick, John Ungerleider, Theuns Eloff, and Helen Gould.

The introductory articles to the case-studies were mostly written by experienced and specialised journalists such as Colleen Scott, Jos Havermans, Johan van Workum, Maaike Miedema, Kees Epskamp, Marc Broere, and Hans van de Veen.

Numerous cases were presented to us from all around the world and we are indebted to all the organisations and individuals who sent us information about their activities relevant to this project.

We have collaborated with Hans van de Veen and his Bureau M&O for a number of years and the relationship has always been a source of great pleasure. Time pressures and the problems of co-ordinating 35 case-studies gathered from around the world made the job of editing and production more difficult than on earlier projects. But Hans managed it with his customary aplomb, for which we offer him our deepest thanks.

Through Bureau M&O, many people have contributed to this book. Besides Karel Meijer (layout) and Niall Martin (English copy corrections), mention must be made of the many journalists who transformed the avalanche of data into concise case-studies. Fitzroy Nation (former editor of the Third World press agency IPS) was responsible for writing a substantial number of the 35 stories. Other 'inspiring stories' were written by Jim Wake, Tjitske Lingsma, Brigitte Ars, Maaike Miedema, Menno Bosma, Elvis Ndubuisi Iruh, Niala Maharaj, and Colleen Scott.

Juliette Verhoeven, project officer at the European Centre, has worked on the project full-time since September and demonstrated enormous commitment in collecting information on different peace-building initiatives from around the world. Due to her dedication it was possible to organise this complex and ambitious project in such a short time frame. Mirjam Pliester collected the photo material and provided assistance in the organisation of this book.

We are also indebted to SIDA (Swedish International Development Agency) and The Abraham Fund, which provided financial support, as well as Minister Pierre Schori, and UNESCO's Director-General Federico Mayor, who graciously agreed to write the preface and the introduction. The prompt decision of SIDA to support us made this publication possible in a very short time frame.

PAUL VAN TONGEREN
Executive Director European Centre for Conflict Prevention
Co-ordinator of the project

Introductions

Inspiring Stories of Peace-building

By Paul van Tongeren*

'This conference could augur well for the coming century. It would unite into one mighty whole the efforts of all States sincerely striving to make the great idea of universal peace triumph over strife and discord.' Count Mikhail Nikolayevich Muravyov, Russia's Foreign Minister, expressed the hopes of many when he spoke of the prospects for peace at the First Hague International Peace Conference in 1899.

One hundred years later we know these hopes to have been in vain. The first international gathering to promote world peace - the event brought together representatives of 26 countries - proved incapable of stopping Europe and the world from marching toward the general war that was the opening event of what British historian Eric Hobsbawm has called 'the age of extremes.' The 20th century was to become the most violent of all ages in history, unprecedented in the scale and intensity of killing and destruction. [1]

One of the considerations that played a part in the birth of this book was the fact that, exactly one hundred years after the First Hague International Peace Conference, a large scale global conference will be organised by The Hague Appeal for Peace in The Hague (the Netherlands, May 1116). A few days earlier, an international gathering will take place in Belfast, Northern Ireland, organised by the Coexistence Initiative of the State of the World Forum. The conference (Diversity and Community in a Global Context: Learning from Europe) will deal with creating a greater understanding of the issues of coexistence and community building.

With 'People Building Peace', due to be presented at the conferences in Belfast and in The Hague, we aim to promote these issues which are crucial global challenges for the 21st century. The initiative for this publication was taken by the European Centre for Conflict Prevention, together with IFOR (International Fellowship of Reconciliation) and the Coexistence Initiative of the State of the World Forum.

One could argue, however, that the need to organise these events makes clear that not much has changed. At the end of the century, the world seems to be more insecure than ever before. Deadly conflict has become a prominent feature of the transition period from the Cold War to the 21st century. With over 30 active internal conflicts and scores more potential trouble spots within and between states, the international community is anxiously asking itself whether and how such deadly conflicts can be prevented.

Searching for an answer to these questions, the group of prominent people who produced the Carnegie Commission's 'Preventing Deadly Conflict' report[2] came to this conclusion: 'First, deadly conflict is not inevitable. Second, the need to prevent deadly conflict is increasingly urgent. Third, preventing deadly conflict is possible.'

The prevention of deadly conflict, the report argues, 'is over the long term, too hard intellectually, technically, and politically to be the responsibility of any single institution or government, no matter how powerful. Strengths must be pooled, burdens shared, and labour divided among actors.'

The time was not ripe for this kind of approach at the first Hague conference. But it is now! Modern foreign policy is no longer the monopoly of very small groups of statesmen and diplomats. Gone are the days when diplomats could conduct policies of which the citizens were unaware.

In the past decade the number of peacebuilders working at all levels of society in places of ethnic and civil conflicts around the world, has mushroomed. The contribution of civilians, whether working from the bottom up or the top down, to resolving the conflicts of our time can no longer be ignored. Churches, women's organisations, the media, and business have all demonstrated their potential for building peace. So too the role of education, the arts and sports is gaining increasing recognition. 'Multitrack diplomacy', as it is called, is flourishing, and provides a major reason for hope of a more peaceful world.

This hope is rooted, as one of the great thinkers on peace-building and reconciliation, John Paul Lederach, writes in this book, 'in the resiliency of people (...) who, in spite of decades of obstacles and violence, keep taking steps toward peaceful coexistence with their enemies.' Hope is also rooted in the fact that the second half of the 20th Century, though rife with violent conflict, 'engendered the most prolific advancement of non-violent conflict transformation activities systematically known in human history, setting the stage for a potential singularity of peace-building in the 21st Century.'

In this book the reader will find many excellent examples of the valuable and frequently successful, initiatives taken by citizens of many countries, to resolve conflict, to prevent violence, and to reconcile parties that have been at war. Apart from introductory chapters written by experts in their particular fields, the book also presents a global overview of the most important organisations.
Aiming at a broad audience, we have chosen to employ a journalistic approach. Almost all of these casestudies have been written by journalists, on the basis of their independent research and documents from the organisations involved. We hope to have given credit to all actors involved, especially in projects initiated by Northern organisations in Southern countries where information was sometimes hard to find.

People from all around the world have contributed to this publication. That cultural diversity is reflected in both the content and the style of the articles you will find collected in this book.

It has not been our aim to promote certain projects or programmes at the expense of others. What we were looking for were 'real-life stories', which give a true account of the possibilities of peace-building by small groups or even individuals, without down-playing the many difficulties involved. We hope the readers will gain more insight into the potential as well as the possibilities of the several tracks involved. We aim to inspire people and local communities working for peace and to support the work of educators, policy makers and international networks. Our intention is to raise the profile of the subject, provide links to organisations dealing with conflict resolution, citizenship, democracy and the longterm promotion of coexistence, peace-building and reconciliation.

Of course, one could argue that despite all efforts for peace in countries like Israel/Palestine, Bosnia or Angola peace is still a very distant dream. We should however realise that peace is a process, to which many of the initiatives described here have given an impetus, relatively small sometimes, but still meaningful. The building of peace is a multiparty effort, including setbacks as well as inspiring steps in the right direction. We should try to learn from both of these!

One of the lessons which can be learned from the inspiring developments in countries like South Africa and Northern Ireland to mention two peace processes which are extensively covered in this publication, is the importance of a coherent and integrated effort involving as many tracks as possible. The multiplier effect which is created this way greatly enhances the chances for sustainable peace. The People to People Programme in Israel is another example of the importance of building peace at the governmental level as well as within the community at the same time.

The potential contribution to conflict resolution, peace-building and reconciliation of some of the sectors described here, is still relatively unknown. Arts and cultural activities as well as sports are tracks that offer many possibilities, amongst other reasons, because of the wide public they are able to reach. Also relatively unknown is the peace-building potential of a powerful segment of society, the corporate sector. Peace is profitable. A fact that has come to be realised by the business communities in South Africa and Northern Ireland. We can only hope that the management of many more companies, Chambers of Commerce, etc. will come to the conclusion that they too can play an important role in the transition from violence to peace and democracy.

Another thing we can learn from the stories presented here is that 'ordinary people' as well as minority groups can make a difference. By means of their creative approaches, their perseverance and compassion, many individuals around the world have succeeded in transforming apparently hopeless situations. We are able to achieve much more than we are sometimes inclined to think!

We feel that, apart from anything else, these case-studies clearly illustrate the potential of multitrack diplomacy. A substantial additional investment in these kinds of initiatives – which in many cases are relatively inexpensive would greatly enhance the chances for peace in many places around the world. To stimulate this, more publicity is a prerequisite. We aim to contribute to the making of video documentaries of several of these cases for television broadcast as we believe this is the way to really reach and inspire large audiences. We should also mention here the decision to produce a Swedish-language edition of this publication. We hope more translations will follow and contribute to the aim of reaching as many people as possible.

The response to our initiative in publishing this collection of inspiring stories, has been overwhelming. At the same time, we have noticed how hard it was in many cases to collect the necessary information. Some of the cases presented here have never previously been described! That is why we have already decided to further pursue this initiative by publishing another collection of peace-building stories in the near future. All suggestions of cases which could be included in this second edition are welcome (preferably before the end of this year). We are especially interested in examples of peace-building in sectors which are not included in this edition, like youth organisations, exchange programmes, trade unions, the academic world, the military, etc.

The two international events previously mentioned provided the direct impetus for this publication. However, we hope the influence of this publication extends beyond the immediate context of its birth. Recently the UN launched the International Year for a Culture of Peace in 2000 and the International Decade for a Culture of Peace and Nonviolence in 2001-2010. We feel that these occasions should be used by people and organisations worldwide to invest in this 'culture of peace'. We sincerely hope this publication will inspire many people to invest in peace-building and create a true culture of peace as we enter the next century. In a way, we owe this to our predecessors.

Notes
1 Ending Violent Conflict, Michael Renner. In: State of the World 1999, Worldwatch Institute.
2 Preventing Deadly Conflict - Final Report of the Carnegie Commission on Preventing Deadly Conflict, Carnegie Corporation of New York, New York, 1997

*Paul van Tongeren *is the executive director of the European Centre for Conflict Prevention and co-ordinator of this project*

Poverty: Prime Enemy of Peace and Democracy

By Pierre Schori*

During my latest visit to South Africa and Mozambique I visited the small township of Mphumalanga in the province of KwaZulu/Natal in South Africa. In the Zulu tongue this name means 'the place where the sun rises'.

I was accompanied by representatives of the non-governmental organization, ACCORD. This peace support organization had awarded its peace prize to Mphumalanga. For years a fierce war had raged in Mphumalanga between the political rivals, Inkatha and ANC. Now peace had returned to the township and Meshack Radebe, the former ANC warlord, served as mayor working side by side with the Inkatha warlord, Sipho Mlaba.

I was taken to the spot where the fighting had been fiercest and was told that for a very long time every day when the sun rose over Mphumalanga it revealed new ruins. A heap of ashes marked the place where the shopping centre had once stood. The two chiefs were anxious for us to stop there, not only to show me the devastation in their village, but also to show me something else. On the other side of the road stood a tall new building - the new school. With great pride they informed me that today, all the children in the township attend that school.

I asked my two guides how peace had finally come to Mphumalanga. They explained that one day they had come upon the idea that they should both write down what they wanted for their township. When they exchanged these documents they discovered their lists were more or less identical. They wanted the same things - housing, water, jobs, schools and health care. And so it came that they began to talk, and soon found themselves moving across the dividing line which had previously marked a free-fire zone. Today, their children attend the same school, and they work for the good of Mphumalanga through politics.

Democracy and development, peace and security must start at home, in the hearts and minds of people. In Mphumalanga, the reconciliation between the ANC and Inkatha warlords has become a role model and marks a first step in the confidence-building that is so necessary for the reconstruction and development of the township and its civil society.

To me, this is a fine example of peace-building in daily, practical work. Nelson Mandela recently made his fourth and last visit to Sweden. President Mandela wished to express the gratitude of the South African people for Sweden's support in the struggle that led to the abolition of apartheid and to peace and democracy in South Africa.

The liberation of South Africa was primarily the achievement of its people. However, international support undoubtedly played a major role. I would describe the 35 years during which Sweden supported the struggle against apartheid as our longest and most successful act of solidarity. During that period, solidarity found expression in many different ways and involved virtually all segments of society. Political parties, churches, solidarity groups and other NGOs all became involved in these activities.

'Global governance is necessary to take responsibility for issues that neither nations nor the global market are able to handle.'

'My first political act as a student,' Olof Palme said, 'was to give blood in support of scholarships to black students in South Africa.' One of the recipients of this support was Eduardo Mondlane, who was later to form the Frelimo liberation movement in Mozambique. Thirty-seven years later, the last major speech Olof Palme gave prior to his assassination was his keynote address to the Swedish People's Parliament against Apartheid. That was in 1986 before an assembly of close to 1,000 representatives of political parties and NGOs.

To me, Swedish support to the liberation of South Africa is a clear illustration that solidarity work -even from a small country so far away- can play a significant role in building peace in the world.

Since then, the importance of the civil society and NGOs has been increasingly recognised. The role of the civil society and NGOs is highlighted by the many fascinating stories contained in this volume.

However, now, when the world has finally overcome apartheid and the Cold War, another gap is growing between countries and people, challenging peace and development. At the same time as globalization generates new wealth and rising incomes, the distribution of that wealth is becoming increasingly uneven, and more and more people live in poverty. We now face the risk of what I would call 'global apartheid'

In an article in El Pais Carlos Fuentes, the Mexican writer, recently compared the world to a village of one hundred inhabitants. In this hypothetical village, 57 people would be Asians, 21 Europeans, 12 Americans and eight Africans. Half of the village's wealth would be in the hands of only six, all of them North Americans. 80 inhabitants would have poor housing. 70 would be illiterate. 50

would be undernourished. Only one person would have a university education and not one of them would own a computer.

Not only is this situation grossly unjust, it is also unsustainable. Indeed, the major threats of our time - human rights violations, war and conflict, mass migration, international crime, drug-trafficking, terrorism and environmental degradation - are rooted in poverty and social inequality. Poverty is the prime enemy of peace and democracy in the world today.

If poverty is to be addressed, we must focus on the interrelation between political, economic, environmental and social development. Poverty is not just a lack of material resources. It is also to lack rights, education and influence.

The key to future development is to change the nature of the relationship with our partners in developing countries. Partnership should be based on a foundation of shared values and mutual trust. Such common values include respect for political and civil rights, democratic ground rules, gender equality, the rights of the child, social and economic rights, and concern for the environment.

This global code of ethics already exists. It is formulated in the Universal Declaration of Human Rights and at UN conferences on the environment, women, children and social development. These global norms serve as a foundation on which we must continue to build. They have persuaded individuals, political parties and the civil society to work together across national borders.

Partnership should also be our guideline in the reconstruction of Central America after the devastating effects of hurricane Mitch.

No country could have put up much resistance to the heavy rain which followed in the wake of the hurricane, but its effects were exacerbated by poor or non-existent planning, a degraded environment, population pressure and wide-spread poverty.

Reconstruction must therefore be used as an opportunity for these countries to build a better society in cooperation with the international community.

Only through growth will Central America be able to generate and sustain the additional resources needed to provide better benefits for the poor and to improve the standard of living for everyone. But if this growth is not accompanied by continued efforts to improve democratic practices and economic equity, then sustainable development will not be feasible. Massive aid must thus be followed by maximum transparency and a crusade against corruption.

Half a century ago, the political leaders of the day restored peace and laid the foundation for a more prosperous and just world, building the United Nations, the European Union and the Bretton Woods Institutions. It is clear that international institutions and cooperation need to be strengthened and reformed. Global governance is necessary to take responsibility for issues that neither nations nor the global market are able to handle.

'The development of thousands of NGOs all over the world will perhaps be the most important contribution of our age to the achievement of a peaceful and just world.'

The most significant development in recent years, however, has taken place in the field of the civil society. The development of thousands of NGOs all over the world will perhaps be the most important contribution of our age to the achievement of a peaceful and just world.

I started by sharing with you a positive experience of reconciliation, compromise and consensus that paved the way for development and security in KwaZulu/ Natal. Let me end with an equally bright picture.

In Mozambique, for so long one of the poorest countries in the world, peace and development can be seen walking hand in hand - almost literally. Young men, former soldiers in the armies of Frelimo and Renamo, are today the ploughshares of peace, clearing the country's soil of reminders of the past - the hundreds of thousands of landmines. They work there shoulder to shoulder, advancing metre by metre. The mistake of one man brings misery to another. Not far behind, the women wait ready with their pickaxes and spades to work the land as it is cleared, the land stolen from them by the war. There again you have a picture of everyday, practical work, where yesterday's enemies are today's partners for a better tomorrow.

* **Pierre Schori** *is deputy Foreign Minister and Minister for International Development Affairs of Sweden.*

Towards a New Culture of Peace and Non-Violence

By Federico Mayor*

On the eve of a new century and millennium, the world is challenged, more than at any time in the past, to transform human history from its domination by war and violence to a new culture of peace and non-violence. What is so unique about this historical moment that the challenge only arises at this time?

I t is a moment foreseen in the correspondence between Albert Einstein and Sigmund Freud in 1932. Freud speculated that for the first time, the abolition of warfare seemed possible, because of 'these two factors - man's cultural disposition and a well-founded fear of the form that future wars will take.' The form of war has changed over the past century and has indeed become universally intolerable. For war now endangers the very existence of our planet. The victims of war have also changed. No longer are the vast majority of the casualties the combatants themselves. Instead, it is now civilians who suffer most: children, women, the elderly and infirm.

It is at this significant point in time that the United Nations General Assembly has taken a series of decisions:

1   proclaiming the Year 2000, the International Year for the Culture of Peace;

2   proclaiming the Decade 2001-2010 the International Decade for a Culture of Peace and Non-violence for the Children of the World;

3   requesting a Declaration and a Programme of Action for a Culture of Peace.

There are many factors in contemporary societies which favour this move towards decisive, concerted action. Humanity's 'cultural disposition' and capacity for common action has been greatly enhanced by modern technology.

By pressing a computer key, a person can make instant contact with others on every continent. This enables people - and, most importantly, the young - to learn about each other, exchange views and begin to coordinate their actions. Unfortunately, extremes of wealth and poverty increasingly divide the world into 'haves' and 'have nots', and many are still excluded from these cyber links. Indeed, we are challenged to ensure the fruits of technology are used to increase human solidarity rather than to divide people further from each other. The 'peace movements' of yesterday have come of age. No longer confined to a single issue, they have diversified into the full range of issues contributing to a culture of peace: human rights, democracy, social justice, protection of the environment, international solidarity, gender equality. No longer restricted to protest against government policy, they are creating new forms of solidarity and positive action, promoting reconciliation, building bridges, cultivating peace.

Peace itself is being redefined. Instead of the absence of war, it is increasingly seen as a dynamic, participative, long-term process, based on universal values and everyday practice at all levels - the family, the school, the community, as well as the nation. Of course, there have been important forerunners of this process. There have been movements for non-violent social change such as those identified with Mahatma Gandhi and Martin Luther King Jr, and organizations such as the International Fellowship of Reconciliation, showing us the way towards a dynamic, active, positive vision of peace.

With the end of the Cold War, and the renewed capacity of the United Nations Security Council to take unanimous action for peace, UNESCO joined in the post-conflict peace-building initiatives of the UN by launching its Culture of Peace Programme. For us at UNESCO, peace has always been our core mission. UNESCO's Constitution, drafted at

'For us at UNESCO, peace has always been our core mission.'

the end of World War II and dedicated to the permanent abolition of war, says 'wars begin in the minds of men,' and adds that therefore, 'it is in the minds of men that the defences of peace must be constructed.' Its words are as pertinent today as the day they were written: 'a peace based exclusively upon the political and economic arrangements of governments would not be a peace which could secure the unanimous, lasting and sincere support of the peoples of the world, and that the peace must therefore be founded, if it is not to fail, upon the intellectual and moral solidarity of mankind.'

In this spirit, UNESCO's Culture of Peace activities work to weave a web of cooperation and understanding in previously divided communities. In programmes such as those in El Salvador and Mozambique, reconciliation was achieved by bringing together those previously shooting at each other and engaging them in jointly designing and implementing human development proposals. In El Salvador, NGOs associated with the former guerilla movement worked together with government ministries to broadcast a radio series providing information on women's rights and giving a voice to poor rural women. The broadcasts were heard throughout the country and were accompanied by a grass-roots educational campaign involving voluntary community peace promoters.

The process of the project was as important as the results - the former enemies were gradually transformed into partners through their participation in a shared initiative. In Mozambique, parliamentarians representing parties on both sides of the former conflict visited their parliamentary counterparts in neighbouring countries to learn how violent conflict can be transformed into constructive parliamentary debate. The experiences in El Salvador and Mozambique -and in many other countries from the Philippines to South Africa, Burundi and Mali- have shown that reconciliation is possible through acknowledgment of the past and working together for a common future.

The United Nations initiatives for a culture of peace mark a new stage: instead of focusing exclusively on rebuilding societies after they have been torn apart by violence, the emphasis is placed on preventing violence by fostering a culture where conflicts are transformed into cooperation before they can degenerate into war and destruction. The key to the prevention of violence is education for non-violence. This requires the mobilisation of education in its broadest sense - education throughout life and involving the mass media as much as traditional educational institutions. Just as violence is a learned behaviour, so, too, is the process of active non-violence. It must be learned and perfected through practice. The skills are many: active listening, dialogue, mediation, cooperative learning, conflict transformation. It may be said that, as we enter a new century, the 'second literacy' of 'learning to live together' has become as important as the first literacy of reading, writing and arithmetic.

The importance of learning cannot be stressed too much. We must all learn the skills and attitudes needed for a culture of peace. It is important, in this regard, to reassure young people that our behaviour is not pre-determined by genes or brain mechanisms. The consensus of leading scientists, expressed in the 1986 Seville Statement on Violence, is that 'biology does not condemn humanity to war .... the same species that invented war is capable of inventing peace. The responsibility lies with each of us.'

While the state, as always, has a leading role in the prevention of violence, it is not alone in this responsibility. The culture of peace is the responsibility of each citizen in his or her daily life, and can be translated into numerous forms of action. One initiative is the Manifesto for a Culture of Peace and Non-violence, written and signed by Nobel Peace Laureates. Individuals are signing the manifesto and their signatures are being collected throughout the world - with a goal of 100 million for the UN Millennium Assembly in September 2000. The Manifesto commits each individual to cultivate a culture of peace 'in my daily life - in my family, my work, my community, my country and my region.' It makes the individual, rather than the state, the central actor in creating a world of peace.

The culture of peace is becoming a global movement - a movement of movements - in which everyone who is working for human rights, non-violence, democracy, social justice, sustainable development, women's equality, join together in a 'grand alliance' of social transformation. The action of nongovernmental organizations working for these varied goals is a particularly powerful motor of social change.

This book is a milestone in the movement towards a culture of peace. It documents how, throughout the world, people are making progress on the various issues that -taken together- contribute to the coming culture of peace and non-violence. I invite the reader to take up this book and learn from the rich experiences and visions documented in its pages. I also invite readers to take up the challenge and emulate these actions in their own communities. It is by joining together that we can make the global transformation from a culture of war and violence to a culture of peace and non-violence.

* **Federico Mayor** *is Director-General of UNESCO*

Part I
Reflections

1 The Challenge of the 21st Century
Justpeace

By John Paul Lederach*

We were seated in a small room, about fourteen of us. Some were under the bunks that lined three walls, some on the top beds with their feet dangling. It was our second, maybe third visit to the room. I remembered our first visit for the defining question that faced our little envoy of mediators and peaceniks. 'Before you start,' they had said, 'we just want to know one thing. What makes you think that violence doesn't work?'

Before we could answer they went on to recount a recent conflict where negotiations had failed, mediation was rejected, but violence brought change. The story served to reinforce a message driven deep into their psyche and experience from childhood up and that had brought them eventually to this room: Only the strong survive. But on this visit it was our turn. We asked what they thought about the just signed peace agreements.

The words of the leader, taking a deep breath, still seem to resonate in my head. 'I fear peace,' he said, 'cause at the end of the day I know I'll be back in this prison visitn' me children's children.' Honest, heartfelt words from the Maze Prison in Northern Ireland.

We were standing on a dirt playground outside an old school building where a tense meeting had taken place. It had been nearly six years since the end of the Nicaraguan war that raged during much of the 1980's. The gathering had brought together former enemies, foot soldiers and their families who had fought for either the Counterrevolution or the Sandinista Government. Driven mostly by their immediate survival needs these former fighters from both sides were engaged in a process of reconciliation and had formed a national network of veterans who were receiving training in mediation, peace-building and micro-enterprise development. At the end of the meeting one of the vets approached the lead facilitator and I overheard him say, 'I need $10.' 'Why,' she asked. 'My sister, she runs around at night screaming like a monkey. She tears at her stomach and says she wants the monkey out.' He fell silent for a moment. 'We went to the Doctors but they say there is nothing to stop the monkey. But, there is a brujo' he stopped in mid-sentence. 'You think the witchdoctor will help?' she went on. I can still remember him looking at his hands, rough from daily work in the fields. These powerful hands carried guns in the war that created the monkey in his sister's belly. But now six years after the war they were empty. 'It's all we know to do,' he said.

As a mediator and teacher many of my tools rely on words. Sometimes, as I found in these two real-life moments and conversations, it only takes a few words in a story to summarize complex aspects of Truth. Both the stories relate to the theme of this book: Peacebuilding and Reconciliation. Both raise questions about the nature and meaning of peace. These questions are not raised as insights from sophisticated observers or theoreticians, nor from the rhetoric of politicians or even the most dedicated nonviolent strategist. No, the questions emerge from the lives of common people, protagonists in the swirl of war and the effects of violence. Their questions are simple. What change will peace bring us? What is to be expected from this peace?

As I look back across 20 years of working for nonviolence, conflict transformation, and reconciliation and as I reflect on the recent decades of peace accords two things stand out. First, objective assessment suggests there are significant gaps in our capacity to build and sustain peace initiatives. Second, direct interaction with these processes provokes contagious hope.

The hope is rooted in the resiliency of people like the two mentioned above, who, in spite of decades of obstacles and violence, keep taking steps toward peaceful coexistence with their enemies. Hope is rooted in the fact that the second half of the 20th Century, though rife with violent conflict, engendered the most prolific advancement of nonviolent conflict transformation activities systematically known in human history setting the stage for a potential singularity of peace-building in the 21st Century. The gaps emerge from a reductionism focused on techniques driven by a need to find quick fixes and solutions to complex, long term problems rather than a systemic understanding of peace-building as a process-structure. In this short chapter I will suggest that we must do two things to address this challenge. We must identify several key gaps that emerge from recent peace-building experiences and we must develop an adequate language appropriate to the hopes we hold.

Three Gaps in Peacebuilding

As a starting point I find the most significant challenges to peace-building in the 21st Century emerge from three gaps. By gap I mean an inability or insufficiency in our conceptual and practice frameworks that weaken our capacity to sustain a desired process. The three I will explore are the interdependence, the justice and the process-structure gaps. Given the brevity of this chapter I will limit myself to summary observations about each aspect and the needs that they suggest.

The Interdependence Gap

The Observation

Interdependence is built on relationships and relationships are the heart and bloodlines of peace-building. In peace-building there are many forms of interdependence. Most recognized is the idea that we build new or rebuild broken relationships across the lines of divisions created through and by the conflict. Using a pyramid to describe a setting affected by violent conflict I refer to this as *horizontal capacity*: the effort to work with counterparts, enemies, across the lines of division (See Figure 1). Most peace-building work, particularly in the sub-field of conflict resolution, has been aimed at improving aspects of relationships through negotiation, dialogue, and mediation by getting counterparts to meet with each other. However, if we ask the question 'who meets each other to develop relationships?' we find this answer: people who are at a relative equal status within the context of the conflict. Community people meet community people, mid-range

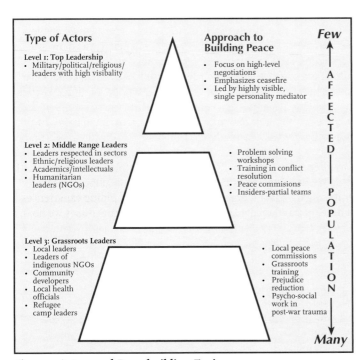

Figure 1: **Actors and Peacebuilding Foci**

leaders encounter each other, and of course, top level political leaders in the limelight sit across negotiation tables. In other words, the emphasis of dialogue has fostered horizontal relationships.

The most significant gap of interdependence we face is rooted in the lack of responsive and coordinated relationships up and down the levels of leadership in a society affected by protracted violent conflict. This is what I have referred to as the *vertical capacity:* the ability to develop relationships of respect and understanding between higher levels of leadership with community and grassroots levels of leadership, and vice versa. To put it simply, high, middle-range and grassroots levels of leadership rarely see themselves as interdependent with the other levels in reference to peace-building until they discover they need them, usually when the process is under enormous stress and time constraints. If pursued the resulting relationship suffers manipulation or instrumentalist superficiality.

Correspondingly, we are hampered in our ability to create and sustain *vertical* and *horizontal integration* strategically necessary for implementing the kind of long-term peace-building we hope to put in place. The challenge of horizontal capacity is how to foster constructive understanding and dialogue across the lines of division in a society. The challenge of the vertical capacity is how to develop genuine recognition that peace-building involves multiple activities at different levels of leadership, taking place simultaneously, each level distinct in its needs and interdependent in effects. Strategic change in a system requires that horizontal and vertical relationships move in tandem on an equal basis. In far too many places and times vertical capacity has been weak. What one level of peace-building undertook was rarely understood by, much less conceived and conducted in a way that significantly involved other levels of the affected society. Yet all levels, at one time or another, are affected by and must coordinate their activities with each other.

In sum, the interdependence gap suggests that sustainability of peace-building require both horizontal and vertical relationship building and coordination. In conceptual and practical terms, the field of peace-building has concentrated more of its resources and capacity-building on the horizontal ignoring the vertical axis, leaving significant insufficiencies in the structure of the peace process to be sustained.

The Need
To address the interdependence gap we must find ways to:
• Increase the recognition that peace-building is an organic system that requires relationships and coordination of multiple activities, multiple roles, at multiple levels. No one activity and no one level will be able to deliver and sustain peace on its own.
• Increase the mutual understanding by each level of the particular

approaches and activities required at the others. The orientation is toward awareness of the unique contribution each brings in order to build relationships of respect, provide greater points of coordination, and decrease the competitiveness of activity and control structures devised to protect turf but which ultimately limit the capacity of change and integration in the system.
- Build relationships before, during and after formal Accords reach ink, between people who are not like-minded, like-focused, and like-situated within the structure of the society. We need to bring an equal emphasis on vertical relationship building as we do to horizontal relationship building.

The Justice Gap

The Observation
Most people involved in protracted conflicts expect peace processes will provide changes both in stopping the direct violence and in addressing the structural issues they feel gave rise to the conflict in the first place. Particularly for settings of internal violent conflict, the latter will almost always require a systemic transformation of relationships in the affected society's political, economic and social policies and ethos. In the past fifteen years peace processes have delivered a reduction of direct violence but have rarely attained the aspirations of desired structural change. Thus, there persists a deep felt perception in many peoples' minds that to reduce violence peace compromises social justice. Let us explore this a bit more.

An expansive time view of any one of the most significant internal wars and their peace accord processes in the past couple of decades suggest an interesting paradox. It starts by the overall progression of conflict and its escalation to war, then negotiations and peace accords. First, situations move from latent status into open conflict and direct violence when people feel there is a significant issue of justice and human or group rights that must change and in which there exist few if any other avenues for achieving due recourse. People who take up *direct violence* are trying to address the perceived injustice or what Galtung called '*structural violence,*' that is, they are trying to achieve systemic changes in the underlying economic, cultural, social, and political structures as those are perceived to detrimentally affect their lives.

As the conflict escalates there comes a time where the choice of means, war and socially sanctioned violence, for pursuing or defending against particular changes reaches a saturation point, or an exhaustion level. Mary Anderson suggests it is when people realize the 'system of violence' has become more oppressive than the initial injustice. In other words *direct violence* added onto the existing latent *structural violence* creates a situation in which everyone perceives themselves as oppressed and worst off than they were before. People then begin the process of re-evaluating their goals and methodologies, and they move toward negotiation and redefining their relationship. In the graph I depicted this as two separate lines, direct and structural violence which criss-cross each other over time.

In the past fifteen years these negotiations have resulted in a series of peace accords. A peace accord means that the *direct violence* line drops significantly, that is, the fighting stops. However, people expect the accords to address the fundamental issues that gave rise to the fighting, the *structural violence,* and that solutions will be produced on the same timeline as the diminishing curve of direct violence. This rarely, if ever has been the case. It results in what I call the *'justice gap.'* The war is over, formal negotiations concluded, and changes have come usually in terms of increased space for political participation. However the expectations for social, economic, religious, and cultural change are rarely achieved, creating a gap between the expectations for peace and what it delivered.

The significance of the justice gap in the context of the challenges we face in the 21st Century is to ask ourselves the question where has most peace-building practice, theory, and funding been invested in reference to the overall progression described above? My observation: Much greater investment has been expended in the study and development of methodologies and practice for reducing *direct violence* than in transforming *structural violence.* We have focused our lenses more on negotiation and peace accord fashioning between groups and their representatives than in understanding the processes of structural change. The justice gap emerges in part because we have not adequately developed a peace-building framework that *reduces* direct violence *and produces* social and economic justice.

The Need
To address the justice gap we must find ways to:
- Increase the capacity of peace-building practitioners, both governmental and nongovernmental to integrate social justice building with direct violence reducing processes, two highly interdependent energies and foci, that are rarely held together at the same time.
- Broaden the understanding of peace-building to integrate the fields of conflict transformation, restorative justice, and socio-economic development. In most post-Accord settings these have shown themselves to be highly interdependent perspectives, practices and skills yet are rarely conceptualized or practised together.
- Reorient our investment (funding, research, and practice) such that we are not negotiation-centric at the expense of developing practices and frameworks for understanding how to create and sustain collaborative, nonviolent processes of structural change.

Former Yugoslavia: just one example of the significant gaps in our capacity to build and sustain peace initiatives

The Process-Structure Gap

The Observation
Peace Accords are often seen as a culminating point of a peace process. In the language of governments and the military the Accords are referred to as an end-game scenario. We fall prey to this thinking when we see the Accords as the way the war ended. In reality the Accords are nothing more than opening a door into a whole new labyrinth of rooms that invite us to continue in the process of redefining our relationships.

This is one reason I have preferred the words conflict transformation over conflict resolution. Resolution lends itself to a metaphor that suggests our goal is to end something not desired. Transformation insinuates that something not desired is changing, taking new form. When we add conflict transformation to peace-building we push the metaphor further. We embrace the challenge to change that which torn us apart and building something we desire. This focus on language pushes us to reconsider the idea of a 'peace process.' Process paints the image that peace is dynamic and ongoing. On the other hand I often hear people ask the question, 'How will the peace be sustained?' This question assumes a metaphor of peace as a product. In both instances our language fails us.

In recent years I have turned to theoreticians in what is sometimes called the New Science and found they encountered similar challenges. This approach includes quantum physics, chaos theory, self-organizing systems theory among others. For me two things stand out in their development. First, they had to shift out of old modalities of thinking in order to enter into totally new ways of looking at old realities. As Einstein was supposed to have said, no problem can be solved with the same consciousness that created it. Second, they had to develop new, or as the case demanded, retool old language to adequately describe the realities. One of their terms was a *process-structure,* a concept used to describe phenomena in nature that are, at the same time, process and structure. I have found this notion especially relevant to peace-building.

When we think of peace as a process we inevitably fall prey to critique that it is an endless dynamic that leads to no substantive outcome. When we envision peace as a result we fall into the trap that it is an end-state, only to discover that is neither an 'end' nor a 'state' and that if we treat it as such our desire to preserve or control it destroy its very essence. I believe that our language has limited our capacity to adequately describe the phenomenon we wish to understand and to the degree possible encourage. It has created a paradoxical hiatus reflected both in our theory and practice, the process-structure gap. Peace is neither a process nor a structure. It is both. Peacebuilding requires us to work at constructing an infrastructure to support a process of desired change, and change is permanent.

I use the metaphor of a river to illustrate this. A river is one of the phenomena the New Science calls a process-structure. When you stand up to your knees in a river what you see, feel and hear is the dynamic flow of water. It rushes around your legs with force and power, changing like the essence of water itself to get around any obstacle put in its way. On the other hand if you stand high on a mountain, or position yourself at a window of an airplane and look down at the river from a long distance what you see is the shape and form it has carved in the land. From a distance it looks static. You see it as a structure not a dynamic process. This is a process-structure. A river is dynamic, adaptive and changing while at the same time carving a structure with direction and purpose.

This is the challenge we face with peace-building. We must engender an adaptive, dynamic and responsive change process. At the same time the very process of change must have purpose and infrastructure to support its flow. In practice we have tended to think about peace as a process up to the point of the Accords, then suddenly, things should translate into structure, too often in purely bureaucratic terms. To conceptualize peace as process-structure moves us away from a myopic focus on agreements and events and toward a commitment of embracing the permanency of relationship building. Relationships are both dynamic and adaptive, yet they also take social, political forms that require accountability, vigilance, and willingness to change. We know this is inherently true of intimate personal relationships. We have been woefully insufficient in conceptualizing social, organizational, political and economic structures as responsive to relational needs and changing environments. When relationship becomes the centre what remains permanent is not a given form but the capacity to encounter and adapt, both of which are processes learned and relearned through conflict addressed constructively.

The Need
To address the process-structure gap we must find ways to:
- Understand peace as a change process based on relationship building.
- Reorient our peace-building framework toward the development of support infrastructures that enhance our capacity to adapt and respond to relational needs rather than being defined and driven by events and agreements.
- Reconceive long-term peace structures such that they reflect the inherent responsiveness often present in periods of active negotiation and avoid the trappings of isolating 'peace' functions in bureaucracies implementing time-bound mandates with little capacity to adapt and change to on-the-ground real-life needs.

Conclusion

The above discussion suggests we should adapt systemic and paradox-based lenses for understanding, responding to and developing the change processes for we wish to put in motion. I believe this must be reflected in our language. As a conclusion let me put forward a modest proposal and challenge that require a shift in practice and language.

At the writing of this chapter I find myself halfway through my fifth decade. If given the grace I may live to see the halfway point of the 21st Century. The year will be 2050, a decade when the last of my generation will pass the torch to our great-grandchildren. A decade when my friend in the Maze feared he would return as an old man to visit his great-grandson. What do we hope can be in place by the mid-point of the next Century?

Inspired by colleagues from the Justapaz Centre in Bogota, Colombia, I propose that by the year 2050 the word *justpeace* be accepted in everyday common language and appear as an entry in the Webster's Dictionary. It will read:

Justpeace \ *jest pés* \ n, vi, (justpeace-building) 1: an adaptive process-structure of human relationships characterized by high justice and low violence 2: an infrastructure of organization or governance that responds to human conflict through nonviolent means as first and last resorts 3: a view of systems as responsive to the permanency and interdependence of relationships and change.

* **John Paul Lederach** *is professor of sociology and conflict studies in the Conflict Transformation Program at the Eastern Mennonite University, USA. He served as director of the program and the Institute for Peacebuilding from their founding in 1993 until mid-1997. Dr. Lederach has extensive experience as a peace-building practitioner, trainer, and consultant throughout Latin America, Africa and the United States, as well as in the Philippines, Northern Ireland, the Basque Country, among other locations. He has pioneered elicitive methods of conflict resolution training and practice, and is a widely published theorist in both Spanish and English. This article is based on his forthcoming publication 'Justpeace 2050'.*

2 The Meaning of Reconciliation

By Hizkias Assefa*

Compared to conflict handling mechanisms such as negotiation, mediation, adjudication, and arbitration, the approach called 'reconciliation' is perhaps the least well understood. Its meaning, processes, and application have not been clearly articulated or developed. A place to start understanding what it entails might be by trying to distinguish it from the other approaches used in peacemaking and peace-building.

I f we were to look at the 'degree of mutual participation by the conflict parties in the search for solutions to the problems underlying their conflict' we could place these approaches in a spectrum as follows. (See Figure 1)

At the left end of the spectrum, we find approaches where mutual participation is minimal. The use of force by one of the parties to impose a solution would be an example of a mechanism that would be placed at this end of the spectrum. Further to the right of the spectrum, we could place

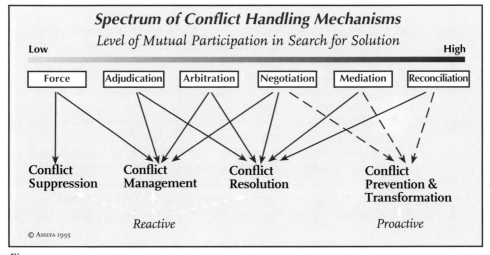

Figure 1

mechanisms such as adjudication. Here a third party, instead of an adversary, imposes a solution to the conflict. However, the mutual participation of the parties in the choice of the solution is comparatively higher here than in the first. In the adjudication process, at least the parties have an opportunity to present their cases, to be heard, and submit their arguments for why their preferred solution should be the basis upon which the decision is made. Nonetheless, the choice of the solution is made by a third party, and the decision is backed by force (enforced) which ensures that the losing party complies.

Arbitration is placed further to the right of 'adjudication'. Here, the participation of the parties is even higher since both adversaries can choose who is going to decide the issues under dispute, whereas in adjudication the decision maker is already appointed by the state. The parties in conflict can sometimes identify the basis upon which their case will be decided and whether the outcome will be binding or not. Although the mutual involvement of the parties in the decision making process is much higher than adjudication, the solution is still decided by an outsider and, depending on the type of arbitration, the outcome could be imposed by the power of the law.

Further to the right on the spectrum we find negotiation. Here the participation of all the involved parties in the search for solution is very high. It is the parties themselves who have to formulate the issues, and find a resolution that is satisfactory to all of them. In this situation, however, particularly in bargaining type negotiations (as opposed to problem-solving type of negotiations) [1], the final choice of the solution might depend on the relative power position of the adversaries rather than on what might be the most satisfactory solution to everyone involved. The party with the higher bargaining leverage might end up getting the most out of the negotiations.

Mediation is a special type of negotiation where the parties' search for mutually satisfactory solutions are assisted by a third party. The third party's role is to minimize obstacles to the negotiation process including those that emanate from power imbalance. Unlike adjudication, however, in the final analysis it is the decision and agreement of the conflict parties that determines how the conflict will be resolved.

Towards the far right of the spectrum we find reconciliation. This approach not only tries to find solutions to the issues underlying the conflict but also works to alter the adversaries' relationships from that of resentment and hostility to friendship and harmony. Of course, for this to happen, both parties must be equally invested and participate intensively in the resolution process. [2]

Before we move on to examine the insights that emerge from this spectrum, it will clarify our thinking if we quickly glance at one more issue of definitions and distinctions.

The conflict handling mechanisms illustrated in the spectrum can be categorized into three groups which we will call conflict management, conflict resolution, and conflict prevention approaches. Conflict management approaches generally tend to focus more on mitigating or controlling the destructive consequences that emanate from a given conflict than on finding solutions to the underlying issues causing it. On the other hand, conflict resolution approaches aim at going beyond mitigation of consequences and attempt to resolve the substantive and relational root-causes so that the conflict comes to an end. While conflict management and resolution are reactive, they come into motion once conflict has surfaced, conflict prevention tries to anticipate the destructive aspects of the conflict before they arise and attempts to take positive measures to prevent them from occurring.

Most of the mechanisms identified on the left hand of the spectrum are conflict management approaches. The use of military force for deterrence or in peace-keeping (separating the conflict parties from each other so that they do not keep inflicting harm on each other) are typical conflict management strategies. To the extent that adjudication, arbitration, and bargaining negotiations do not become avenues to solve the underlying issues of the conflict, and in most instances they do not, they become mere stop-gap conflict management measures. But if they provide an opportunity to work out not only differences on substantive issues but also negative relationships, they can become conflict resolution mechanisms.

'Justice is a necessary but not sufficient condition for reconciliation.'

Observations

We notice that as we move from the left to the right on the spectrum, i.e., as the participation of all the parties in the search for solution increases, the likelihood of achieving a mutually satisfactory and durable solution also increases. We know that solutions imposed by force will only last until the vanquished is able to muster sufficient force to reverse the situation. Solutions imposed by adjudication and arbitration, unless somehow the loser gives up, can always be frustrated by the latter's endless appeals or lack of cooperation in the implementation process. If, however, the parties are engaged earnestly in the search for the solutions and are able to find resolutions that could satisfy the needs and interests of all involved, there could be no better guarantee for the durability of the settlements. It would be in the interest of every one to see to it that they are fully enforced. This is what we believe problem-solving negotiations, mediation, and reconciliation can do.

What is noteworthy however is that as we move from the left to the right end of the spectrum, although the likelihood of effectiveness and durability of the solutions increases, our knowledge and understanding of the approaches to be utilized become sketchy, less developed and unsystematic. Our knowledge and methodology of conflict management approaches (the mechanisms on the left hand side of the spectrum) such as the use of force, adjudication, or arbitration are quite advanced. They are highly developed disciplines within institutions that command high respect and resources devoted to training and practice. Military and police science, jurisprudence and legal studies, as well as the entire military and police academies, law schools, ministries of defence and justice, police departments, courts, prison systems, are examples of these disciplines and institutions that advance the practice of these approaches. In contrast, conflict resolution approaches such as problem-solving negotiation and mediation are less developed and institutions and resources devoted to their training, advancement and practice are meager. Whatever is in place is voluntary and ad-hoc. Then, when we come to reconciliation, let alone establish procedures and institutions charged with the application of the concept, there is not even much understanding of what it means, especially, among social scientists. Religious people and theologians are a bit better equipped to discuss the concept. But even there, there is a great gap between articulation and translation of the ideas into practice.

Healing and Reconciliation

Despite the lack of knowledge about how to operationalize reconciliation, there is however no question about the tremendous need for it. In fact, it could be said that the need in today's world is much greater than at any other time in the past.

One reason is that conflict management strategies are not adequate to deal with the kinds of contemporary conflicts raging in many parts of the world. Especially since the end of the Cold War, civil wars have replaced interstate wars as the most predominant large scale social conflicts. To a certain extent, in interstate conflicts strategies aimed merely at separating the conflicting parties might suffice. Even if the underlying issues of the conflict are not resolved, the separation could help avoid the recurrence of the conflict. Because states tend to isolate themselves from each other by their national boundaries, the task of separating them by peace-keeping forces is relatively easier.

However, in civil war situations the relationships between the protagonists is much more intimate and complex. In most cases, the parties share the same geographic area and even community, there might be strong economic interdependence between them, they usually have all sorts of social ties among each other including intermarriages. In these instances it is quite difficult to separate the protagonists since the boundaries between them are very difficult

Tuareg leaders on their way to the Mali Flame of Peace ceremony, 1996

to draw. Even if it is possible to do it for a short while, it is not feasible to think of conflict management strategies such as separation as long term solutions. For that matter, even decisions imposed by adjudication or other such processes will not be solutions since the winning party cannot expect to enjoy its victory without facing the consequences of the loser's wrath. Therefore, in civil war situations conflict management strategies are not adequate. One has to move towards conflict resolution and reconciliation processes where not only the underlying issues to the conflicts are resolved to everyone's satisfaction but also the antagonistic attitudes and relationships between the adversaries are transformed from negative to positive.

Moreover, even in interstate relations, we are increasingly realizing that the components of the modern international system are no more the 19th century autarchic states. The globe is shrinking and the fates of peoples of the world are becoming more and more inextricably intertwined. Thus, it would be increasingly difficult to expect unilateral approaches to handling conflicts such as imposition of solutions by force as viable approaches. In an interdependent and closely interconnected world even those that are supposedly weak can have their own way of subverting or undermining the imposed order. Therefore, those groups must somehow be enabled to participate in the search for solutions in their conflicts even with the more powerful actors. In fact, the democratic values that the current international order is trying to promote as a universal value in all societies of the world necessitates movement more and more towards integrative negotiation, mediation and reconciliation as the predominant ways of dealing with conflict instead of unilateral measures that entail the use of coercion.

What Does Reconciliation Entail?

Reconciliation as a conflict handling mechanism entails the following core elements:
a) Honest acknowledgment of the harm/injury each party has inflicted on the other;
b) Sincere regrets and remorse for the injury done:
c) Readiness to apologize for one's role in inflicting the injury;
d) Readiness of the conflicting parties to 'let go' of the anger and bitterness caused by the conflict and the injury;
e) Commitment by the offender not to repeat the injury;
f) Sincere effort to redress past grievances that caused the conflict and compensate the damage caused to the extent possible;
g) Entering into a new mutually enriching relationship.

Reconciliation then refers to this new relationship that emerges as a consequence of these processes. What most people refer to as 'healing' is the mending of deep emotional wounds (generated by the conflict) that follow the reconciliation process.

A very important aspect of the process of reconciliation and one that distinguishes it from all the other conflict handling mechanisms is its methodology. In most of the conflict handling mechanisms such as adjudication, arbitration, and for that matter even negotiation and mediation the method used for establishing responsibility for the conflict or its consequences is adversarial. In these processes, the parties present their grievances and make a case for the adversary's fault or responsibility, thereby demanding that it should be the latter that should make amends. Each party begins by defending its own behaviour and denying its own guilt or responsibility until the opponent proves it to his or her satisfaction or to the satisfaction of outside observers, be they judges or mediators. In such a process, one's behaviour is always explained as a reaction to the behaviour of the adversary. The typical pattern of the interaction is: 'I did this to you because you did such and such a thing to me!' The aim is to get the adversary to change his or her future conduct by proving the person's guilt. Of course, the expectation is that both parties will change each other in this way and will eventually transform their relationship from negative to positive.

On the other hand, the essence of reconciliation is the voluntary initiative of the conflict parties to acknowledge their responsibility and guilt. The interactions that transpire between the parties are not only meant to communicate one's grievances against the actions of the adversary, but also to engage in self-reflection about one's own role and behaviour in the dynamic of the conflict. In other words, in this kind of dialogue, as much as one attributes guilt and responsibility to the adversary for the damage generated by the conflict, one has to also be self-critical and acknowledge responsibility for his or her own role in the creation or perpetuation of the conflict and hurtful interaction. The aim of such interaction is that, in the final analysis, each of the parties acknowledges and accepts his or her responsibility and out of such recognition seeks ways to redress the injury that has been inflicted on the adversary, to refrain from further damage, and to construct new positive relationships.

'Despite the lack of knowledge about how to operationalize reconciliation, there is no question about the tremendous need for it.'

It is true that in both reconciliation and other conflict resolution mechanisms the process of dialogue is expected to generate change and transformation. In reconciliation, however, the forces for change are primarily internal and voluntary; while in the other approaches they are external and to a certain extent coerced. In the situation where the source is external it is possible that it might be the adversary's skill in marshaling and presenting its arguments; its strong will and intransigence; or its capacity to manipulate, exert pressure, or administer punishment that might intimidate the other party into accepting responsibility and settlement. Under such circumstances, therefore, it is questionable to what extent reluctant acceptance of guilt can serve as a force for significantly altering the future conduct and relationship between the adversaries.

This is not to imply that it is not possible to induce change in behaviour and relationships by forces outside the person, nor that every person changes his or her behaviour and relationships wilfully or voluntarily. The point here is that unless the need for change is internalized, the change is likely to be only temporary. The relationship would not have been significantly altered, and the conflict would not have found enduring solutions. It would emerge again as soon as circumstances change. More enduring transformation is likely to emerge when motivated by an internal need to change, especially when it emanates from self-reflection and criticism.

Reconciliation and Justice

Here it would be important to clarify the often misunderstood relationship between reconciliation and justice. Especially in horrendous conflict situations like Rwanda, Yugoslavia, Cambodia and others, many have argued that reconciliation is not appropriate because it is too soft on criminal conduct of offenders, and might even encourage it. They feel that justice (usually meaning the punishment of the offenders) precedes reconciliation. However, this argument presents a false dichotomy. An attempt at reconciliation without addressing the injustice in the situation is indeed a mockery and belittling the suffering of the victim. There cannot be reconciliation without justice. Justice and equity are at the core of reconciliation. The central question in reconciliation is not whether justice is done, but rather how one goes about doing it in ways that can also promote future harmonious and positive relationship between parties that have to live with each other whether they like it or not. Justice is a necessary but not sufficient condition for reconciliation. Reconciliation takes the concern for justice a step further and is preoccupied with how to rebuild a more livable, and psychologically healthy environment between former enemies where the vicious cycle of hate, deep suspicion, resentment, and revenge does not continue to fester.

For this reason, the methodology used to arrive at justice in the reconciliation process is different from that used to arrive at justice in the conventional (juridical) approach. The aim of the latter processes (particularly of the criminal justice process) is primarily to identify guilt and administer the punishment that the law requires with little attention to healing the bitterness and resentment that exist between the parties in the conflict. Identifying ways in which offenders are assisted to redress the material and emotional damage they have inflicted through self-reflection, acknowledgment of responsibility, remorse, and compensation would be an important step towards establishing an environment of reconciliation. The approach known as 'restorative justice' as opposed to 'retributive justice' brings us closer to the point where justice can be done but at the same time the possibilities for reconciliation are enhanced. [3]

Applying this concept in some of the catastrophic situations like Rwanda, Yugoslavia, Cambodia or Chile, reconciliation does not mean that the offenders are just pardoned. It means creating a process and an environment where the offenders take the responsibility to acknowledge their offense and get motivated to change the situation and relationship in a positive and durable manner instead of keep denying their guilt until it is proven to them by the juridical process.

The important thing to note is that to the extent the offenders keep denying their guilt, even if their responsibility is proved juridically and they are punished, the internal change that needs to take place to change the relationship from destructive to constructive, from hate to cooperation and harmony may not happen. Particularly in group conflicts, the punishment of the offenders alone does not prevent them or their followers and (at times, even their descendants) from continuing to hate and desiring to retaliate against those that punished them or their forefathers. Reconciliation has a much better chance of stopping the cycle of violence and hatred that sometimes transcends generations than any other conflict handling mechanism. Although flawed in many ways, this is what the experiments with Truth and Reconciliation Commission in conflict-ravaged societies are trying to do. In a number of instances, these commissions have been able to go as far as obtaining voluntarily acknowledgment of guilt by offenders. But they have not gone far enough to get them to demonstrate sincere remorse, or take active steps to compensate and repair the relationship vis a vis their victims. [4]

Notes

1 See Roger Fisher and William Ury, Getting to Yes, for the distinction between the bargaining type (distributive) and problem-solving type (integrative) negotiation approaches.

2 Of course these categories are neither exhaustive nor water-tight. There are many more mechanisms that mix the various types and fall somewhere in between. One example is a mechanism that has come to be known as med/arb, where the process starts as mediation with the voluntary and full participation of the parties, but if that fails in resolving the problem, the solution is determined by a third party, an arbitrator. There are also other non-formal processes such as advocacy by interest groups, political mobilization at the grass-roots level in order to put pressure on leaders, etc. that can be placed at various points on the spectrum. 'Advocacy' operates in the adjudication framework although the body to whom the appeal is done might be the courts of national or international pubic opinion instead of the regular courts of law. 'Political mobilization' could be seen as a tactic in the negotiation process in which the adversaries are marshaling their forces to improve their bargaining leverage or capacity to be heard and be taken seriously.

3 See Howard Zehr, Changing Lenses, (Scottdale, Pennsylvania: Herald Press), 1990

4 For a critique of Truth and Reconciliation Commissions and more detailed elaboration of concepts, approaches, and methodologies, and examples see Hizkias Assefa, Process of Expanding and Deepening Engagement, Reconciliation Methodology in Large Scale Social Conflicts (forthcoming).

*Hizkias Assefa is Professor of Conflict Studies, Conflict Transformation Programme, at Eastern Mennonite University, USA, and a Distinguished Fellow at the Institute of Conflict Analysis and Resolution at George Mason University, USA. He is the founder and co-ordinator of the African Peacebuilding and Reconciliation Network in Nairobi, Kenya. He works as a mediator and facilitator in civil war situations in many parts of Africa from his base in Nairobi. He is the author of several books, including Peace and Reconciliation as a Paradigm: A Philosophy of Peace and Its Implications on Conflict, Governance and Economic Growth in Africa (Majestic Press, 1993), and Process of Expanding and Deepening Engagement: Methodology for Reconciliation Work in Large Scale Social Conflicts (forthcoming).

3 Telling the Truth in the Wake of Mass Violence

By Michelle Parlevliet*

Since the mid-1970s, a growing number of states around the world have tried to come to terms with a legacy of gross human rights violations that had been committed in their recent history, whether during military or authoritarian rule or in the course of an armed conflict. An approach which has steadily gained prominence in this respect is the investigation and recording of past atrocities by so-called truth commissions. Some twenty such commissions have operated across the world in the last fifteen years of which those in Chile, Argentina, and most recently, South Africa, are the most widely known.[1]

Without much international attention, a truth commission recently completed its work in Guatemala, whereas investigations continue in the southern provinces of Sri Lanka. Discussions regarding the establishment of a commission have been ongoing for some time in Surinam, where human rights violations committed during the 1980s continue to haunt society. In Indonesia, the fall of Suharto has allowed civil society to take up the issue and to start considering confronting the past. A commission has been proposed for Bosnia-Herzegovina, one suggested for Northern-Ireland, and one called for in Namibia and Sierra Leone.

The recent proliferation of truthtelling bodies warrants a closer look as their establishment generally relates to addressing old conflicts and preventing new ones. This chapter clarifies the meaning and practice of such commissions and seeks to shed light on their relation to furthering reconciliation in a society. Besides explaining the motivations behind their establishment, it describes their general features and activities and indicates how they may contribute to reconciliation. Challenges are pointed out that a truth commission may encounter in this regard and some factors are highlighted that might affect the impact and effectiveness of a truth commission. An in-depth examination of these matters is, however, beyond the scope of this chapter which therefore has the character of an overview.

Truth Commissions - What For?

When countries move out of protracted periods of violence, societies and leadership alike need to decide whether and how to deal with the widespread human rights violations that have been committed. In considering whether to close the book on such abuses or to investigate what happened and hold individuals accountable, ethical and political considerations need to be balanced: the demands of justice must be weighed against what is politically feasible. A tension is then often perceived to exist between the pursuit of both justice and peace, given the politically precarious nature of a transition. It is feared that the former may jeopardize the latter when a democracy or peace agreement is still fragile.

More and more, however, it is recognized that justice is part of the positive contents of peace and that addressing justice-related issues may contribute to reconciliation on the long term. Consequently, accounting for past abuses is increasingly deemed important for the development of an enduring democracy or a lasting peace. It is felt that any failure to do so may well lay the foundation for renewed violence by reinforcing a sense of impunity and feelings of resentment, allowing for conflicting versions of the past [2] and perpetuating enemy images. Redressing past violations, on the other hand, can reassert the rule of law, create awareness of human rights, and legitimize structures of governance, thus altering the conditions in which serious crimes occurred. While the past cannot be undone, it may be possible to mitigate its negative impact on society.

Telling the truth originally came up as a way to deal with a legacy of abuses because the political circumstances often precluded bringing perpetrators to justice. 'Bringing truth to light' then at least ensured that knowledge of past crimes would be preserved. Memory, it has been argued, is the ultimate form of justice. Truth has further been emphasized in relation to the type of violations that occurred, many of which evolve around secrecy and denial (such as disappearances, torture, killings by anonymous death squads.) It is seen as a direct response to such crimes, which indicates that it is not only knowledge of the truth that counts, but as much the acknowledgement thereof. It counters the atmosphere of silence and deceit in which such crimes could be committed [3]

Over time, the importance of truth has become so widely accepted, that 'a right to truth' is gradually recognized to exist for both societies and individuals. For the former, it is considered essential to avoid the repetition of crimes in the future. For the latter, it is part of an effective remedy for violations endured. This right is now also included in a set of principles prepared for the United Nations with a view to combating impunity (the 'Joinet-principles.')[4]

Truth commissions, meanwhile, are increasingly considered to be valuable in their own right, because of their broad scope of inquiry, inclusive character, impact on victims, and their forward-looking nature - far from being a mere second-best.[5]

Forms and Activities: Variations on a Theme

Arguably most remarkable about truth commissions is their hybrid nature. They have come in a wide variety of forms and sizes, and new models will continue to be developed as each situation presents its unique set of circumstances, constraints, and demands. The historical, political, and cultural context of a particular country is of major influence on the shape that a commission will eventually take, precluding any easy categorization of the truth commissions that have existed to date. Nevertheless, a general description can be made.[6]

Features
Truth commissions can be defined as official bodies which are to investigate, within a limited time-frame, past human rights violations in order to paint the overall picture of abuses that occurred in a particular country over a specific period of time. Their mandate is limited to serious violations, which are either specified in detail or are broadly set out, leaving it to the commission to interpret which abuses to include in its investigation. The Salvadoran Commission on the Truth, for example, was charged with investigating 'serious acts of violence that have occurred since 1980 and whose impact on society urgently demands that the public should know the truth.'[7]

Commissions may investigate violations by the armed forces of the state, those committed by the opposition, or both. Focusing on the past yet also intended to impact on the future, truth commissions are charged with making recommendations with regard to both.

Sponsorship
Most commissions to date have been state bodies, established by the head of state or by parliament, and consisting of nationals of the particular country. In El Salvador and Guatemala, commissions were established under auspices of the United Nations in the context of peace agreement between government and guerrilla forces overseen by the UN. Their membership was wholly or partly international, appointed by the UN Secretary-General, due to the strong polarization in the countries. At times, national human rights organisations or church institutions have undertaken projects that resemble such official commissions in the absence of any government effort. In Brazil, for example, the Archbishop of São Paulo secretly compiled a comprehensive report on state repression, 'Brasil: Nunca Maís'.[8]

Since 1995, the 'Recovery of Historical Memory' (REMHI) project has been conducted in Guatemala by the Human Rights Office of the Catholic Church, in order to complement the official truth commission later to be established. The 1994 constituting accord of this official body was considered seriously flawed.[9]

Activities
In contrast to the judicial process which is more geared towards (alleged) perpetrators, truth commissions tend to focus on victims and relatives. They usually are the main source of information for a commission and much emphasis is put on allowing them to relate their accounts. Few restrictions are placed on participation. Only in South Africa did the commission receive much information from perpetrators, which primarily stemmed from its capacity to grant amnesty in exchange for disclosure about crimes committed. Activities may be conducted in public or private depending on security considerations, the mandate of a commission, and the national context. Publicity increases the transparency of a commission but may also draw it more easily into the political arena. Some commissions attempt to investigate all abuses brought to their attention, others focus on a sample of cases.

Quasi-judicial
Truth commissions are not judicial, but quasi-judicial bodies. They do not make findings of criminal responsibility, their reports do not have judicial effects, and they often have limited powers. It is sometimes specified in the mandate of the commission what its relation is with the judicial process, for example, whether criminal evidence should be forwarded to the courts. Two issues have been particularly controversial: whether any names should be mentioned, and whether violations by both governmental and oppositional forces should be investigated. Traditionally, only state agents can commit human rights violations, not non-state actors. It has been questioned whether investigation of all abuses would equate blame between them, thus down playing the degree and gravity of state repression.[10]

On the naming of perpetrators, many argue that the truth is incomplete without individualizing responsibility and that it is the only way to break impunity. Others raise considerations of due process since a commission is not a court of law. Generally, the terms of reference have left the decision to the commissions whether or not to name names.[11]

Reporting
The final reports compiled by truth commissions are usually very comprehensive, in line with their task 'to paint the overall picture.' The overall pattern of abuses is indicated, the political and historical background is explained. An analysis of legal structures may be included as well as the role of different societal actors, thus establishing the context in which serious

violations of human rights could be committed. If not naming names, most commissions have laid out institutional responsibilities. The findings are usually presented by listing all cases, or by describing some representative ones in depth to illustrate general trends. Testimonies of victims are sometimes used to convey the emotional and social impact of human rights violations. Finally, extensive recommendations are made, outlining needed reform (such as restructuring the police, strengthening civilian command over the military, human rights education, change of personnel) and suggesting reparative measures (compensation, access to health care and education, renaming of public spaces.) Most commissions have made recommendations regarding the prosecution of perpetrators, irrespective of concurrent amnesty measures.

Follow-Up
In most cases, the reports have been widely released to the public. Some heads of state publicly accepted responsibility and apologized to the victims following the publication of a report. The Chilean President, for example, did not only make a televised apology appealing for forgiveness, but also sent a copy of the report to the family of each victim named therein. The truthtelling process may set other efforts related to dealing with the past in motion: in South Africa and Guatemala, for example, a process of exhumations and reburials has started which has gone some way in addressing the grief of relatives. The record of judicial follow-up to truth commissions is generally mixed. In several countries, blanket amnesties had already been declared before a commission came into being; elsewhere, governments declared an amnesty soon after the publication of a report.

> '*The past cannot be undone, but it may be possible to mitigate its negative impact on society.*'

Seldom has the (former) military and political leadership acknowledged responsibility for past human rights violations, nor have individual perpetrators been much prompted to come forth either. In most cases, however, society at large has acknowledged the abuses.

Limitations
Commissions operate in an tense political environment, which often place serious limitations on their activities. The balance of power between the different political and societal actors during the transitional period determines the scope and depth of the truthtelling process. If, for example, those responsible for past abuses continue to hold much power, a successor government can only press for investigation to a limited extent. In Namibia, the government has been resisting the establishment of a truth commission in order to avoid having its own past behaviour be subjected to scrutiny. The continuing dominance of the Guatemalan military ensured that the mandate of the Historical Clarification Commission did not allow for individualizing responsibilities nor for handing the material collected to the courts once the

commission had completed its work, despite strong pleas from national human rights organisations to include both.[12]

Challenges during a truth commission's existence may include lack of powers and/or resources, intimidation of witnesses, restricted access to information, attempts at political manipulation. Afterwards, the political parameters may impede the implementation of recommendations.

Enhancing the Prospects for Reconciliation

Establishing the contributions of truth commissions to reconciliation in any exact manner, is hardly possible. 'Reconciliation' itself is difficult to define, and, aside from its final report, the outcomes of a truth commission are not always that tangible either. Yet, reconciliation is not beyond our power to conceive nor do we lack examples of how truthtelling can affect societies. Experiences to date indicate that there a number of ways in which truth commissions can enhance the prospects for reconciliation in countries divided by their past: these exist on the social, factual, political, and moral level.

- Social: Breaking the silence about the past and officially acknowledging what happened can be essential for healing the wounds that exist in society. It breaks through the fear and isolation that serious violations generate and undermines a practice of denial and deceit by those who are responsible for them. It can also have a profound psychological impact on victims as their pain is recognized for the first time. A truth commission gives them the opportunity to tell their stories, air their anger, and be heard, which is a form of redress and rehabilitation. It may not only ask about what happened, but also how the violations effected people's life and how they coped. The process of truthtelling is increasingly considered to be as important as its final product (the written record) because it allows people to become actively involved and to regain some authority and dignity. The official nature of a commission enhances this vindicative impact for it symbolizes that the state acknowledges the stories and takes responsibility for the past.

- Factual: A commission can work towards a collective understanding of the past. By investigating what happened, it creates a factual record that impedes future distortion or manipulation of the past. It is not so much that one, definitive, account of truth can be established that everyone will share; rather, a framework is established in which further discussion on the past can take place.[13] In evaluating different claims in light of the information gathered, a commission will find that some cannot be upheld and that others are validated. In Argentina, it has become a matter of public record that people were thrown into the sea from helicopters while still alive. In South Africa, it can no longer be denied that a systematic practice of torture in detention existed that was, if not ordered, at least state-condoned. Yet the value of a truth commission also lies in exposing the many accounts that exist of what happened and why it happened, because that challenges perceptions and undermines a rigid black and white picture. The complexity related to the past is revealed; people learn about parts of the past of which they were not aware.

- Political: A truth commission can help to lay the foundations for a democratic culture of discussion and participation in which disagreement is managed in a non-violent way. People are given a voice which they may not have had before, and pluralism is encouraged by juxtaposing different versions of history. Processing a legacy of violence draws people into debate - about citizenship, the organisation of society, the governing of the state. Establishing the facts about particular events or prominent cases can also facilitate interaction between opposing parties in the public sphere. 'An official accounting and conclusion of the facts can allow [them] to debate and govern together without latent conflicts and bitterness over past lies,' Hayner writes.[14] The official nature of the commission may serve to restore the state's legitimacy, signalling its commitment to break with the past and to respect human rights.

- Moral: A commission can contribute to an awareness of fundamental values as it evaluates the past on the basis of a normative framework that evolves around human dignity and integrity. Investigating the past becomes a way for society to learn anew what ought be and what should not - to base itself on the very ethical values it needs to survive, allowing for the recognition of a common humanity. 'The tales of war,' Krog puts it, become 'part of an ethos relating to how people should behave towards one another.'[15] Truthtelling involves an examination of how conditions could arise that nurtured mass violence. Ultimately, it can bring people to reflect on their own role and responsibility, whether direct or indirect.

The positive impact of a truth commission in these areas can be significant. Yet a process of reconciliation involves many aspects and takes place on a number of levels. A commission will encounter challenges in furthering reconciliation, three of which are identified below.

Impartial?
A polarizing issue around truthtelling regards the interpretation of principles such as 'impartiality' and 'objectivity' that guide a commission in its work. A commission cannot escape making moral judgements on the past as its findings are made in light of human rights norms: it determines what was wrong and why it was wrong. The findings may also reflect whether one side

Archbishop D.M. Tutu and F.W. de Klerk (Former President of South Africa)

committed much more abuses or was disproportionally victimized. A truth commission can - and must - be impartial, but it cannot be neutral. 'Evenhandedness' means treating all violations fairly, not putting them on a par and apportioning equal blame to the different parties per se. This view is often contested by those who are (most) responsible for violations: they consider it proof of bias and may appeal to the commission to acknowledge that 'all sides committed abuses.' The tense environment in which a commission operates accelerates accusations of bias, especially because the findings may have political implications. The political wrangling around a truth commission is thus intensified as some seek to seize on its findings and others denounce them.

Coping with Conflict?
The above highlights that a truth commission may be caught between two roles that are contradictory rather than complementary: a non-partisan facilitator, supposed to bring different actors together to set forth and discuss their version of the past, and an advocate, expected to attribute responsibility and judge the severity of abuses. [16] A truth commission is, however, by origin much more the latter than the former. This suggests that it could be more complex for a truth commission to deal with horizontal (intercommunity) violence than with vertical (state-sponsored) violence: then, the abuses may be less overwhelmingly concentrated on one side and a commission can less fall back on the specific responsibility of the state to respect the right of its citizens. It also implies that a truth commission can probably not function in an on-going conflict nor can it resolve an actual conflict.

Reconciling the Personal?

The contributions of truth commissions to reconciliation are primarily concentrated on the national level. They can less affect the individual or community level, partly because of their temporary existence, but also because it would probably involve bringing people directly together - which a truth commission is generally unable to do in the face of the sheer enormity of its task to compile a comprehensive record within a short period of time. It has also been noted above that it is questionable to what extent a truth commission really prompts individual perpetrators to own up to their acts and elicits genuine repentance. In part, this may be a question of time; a truth commission has then created a space in which such acknowledgement can occur.

Affecting the Impact of a Truth Commission

If anything, experiences to date teach us that there can be no standard model for a truth commission nor a recipe for success given the extent to which a commission is shaped by the particular national context. Nevertheless, increasingly insight is gained into the factors that might affect the impact and effectiveness of a truth commission, of which the political parameters during the transitional period are probably the most fundamental, determining whether a commission is to be established, its terms of reference, powers, and general strength. These may further include, amongst others, the following:

- **Willingness to deal with the past and to share a common future** (or a recognition of a need to do so.) Genuinely coming to terms with the past is an inherently difficult undertaking, generating a public process of accounting that throws up controversial issues and poses painful questions. It implies that a truth recovery process cannot be imposed on a society by external actors; they can only support it once it is embarked on from within. It should be noted here that a popular desire for redressing past violations does not necessarily exist in any given context. Cambodia and Mozambique seem cases in point. In the case of a strongly divided society, moreover, participation by all major constituencies or communities is essential to ensuring the credibility of a commission. If, for example, a commission were to be established in Bosnia-Herzegovina in which only two of the three ethnic groups would take part, it could easily be perceived (or pictured) as merely slamming the third.

- **Support by the political and military leadership.** This may enhance the commission's authority and reach, and will influence the resources at its disposal, its ability to access information, and the extent to which any effects are given to the commission's findings and recommendations, whether judicial, institutional, or reparative. Such backing should, however, not affect the independence of a commission. Even if not actively supported, a commission may still be able to function fairly effectively as long as outright interference or obstruction is avoided. The Chilean Truth and Reconciliation Commission, generally regarded in a positive light, operated despite Pinochet's continued command of the armed forces. A similar situation could evolve in Surinam if a commission is established while former junta-leader Desi Bouterse remains Advisor of the State.

- **Legitimate and feasible mandate.** A number of issues arise in this regard. A commission might be accused of being mere window-dressing if its mandate does not cover those violations that were among the most frequently experienced. For example, the Uruguayan truth commission had a mandate limited to disappearances while torture and illegal detention were far more common during the period under investigation.[17]

  'A truth commission can set a much longer-term of transformation in motion, especially when it is embedded in a broader program of reform.'

  A degree of flexibility in the phrasing of its mandate allows a commission to investigate abuses as it deems fit. While the mandate of the South African Truth and Reconciliation Commission specified killing, abduction, and torture as gross human rights violations to be investigated, it also included the undefined notion of 'severe ill-treatment.'[18] This enabled the commission to look into crimes such as rape and poisoning as well. Further, the Joinet-principles prepared for the UN advocate that all abuses are investigated, whether committed by governmental or non-governmental forces,[19] which is relevant with a view to furthering reconciliation. A practical consideration regards the proportion between the period under investigation and the period of operation. The fact that the Accord on the establishment of the Guatemalan Historical Clarification Commission only awarded six months (with a possible six-month extension) to investigate a 36-year period of armed conflict undermined the commission's credibility before it even came into being.

- **Composition and procedures.** The degree of impartiality and representativeness of the commissioners will influence the acceptance of the commission amongst the broader public and political groupings. The credibility of the South African TRC was enhanced by the consultative procedure adopted for the appointment of commissioners, which included nominations by the public and public interviews of the nominees. The Joinet-principles suggest that the public be informed of the criteria used for the selection of commissioners.[20] Fair procedures are important for ensuring a just treatment of all parties.

- **Public participation and strength of civil society.** Involvement of the public and of civil society can contribute to the phrasing of the mandate and creates a general understanding of what a commission is supposed to do. It generally increases the democratic value of the truthtelling process. Thus far, extensive public debate preceding the establishment of a commission has only taken place in South Africa but a trend may have been set, considering current developments in Indonesia and Suriname. Non-governmental organizations often have a wealth of material on past human rights violations that will aid investigations by a commission. They can further be involved in collecting statements, providing information to the public, and supporting witnesses. The role of the media is also relevant in this regard, especially when the activities of a commission are conducted in public. Reporting can extend a commission's reach and accessibility considerably, yet if the media lack independence it may also undermine the truthtelling process.

- **Broader program of reform.** Whether a commission can help to overcome a legacy of past abuses is strongly influenced by the extent to which it is embedded in a broader process of social, economical, and political transformation. In particular when large scale violence was accompanied by structural repression, many consider reconciliation to be directly related to the division of resources and opportunities; truthtelling must then be complemented by a focus on social justice and socio-economic conditions. While not able to institute any change itself, a commission can contribute to reform through the recommendations it leaves behind. These can encourage changes on the long term if the political and economical context do not allow for immediate implementation. For example, despite the fact all members of the Salvadoran Supreme Court -which the truth commission had recommended be dismissed- refused to step down initially, none of them was reelected by parliament when their term had ended. President Menem of Argentine might have first down played in public the report of the National Commission on the Disappearance of Persons, he later silently slashed the military budget.[21]

- **Timing.** Establishing a commission early on in a transitional period may allow it to seize the momentum for dealing with past violations to the full extent, yet the political situation may then still be very fragile and emotions easily run high. In Northern-Ireland, for example, it is felt that the situation may not sufficiently have stabilized yet for a truthtelling process to be undertaken at this point.[22]

It seems important that the violence should have abated. The South African TRC has been notably less active in the province KwaZulu-Natal where a large threat of violence remains. It feared that truthtelling might seriously jeopardize the situation there.[23]

The above are but a few of the range of factors that influence the effectiveness and impact of a truth commission. Other issues include logistical and practical matters, support by the international community, access to outside sources of information, the level of fear amongst witnesses, and the role of external actors in the violence. The investigation of the latter might be fraught with difficulties but could be particularly important in situations such as Northern-Ireland. The relative strength of such factors and the way in which they are linked together will depend on the specific circumstances of each case.

Conclusion

Truth commissions have become very popular in a brief fifteen years and it is unlikely that their rise will be checked any time soon. As more insight is gained in their functioning and the ways in which they may affect societies, commissions are increasingly deployed in coming to terms with a legacy of violence. A development in this regard is their growing launch in situations of armed conflict, which possibly present a truth commission with more complex challenges than transitions to democracy do. Attention also seem to shift from merely breaking the silence and telling the truth about what happened to looking into the contextual circumstances and the root causes of the conflict.[24]

While a commission is suitable for doing so considering its broad scope of inquiry, a socio-historical analysis of a conflict is also more susceptible to varying interpretations. Time will tell how this will work out.

The rise of truthseeking bodies is not any longer primarily related to the limited applicability of a judicial approach in transitional situations. Rather, it is realized that a truth commission can set a much longer-term of transformation in motion, especially when it is embedded in a broader program of reform. It generates a process of reflection that blurs the hard edges of perceived reality, highlights the need for addressing relationships and attitudes, and makes people think about the organization of society and the governing of the state. The increased level of public involvement in establishing truth commissions is valuable in this respect, signifying how dealing with the past is a collective effort. While a truth commission cannot institute change itself, it can create an environment in which other measures are more likely to gain a foothold. The past may be there to stay, yet a truth commission can allow it to be processed and managed in a non-destructive way based upon the recognition of human dignity and integrity.

Notes
1 For an overview of truth commissions, see Priscilla Hayner, 'Fifteen Truth Commissions - 1974 to 1994: A Comparative Study,' Human Rights Quarterly, Vol. 16 (1994), p. 597-655; and Daan

Bronkhorst, Truth and Reconciliation. Obstacles and Opportunities for Human Rights, Amnesty International, Amsterdam, 1995. There is no exact figure of truth commissions to date as slightly different definitions are being used which are more or less inclusive.

2 This is the main consideration in a recent proposal, put forth by the United States Institute of Peace, to establish a truth commission for Bosnia-Herzegovina. Check reference Kritz.

3 Juan Mendez,'Review of 'A Miracle, A Universe: Settling Accounts with Torturers'. By Lawrence Weschler (New York, Pantheon, 1990)' New York Law School Journal of Human Rights, Vol. VIII, part II (Spring 1991): p. 583-4.

4 'Set of principles intended to strengthen action to combat impunity,' Annex II to The Administration of Justice and the Human Rights of Detainees. Question of the impunity of perpetrators of violations of human rights (civil and political rights): final report prepared by Mr. L. Joinet, pursuant to Subcommission resolution 1995/35, UNDoc E/CN4/Sub2/1996/18, 29 June 1996. Joinet is a member of the UN Subcommission on Prevention of Discrimination and Protection of Minorities.

5 For an analysis of truth and truthtelling in relation to redressing human rights violations, see Michelle Parlevliet, 'Considering Truth: Dealing with a Legacy of Gross Human Rights Violations,' Netherlands Quarterly of Human Rights, Vol. 16, No. 2, June 1998: p. 141-174.

6 The description in the following section is in part based on Hayner (note 1): 600-606.

7 Report of the Commission on the Truth for El Salvador, From Madness to Hope: the 12-Year War in El Salvador, UNDoc s/25500/1993: p. 11.

8 Lawrence Weschler, A Miracle, A Universe: Settling Accounts with Torturers (New York: Pantheon, 1990.)

9 Richard Wilson, 'Violent Truths: The Politics of Memory in Guatemala,' Accord, Issue 2, 1997: p. 18-27; and Frank LaRue, 'Truth Commission Accord Fails to Address Concerns of Guatemalan Civil Society and the People's 'Right to Truth,' Center for Human Rights Legal Action, 21 July 1994.

10 In the traditional understanding, only the state can violate human rights because such rights exist in the relation between citizen and state as a limit to state power; private persons (which includes guerrilla/opposition forces) cannot violate human rights. Most of the discussion on this issue has revolved around the Chilean Commission on Truth and Reconciliation, which interpreted the concept 'human rights violation' to include acts committed by government and non-governmental actors, arguing that this broader interpretation had become dominant in public opinion.

11 Hayner (note 1): 648-9. The Salvadoran commission named, amongst others, the Minister of Defence and the President of the Supreme Court. See also Cassell (who served on the commission) for the motivation of the Salvadoran commission to name individuals; Douglas W. Cassell, Jr. 'International Truth Commissions and Justice,' The Aspen Institute Quarterly, Summer 1993, Vol. 5, No. 3: p. 69-90.

12 Wilson; LaRue (note 9).

13 Ignatieff speaks in this context of 'narrowing the range of permissible lies,' see Michael Ignatieff, 'Articles of Faith,' Index on Censorship, Vol. 25, No. 5, 1996, Issue 172: p. 110-122; and Michelle Parlevliet (note 4): 158-160; 168.

14 Priscilla Hayner, In Pursuit of Justice and Reconciliation: Contributions of Truthtelling, paper presented at Conference on Comparative Peace Processes in Latin America, Washington D.C, 13-14 March 1997: 9.

15 Antjie Krog, in Alex Boraine, Janet Levy, and Ronald Scheffer (eds.), The Healing of a Nation?, Justice in Transition, Cape Town (1995): 115.

16 Michelle Parlevliet, 'Between Facilitator and Advocate: the South African Truth and Reconciliation Commission,' Forum (forthcoming)

17 Hayner (note 1): 616 .

18 National Unity and Reconciliation Act (1995): check reference

19 Joinet-principles (note 4): 11 (principle 7.)

20 Ibid.

21 Margaret Popkin and Naomi Roht-Arriaza, 'Truth as Justice: Investigatory Commissions in Latin America,' Law and Social Inquiry, Vol. 20, No. 1, Winter 1995, p. 79-116: p. 103; Lawrence Weschler in Truth Commissions: a Comparative Assessment, Harvard Law School Human Rights Program, 1996: p. 63.

22 Brandon Hamder, 'Conclusion: A Truth Commission for Northern Ireland?,' in Brandon Hamder (ed.), Dealing with the Past in Northern Ireland and Societies in Transition, INCORE, Londonderry (1998): 79-86.

23 Interview with Dr. Alex Boraine, Vice-Chair of the South African Truth and Reconciliation Commission, 15 May 1998.

24 I thank Ron Slye, University of Seattle, Factulty of law, for bringing this to my attention.

Michelle Parlevliet is Program Manager of the Human Rights and Conflict Management Training Program, at the Center for Conflict Resolution, South Africa. She has previously worked in the Prosecutor's Office of the International Criminal Tribunal for the Former Yugoslavia and as a researcher at the South African Truth and Reconciliation Commission. MA Political Science (University of Amsterdam, the Netherlands); MA International Peace Studies (University of Notre Dame, USA)

4 Europe: From Warfare to Coexistence

By Georges Berthoin*

Emerging from World War II, whether victorious or defeated, we experienced as individuals or as groups the total annihilation of peoples, riches, institutions, values. Naturally we shared, with the same intensity, the same desire that it should never happen again. Total war led to a resolute quest for peace.

We knew that peace could not be established merely through the rhetoric of speeches or through good intentions. To build peace we had first to understand war. Why and how had our European civilization fallen into destruction on such a scale that the very fabric of our societies had almost collapsed? This meant undertaking a fundamental critical review of our history and its effects on individual and collective psychology. After this review we would be able to make concrete suggestions and take the necessary steps. Change would result from facts as much as from ideas or perceptions.

In order to exist, all living entities must fulfil three functions: they must find 'their' place, learn to survive, and to receive and transmit life. None of these functions encourages a passive attitude: to exist is to fight.
If one of the three functions is denied, the intensity of the fight increases to a level where violence becomes unavoidable. Consequently, we must recognize that fight is a natural instinct, an element of human culture. From the schoolyard, to the football stadium through to war and the battlefield.

The first step towards coexistence is existence itself: an awareness of one's identity with neither a superiority or inferiority complex, acceptance of the other within a system which guarantees not only one's equal acceptance, but is considered by all as legitimate and fair to each of its components' interests. To reach coexistence, channels providing adequate and lasting answers must be developed. Acceptance is only workable if at each level there exists a corresponding institutional and symbolic framework which is mutually accepted. If such a context does not exist, each group will try to prevail according to its own logic. Violence then becomes the ultimate resource.

Through the centuries our societies have prepared for such eventualities by awarding war and the warrior a special place and prestige within their organisation, by according them a moral and even religious recognition.

The man of peace encounters great difficulties in competing with the traditional heroic, epic, romantic image of the soldier. The peacemaker must choose his circumstances, project and conditions very carefully if he is not to be perceived as an appeaser, a de facto agent of the enemy, a traitor. If peace is a universal human dream, its quest and implementation are extremely complex and hazardous. It is only if society feels itself to be secure and that its dignity is fully recognized that any peace initiative is workable.

The challenge is therefore to go against instinct and tradition, in order to demonstrate that war does not pay; that many means exist which can help to reach peace. This effort requires not only an individualised psychological approach and a sense of history but a thorough understanding of the influence of context on people's behaviour, and an ability to change the overall context through social engineering.

Discrimination between victors and defeated breeds future conflicts. Without full, free and equal access to the economic, political and cultural order resulting from victory, the defeated do not feel involved in its preservation. Under a surface appearance of acceptance, revenge awaits its opportunity to bring about change. A new peaceful order cannot prevail if its legitimacy is not as fully recognized by the defeated as by the victor. This poses a difficult challenge which can be met only when the victor offers principles which by their own nature are common to both parties. Sovereignty of the people - democracy- is the only principle which, by its very nature, finds legitimacy equally rooted in both existence and dignity.

'Recent European history shows that institutions can build peace.'

The psychological ability to overcome the past, recent or ancient, is of cardinal importance as practically all organized human groups were at one moment of their respective history in a master-victim relation. To ask them to forget or to forgive is asking the impossible. People remember. The past cannot be changed. But it can be placed in a new dynamic process, and even transformed into a driving force for peace if the will to build the future together prevails. In post-War Europe, in freeing ourselves from an obsession with the potential enemy we also freed ourselves from the curse of past history and were able to join forces to discover and manage our new awareness of common interest.

The attraction of realizing this common future became for all of us the driving force for peace manifest in the creation of the European Community. It was and remains the most concrete answer to this challenge.

In one of the early texts of modern political theory, The Federalist issue no. 10, James Madison wrote:
'The latent causes of faction are....sown in the nature of man. Since the causes of faction cannot be removed....relief is only to be sought in the means of controlling its effects.'

We did not share that view and felt that in changing the causes we could find the relief.

So in order to establish the context which was able to change the psychology of individuals and nations alike, we looked for limited but decisive areas where fundamental and competing interests could be objectively recognized as common: coal and steel for Western Europe, (or, one day, water for the Middle East).

Common institutions based on the principle of non-discrimination were established in order to help recognize and manage such potentially divisive interests as common to all.

From this joint awareness and administration, a confidence building process emerged which demonstrated progressively the practical rewards of peace. Gradually the construction of this new context gathered momentum. A feeling of security began to replace the ancestral fear of the other. Through new habits and perceptions and the existence and work of common institutions, the partnership was enlarged to new areas and more and more potential conflicts were put into the category of those which could be prevented by being channelled into a process, which we all recognized as effective, practical, fair and legitimate.

This strand of recent European history shows that institutions can build peace. The more distant past also shows that without effective institutions, no lasting peace is possible.

However, it requires a special kind of institution to fulfil this role. It must be able to make and enforce decisions. It cannot be a coalition created by the victorious side in order to impose their will, because this would provoke a growing feeling of resentment among the defeated and a corresponding desire for revenge. Neither could it be a system where each participant would enjoy equal sovereign power or its effectiveness would be restricted by the constant risk of veto. The possibility of creating an authority which would give its orders to different national entities seemed to be the most efficient answer. But this would also involve ignoring the new and powerful trend which sees all types of human communities fighting for recognition. Coexistence today involves more and more actors. Accordingly, through trial and error, we came to understand that a new type of governance had to be invented. Despite the lack

PHOTO LINDA GRAHAM

The Bosnian city of Tuzla managed to preserve its multicultural character

of a precedent, we succeeded. One day the European Union may be recognized not only for its role in solving nineteenth-century problems but also for having helped to create harmony between diversities in need of recognition and the universalist logic of modern technologies in the twenty-first century.

This is now the central issue confronting national bodies of every kind.

Through a process which was in many cases very dramatic and chaotic, national orders prevailed. In order to allow coexistence between them, the European union had the choice between adopting a traditional international method where all governments enjoy an equal veto right or the more effective approach in which an independent authority imposes its ruling over the member States - the supranational method.

The latter alternative was used at the beginning of our unification process. It worked and was accepted because it involved a limited sector with limited functions. But its adoption became more problematic when more and more - and finally all- aspects of economic, social and political life were incorporated in its jurisdiction.

The way out of the dilemma was to create a pragmatic balance between each of the participants' respective sovereignty and the group representing the common interest of the 'collective' sovereignty. The answer was found in adopting a horizontal model of decision making in place of the traditional vertical chain of command. In the vertical model, proposal for action is submitted to a superior authority whose executive authority is exclusive. In the horizontal model there is no hierarchical authority between those making proposals and decisions. Both enjoy equal but different sources of legitimacy, one European, one national.

The European Commission enjoys the exclusive right to make proposals. It represents the common European interest and has no link with any Government or coalition. At the same time, while it is designated through the joint action of the member States, it is confirmed by, answerable to and can be dismissed by the European Parliament which is democratically elected by the people of the Union, on the basis of direct universal suffrage. Thanks to this dual legitimacy and independence, the Commission can consult with all interested parties in the official world and civil society. It can then investigate and submit proposals, which are by definition representative of the common interest. The fate of these proposals then becomes the responsibility of the different national sovereignties as expressed through the deliberations of the Council of Ministers. At this stage the Commission takes on the additional role of facilitator.

'The extranational experience of the European Union might help elaborate a method for the prevention of conflicts.'

For national governments concerned about losing face, it is far easier to accept a proposal elaborated through a process grounded in common-interest-legitimacy, which by definition, also represents part of the national interest, than to bow to the will of other national sovereignties.

I had an opportunity to present this new form of governance in a more systematic form at a workshop chaired by the Hon. Harlan Cleveland in Aspen, Colorado, in 1975. I gave it the name: 'extranational' to distinguish it from international or supra-national institutions.

The extra-national experience of the European Union might help elaborate a method for the prevention of conflicts.

If a danger of conflict arises or even when the conflict already exists, the first step to be taken should be to find an authority which both sides recognize as legitimate and well intentioned.
Then through its help, to find out what the potential opponents share in common. To make them aware that they share the fact that they are in

opposition; that their conflict might escalate; that their joint challenge is to weigh how a peaceful approach might be more productive than war.

To share this recognition is almost impossible without the help of a third party. Arbitration of all kinds is a well known method used on an adhoc basis where the situation is tense, or under the pressure of an outside element or when both sides freely agree to abide by its conditions, hoping, as in war, that they might win.

If a permanent institutional framework or body were to exist, which potential opponents could recognize as legitimate and fair, they might more easily share the same willingness to understand what each party is trying to achieve and finally conclude that peaceful approach might bring about better results.

Then, but only then, as a third stage, negotiation on the contested subject could start with a reasonable chance of success.

In most recent conflicts, in Yugoslavia, the Middle East, and Rwanda etc., the mutual interest of the opposing parties did not get a chance to be explained in a manner acceptable to the antagonists because the legitimacy of the so called 'international community' was always challengeable and challenged by the main powers. The mandate and legitimacy of the third element which should have been the UN, was in fact the product of the different and even conflicting agendas of the five permanent members of the Security Council. The Secretary General who was trying to resolve the conflict, saw his authority challenged when he was about to become the independent facilitator that the situation required. Finally he ended up as a ping pong ball between opponents and major international actors alike. He was effectively reminded that he was in the final analysis merely the highest ranking civil servant in the organisation. A change in his statutory position is imperative if we intend to prevent or end conflicts worldwide.

This is where the value of the European Union's example lies. It comes from the fact that almost 50 years of practical experience are available to be studied as a realistic precedent because it managed to establish the conditions of a lasting peace between old sovereign states after centuries of wars and at the end of the most destructive conflict of all. This is a tried answer to conflict prevention for all to emulate.

The new extra-national approach can be used at any level where tensions occur. With proven credibility, this system could be used on global, regional, tribal, or local levels, as a non utopian answer to aspirations for peace common to the human race. It would transform the necessary fight for existence into a civilized process.

Jean Monnet instinctively referred to this institutional solution in the very last sentence of his Memoires:
'the sovereign nations of the past no longer provide the framework within which today's problems can find their solutions. And the Community (today the European Union) itself is no more than a step towards the types of organization of tomorrow's world'.
I would like to conclude with the comment that the world of tomorrow needs peace to survive. We have the means, we need the will.

I hope that among those who happen to read this text somebody somewhere will take up the challenge and make a difference in considering the extranational solution. We all need it. The bottle at sea might not be lost, after all.

*****George Berthoin** *joined the French Resistance in October 1940, aged 15. For his activities, he was awarded the Legion d'honour, Médialle militaire, and Croix de Guerre. He studied at Grenoble and read Sciences Politiques in Paris and Harvard. He was involved at the inception of the European Community as Head of Staff (1952-55) and then acted as personal advisor (up to 1979) of Jean Monnet. In 1956 he was appointed deputy head of EC diplomatic mission to the United Kingdom. He acted as ambassador until the UK joined the EC in 1973. Co-founder of the Trilateral Commission, he acted as its European chairman for 17 years (1975-92). He was international chairman of the European Movement 1978-81 and member of the Wise Men Group in Africa. He presently serves as an Executive member of the International Peace Academy in New York and of the Aspen Institute in Berlin. He is also honorary international chairman of the European Movement, honorary European chairman of the Trilateral Commission.*

5 What is Co-existence?

By Kumar Rupesinghe*

Learning to live together, to coexist, to learn to accept difference, and make the world safe for difference will be one of the great challenges for the 21 Century. coexistence is a term that has been used synonymously in several contexts and used as a key phrase in the emergence of a number of great social and political movements. The key characteristic in the definition of the word coexistence is its relation with its 'others' and the acknowledgement that an 'others' exists.

Coexistence means learning to live together, to accept diversity and implies a positive relationship to the other. Our identities are defined in relation to the other. When relationships are affirmative and equal it enhances dignity and freedom and independence. When relations are negative and destructive this undermines human dignity and our own self worth. This applies to personal, group and interstate relationships. After experiencing two world wars and countless wars of destruction and genocide the promotion of coexistence at all levels remains an imperative for the 21st Century.

One of the basic conceptions in the history of Western culture in general, and of modern philosophy in particular is that the actual validity of a certain entity with its specific qualities exists only when it is recognised by another subjectivity. According to Hegel, the essence of his conceptualisation of the term is that 'existence' is already, fundamentally 'coexistence'. This is true for individuals, groups and classes. Mutual recognition is required as a necessary condition (even as a constitutive one) for freedom and independence. There are many excellent examples of the struggle for recognition, and the assertion of independence in the history of social movements. A significant example is the struggle for coexistence between men and women from Patriarchy to the struggle for the emancipation of women and gender equality. The struggles against slavery, and against feudal bondage are well known. Today the struggle for coexistence continues with the transformation of the former Soviet Union, the peaceful revolution in Eastern Europe.

In the modern political vocabulary the term 'peaceful coexistence' has been conceptualised as a strategy of survival and existence between war in the literal sense and peace in the ideal sense. Peaceful coexistence in this sense means the peaceful relationship between states. With the development and the centralisation of the state, coexistence between states and the non-interference in the internal affairs of other states has been a central tenet of state diplomacy. It was Lenin who first articulated peaceful coexistence as a state policy of the revolution. During the early phase of the Russian revolution he used it to describe periods in which Soviet policy would abandon the all- out attack on every front against the non-communist world and replace it by the more subtle tactics of concluding agreements with some governments in some areas, while keeping up intense pressure elsewhere. The purpose of coexistence, according to Lenin, was purely tactical and the phase strictly temporary. By changing the nature of the attack and relaxing the pressure, divisions in capitalist states, which were always inherent, would be allowed to develop and thus weaken the enemies of communism.[1]

However in the Cold War context 'peaceful coexistence' enunciated by Khrushchev made a strategic shift in focus where it was explicitly recognised that the continued conflict between the two systems would lead to the mutual destruction of the entire system. coexistence according to Krushechev meant continuation of the struggle between the social systems -but by peaceful means, without war, without interference by one state in the internal affairs of another. It will be a competition of the two systems in a peaceful field.[2]

Another shift in meaning came with the Bandung Conference where the concept of 'coexistence' was used with the aim of creating a more peaceful international environment. Nehru outlined his conception of peaceful coexistence between the two superpowers in terms of the Five Principles, or the *Pancha Shila*: mutual respect for territorial integrity and sovereignty, non-aggression, non-interference in one another's internal affairs, equality and mutual benefit.[3] Nehru was convinced that India might contribute to bringing about reconciliation between the United States and the Soviet Union through this 'bridge-policy' which was rooted in the Gandhian strategy of *satyagrahya*, or non-violence. Although these principles may now be regarded as aspirations of the newly emergent independent nations of a number of Asian and African states, the fact remains that they brought to the forefront the acknowledgement of this concept in international policy making.

Coexistence as a paradigm should not only relate to inter-state relations but intra-state relations as well. Coexistence between different peoples, races, religious groups, clans, tribes within a spectrum of identities is the great challenge for the 21st century. Coexistence between peoples has become an imperative in the next phase of evolution of civilisation. On the one hand the struggle for self-determination of peoples, a major factor in nationalist wars of the 20th century culminated in the completion of the decolonisation process. Currently the civil wars and ethnic identity conflicts are challenges to the existing state system.

There is a continuum of struggles for recognition of new identities and, of contestation and challenges to the unitary state. In some cases such contestation and war has led to the separation of states. Recent examples abound, such as the separation of Pakistan from the Indian polity, the separation of Bangladesh from Pakistan and the recent breakdown of Yugoslavia. On the other hand there has also been the expansion of larger entities, where the expansion of the European Union is only one classic example. The formation of the European Union is a good example of the decision to suspend warfare, between the Great Powers. The work of Jean Monnet and others in crafting a normative framework, to develop peaceful coexistence between France and Germany, through economic co-operation and then to extend the concept to Europe as a whole provides an excellent example of recognising diversity and maintaining coexistence.

Identity, ethnicity and coexistence

When closely examined, the overwhelming majority of the nation states in our global community reveals significant internal cleavages based upon ethnicity, race and religion. The significance of these differences in the social and political process varies widely, as does the degree of saliency, intensity and politization of communal segments both within and between states. The most fundamental proposition after the proliferation of ethnic and identity conflicts, particularly after the Cold War is the realisation that cultural pluralism is an enduring attribute of contemporary political life. There is no longer any justification for clinging to the belief that the array of processes commonly known as 'modernisation' would automatically lead to a notion of a single nation, or lead to the erosion of cultural solidarity, ethnicity or religion. Rather the reverse may happen. Social change tends to produce stronger communal identities. Studies, which focus on the individual as the primary unit in the analysis of conflict, point to the need for identity as fundamental to the survival and well being of the individual and the society in which that individual exists. Burton for example points to such complex and protracted conflicts as the Arab-Palestinian conflict, the Cyprus conflict and the Northern-Ireland conflict as being based on the need for identity which humans will seek to satisfy irrespective of contextual circumstances or degrees of coercion.[4] The 'basic human needs approach' therefore sees the recognition of identity both as a universal need and as an essential requirement for individual development.[5]

'Coexistence between peoples has become an imperative in the next phase of evolution of civilisation.'

There are of course detractors who are sceptical about the value and operational viability of using the concept of coexistence. One school of thought would argue that relations between contending groups couldn't be changed, that they are primordial and not transformative. Others would argue that coexistence means accepting the status quo. A more powerful variant of this argument is that coexistence is a term used by majorities to assert dominance over the minorities. They would argue that hegemonic majorities would wish to retain their dominance by proposing forms of coexistence, which do not undermine their dominance. I would argue however, that coexistence between communities and groups is fundamentally a transformative relationship, which is dynamic and positive. The term implies that identity is a fundamental driving force in human development and that coexistence evolves from a minimum condition of recognising difference and accepting diversity and the mutual recognition of the other to a transformative relationship where communities over time may find appropriate mechanisms and institutions to coalesce and a higher level of meaning.

Approaches to promoting coexistence

There are a variety of approaches, which are currently being used in the promotion of aspects of coexistence between peoples. Some social movements have defined themselves as promoting conflict resolution or conflict management. Conflict resolution or management is normally defined as bringing parties to the negotiating table. Other variants of conflict resolution refer to the various methods and approaches developed in two track diplomacy where the efforts have been developed to support the formal negotiations process by complimentary approaches such as promoting problem solving approaches and working towards building peace between communities. Numerous efforts are being made, largely by citizen based groups to create space for dialogue to improve coexistence between communities. The environmental movement for example is a classic example of extending coexistence to nature so that nature is seen as an aspect of our planetary existence. The gender movement is another example where the focus is on recognition, emancipation, and the struggle for equality and freedom. Typically, the concept of conflict resolution means the steps taken to promote political coexistence between different parties to a conflict.

Conflict Resolution was however too narrow for those who felt that the concept implied merely a negotiated settlement between parties to a conflict. This approach it was felt did not involve peace building between communities. Often negotiated settlements would fail if due care is not taken to sustain building efforts between the communities. This is why another concept was then introduced, called conflict transformation. Conflict transformation implied a wider concept where the critical aspect of conflict resolution is the transformation of social relations between groups and identities in society. Another concept, which came into vogue immediately after the Cold War, was the concept of conflict prevention. Concerned with the proliferation of internal conflicts and civil wars within states and wars between peoples within a state, conflict prevention was introduced to mean the prevention of conflict before

Building the basis for coexistence

Photo Oliviero Toscani

violence actually occurs. A more sophisticated variant of conflict prevention was the reduction of violence in any point in the conflict cycle. However this concept was also confronted with terminological difficulties. There are those who argued that the term conflict prevention presents a negative connotation, suggesting that conflicts are endemic to human coexistence and therefore necessary in the course of human evolution. However, what the concept was meant to imply was the prevention of violent conflict.

Political coexistence and community coexistence

Policy initiatives that have been presented to stem conflict between communities have been directed towards institutional management in the highest echelons of governments and in the hands of the political elites. The biases and prejudices of party politics and populist policy often entangle these policies. Policy initiatives to address community coexistence have been far less a priority. Much of the inter communal conflict that exists in society today are due to policy makers resorting to the easier and less resourceful method of initiating policy directed at the centre with the hope that the 'trickle down effect' would reform community institutions in grassroots levels as well. They address only the needs of political coexistence through the implementation of constitutional safeguards and side stepping policy making with regard to community coexistence. A distinction needs to be made between the promotion of political coexistence and community coexistence. Political coexistence means the development of systems of governance which can better accommodate ethnic diversity and pluralism. This means the search for constitutional forms of governance ranging from federalism to forms of autonomy and self-governance. It may also take the forms of different types of electoral systems, which can best accommodate and balance ethnic groups in a society.

What is however distinctive about community coexistence is that often different groups, whether they are ethnic, or religious share a common living space, and thereby have to define their relationship to each other. How these relations are developed, sustained and nurtured is a major challenge for the 21st century. For it is at the community level that perceptions are developed transmitted and socialised to the other. According to Mari Fitzduff, 'Earlier definitions of the objective of community relations work seem to have primarily concerned themselves with emphasising the idea of a harmonious existence between differing groups with the intended goal of integrating the minority groups into the wider community as quickly as possible. Later definitions of objectives have put a far greater emphasis on the idea of equality of basic rights and opportunity for all groups, whilst simultaneously encouraging cultural diversity, as being preferable.[6]

In an assessment of Community Relations Work in Northern Ireland Mari Fitzduff argues, 'It is increasing recognised that such work focusing on differences e.g. of a political or theological nature in some instances is likely to be limited, unless work designed to facilitate free discussion within communities is carried out productively. If such intra-community work is not done, which is often the case because of fear and intimidation and lack of available structures through which to do the work - mutual understanding work is more likely to produce defensiveness and be therefore less effective.'

Building the basis for coexistence: education

An attempt to release the child from the confines of the ethnocentric straightjacket and to awaken him to the existence of other cultures, societies and ways of life and thought. It is intended to decondition the child as much as possible in order that he can go out into the world as free from biases and prejudices as possible and able and willing to explore its rich diversity.[7]

As the twenty first century draws to a close, countries the world over are preoccupied by the challenge of finding new and improved ways to educate their citizens for living in diversity in the next millennium. There are over 2 billion children who will inherit the earth.
The right to education is a fundamental right recognised by all countries. It is

however a fact that still a majority of our children is without proper schooling and facilities. Therefore building a basis for coexistence is that every child has to have access to education and participate in making decisions about her education. Education and learning is a principle means of learning to live together. This means that the school becomes a major institution for teaching coexistence, multicultural learning. The International Commission on Education for the 21st Century in its report on education for the 21st century outline the 4 pillars of education, of which Learning to Live Together is identified as a central challenge. (See Introduction Education)

How can we inculcate the respect and need for existence and the need for coexistence amongst school children? The process of educating about coexistence needs to occurs on every level, from the informal level ranging from teacher's colleges, to schools themselves; to community groups; governmental organisations to media and corporations; and all the informal modes including families, celebrities, writers and poets. It is clearly challenging in culturally diverse societies to reflect satisfactorily the needs of all socio-cultural groups in the curriculum. Adapting a common core curriculum to local needs and traditions is of vital importance, but potentially divisive. If social sciences and humanities curricula are to adequately reflect international, national and local concerns in today's increasingly pluralistic, multicultural societies, curriculum development processes need to become more democratic, adopting decentralized approaches which permit input and participation by all interest groups.

'Ministries of Coexistence could be set up in all countries, as Ministries of Environment were set up in the 1970s.'

Multicultural education is a viable means of social engineering drawing students to appreciate the plural societies from which they come.[8] Teaching and learning are always cultural processes in that they encompass the dynamics of a particular social fabric. Although students learn better using examples drawn from their own cultures -retaining their own culturally specific examples-[9] there is a growing need for multicultural education as an agent for helping to defuse deeply held mindsets, biases that have been infused by the conditioning of the environment of a particular culture as being an integral part of that person's perception of self and others. However, if multicultural education is to succeed in its aims it cannot be a mere ad hoc program implemented at critical junctures of a conflict in a lame attempt to reconcile differences between conflicting social groups but should be a long-term project. Multi-cultural education deals directly with identity. Just as peace education was a reaction to Cold War politics, multicultural education should be looked as an essential tool developed to stem ethnic conflict.

An important instrument in promoting coexistence education is the curricula. At the end of the 20th century, it is more or less universally recognised that curricula should be open, active, flexible and intercultural. But the translation of this ideal into meaningful reality into schools and classroom is an enormous challenge in all countries. A core curricula needs to be adapted to local conditions and take account of local identities. It also requires a participatory approach to curriculum development. The stakeholders need to be enlarged beyond the policy makers in the Ministries of Education and be included and specialised education personnel, parents, teachers, community leaders, religious leaders and the students themselves.

The need for a policy shift

Conflict exists on every level of human behaviour - however this is not always reflected as a determinant in policy making. The fact that conflicting perspectives exist need to be legitimised and ways of living together must be found despite these differences. Whilst many people are involved in coexistence work, these initiatives are not always reflected at the policy level. Politicians, governments and opinion leaders must accept that coexistence is a legitimate goal. One suggestion is to set up a special department or Ministry of Coexistence in all countries as Ministries of Environment were set up in the 1970s.

Learning to live together does not fall from the sky. It is clear that coexistence is learnt behaviour, which requires a sustained process of learning both at school, within the communities and in society as a whole. This requires structures, and institutions which sustain and enhance coexistence through a multitude of projects and programmes. Further, it requires financing such efforts and a commitment by the central government. An excellent example of such efforts is the work of the Community Relations Council in Northern Ireland. Here the government commits resources to the Council to promote community coexistence. Such a model needs to be repeated in other countries. There needs to be government commitment and resources provided for the Council to be effective.

Another form of legitimation is through the work of municipalities and local government bodies. These institutions are in the front line of coexistence work. They are located in spaces where many communities live together. Here much can be done to develop understanding, through a variety of schemes and programmes. They can range from the provision of resources for supporting community centres where all communities can come to learn and play. They could be in the provision of encouraging games and sports amongst the various communities. There can be programmes for learning other languages, to encouraging encounters between the two communities and learning about each others history. Municipalities and local government bodies are also democratically elected bodies, which have the power and the resources to provide substantive support for community building work.

Donor organisation and foundations need also to be sensitised. The Abraham Fund is one of the leading foundations doing this work, supporting over 200 hundred initiatives on coexistence between the Jewish and Arab populations each year. (see case-study)

The principled method used by the programmes of the Abraham Fund seems to be to encourage encounters between the two peoples and two cultures. These encounters are encouraged at a variety of levels. Given the level of hostility, misperceptions, and trauma that the peoples have experienced these encounters are not easy and have to be managed with great facilitation skills.

It has been very clear to me in my very brief visit to Israel that the support for these grass roots efforts and initiatives has influenced the politics of coexistence. In fact these grass roots efforts will be the necessary building blocks for the politics of coexistence.

These encounters between the two peoples are not easy. Although the two peoples have lived as neighbours, many do not know or understand each other's history, culture, and traditions. Therefore these encounters may result in the following dynamics:

- Confrontation: stating ones grievances and complaints;
- Understanding that each side has a point of view which needs to be recognised;
- Reconciliation where a higher understanding may be reached and friendships begin to be formed;
- Transformation where relationships of equality are manifested in the elaboration of joint projects at the level of the community.

The significance of the projects is that it promotes encounters and the two sides experience the transformation. A significant aspect of the projects is that the formulation and implementation of the project requires the participation of both sides. Therefore a prerequisite for funding a coexistence project is the requirement that both sides are represented in the decision making process.

Conclusion

Promoting positive coexistence between states and between peoples is a major challenge for the 21st century. There are fortunately today social movements, which have begun to grapple with these issues, both at the international and national level and at the political, and community level. What we are have argued is that political coexistence to be successful requires investment in coexistence at the community level. We need to accumulate the experiences, and the energies of a variety of citizen based movement, and build a multi-faceted approach to these issues. Social movements necessarily work on aspects of coexistence and it is the combination and the cumulative effects of these movements that will create the space for coexistence.

A principle pillar for coexistence is the education system. The education system requires a major paradigm shift in focus where living together in diversity becomes a principle value in the education of the child. We need to invest heavily in our children. This means that our attitudes towards education require fundamental reassessments where education should be seen as an interaction between the community, the school and the child. It is the relationship, which can create space for tolerance and the acceptance of diversity. Investments in the education of the child are a solid investment in ensuring a world safe for difference.

Notes
1 Hugh Gaitskell, 'The Challenge of Co-existence', 1957 p.8
2 The New York Times, 14 October 1959.
3 These 'Five Principles,' announced by Mr. Nehru at the Conference of Asian -African countries at Bandung in 1955, were accepted by all powers represented, including Communist China. They have also been incorporated into treaties made by India with its neighbours including Soviet Union and China.
4 Identity and collectivity p.122 Jabri
5 Jabri p.123
6 Mari Fitzduff (1991) Approaches to Community Relations Work. Community Relations Council, Belfast
7 Parakh B.(1986) The concept of Multicultural education. In S. Modgil, G.K.Verma, K.Mallick & C.Modgil(Eds.) Multicultural Education The Interminable Debate. S.Modgil London: Falmer Press, p.16-17
8 p.10
9 Geneva Hayp.9

Kumar Rupesinghe joined the State of the World Forum as the director of the Coexistence Initiative after spending six years as secretary general of International Alert (UK), an NGO mandated to prevent and mitigate violent internal conflict. Previous to this, he served as director of the program on Ethnic Conflict and Conflict Resolution at the International Peace Research Institute. Kumar was appointed Co-Coordinator of the Program on Governance and Conflict Resolution at the United Nations University, Tokyo. A native Sri Lankan, he was intimately involved in the political life of his country and engaged in many efforts to seek a solution to the national conflict between the two communities in the country. He is a prolific writer, author and editor of over 25 books and numerous articles.

6 Multi-Track Diplomacy in the 21st Century

By Louise Diamond*

A freedom fighter, struggling against the military occupation in his land, is encouraged by a religious-based peace mission to try another approach. He puts down his weapons and opens a centre for conflict resolution, to mediate local disputes and promote dialogue and non-violence. A village elder, with modest financial help from an international agency, arranges a traditional ceremony of reconciliation to re-integrate child soldiers who committed atrocities, under duress, against their own families during a recent civil war.

Mid-level community and political leaders attend a series of facilitated discussions with their counterparts across the communal divide of their conflict. Several years later, many are in important government positions, and ideas generated in those conversations begin appearing in the political discourse. An influential journalist meets with his colleagues from 'the other side' of an ethnic conflict in an NGO-sponsored dialogue, and subsequently refuses to use stereotypical or derogatory language about 'them' in his news coverage. A rural affairs specialist working for a relief organization in the developing world, after attending a training program in conflict resolution, mediates a successful agreement to a chronic dispute between pastoralists and agriculturalists.

Multiply these stories many thousand times over, and a picture of multi-track diplomacy in the late 20th century begins to emerge. People from all walks of life and wielding influence over various sectors of their society, find myriad ways to promote peace in settings of violent conflict. Working at different levels of social organization, from the political to the institutional to the social, these individuals, and the organizations and institutions through which they operate, are the visible manifestation of the multi-track approach.

Many who step forward as local peacebuilders in their own communities are influenced by third party actors, a growing force of professionals and private citizens who design and implement programs of peace-building or conflict prevention, management, resolution and transformation in places of conflict around the world. In some cases, these individuals become so committed to the practice of peace-building that they themselves become professionals or para-professionals in the field, creating institutions of their own and operating as catalysts and third parties to others.

Only short while ago this body of peace-builders hardly existed. Now they are legion, operating out of university programs, mediation centres, democratization institutes or conflict resolution NGOs. They are associated with citizen diplomacy initiatives, with religious groups, with business or professional associations or with political parties. They come from humanitarian relief and development agencies, from human rights organizations, from grassroots women's networks or from prestigious think tanks. They may be psychologists, lawyers, sociologists, activists, political scientists, journalists, public servants, artists, organizational consultants, government officials, academics or housewives. In short, the community of peacebuilders actively working throughout all levels of society, from the top down and the bottom up, in places of ethnic and civil conflicts around the world, has mushroomed, and multi-track diplomacy is flourishing.

Why this should be so is a topic that could reasonably be considered in an article by itself. Here, however, we will start from the present and look forward, identifying the challenges to global security in the 21st century, and the possible ways in which multi-track diplomacy might make a contribution in the world of the new millennium.

A Look at the World of the 21st Century

Multi-track diplomacy, then, enters the 21st century as an established presence; a systems approach to peace-building that embraces a large network of organizations, disciplines, methodologies and venues for working toward the prevention and resolution of violent conflict around the world. It has its success stories, told elsewhere in this book, and its best practices; its challenges and edges for growth.

To understand how multi-track diplomacy might play a role in the world of the 21st century, it is necessary to examine some of the trends in world affairs that are looming on humanity's horizon as potential threats to global security in the coming era. Let us examine eight of these trends in some detail:

1. The Globalization of Violence
The benefits of globalization that have so affected our communications and economic systems have also been available to those forces in the world bent on destruction, greed and violence. With increased access to world-wide markets, the internet, cellular communication, international banking facilities and other tools for moving information and resources across great distances at high speed, those involved in such nefarious pursuits as drugs, the illegal

arms trade, the sex trade, terrorism, gambling, money laundering, the black market, racketeering and other such nasty past times have been able to be more effective in their own endeavours, and to take advantage of the increase in power and reach that comes with working together. The illegitimate industries, like their legitimate counterparts, are cooperating, consolidating and diversifying their interests, forming a shadowy infrastructure that covers the globe, de-stabilizes vulnerable systems, and thrives on chaos. Many of these actors are involved behind the scenes in conflict situations, benefitting from the continuation of the violence while having no direct interest in the particulars of that conflict. Though they will never come to the table as part of any formal peace talks, their power is great, especially in certain high political circles without whose connivance they could not operate.

2. The Breakdown of Systemic Integrity

All kinds of systems are losing the strength and certainty of their boundaries at the end of the 20th century. Cells cannot hold their integrity, as new viruses and diseases pose epidemic threats to large populations. Environmental systems cannot maintain their ability to function properly, as species necessary to the balance of nature die out and the natural world becomes polluted beyond its ability to either sustain or purify itself. Families fall apart; moral systems degenerate; educational systems in some places lose their capacity for operating as learning centres and become, instead, warehouses for the social control of desperate children. Economic systems that have sustained great prosperity over time dissolve in an instant, erasing the possibility of a decent standard of living for millions of people anytime in the near future. Political systems disintegrate, leaving thugs, ad hoc militias and greedy despots in charge of whatever patches of land they can hold by force and threat. Whole nations disappear into the chasm of chaos, or seem poised to do so momentarily.

'The work of peace-building is at the forefront of our planet's evolutionary journey in these times.'

3. The Rise of Rogues

Partly as a result of this disintegration of integrity, rogue individuals and nations are emerging in record numbers. People and institutions that function outside any traditional boundaries of law, persuasion or sense of the common good are establishing their capacity to operate across established boundaries at will. Narco-terrorism, nuclear terrorism, the threats of germ and biological terrorism, private armies under the control of warlords and profiteers, maverick states that respond not at all to international pressures or sanctions - these manifestations of uncontrollable, dangerous rogue forces pose untested threats to the world and its institutions of civilization.

4. The Depletion of Natural Resources

Both a cause and an effect of some of the phenomenon already described, the degradation and depletion of earth's natural resources are posing a major threat to the sustenance and stability of life on the planet. Water, oil, land, forests and breathable air are in increasingly short supply, and reserves of precious minerals necessary for the continuation of modern technology are dwindling. The imbalance of overpopulation with the means to sustain life has already contributed to some of the past decade's worst conflicts, such as in Rwanda. The hole in the ozone layer, global warming and the poisoning of the oceans, direct results of our industrial and economic systems, are, in turn, contributing to the very breakdown of systemic integrity we discussed earlier.

5. The Institutionalization of Polarization
While there have always been factions and differences in human society, the deepening of polarization as a norm of social, political and economic interaction has become apparent in the last decade. In the U.S., the two main political parties have descended into an entrenched adversarial relationship in which bipartisanship and cooperation are increasingly rare. The North and the South, the developed and the developing worlds, are still deeply divided over power and resources, and the distance between the economic 'haves' and 'have nots' in many countries is growing, and dangerously so. With intensified polarization comes extremism. Throughout the latter part of the 20th century, we have witnessed the threat to regional and global security posed by the rise of nationalistic and religious extremism. As these movements attain power, stature, and resources -such as in the case of the Taliban in Afghanistan, the far-right wing in Israeli politics or, the BJP/Hindu nationalist party in India- they become woven more thoroughly into the fabric of modern life. Less on the fringes, where they can be ignored, they have migrated to the centre of our world screen, where the threats they pose are highly visible - and highly volatile.

6. Challenges to the Nation State
As empires fall, political boundaries change, and ethnic groups gain access to arms and world attention for their causes, the familiar system of nation states which has ordered the global political and economic systems for so long is being tested from all sides. With between 5,000 and 10,000 different ethnic groups in the world, and only 185 member nations of a UN which affirms in its Charter the right of self-determination, the stage is set for potential conflicts. At both ends of the spectrum, from consolidation to disintegration, the nation state system is facing challenges. As Europe seeks its union, Quebec seeks dis-union. As the Czech Republic and the Republic of Slovakia find a relatively easy way to separate, the Kurds, the Chechens, and the East Timorese have not been so fortunate. The new millennium will require humanity to be creative in designing ways that peoples and national groups can experience the dignity and integrity of their identity while simultaneously maintaining the unity and viability of a world order based on law and mutual respect.

Millions of people are suffering massive trauma from recent wars   Photo Rob Hof

7. Changing Power Blocs

The fall of the Soviet Union and the rise of the United States as the single superpower in the world is not the end of the story. Far from it. Much is in play in Europe, with the evolution of the European Union and NATO, and in Asia, with the awakening of China to its potential for power in the world. Turkey, poised between East and West, could shift its sizable weight in one of several directions, not all of which bode well for security in Southeastern Europe. The disintegration of Russia could lead to any number of scenarios in which powerful entities might rise from the ashes of that state so recently a major player in world affairs. These are but a few examples of the shifts that are taking place -seismic shifts- in relative strength, alliances and relationships as old and new nations flex their muscles and take or lose advantage on the world stage due to some of the other phenomenon previously mentioned.

8. The Traumatization of the Human Family

Millions of people around the planet are suffering massive trauma from recent wars and associated famine, displacement and destruction. As civil wars increasingly target women and children, and group massacres, large scale atrocities and rape become common weapons of war, large populations are profoundly wounded, in body, mind and spirit. In some countries, whole generations are debilitated, especially in those places where child soldiers have formed the backbone of the fighting forces. In others, the psychological debilitation is already moving into the second, third and even fourth generations. Post Traumatic Stress Disease (PTSD) is probably the most widespread disease on the planet. This means that many places in conflict remain vulnerable to political manipulation and ongoing cycles of violence, as the people are lacking the personal strength and inner resources to resist the forces that call for retribution and revenge.

Implications for Multi-Track Diplomacy

These trends present a sober picture indeed of the world of the 21st century. The realm of multi-track diplomacy, as one small player in the global drama, exists within this context, yet brings a perspective, a commitment and a set of methodologies that are at humanity's leading edge for dealing with these most difficult issues. In fact, I would go so far as to suggest that the work of peace-building is at the forefront of our planet's evolutionary journey in these times.

The very dangerous conditions described in the section above arise from, and thrive in, a worldview and set of assumptions about the world as a place of separation. Separative consciousness sees duality and difference as opportunity for superiority, dominance and control, and breeds materialism, greed and violence. For many centuries the dominant western world organized its political, social and economic systems on this basis. The general breakdown in the global (and environmental) environment we are seeing now can be understood as the natural ripening of the inherent seed of destruction in the separative worldview, for when only the parts are seen, without reference to the whole, duality will play itself out in struggle, contest and conflict indefinitely.

We live at a time when large numbers of people on the planet are discovering that there is another worldview, a holistic or unitive view, that acknowledges the parts as inherently inter-related and part of a larger innate wholeness. Beyond the duality we share a common human experience, a common spiritual source, and a common capacity for connecting through that source to ways of being that will honour both the diversity and the unity in the family of life. The world is living through a major period of transformation, as the bankruptcy of one worldview becomes apparent, while the new worldview is still in its infant stages. This produces both the potential for chaos and the potential for great creativity. The peacebuilders of the world, and the multi-track approach to peace in particular, because of its systems orientation, carries that creative potential and is, therefore, a vehicle for humanity's evolution into a new state of consciousness.

In addition to these obvious activities, multi-track diplomacy can face the unique challenges of this transformational period in seven quite specific ways:

1. Maintaining Flexibility in the Face of the Unknown

The state of world affairs is, as we have seen, in a period of great flux. Many events that we can reasonably anticipate may or may not occur. Others that we have not considered may happen tomorrow. A single event of biological terrorism, for instance, could easily change the face of life on this planet as we know it. A single expansive move by China, or new confrontation in the Balkans or the Middle East, could re-configure political relations for many years to come. The truth is, peacebuilders need to be prepared to move in several directions at once, both responding to whatever opportunities present themselves for positive and effective work for peace, and also being pro-active in turning challenges into opportunities. To maintain this flexibility as a whole field of endeavour requires greater reflexivity, discourse and coordination among theory builders and practitioners from all parts of the world.

2. Recognizing Healing as the Key to Transformation

Because of the profound human trauma discussed earlier, and the brokenness of many systems, healing and reconciliation are critical aspects of any multi-track diplomacy process. New and sustainable peace systems must take into account the mending process that comes with acknowledgement of the harm done, apology and forgiveness when possible, completion of mourning, and healing at the individual and group levels. One of the greatest challenges facing peacebuilders today is not just how to engage individuals in this type of healing, but how to engage whole systems, and especially the leadership, for unless humanity learns how to heal itself, the trauma will condemn us to repeat the same cycles of violence from generation to generation.

'Exercising our power to empower means generating more stories like those shared elsewhere in this book, building a base of success from which we can all learn and draw.'

3. Building the Infrastructure for Peace

The forces of war have an existing infrastructure that enables them to mobilize and actualize their aims - they have armies and arms suppliers; transportation, commerce and communication systems; banking, taxing and other funding methods; media, education and propaganda systems; and government ministries, clans, villages, political parties and other entities capable of taking action. The forces of peace have little of this. We have come a long way in recent years toward developing organizations and networks that can serve as vehicles for carrying and coordinating peace-building activities, with an accompanying research, education and media capability as well. Much more needs to be done to create both a human and an institutional infrastructure for peace-building, in order to concretize these methods and approaches in social, political and economic systems that can both stand on their own and work together toward a shared goal. In addition to such institutions, we need the capacity to move money, materials, people and technologies rapidly and efficiently to wherever needed on the planet. In this way the transformation of consciousness is assisted by building alternative structures so that as the old collapses, there is something in place to sustain that which is being birthed.

4. Taking the Holistic and Positive View
One of the hallmarks of a multi-track approach is the capacity to see the whole, and the inter-relationship of the various parts. We know that development and peace are mutually interdependent, for instance, and that democratization requires the capacity for conflict resolution and problem solving at a group level, so we see the natural interface of several disciplines. This kind of relational awareness is critical to building peace systems, for it encourages the kind of connections, bridges, alliances and networking that are essential to the ongoing support of the change process. Stepping back and seeing the whole picture, especially that of the evolutionary moment in which we stand, allows us to hold the gate open for a new range of possibilities. It also allows us to affirm the positive view that, despite all the problems in the way, peace is indeed possible. In this way we energize the potential rather than the despair, and keep hope, that precious and fragile flame, vibrant and alive.

5. Making Peace From the Inside Out
People whose life is given to peace-building, whether as outside third parties or actors within conflict systems, are generally motivated to service, and as servers, may be prone to work themselves beyond the point of balance. Certainly working in war zones, with wounded people and in tense and violent circumstances can produce symptoms of secondary trauma, compassion fatigue and burn-out. Because multi-track diplomacy is a systems approach, in which even the intervenor is part of the system, and because it is a multi-level approach, in which the personal level is just as important as the inter-group level, those involved in this field have the opportunity to use our own technology with ourselves, becoming agents of peace in our being as well as in our doing. When we are taking the time to integrate what we teach about peace in the outer domain with our deep experience of peace within, we can be much more effective, at the individual and at the institutional levels, in two ways: we are clearer and stronger channels for the outer work when we take time to reconnect with our own inner source of peace, and we are better models for others, showing by our presence as much as by our actions that peace is a viable and dynamic state.

6 Creating New Pathways for Shifting Consciousness
A colleague, Robert Fuller, once spoke about finding 'a better game than war.' Peacebuilders taking a multi-track approach are engaged in this endeavour. We know that the 'war option' is a lose-lose game; we come offering a better way, a way that goes even beyond win-win toward the transformation of the consciousness that would allow us to build truly just and peace-able societies.

Because the methods and pathways for this shift are inherent in the principles and practices of peace-building with a holistic view, we occupy a position in the world analogous to the early road or railway builders. We are opening the paths, setting the tracks in place, laying down the rails, making clear the direction that will shape the future of our planet. Our tools -methods for cooperation, creative joint problem solving, reconciliation, prevention, dialogue, mediation, negotiation, and communication, among others- are the tracks that we are setting down, so people will be able to transport themselves across old territory in new and better ways. As with all road building, once we open a path, more and more travellers will use it, especially if it carries them to where they want to go. The ways of thinking and acting we are inviting people into is a different, and a better game than war, and our work makes it possible for people in large numbers to make that shift. Knowing this, we can be more intentional about it.

7. Empowering Peacebuilders for Local Action
Multi-track diplomacy invites everyone into the game of peace-building. It says that there is a place and way that people from any sector of society can make a contribution to peace. Those of us engaged in travelling to places of conflict to make interventions there realize that building peace is primarily a local task. What we can offer is to give people a view and a direct experience of what is possible, help them do what they want to do faster and better, and perhaps strengthen their capacity to use appropriate tools and skills. We can motivate, catalyze, inspire, instruct, facilitate, encourage, support, assist, demonstrate, and convene. We can present possibilities, open minds to new ways of thinking, and cheer people on as they take charge of changing the systems they live in. We can articulate theories and best practices, provide a safe space where people can meet 'the other', or elicit inner individual and cultural wisdom about peace and conflict resolution. What we can never do impose our solutions on others, or build their new systems for them.

Our power to empower is perhaps the most important role we can play in the 21st century. The more individuals who feel empowered to work in their own systems for peace and conflict transformation, the closer the world comes to that critical mass that will allow for a massive leap in consciousness, allowing new processes for peace that were previously unimaginable to become normative, and easy.

Exercising our power to empower means generating more stories like those shared elsewhere in this book, building a base of success from which we can all learn and draw. It means enabling people to have that critical understanding of what true power is, the very opposite of the power of domination and control that characterizes war systems. Ultimately, exercising our power to empower means that the next article written on the role of multi-track diplomacy will have infinitely more peacebuilders -like those mentioned in the very beginning of this article- to showcase as examples of those engaged in the courageous act of creating viable, sustainable peace systems on this precious planet we all call home.

*Dr. Louise Diamond is co-founder and Executive Director of the Institute for Multi-Track Diplomacy in Washington, D.C., which works with ethnic and regional conflicts around the world. There she is engaged in diverse projects that address theoretical and practical aspects of international peacemaking and peace-building from a systems perspective. In addition, she offers workshops and classes on various issues relating to peace and peacemaking, and is the Educational Director and Training Supervisor of an international peace education programme, the 'Peacekeeper Mission'. She writes extensively, bringing a peacemaking perspective to current events.

7 Changing History - Peace Building in Northern Ireland

By Mari Fitzduff*

On Good Friday, April the 10th, Northern Ireland politicians stumbled out from the portals of Stormont into the breaking daylight.[1] Many of them were not far from tears. All were obviously exhausted by the roller coaster of adrenaline and the lack of sleep they had incurred during the last few days and nights of the talks, as deals were crafted, walk-outs were threatened and averted, and the apparently insuperable barriers on decommissioning and other issues were overcome. Both the British and Irish Prime Ministers had been called upon to provide support in the last few days and even President Clinton had assisted by encouraging telephone calls. The waiting populace held their breath alternating between despair and hope.

The hope was justified - the miracle happened, the Belfast Agreement was reached. After thirty years of a bloody civil war, Northern Ireland's political parties finally achieved consensus on the principles, and in some cases the practice, necessary to govern a society divided on constitutional, political, and cultural perspectives. Six weeks later, by a vote of over 71%, and despite the best efforts of fundamentalist nationalists and unionists, the deal was endorsed by the peoples of the island of Ireland, North and South. The road to peace appeared to have been secured.

What had brought Northern Ireland to this particular turning point? What had been the major developments in eventually securing the peace? While obviously the debates about such developments will continue for some decades, the following would appear to have been the most important in creating a positive context for a political solution.

A. Community Development/Community Relations work within and between communities which opened up new possibilities for dialogue and co-operation between them.

When civil violence broke out in 1969 in Northern Ireland and particularly in the aftermath of the riots in Belfast and Derry/Londonderry in August 1969, the British Labour Home Secretary, James Callaghan announced the establishment of a Ministry for Community Relations and a Community Relations Commission which was charged with the promotion of policies which would improve community relations. [2]

The Commission decided to adopt as its main strategy the initiation of local community development programmes across Northern Ireland, based on the belief that communities which lacked self-confidence were more likely to relate aggressively to one another. Furthermore, it believed that the problem, particularly for people in more socially marginalized communities, of relating to the structures of power, contributed to feelings of helplessness and resentment which in turn contributed to community tensions. (Hayes) The Commission survived until the Sunningdale Agreement in April 1974, which set up a new power sharing assembly for Northern Ireland. In one of its first actions, the power sharing assembly abolished the Community Relations Commission on the basis that henceforth the politicians themselves would be responsible for community development and community relations issues. Ironically, the new assembly itself only lasted five months due to disagreement among the politicians about the remit of cross-border bodies which had been set up as part of the Agreement, and a loyalist workers strike which paralysed Northern Ireland.

However, the process of community development remained an important method of facilitating communication within communities, and between government and communities, and this process continued to underpin many programmes subsequently initiated and funded in the last two decades.

Over a decade later, in 1985, the Standing Advisory Commission on Human Rights commissioned a report on the current state of community relations work, and its potential for future development. (Frazer & Fitzduff) This report on the under resourced, underdeveloped and unstrategic nature of much of the work, suggested a theoretical framework for its development, and suggested some practical structures that should be considered if the government intended to take the work seriously. It suggested the creation of a specialist community relations unit within government and the creation of an independent community relations body which would address issues of policy, training, and funding community relations work. In 1987, the Central Community Relations Unit (CCRU) was set up, which was located at the heart of government and in 1990, the independent body, the Community Relations Council (CRC) was established.

Community Relations 1990-98
In drawing up its initial strategic plan the CRC decided not to concentrate on developing more 'reconciliation' groups, but expanded its remit to include bodies who had not previously been working actively at peace-building e.g.

business, church and sports groups, health and education boards, etc and many groups from the voluntary and community sector. It also worked closely with the Trade Unions who had, since the late 1980's, been developing anti-intimidation and anti-sectarian programmes for the workplace.

Subsequently there was a significant expansion of the number of groups working at peace-building much of which growth was facilitated by a hugely increased financial investment in such work [3] so that by 1998 the number of civic groups engaging in contact work, and developing programmes and training to address issues of human rights, cultural diversity, co-operation on social and economic issues, single identity work, neutral venue work, anti sectarian work, anti-intimidation work as well as political dialogue and mediation work had increased significantly i.e. from 40 in 1986 to 140 in 1996 [4].

As the theoretical framework for such a focus expanded the work also began to engage a much wider spectrum of people, including those who had previously been cynical of the 'peace and doves' stereotype attached to the work. (Fitzduff) It therefore became more possible to build a coalition of people and organisations addressing both the 'softer' issues such as understanding and co-operation, as well as the 'harder' issues of inequality, rights, policing and political and constitutional differences.

In addition, the programme begun in the 70's of more substantially resourcing community development began to pay significant political dividends. Such work, in the absence of local democracy, had provided for community participation in governmental consultation processes, about social, economic and political issues. By the 1990's, however, it had also helped to generate a new breed of 'community' politicians who developed loyalist, republican and feminist thinking in a way which significantly enriched the political mix of parties who were eventually able to sign the Belfast Agreement. Parties such as the PUP, the NIWC and Sinn Fein all have considerable experience at community and social politics. [5] Such work also provided them with fruitful contacts gained from their collective experience in addressing local social issues together, and such experience should augur well for the social and economic tasks that face them as representatives in the new Assembly.

'Governments also often lack the flexibility to develop creative processes for the management of diversity.'

External assistance offered by the European Union was also of significance. When the ceasefires were declared in 1994, the EU decided to help to underpin the peace by allocating £250,000,000 to help build up the economy and establish peace. Such funds have been useful, as their criteria for distribution included in many cases the need for communities to work together on funding decisions. Such processes ensure that communities can no longer continue to be unaware of each other's social and economic needs, and have in many cases provided very useful training for future collaborative government at both local and regional level.

B. Political Dialogue and Development work which focused on work with politicians and others on political divisions and political options.

Given the small size of Northern Ireland -less than 3 hours drive from end to end- it is hard to imagine just how difficult it is to facilitate and promote political dialogue. This is partly because of the culture of silence which is adhered to between the communities where raising any issues of cultural or political difference is seen to be either impolite or dangerous, depending upon the circumstances. For politicians, who exemplify community differences, being seen to have any meetings outside of the context of formal dialogue - which dialogue is usually characterised by hostility is almost impossible. And for much of the conflict, it was almost impossible for the government, and most political parties to have any dialogue at all with Sinn Fein, because of their perceived association with the IRA and paramilitary violence. [6]

In such circumstances, much ingenuity was needed on the part of many groups to facilitate political dialogue and to eventually achieve sufficient consensus between the parties to move into inclusive dialogue.

Primary among these dialogues processes were those conducted by the Quakers and others with and between politicians, particularly during the early nineties and which kept open dialogue through processes of shuttle mediation. In addition, some academics were extremely useful in organising workshops for politicians and others, often outside of Ireland, in places like Washington or South Africa, where it was easier to meet than at home. Often such conferences gave the participants opportunities to address wider perspectives and possibilities for conflict resolution, as well as providing opportunities for relationships to form between the politicians - which relationships could never have formed in the socially and politically constricting circumstances of Northern Ireland.

Another particularly useful initiative was that by a small group of Protestant clergy who opened a confidential process of dialogue with Sinn Fein, at a time when such processes were viewed with deep opprobrium by most political parties, and who provided a useful context within which Sinn Fein could address the reality of their perceptions of the hopes and fears of the Protestant/Unionist community. Other groups such as the Glencree Centre for Reconciliation, just outside of Dublin, also involved itself in workshops with politicians, particularly following the ceasefires of 1994. And community

PHOTO BELFAST EXPOSED KING ST.

The hope was justified - the miracle happened, the Belfast Agreement was reached.

workers themselves -some of whom were ex-republican and loyalist prisoners-
eventually began to find many creative ways, despite the danger to them from
their own and their opposing community, to involve themselves in processes
of dialogue and relationship building through their common social and
community concerns.

What was important about all of the above processes was that they were almost
all conducted in confidence and thus provided a safer context within which
politicians fears and hopes could be constructively addressed. Such dialogue
processes -in addition to those eventually developed by the Government and
between political parties- were to prove invaluable in accumulating the
possibilities, and the beginning of enough understanding and trust on the part
of at least some politicians, to enable the peace process to truly begin.

What was also useful was the eventual emergence of a party that was not
dedicated to a particular political position - but to the dialogue process itself.
This was the Northern Ireland Women's Coalition which was formed just six
weeks before the election to the Northern Ireland Forum for Political Dialogue
in 1996. It was formed in response to the dismay felt by many women in

Northern Ireland at the lack of response by existing political parties to the need to include women in Northern Ireland politics.[7] The party included nationalists and unionists, and was jointly chaired by two women from both perspectives. Its members came from all classes of life e.g. community workers, professionals, academics, nuns, trade unionists, etc. and they fought the elections on a cross-community approach. They secured a place at the negotiating table, focusing on principles of equality and inclusion. Although originally treated with sexism and hostility by many parties, particularly the unionist parties, they were eventually able to play very useful part by facilitating discussions between the parties -often using a shuttle-mediation approach- on difficult issues like the release of prisoners and decommissioning.

Another newcomer to the peace process was the business community who began to develop their approach to the ending of violence in the early nineties. Whereas before they had been content to complain about the effect of the violence on business from the sidelines, they now began to coalesce with the Trade Unions to see if a more strategic approach could be put into place which would put pressure on both republican and loyalist paramilitaries to end their campaign, and to pressurise the politicians in getting down to the business of building an agreement. Groups like the Chamber of Commerce, the Institute of Directors, the Confederation of British Industry, and all the major trade unions joined together and began to make statements urging the need to end the war, and the need for serious political negotiation. In addition, they involved themselves in dialogue with all the political parties, including Sinn Fein, even before the ceasefires were announced in 1994. Their influence was very salutary, particularly on the Unionist political parties, who began to feel the need to respond to the pressure from them to enter into serious political dialogue.

During the nineties, the United States was also of substantial assistance in helping to develop and secure dialogue and peace. The US had gradually developed a perspective which was able to take account of the needs and fears of Unionists as well as nationalists, and -spurred by the interests of the huge Irish vote in the USA- they began to focus on ways of ending the violence. People like Congressman Bruce Morrison, and business men like Bill Flynn and Charles Feeney visited Ireland to persuade the IRA of the need to end the military campaign, and to engage with the unionist community. Clinton granted a visa to Gerry Adams to enter the US in 1994 while the IRA was still bombing cities and killing people, in the hope that it would assist his alleged quest for a solution. Although such activities were initially viewed with suspicion by many within the British Government, many subsequently came to appreciate the assistance which such interventions were able to offer. Such assistance was particularly exemplified by the assistance of Senator George Mitchell who acted as Chair of the talks process for almost two years and whose efforts were invaluable to its success.

C. Equality work which ensured equal access to power and resources for Catholics as well as Protestants and economic development to assist this.

The outbreak of civil violence in 1969 in Northern Ireland which cost over three and a half thousand lives was significantly attributable to the failure of policies of equity in Northern Ireland since its inception as a state in 1921. Although the newly formed region of the UK contained within its borders a substantial number of Catholics who were unhappy with their status within Northern Ireland, few efforts were made by the newly elected unionist government to sufficiently address their responsibilities involved in governing a divided society. [8] Such a failure with its concomitant patterns of inequity, biased voting systems, unrepresentative policing, a maintenance of ghettoisation in education, housing, and workplaces, and a significantly alienated minority created the context for the eventual development of a civil war.

In 1972 the Unionist Northern Ireland government was dismissed by the British government, and direct political and security control for the region from London began, Such belated interest from London -which had previously shown little care for on-going inequities in the region- eventually helped to ensure the development of a more equitable and culturally representative society in Northern Ireland.

Equality legislation
In August 1969 the British government declared that every citizen of Northern Ireland was entitled to the same equality of treatment and freedom from discrimination as obtains in the rest of the United Kingdom, and a series of legislative reforms to address existing inequalities was introduced, first by the Northern Ireland parliament and after it had been dissolved in 1972, by the Westminster parliament.

In 1969 legislation was introduced to investigate complaints of maladministration by government departments, and in 1972 a commission was established to promote fairness in staff recruitment in the local councils, which had been so noted for their discriminatory nature. In 1973 the Northern Ireland Constitution Act provided for a legislative assembly to address discrimination on the grounds of religious or political belief and the Act also established the Standing Advisory Commission on Human Rights to monitor the effectiveness of laws against discrimination.

As discrimination in housing had been a major grievance, control of all public housing allocation was transferred from local council authorities to a regional authority, and voting reforms were introduced i.e. house ownership was no longer deemed a prerequisite for voting rights, and the multiple vote given to business owners was abolished, as both of these had effectively discriminated against Catholics. Local council boundaries were redrawn more accurately to represent the reality of citizen distribution, and a proportional representation system of voting was introduced which increased nationalist chances of gaining power where their numbers were substantial enough, and increased the number of councils under nationalist control.

Employment Inequities
Following the civil rights disturbances of 1969, major disparities in employment levels in Northern Ireland had been confirmed. (Cameron 1969, Rose 1971) In 1971 it was estimated that 17.3 per cent of Catholic males were unemployed, compared to 6.6 per cent Protestant males. In 1976 the Fair Employment Act was passed, making discrimination in employment on religious or political grounds unlawful and a Fair Employment Agency (FEA) was established to receive complaints of discrimination in employment and to investigate the extent to which there was inequality. This agency was eventually replaced in 1989 by the Fair Employment Commission (FEC) which was given extra resources and powers by the government in pursuit of its task i.e. monitoring of the religious composition of workforce was introduced, and indirect discrimination was made illegal.

Targeting Social Need
However, by the early 1990's, after two decades of government attempts to address equity issues in Northern Ireland, the indicators still showed that the Catholic community in many areas remained seriously disadvantaged e.g. forty-five of the top fifty unemployment blackspots areas in Northern Ireland were almost exclusively Catholic. Faced with a major challenge of the continuance of marginalised ghetto areas (mainly Catholic, but also some Protestant areas) and the link between such areas and the use of paramilitary violence, the government decided that a major initiative was needed to address such alienation. (Poole) It set up Targeting Social Need (TSN) programme to tackle areas of social and economic differences by targeting government policies and programmes more directly to those areas or sections of the community suffering the highest levels of disadvantage and deprivation.

'The agreement has broken the much out-dated notion that nationality, ethnicity and territory are necessarily legally or constitutionally overlapping.'

Extra attention was also given under the TSN programme to providing further opportunities for training, to increasing development work for indigenous industry creation, particularly in the most marginalised areas, and to ensuring that individual job creation agencies further biased their work towards those areas that were most seriously disadvantaged.

Policy and Fair Treatment

In 1994 the government introduced a new initiative called Policy Appraisal and Fair Treatment (PAFT) to ensure that issues of equality condition policy making and action in all spheres of government activity, and to ensure that considerations of equality, equity and non-discrimination (not just in relation to religious/political affiliation, but also in relation to other areas of inequality) are in-built from the outset to the preparation of policy proposals, including legislation and strategic plans for the implementation of policy and the delivery of services. These guidelines now apply to all Northern Ireland government departments and all government agencies

Two decades later, under the jurisdiction of direct rule from London, many inequities have been addressed. Complaints are no longer heard in Northern Ireland about rigged voting systems, unfair housing allocations, or unequal educational funding. Only primarily in unemployment -where levels of long-term unemployment among Catholic males is still twice as high as among Protestant males- does a significant problem remain, despite the various legal and social initiatives which have been undertaken to address the issue. Such advances mean that the anger and resentment many Catholics felt at being excluded under a Unionist regime is no longer as potent a factor in continuing the support for violence.

D. Education work which provided new possibilities for contact and mutual understanding between children and young people.

The educational systems -like most systems in Northern Ireland- is sectarian, with almost all children attending single identity schools. In 1981, the first integrated school for both Catholic and Protestant children was opened, and since then more than thirty have been established through the hard work of parents. [9] Although still only serving a small minority of children (3%) they have served as a vital initiative in transforming the existing education system. Under pressures from such schools, some of the existing schools are now willing to consider opening up participation to pupils from other communities.

Significant work has also been undertaken to ensure that, even within segregated schools, pupils have an opportunity to address existing cultural and political divisions.
By the early 1990's, through the dedication of academics and teachers determined to address cross-community misunderstanding and division, programmes within schools designed to increase understanding among children and young people e.g. Cultural Heritage, Mutual Understanding and Contact programmes were an obligatory part of every schoolchild's curriculum. And by 1990, a common history curriculum was being taught in all schools in Northern Ireland, whereas before 1990 Catholic and Protestant

schools often taught completely different versions of history. By 1994, a common religious curriculum was inaugurated. Through such initiatives, the power of the schools as a purveyor of perspectives which often increased mistrust and prejudice between communities had been diminished.

E. District Council Community Relations programmes which established locally led initiatives to address issues of division between the communities.

Northern Ireland has twenty six local councils which have, with varying degrees, exemplified the hostility which has pervaded much of Northern Ireland public life. In many cases they were significantly responsible for the kind of discriminatory behaviour that led directly to the civil unrest of 1969. Their abuse of powers was so obvious that they were all stripped of most of their responsibilities in housing, health care, and social services which were all centralised. Even when using what limited powers were left to them their work was often characterised by acrimony, hostility and in some cases physical violence.

However, a decision was made by the Central Community Relations unit to involve these councils in community relations work and in 1990, a District Council community relations programme was developed which was eventually established within all Councils despite deep resistance by most of them. Each of the twenty six district council now has at least one full-time community relations worker addressing coexistence needs in its local area and as their programmes has had to ensure an overall commitment from what are often very divided councils, their very existence has marked a substantial sign of progress in the field.

Such programmes involved contact work, co-operative economic development programmes between the communities, cultural events such as concerts, drama etc which exemplified cultural diversity, mediation, problem solving and political discussion workshops. The evidence is that where such relationships have been active for at least two years, relationships between communities have significantly improved. (Knox and Hughes)

F. Cultural Traditions work which developed programmes to exemplify cultural differences as positive, rather than negative. This included Media work which validated cultural diversity and promoted discussion on issues of difference.

For the entire period of the existence of the state, expressions of cultural and political identity have been contentious. Flag flying, the use of the Irish language, language and unionist and nationalist parades, have all been seen as a threat to the political realities and aspirations of the other side. In a contested territory, such expressions have a significant potential to accrue into civil disorder. (Mc Cartney 1994)

Since 1921, many such expressions on the part of nationalists in Northern Ireland were deemed illegal. Several legislative Acts (1951 and 1954) outlawed the flying of the Irish flag, and laws were also passed forbidding the use of Irish language street signs (1949) or the use of any language other than English in court (1739). All transactions with the government had to be conducted in English. [10] Such laws contributed to significant community tension and defiance - e.g by 1992 over 550 Irish language street signs had been erected in nationalist areas in clear defiance of the law and many nationalists also began to use the Irish language and its lack of official support as a cultural weapon with which to challenge the authorities.

Much of this has now changed - mainly due to the work of the Cultural Traditions Group (CTG), a group of academics, practitioners and policy makers, drawn from both the nationalist and unionist communities, an operating under the auspices of the Community Relations Council. [11] Many within this group recognised that the negative government response to the Irish language had been both short-sighted and unnecessary. They established and achieved government funding for the Ultacht Trust, a group set up on a non-sectarian basis to develop and fund the Irish language. The government were also persuaded to fund those schools that taught through the medium of Irish on the same basis as other schools, and to assist with the funding of a daily newspaper in Irish.

'Conflicts do not end - they just change.'

Eventually, in 1992 the Secretary of State for Northern Ireland announced that where there was a local demand, street names in Irish could be erected alongside the English name. Correspondence in Irish is also now dealt with by the government, and although there is as yet no official policy on publishing official documents in Irish, this does happen when requested e.g. the Belfast Agreement was published in Irish.

In broadcasting, there were also many issues that were a source of considerable contention to the nationalist minority. There was an exclusion on the reporting of minority cultural issues, including sport, and the Irish language was banned from radio and television for almost the first fifty years of the Northern Ireland state. Following the Civil Rights campaign, the new-found culturally assertive capacities of the nationalist community began to achieve some successes in the early 1970's when the British Broadcasting Corporation (BBC) was persuaded to introduce occasional radio programmes in the Irish language. Although there was considerable resistance from many unionists, the BBC persisted with the experiment, and were eventually persuaded to introduce a regular Irish-language programme in 1981, followed by some schools broadcasting in 1985. In 1991 the BBC broadcast its first television production in Irish. Although the total hours broadcast in Irish are still minimal, particularly when compared to those available in Gaelic in Scotland, or in Welsh in Wales, the barriers to the use of Irish in broadcasting have now substantially disappeared.

In addition to its work on the language, the Cultural Traditions Group also helped to further develop the work of the broadcasting companies by encouraging, and in some case funding, initiatives which exemplified cultural diversity programming and encouraged debate on political and cultural issues. Such work has assisted a context of diversity and challenge which has eventually led to a much healthier and open context for discussion on the many issues which were eventually pertinent to the Belfast Agreement and the setting up of the subsequent Assembly. The use of the Irish Language, and expressions of nationalist and Irish identity have now receded as a significant source of political tension. The community are now used to hearing regular Irish language programmes on radio and television, the tricolour usually flies freely, without official interference, and street names in Irish are now accepted as delivery addresses by the postal services. A constructive framework for valuing diversity has now at last been laid and has ensured a much more positive context for the agreements on cultural pluralism that were made in the Belfast Agreement.

Lesson Learnt

The need for civic society involvement
In a situation like Northern Ireland where the state retains some coherent and credible levels of governance, it is of vital importance that the government itself should be engaged in processes of conflict management which can assist peace building through e.g. the development of policies that promote patterns of equity and inclusiveness through legislation, resource allocation and appropriate policies to ensure such principles. However, even where the state appears to function in a cohesive fashion -as was the case for much of the Northern Ireland conflict- it will often not of itself be able to either start processes of equity, inclusiveness, and political dialogue and agreement without pressure -and support- from civil society.

Investing in a top-down, hierarchical approach to the management and transformation of an ethno-political conflict is unlikely to succeed for a variety of reasons. Governments themselves are often seen as part of the problem by minority groups because (as was the case in N.Ireland) they are often seen to have validated and resourced their particular groups and ignored or excluded the needs of other groups. Governments also often lack the flexibility to develop creative processes for the management of diversity and indeed experience in places like Northern Ireland, South Africa and the Middle East has shown that training for such diversity is often in the first instance developed through the more independent processes of NGOs and others, where bureaucracy is often lighter, and independent funding sometimes ensures a more open approach to such issues.

Primarily, however, governments find it hard to deliver on political agreements because politicians are often the people who find it the hardest to develop policies of diversity in the face of the fears of their electorates. Thus there is often a need for a constituency for such validation to be developed by their electorate which can enable or permit them to move with energy on such policies, and here NGOs and others can play a crucial part. Such was the case in Northern Ireland where the work of the NGOs was crucial in developing processes of dialogue, models of training, and constituencies for political agreement both during the pre-agreement phase of the peace process, and the 'YES' campaign that followed to secure its endorsement.

The need for a variety of approaches to peace-building
Unfortunately, fundamental disagreements between theorists and practitioners about priorities in approaches to conflict resolution work have often limited its development. This was certainly the case in Northern Ireland where throughout much of the seventies and eighties there was major dissension between those who see such work as primarily needing a structural approach to management and those who see the work as needing primarily a psychocultural approach. (Ross) Those focusing on structural work -who saw the problem as one of incompatible interests which arise from the structure of a community- concentrated on issues of justice and rights, equity and political issues. Those approaching the work from a psychocultural perspective -which emphasises the need to develop relationships between conflicting groups- concentrated in the first instance on eliminating the fears, ignorance and hostility between communities through contact and co-operative possibilities which provided access to groups about each other's histories, religions, cultures, and fears.

Both approaches of course have their limitations, and tension between groups and institutions about prioritising such approaches was both limiting and unnecessary. [12] Eventually, groups focusing on relationship building began to energetically included dialogue on difficult issues of structural problems as part of relationship building, and those involved in such structural work began to avail of the skills of those who could provided the productive context within which such dialogues could take place. [13]

Reframe the problems where possible
A major factor in trying to end the obstacles to dialogue and agreement has been attempts that have been made to circumscribe accustomed or declared stances on such issues as dialogue, and constitutional possibilities. These have

included e.g. the use of 'unauthorised' and 'deniable' contacts to facilitate dialogue where such was deemed either useless, obnoxious or in some cases illegal; the presentation of a common social focus as an excuse for assisting talks between loyalist and republican community workers in Belfast; the use of parallel or proximity talks to ensure that all political parties could be include in discussions; and the use of shuttle mediation in such situations were examples of lateral thinking that was useful in difficult situations.

When very contentious issues arose in multi-party talks -such as decommissioning or policing- and began to slow down the talks processes, the use of independent commissions to discuss these issues with neutral facilitators was very helpful. Prime examples of these were the Independent Commission on Decommissioning and the newly formed Independent Commission on Policing. Such developments meant that these issues were not allowed to derail the various talks processes.

Perhaps the most major creative success is the Belfast Agreement itself, which has developed a unique constitutional framework which secures a system of overlapping and interlocking national and cultural loyalties, and which has effectively brought an end to the idea of any possible identity or loyalty hegemony in Northern Ireland. All citizens can now legally avail of both British and/or Irish passports. People can choose to look to London or to Dublin -or to Northern Ireland- for their cultural identity and heritage. The agreement has broken the much out-dated notion -in this world of increasing ethnic mobility- that nationality, ethnicity and territory are necessarily legally or constitutionally overlapping.

The Future

It is a well established fact to those of us working in conflict that in fact conflicts do not end - they just change. Undoubtedly significant challenges remain to be addressed. [14] Among these can be numbered the possible further development of some of the splinter groups who have split from the main paramilitary movements, and the need for the existing Assembly parties to constructively and collectively deal with this challenge. The issue of contentious parades still remain unresolved and there is the continuing difficulty of the possible destabilisation of the Assembly through the growth of more 'anti-agreement' representatives who could coalesce around such issues as the failure to agree to a process of decommissioning and the difficulties in re-developing a police service that is more acceptable to nationalists. However, thanks to the previous work undertaken, and to the nature of the Belfast Agreement itself, there is now in place a variety of very useful mechanisms which have been designed to deal with these and other inevitable difficulties that will arise over the coming years.

Effectively, the war is ended. For many, committee papers have been substituted for guns. Meetings with British civil servants -and even British Prime Ministers - have become part of daily life for erstwhile Sinn Fein/IRA and Loyalist activists many of whom are now full or part-time engaged in national and local politics and who are now having to depend upon the use of politics rather than force to address the myriad local and regional issues that are now their collective responsibility.

The road to such an agreement has been long, complex and often bloody. Almost thirty years and three and a half thousand dead have been the result of the fear, discrimination, intransigence, anger and violence with which communities and government have limited their much surer and swifter progress towards peace. The peace has been long in the coming, and hard in the making. It does, however, at last appear that the hard work and the courage of many, creative approaches to both dialogue and constitutional solutions have eventually yielded enough to take Northern Ireland to a future where politics and not violence will primarily prevail. If this proves to be the case - it will truly be a new beginning for Northern Ireland.

References

Disturbances in Northern Ireland - Report of a Commission appointed by the Governor of Northern Ireland, Cameron Report. Belfast, Her Majesty's Stationery Office, 1969.

Adding Insult to Injury, Committee on the Administration of Justice. Belfast, CAJ 1992.

A Typology of Community Relations work and Contextual necessities, Mari Fitzduff. Belfast, Policy and Planning Unit, Northern Ireland Office, 1989.

Improving Community Relations, Hugh Frazer and Mari Fitzduff. Belfast, Standing Advisory Commission on Human Rights, 1986.

Policing a Divided Society, Andrew Hamilton. Coleraine, Centre for the Study of Conflict, University of Ulster, 1995.

The role of the Community relations Commission in Northern Ireland, M. Hayes. London, Runnymede Trust, 1972.

Community Relations and Local government, C. Knox and J. Hughes. Coleraine, Centre for the Study of Conflict, University of Ulster, 1994.

Clashing Symbols?, Clem McCartney. Belfast, Institute of Irish Studies, Queen's University, 1994.

'The Geographical location of Violence in Northern Ireland' Political Violence, Michael Poole. Belfast, Appletree Press, 1990.

Governing Without Consensus: An Irish Perspective, Richard Rose. London, Faber, 1971.

The Management of Conflict, Mark Ross. Yale University Press 1993, and Why do they do what they do? Theories of Practice in Conflict Management. Paper presented to the European Conference on Peace and Conflict Resolution, Belfast 1998.

Notes

1 Stormont is the traditional seat of government in Northern Ireland, just on the edge of the city of Belfast.

2 The city is usually called Derry by Catholics, while Londonderry is the preferred name of most Protestants

3 e.g. from a quarter of a million pounds in 1990 to approximately £7 million per annum by 1997

4 Single identity work is work which is done within a community to increase confidence building prior to contact/co-operative work. Neutral venue work addresses the need to develop physical meeting places which were acceptable to both community - much needed in Northern Ireland when most local venues were sectarian. Anti-sectarian work examined exclusion and discriminatory processes by groups and individuals, against other groups, and developed programmes to address these phenomena i.e. reviewing the cross-community nature of staff and management, patrons, choices of holidays, and cultural practices within institutions which were alienation to one or other community. Anti-intimidation work includes work addressing the difficulties of divided workplaces where contentious issues of flag flying and discrimination have frequently resulted in violence and sometimes in murder and included the implementation of staff policies and training to deal with such intimidation.

5 The (PUP) Progressive Unionist Party, and the NIWC (Northern Ireland Women's Coalition) all have their basis in local community work. Sinn Fein also draws much of its support from such work.

6 It subsequently emerged of course that the British government had eventually involved itself in 'deniable' dialogue with the IRA, and in the late eighties/early nineties, John Hume, the leader of the SDLP (Social Democratic and Labour party) began a dialogue with Gerry Adams, which was received with much hostility by most parties. These talks addressed a possible pan-nationalist, non-violent approach to achieving their common goal of unity in Ireland as well as the talks between Sinn Fein and the Irish government which were assisted by the efforts of several Catholic priests.

7 There are no women members of parliament from Northern Ireland, and only 11% of local councillors are women.

8 Catholics constituted approximately a third of the population in 1921.

9 Initial establishment and fund raising for such schools has to be undertaken on a voluntary and private basis. When schools have established viability of pupil numbers, the Government will in some cases provide funding for the schools.

10 Ten per cent of the population claim to have a knowledge of the Irish language. (Census Report 1990)

11 The Community Relations Council (CRC) was an independent body set up in 1990 to promote community relations. The Cultural Traditions Group (CTG) was part of the Council.

12 Mari Fitzduff, Beyond Violence: Conflict Resolution Approaches in Northern Ireland UNU Press 1996. Chapter 2.

13 A very effective example of this was the distribution of peace funds from the EU in Northern Ireland much of which was undertaken by and through NGOs, often working in partnership with politicians and business people. Initial evaluations are endorsing the effectiveness of this model.

14 For an expanded discussion on many of these issues see Mac Ginty, R 'The Northern Ireland Agreement: Threats and Opportunities' Paper prepared for a seminar in the university of Kent, June 1998.

*Mari Fitzduff *is currently Professor of Conflict Studies, and Director of INCORE (Initiative on Conflict Resolution and Ethnicity). INCORE is a joint initiative of the University of Ulster and the United Nations University whose aim is to address the management of conflict through an integrated approach using research, training and policy development. Previously, she was Director of the Northern Ireland Community Relations Council which works with government, statutory bodies, trade unions, businesses, and community groups developing programmes addressing issues of conflict in Northern Ireland.*

8 A Joint Effort - The South African Peace Process

By Peter Gastrow*

The tumultuous political transition that occurred in South Africa during the 1990s, variously described as the South African 'miracle', the 'negotiated revolution', or the peaceful change from apartheid to democracy, is a success story that should never be taken for granted. The determined actions and sacrifices of many individuals and organisations, as well as national and international developments, shaped this process. There was nothing inevitable about it - in fact at various stages of this process the prospects of peaceful progress or civil war were balanced on a knife-edge.

When, in February 1990, Nelson Mandela was released from 27 years in prison, and liberation movements such as the African National Congress (ANC) and the Pan Africanist Congress (PAC) were unbanned, South Africa had just gone through a debilitating year of political violence. With 1,403 people killed, 1989 had been the worst year of political violence in modern South African history. A political and strategic deadlock between the Apartheid State and the anti-apartheid forces had developed. The release of Mandela fuelled expectations of constitutional negotiations that would lead South Africa out of its political cul-de-sac. It was assumed that political violence would abate and that peace was at last within reach.

This optimism was largely misplaced. Violence did not abate. Fierce clashes between ANC supporters and supporters of the largely Zulu based Inkatha Freedom Party (IFP) took place. In many instances, the security forces were playing a sinister role of fuelling such conflicts. In fact 1990, the year that many thought would be the precursor to liberation, democracy and stability, became a year of unprecedented political strife and killings. 3,699 people were killed through political violence, a 163 percent increase over 1989. Hopes for a peaceful change dimmed as the increased political violence prevented constitutional negotiations from commencing. It became clear that if South Africa was to break out of the growing spiral of violence and polarisation, political leaders would have to manage the coming transition more effectively, and rules of conduct would have to be agreed upon in order to minimise the political violence and intolerance.

In the face of these developments, an embarrassed South African political leadership began realising that they were incapable of stemming the violence on their own. Bilateral meetings between Nelson Mandela, then deputy president of the ANC, and Chief Minister Buthelezi, leader of the IFP, took place. One day after Mandela and Buthelezi had announced a 'watershed agreement effectively outlawing violence, intimidation and political intolerance among their followers' a fierce battle between more than 2,000 supporters of the ANC and the IFP took place in the province of Natal. At least 8 people were killed, 60 injured, and about 56 houses burned to the ground. The calls for peace by political leaders had no effect.

President de Klerk and his ruling National Party were embarrassed by their apparent inability to contain the violence that weakened their negotiating power. Growing allegations of 'third force' involvement and of the active participation and fuelling of the violence by de Klerk's security forces were strongly denied by him.

The impression therefore gained ground that violence was out of control and that neither South Africa's political leadership or De Klerk's security forces were able to address it effectively. Interventions from national role players other than the government and political leaders seemed to present the only hope to stem the worsening political violence and instability.

The church was the institution that first attempted a national intervention at the beginning of 1991. This was one year after the release of Mandela. The South African Council of Churches (SACC), an umbrella body for many churches, including the Methodist and Anglican Churches, called for an urgent national meeting of all leaders of strife-torn communities. The SACC, which had over many years been a strong critic of apartheid, did not represent Afrikaner churches and was distrusted by some of the political opponents of the ANC, including Chief Minister Buthelezi of the IFP. It was therefore not surprising that Buthelezi was sceptical about an SACC sponsored meeting. This was one of the main reasons why it never got off the ground.

South Africa's business community, primarily white, was also experiencing anxious times. The initial optimism that the release of Mandela would lead to political stability and the lifting of international economic sanctions, and therefore an economic upswing, had proved to be groundless. One interest group within the business community, namely the Consultative Business Movement (CBM), decided to take up the challenge. It was a voluntary organisation of senior and more progressive South African business leaders who acknowledged and supported the need for fundamental transformation in the country. In a low-key manner, the Consultative Business Movement met with the ANC, the South African Communist Party, Chief Minister Buthelezi and the Central Executive Committee of the IFP, a delegation of cabinet ministers from the National Party and with the leaders of the largest labour federation in the country, the Congress of South African Trade Unions. At all these meetings, the violence in the country was discussed. Nothing concrete emerged, but the CBM had placed itself on the map as an organisation with a potential facilitating role.

Whilst political violence was escalating to alarming levels, President de Klerk organised a 'Peace Summit' to which he invited all political groupings in the country. Some of the major political forces, for example, the ANC, declined to participate. They saw him as part of the problem of violence and not as the one who could provide a solution. His inability to deal with the violence through his government's security forces highlighted his impotence. It had become clear that without the involvement of the ANC, his Summit would not achieve much.

'A peaceful political transition was pursued through a multi-track approach involving all sectors of South African society as well as the international community.'

The frustration and helplessness being experienced by South Africans in general contributed to a gloomy future scenario of ongoing violence, growing instability and even prospects of a low intensity civil war. Commentators, both locally and abroad, predicted a bloody future. All efforts at bringing political violence under control had failed: the political leaders had been unsuccessful in stamping their authority on their followers. The churches were not trusted by all. De Klerk himself and his government had no credibility among the majority of black South Africans and big business was too close to the government to be trusted by the ANC.

The success in turning this critical and depressing situation into one of hope, lay in attempts to find more creative multi-track approaches towards achieving peace. No bilaterals or single organisations had succeeded in bringing South Africa's main political leaders together to talk peace.

The various initiatives that followed, and that contributed to the eventual peaceful political change in 1994, involved a whole range of interest groups and role players. Leaders of the South African Council of Churches and the CBM took the step of jointly exploring what role civil society could play to halt the slide towards growing polarisation of South African society. They expanded their discussions to include the leadership of the Congress of South African Trade Unions and also made contact with de Klerk's office. In further discussions (these were all informal and low-key), key figures from the Dutch Reformed Church, such as its former moderator, were invited. The Dutch Reformed Church was regarded as an Afrikaner church with influence over the Afrikaner establishment. The church and business leaders from the SACC and CBM then met with Buthelezi as well as with President de Klerk.

What they were seeking was an understanding for the need to call a peace meeting through the joint offices of the churches and business. The initial responses by Buthelezi and de Klerk were sceptical. De Klerk stressed that the government did not need the help of facilitators because it was in direct communication with all relevant parties. He did, however give a mandate to a trusted senior figure in the Afrikaner establishment who had attended De Klerk's failed peace summit, to meet with church and business leaders to explore the possibilities for a more representative peace meeting.

These informal discussions gathered momentum. Participants soon conceptualised the process that would have to be followed if violence was to be reduced. A meeting, referred to as a 'think tank for peace', to which all relevant political groups and others would be invited, was planned for 22 June 1991 in Johannesburg.

The response to the invitations was very encouraging. Never before in South Africa's history had so many diverse political groupings agreed to meet on one platform to talk peace. During the daylong meeting, which was held in the sumptuous offices of a large business concern, Archbishop Tutu played a crucial role in steering the ship through some dangerous rapids. Behind closed doors, different perspectives of the political violence and the political intolerance were considered.

South Africans at large received the outcome with a sigh of relief. It was agreed to establish a new preparatory committee, this time consisting mainly of representatives of various political parties but chaired by a prominent non-partisan businessman. The committee decided to establish five working groups that would look at the following issues :

Group 1: Code of conduct for political parties
Group 2: Code of conduct for Security Forces
Group 3: Socio-economic development
Group 4: Implementation and monitoring
Group 5: Process, secretariat, and media

Each Working Group was to consist of three nominees from the government/National Party, three nominees from the IFP, three nominees from the ANC/South African Communist Party/Congress of South African Trade Unions alliance, one religious leader, and one business representative from the preparatory committee. September 14, 1991 was set as the target date by which the reports from the five working groups had to be completed and on which a National Peace Convention would be held to ratify and sign the agreements. South Africa's political, church, trade union and business leaders would be invited to attend.

Whilst the political leadership backed the work of the five Working Groups, there was no let-up in the violence and killings between their supporters and the security forces on the ground. To an increasing extent, South Africans realised that, unless the planned National Peace Convention was successful, the chances of commencing constitutional negotiation were slim and so were the chances of peace and stability. The Convention therefore had to be successful. And so it was.

The National Peace Convention was a remarkable occasion. The written reports from the working groups had been collated to form what was from then on referred to as the National Peace Accord. With the exception of three white right-wing parties, the national leaders of all South Africa's political groups attended. This had never happened before. For the first time Mandela, de Klerk, and Buthelezi were together and actually sitting next to each other. Add to that the leaders of the South African Communist Party, the Pan Africanist Congress and a number of smaller parties, and it becomes clear why the National Peace Convention represented a breakthrough for South Africa. It showed that the deep-seated differences that existed would, in future, not prevent the various parties from speaking to each other about common interests.

Leaders from various religious denominations were there. So were trade unions, the business community, the diplomatic corps, Zulu king Goodwill Zwelithini, traditional chiefs and newspaper editors. The symbolic significance of such a gathering was powerful, something that the media conveyed with full fanfare.

Witnessed by all those present, the political leaders signed the National Peace Accord and undertook to make it work. This was to be a daring experiment in conflict resolution on a national scale. The Accord provided for the establishment of a network of representative peace committees at national, regional, and local levels. Basic democratic norms would have to be abided by, political intolerance would not be allowed, dispute resolution mechanisms were built in, a code of conduct was provided for both political parties and the police, and a programme of socio-economic development was to be initiated. The first broad outlines of the new South Africa were established. As an evaluation mission from International Alert concluded, 'Its [the accord's] significant success lies in developing a 'peace culture', in securing an ideological commitment from the principal political actors to 'political tolerance', and in being able to establish procedures and mechanisms for crisis management.'

This approach towards achieving peace, in which the elite as well as ordinary communities had a role to play, and in which labour unions, churches, business, traditional leaders, other civil society structures as well as political

Emotions at Amnesty Hearings

parties were involved, meant that people from across South Africa became part of a peace process with a common objective in mind. By April 1994, when the first democratic election was held, one national peace committee, eleven regional, and 250 local peace committees had been established throughout the country.

After the signing of the National Peace Accord, political leaders soon turned their attention to the next major challenge that required urgent attention, the proposed multi-party conference to negotiate a new democratic constitution for the country. Political expectations were high; something the Peace Accord was unable to address. It was not geared to transform the country from apartheid to a democracy. It was also not geared to deal with the danger presented by the multiplicity of military forces in the country. Nor was it capable of defusing the threats of sabotaging of the negotiated change by armed white right-wing groups. A number of simultaneous and multi-track approaches to deal with these threats were initiated.

By the end of 1991, the Conference for a Democratic South Africa, CODESA, had constituted itself as the multi-party forum through which constitutional negotiations would take place. The country's political leadership participated in these often tension-ridden discussions, week after week, for many months, while their supporters were attempting to make the Peace Accord work on the ground. All the Peace Committees could achieve was to help contain political violence to levels that would otherwise have been even worse.

After a particularly brutal massacre in June 1992, in which 48 people, mainly women and children were killed, local and international outrage followed and the constitutional negotiations came to a grinding halt. After an appeal to the United Nations by Nelson Mandela, the General Assembly decided in August 1992 to deploy UN observers to South Africa. Within the next few months they were joined by monitors from the Commonwealth, the Organisation for African Unity and the European Community. In terms of the UN resolution, they attached themselves to peace committees in various parts of the country where they made a significant impact. With their distinct uniform or flags, they were seen by friend and foe as 'the ears and eyes' of the international community. This enabled international monitors to have a restraining impact on potentially violent situations such as huge political rallies or protest marches. Their contribution to the eventual successful political change should not be underestimated.

'The successful peace process over the past ten years will always provide justification to South Africans for the belief that should national crises occur, they have it within themselves to pull together and overcome such crises.'

In order to assist in preparing citizens and institutions for a totally different political and social future, many civil society structures were busy facilitating contact and interaction between erstwhile enemies or with state and other institutions that faced fundamental transformation. These were crucial initiatives: communication and joint planning for the future was facilitated between the South African Defence Force and the military wing of the ANC. Afrikaner establishment figures from sports, the arts, business and the media were introduced to leading politicians and others from exile in a systematic way. Low-key contacts with white right-wing groups were established with the hope of staving off any serious attempts to derail the coming election and to secure their participation in the elections. Some non-governmental organisations focused on research and policy changes that would soon become necessary. Many other examples could be mentioned. All these efforts constituted a productive and multi-faceted approach by civil society structures towards achieving a peaceful transition from apartheid to a democracy.

During the entire pre-election period, international economic and financial sanctions remained in place and were used to apply pressure for change on de Klerk's governing National Party and on the business community. Even sanctions played their part in the eventual successful outcome of this process. A peaceful political transition was therefore pursued through a multi-track approach involving all sectors of South African society as well as the international community. The peace process resulting from the National Peace Accord was merely one of the tracks that brought South Africa to its first democratic election. Coming soon after the Peace Accord, CODESA was the track on which the actual new dispensation was brokered, and for almost two years, these two processes worked in tandem. Other tracks involved civil society structures, the international monitors, and informal interactions by non governmental organisations and a variety of groups.

All these initiatives went through testing times. Although deaths as a result of political violence had peaked in July 1993, shortly before the elections, in March and April 1994, a serious escalation of political violence suddenly occurred. During March alone, 552 persons had died. A state of emergency was declared in the province of KwaZulu-Natal and security forces were placed on the alert.

An inexplicable change occurred during the last week before the election was due on 26 April 1994. Violence subsided. An almost eerie absence of political violence and death during the four voting days occurred. The co-operation and goodwill that was exhibited between South Africans from across the spectrum created a new sense of national unity and optimism for the future. It had a major influence on the national mood for a year or two.

As was to be expected, however, the post election honeymoon has since lost a lot of its sparkle. Despite the miraculous transition in South Africa, enormous challenges and problems face the country. The successful peace process over the past ten years will, however, always provide justification to South Africans for the belief that should national crises occur, they have it within themselves to pull together and overcome such crises.

Peter Gastrow has played a key role in the promotion of peace in South Africa in the past decade. As a lawyer and a Member of Parliament, he participated in the establishment of the National Peace Accord and served in a number of its structures. He chaired the Law and Order Sub-council of the transitional government prior to the 1994 elections and thereafter assumed the position of special advisor to the Minister of Safety and Security. Gastrow is presently the Cape Town Director of the Institute for Security Studies; an independent applied policy research institute that focuses on human security in Africa.

9 Israeli-Palestinian Peace-Building: Lessons Learnt

By Manuel Hassassian and Edward (Edy) Kaufman*

We would like to share our thoughts on the relevance of Israeli-Palestinian case to work conducted worldwide from coexistence to peace-building and reconciliation. While ours is a particular case -and we often think that our conflicts present unique features when explaining the difficulties in resolving them- we should be also aware that it shares similarities and differences with other ethnopolitical disputes. In fact it belongs with many others to the category of protracted communal conflicts, the prevailing category of violent disputes in the post-Cold War period. From this perspective, the Israeli/Palestinian conflict perhaps shares less attributes with the Syrian/Israeli border dispute (over territorial claims on the sparsely populated Golan Heights) than with other identity-driven confrontations in former Yugoslavia, Cyprus, Sri Lanka or Indonesia.

We will centre our comments on the last decade of joint work conducted on the part of non-governmental organizations, academics, and other professional groups interested in a historic compromise based on the search for common ground. Our wish is to present a critical introspect, although it may be difficult to retain objectivity when we are both so centrally involved in the process itself. In the next pages we would like to present a brief background followed by a diagnosis of the obstacles, as well as the achievements, of the groups presented in the book in different sectors. The article concludes with some prescriptive comments applicable to others.

Framing the Issue

After over a century of discord, marked both by intermittent acts of violence and officially declared wars (about one a decade), the Israeli-Palestinian conflict has eventually resulted in a lengthy peace process. The current process was inaugurated at Madrid in October 1991 as a regional enterprise and took shape as a bilateral understanding through the 'Oslo channel', which was endorsed by both sides in the famous signing of the resultant accords on the White House lawn in September 1993.

Israel's first agreement with Egypt in 1978 failed to lead to a subsequent reconciliation with its other Arab neighbours, leaving the core dispute with the Palestinians active for another two decades. The 1988 recognition by the Palestine Liberation Organization (PLO) of a 'two-state solution' did not meet with the approval of the then Likud government in Israel, and it was only in the aftermath of the 1991 Gulf War that negotiations were able to progress. The process launched in Madrid that same year came at first to a diplomatic impasse in Washington, but this was followed by a complex, but effective, track two process in Oslo.

The rise to power of Prime Minister Netanyahu's hard-line government in 1996 slowed down the implementation of the interim agreements and totally disrupted the timetable established for completing an agreement of final status issues (including borders and security, Jerusalem, Jewish settlements, Palestinian refugees and other issues such as management of water resources). The parties were expected to reach an agreement on these important issues by 1999, but by now it seems that the situation will remain an open challenge at the dawn of the 21st century.

We would like to focus on the interaction of Arabs and Jews across the Green Line that has separated the 'small' Israel from the territories of the West Bank and Gaza that were occupied in the June 1967/Six Days War. These areas have seen only partial re-deployment in areas now under the control of the Palestinian National authority, while the rest of the occupied lands remain under shared rule but total Israeli military control. The larger part of the West Bank and a smaller portion of Gaza are still in Israeli hands and this territory includes not less than 130 new Jewish settlements.

This delimitation of scope is important since within the 'small' Israel there has been a longer history of rapprochement between Jews (80% of the population) and Arabs (20%), efforts often described as a drive towards 'coexistence'. This last term is not popular amongst Palestinians, and to a lesser extent amongst Israelis, who are involved in 'peace-building' as a complement to the efforts at 'peacemaking' among their leaders. The issue at stake is found within the former term, since a Palestinian state has not yet come into existence and any efforts towards any other solution are considered to be insufficient for eventually ensuring a 'real peace' that can cement the post-negotiation stage of 'reconciliation'. Hence, 'coexistence' across the yet undefined borders is often perceived as a false 'normalization.' The term for this in Arabic (tatbyeh) connotes unilateral acceptance of the Jewish state without first securing the full recognition of the individual and collective rights of the Palestinian people.

Meanwhile, the Jewish side achieved its political independence fifty years ago and has since worked to secure it through military superiority over coalitions of Arab states, and surely over the Palestinians. It has also worked to consolidate its presence in the Middle East through peace accords with Egypt (the most important and strongest Arab country) and the Hashemite Kingdom of Jordan (with which Israel shares its longest current border). The State of Israel has also developed a vibrant economy stimulated by generous foreign aid and consolidated democratic institutions.

What makes this conflict even more difficult to resolve is the fact that the people of both nations have historically claimed the full possession of the entire land of Greater Israel or Palestine, and that throughout history there have been few moments of convergence of objectives between their respective leaderships. Yet, from within the context of these constraints, there has been a growing recognition by each party of the rights of the other to self-determination and support of the Oslo peace process has reached a high of 75% in both societies. Still, only a small segment of this population actively strives towards the fulfilment of this goal either separately or together with their counterparts.

At the other end of the spectrum we find a militant extremist minority often driven by 'divine inspiration' to commit acts opposed not only to the particularities of the Oslo Peace Process, but to any reconciliation. This contingent perceives the conflict in terms of a zero-sum game and claims that its side (these sorts exist on both sides of the conflict) has absolute rights and that there is no room for compromise. Their use of various acts of violence and terror, as well as civil disobedience, provides them with a relative advantage as compared with the mostly reactive and law-abiding protesters from the 'peace camp'. The Israeli silent majority seems to have been more affected by the zealots' opposition to the peace process than by the support it receives from pragmatics and moderates.

Obstacles and Opportunities

To what extent can we establish the success or failure of such endeavours made in support of peace? No clear methodology has been found yet. One could argue that the situation could always have been worse. For instance, the conflict is now considered to be of a 'low intensity level' compared with its past stages or the current situation with similar conflicts elsewhere around the globe. It could be argued that without the sustained efforts of NGOs on both sides there would not have been a sense of hope for the resolution of the conflict; that without peace demonstrations and human rights monitors, the suffering of the Palestinian side would have been greater.

At the same time, it is quite depressing to realize that only a small fragment of the population of both societies has been involved in peace-building activities, and that the fragility of such undertakings have often declined as a result of terror by committed fundamentalist extremists from both sides. Even the most insignificant minorities when driven by 'God's will' can effectively disrupt the peace process. A serious impediment to face-to-face contacts results from the closures of the Palestinian areas that often follow incidents of terror. Still, there is a need to recognize the presence not only of physical barriers, but also of psychological barriers that are no less difficult to overcome while neither side is still unable to display significant levels of reciprocal compassion.

The facts on the ground have placed Israel in the position of relative strength, generating an asymmetric relationship with the Palestinians that makes joint efforts towards peace-building more difficult. The Palestinians will not assent to claims of a 'lasting' peace before the Israeli power and the international community both recognize some basic aspects of 'justice'. Thus we find the first gap between the goals of the Israeli side -with a noticeable and at times very active 'peace movement' -Peace Now in its best moments could gather more than 200,000 in Tel Aviv- and a much smaller constituency led by a significant number of skeleton NGOs that make up the 'human rights community.'

'Extremist groups using violence, civil disobedience, and insubordination on both sides have bypassed the cumulative impact of the many activists involved in 'people-to-people' activities, despite the fact that the former group constitutes a smaller portion of activists.'

One the one hand, for many Israelis the search for a 'lasting peace' is an act of enlightened self-interest. On the other hand, many Israelis find it difficult to express solidarity with the demands to refrain from human rights violations of the 'other' when this means identifying with members of a nation from which a small minority of the population is still perpetuating horrendous acts of terror towards them.

After the June 1967 war, the first Palestinian NGOs were established to prevent human rights violations and, during the Intifada, they grew into a self-reliant driving force working in the absence of an elected authority. After the Oslo accords, more NGOs were established to raise awareness among the public on women's rights, democracy, and transparency. Only lately, several NGOs were established in support of the Peace Process. What makes the relationship between the two parties more difficult is that among the Palestinians there has been a widespread disillusionment with their Jewish counterparts who have not made their struggle for peace a top priority in their lives. The occasional participation in a demonstration or signing of a petition falls significantly below their level of expectation. Indeed, few Israelis have joined those involved as paid staff or volunteer board members of human rights NGOs. Yet, it is important to recall that those few are strongly committed Israeli activists that have been fighting against administrative detention, housing demolition, the use of 'moderate physical pressure' (that amounts to torture) in interrogations, and other violations.

We detect a certain level of tension around these issues. It has been difficult to generate an atmosphere of cooperation when the asymmetry on the ground is so clear. The practical limitations on the freedom of movement and the effect of humiliation by Israeli security forces combine to generate a mood amongst Palestinians that is adverse to voluntary participation in cooperative endeavours with Israeli partners. Furthermore, the unequal number of Israelis (five million Jews and one million non-Jews) and Palestinians (two and a quarter million), the gaps in the educational, technological, and socio-economic levels, and years of consolidation as a democratic entity - all of these factors increase the disparities. One of the consequences is that we often find more Israelis seeking Palestinian partnership than vice versa - a problematic situation when planning activities based on equality which also means numeric parity.

Lastly, we need to recall that in the not remote past, and for a long period of time, the Palestinian leadership first and then the Israeli leadership later forbade any contacts amongst our peoples - although there has been direct contact since 1967. Palestinian dialogue pioneers have been killed by extremist groups and -no doubt a more moderate level of limitation- Israeli peaceniks have been jailed, or politically ostracized, for talking to PLO representatives. While academic and intellectual projects and encounters have been developed since the Intifada (the Palestinian uprising in the West Bank and Gaza that started in November 1987), most of the dialogue and cooperation programs started after 1993 through the support of 'People-to-People' initiatives of friendly governments, with Norway in the lead.

This structural weakness in 'peace-building' has marked the cooperation within this area, where people of goodwill tend to act separately, or at best in short-term projects of bilateral cooperation between NGOs, and even less so among professionals under the umbrella of public institutions such as universities. The official Palestinian policy is still to reject such 'normalization' in the face of existing inequalities. Yet, there have been not a few NGOs ready for cooperation and some of them have even utilized such contacts in their defense of Palestinian rights, both in relation to the Israeli and Palestinian authorities.

Another concern lies in the ability to understand the culture and tradition of the 'other'- from how to share the grief when facing acts of terror and violence to the differences in group dynamics in the conduction of meetings. Though

The enthusiasm for cooperation has decreased with the decline and eventual halt of the Peace Process

many Palestinians know Hebrew, few Israelis understand Arabic, and as a result most of the peacebuidling activities are conducted among those who speak English, thus omitting the real grassroots people, who are often more emotionally antagonistic to each other. Furthermore, there are only a handful of joint Israeli-Palestinian NGOs, and most of these are more radical than liberal in their political orientation, and therefore unattractive to the majority of activists on either side.

This marks a major difference from the Arab-Jewish coexistence activity within Israel, where the tendency has been prevailingly to work together in common institutions. In peace-building across the divide, the majority of interactions are conducted by separate Israeli and Palestinian NGOs acting together for a specific period of time. While this mode may more appropriate for what eventually is heading into two distinct but intertwined states, there is still a long way to go for each side to reach out to other similar organizations in its own civil society. For instance, the possibility for a joint Israeli/Palestinian peace education project that would have a multiplying effort in involving or getting interested other NGOs in each side interested in education. Paradoxically, even if progress in coexistence work can be noticed, we cannot expect a high level of success for Arab/Jewish cooperation efforts in Israel without reaching an effective peace-building among Israelis and Palestinians. The remaining level of conflict in the latter relation makes it impossible to reach the attainment of equal rights in the first. This is not meant to belittle the importance of a pluralistic commitment to work simultaneously in seeking the fulfilment of both goals. Rather it is intended to simply stress the need to prioritize and understand that real reconciliation will not occur unless we put more energy in producing changes of leadership conducive not only to the reactivation but also towards the 'humanization' of the Peace Process. Implicit in this is the necessity to fight simultaneously both for the respect of human rights and conflict resolution.

Although the scale of cooperation remains limited by the above mentioned obstacles, we need to stress that the diverse projects of schoolchildren, youth, artists, professional groups, women, and political movements of both sides have shown a high level of creativity. In many ways the Israeli/Palestinian laboratory is an exemplary reservoir of ideas to be emulated elsewhere. Needless to say, we also acknowledge that there is a lot to learn from peace-builders elsewhere. The numbers and qualities of joint projects have increased over time, and it is true that they have done so with the help of generous funding from abroad. In most cases, they have managed to endure the downs of the Peace Process, and that in itself can be seen as an achievement. We do not have space to systematically point out to the many success stories, some are described elsewhere in this volume, and we will confine ourselves to relate briefly to the categories analyzed in this book, with a few illustrations.

Track Two Diplomacy
While the national leadership received the international recognition for the historic signing of the Oslo accords on the White House lawn, these agreements would never have been produced if not for the initiative of non-official second track diplomats. The Israelis and Palestinians who worked through the secret channel in Oslo to produce the framework for the current peace process stand as the most prominent example of the potential of second track diplomacy to make real and lasting advancements in the building of peace.

Media
While the media has perhaps the greatest potential for reaching the masses in whose opinions the fate of the peace process may ultimately lay, the existence of joint endeavours in this sector is really quite limited. Elsewhere we advocate co-authored newspaper editorials as a means for affecting public opinion. While we maintain that such work is important it is relevant that we point out that there is no structural cooperation between Israeli and Palestinian media.

Two examples of genuine, ongoing cooperative media projects may be cited, and commended; but it must be stressed that by the nature of their target audiences they have no real effect on the mass population. First is the Israeli-Palestinian Sesame Street television program that may foster in the next generation a culture of peace but cannot have an impact on the politics of the day. Second are the publications of the Alternative Information Centre, a radical left-oriented organization of Israelis and Palestinians critical of the two leaderships and of the Oslo process, but little resonance in both societies.

Religion
Christian, Jewish, and Muslim moderates have met in various different initiatives aimed at using religious leadership to foster support for peace, finding more common ground than expected. The response of those involved in such projects tends to be initially quite positive. But in the long run little inroads have been produced on their respective clerical establishments. No doubt, given that the main dimension of our national conflict is now related to religion, the need to continue to invest on this area needs to be more recognized

Education
It is possible to point out numerous joint projects in the field of education, yet almost without exception these projects are conducted between Israeli Arabs and Israeli Jews. As noted elsewhere, such constructs, confined to the bounds of 'small' Israeli, tend to draw attention away from the greater picture of the Israeli-Palestinian situation. The barriers to cooperation between academic institutions imposed from above on both sides are also existent for the large public school sectors. On the part of the Israelis, the tremendous influence of the orthodox religious in the educational leadership must be weighed. For the Palestinians there is a refusal on the part of the leadership to engage in cooperative endeavours with Israeli institutions until it is possible for schools in the West Bank and Gaza to enjoy free exchange of students.

Women's Issues
Women are among the most prominent individuals working for peace and are involved in large numbers on the Israeli side. This seems not be the case on the Palestinian side where most women leaders seem to devote more energy in the struggle for equality and to show a tougher stand towards normalization with their peers. Few organizations exist and one of the most active over a sustained time has been 'The Jerusalem Link', a coalition of two Israeli and Palestinian feminist peace organizations in East and West Jerusalem, active in promoting both peace and human rights through a two-state solution. It is often responsible for organizing protests against housing demolitions, and other acts by officials that endanger the progress of peace.

Private Sector
Israeli and Palestinian individual businesses have been inclined to trade and seek join ventures or deals, making this cooperation more attractive perhaps than any other. Yet in the motivation for their compulsion to work side by side can be found the very factor that yields private enterprise cooperation ineffective in directly affecting peace-building. That is, the private sector tend to be apolitical, and businesses are inclined to foster only good will and obviously the individual interests of the beneficiaries.

Individual/Community-Based Initiatives
Given the constant tension, the animosity resulting from individual violent acts and collective reprisals, the reduction of the resulting hatred is a top priority in setting the atmosphere for peace-building activities. Unfortunately, only a few initiatives have been undertaken in this field. Dialogue groups have been in existence for a while, such as the Rapprochement Centre in Beit Sahour. But in the long run the effect of talk that does not lead into action has been detrimental to its continuity as a whole. One of the most recent projects is the Parents' Circle, a group formed by a religious Jewish Israeli man who lost his son through an act of Hammas terror. He refuses to join in the ranks of the families of victims of terror organized in Israel to actively oppose the peace process on the basis of the persistence of such acts. Instead, he has been bringing together Israeli and Palestinian bereaved parents who have lost a member of the family through politically motivated or military violence. They work together to convince the leaderships on both sides that only through establishing a genuine peace will the two peoples be able to put an end to the terror.

These observations can be put within a larger context to affirm that the lack of progress in the peace process has negatively affected democracy in Israel and the process of democratization in the Palestinian Territories. There have been many indications that the quality of life, not only in economic terms, but also in terms of basic freedoms and political/civil rights is increasingly restricted by the procrastination in the advancement of peace. This message has not been successfully communicated to large sectors of the population on both sides, and it still remains a task for those involved in coexistence and peace-building work to undertake as part of their efforts to make the connection between democracy and peace. To get out of this vicious cycle there is a need for the liberal civil society to realize that fragmented efforts need to be understood within a wider picture. On the positive side, there is a connection between democracy and peace (the popular formulation is that democracies tend not to fight wars with one another), and, on the negative side, the first of these deteriorates as a result of paralysis in securing the latter.

'Coexistence across the yet undefined borders is often perceived as a false normalization.'

In retrospect, we should convey our concern that the dedicated efforts of a small but active part of both Israeli and Palestinian civil societies do not seem to have been effective in positively redressing the adverse trends in the peace process. Extremist groups using violence, civil disobedience, and insubordination on both sides have bypassed the cumulative impact of the many activists involved in 'people-to-people' activities. This despite the fact that the former group constitutes a smaller portion of activists. It may well have to do with the enormous impact of the use of violence, terror, and collective punishment, and the peace forces may revise again the inventory available for effective engagement in civil disobedience and other non-violent methods. The enthusiasm for cooperation has decreased with the decline and eventual halt of the Peace Process. Paradoxically, at times when peace-building is more necessary than ever, the level of motivation of the civil societies to work hand in hand is lower.

For Israeli NGOs it is necessary to fight simultaneously for the end of occupation while at the same time minimizing the day-to-day suffering of the Palestinian population. For Palestinian NGOs it is crucial to transcend their sense of frustration with the lack of 'peace dividends' by still showing public concern and rejection of the use of terror against Israeli civilians. During this last electoral campaign in Israel, the impact of such acts by rejectionist groups is feared; but so far no strong peace message has been coming from the Palestinian civil society as a preventive measure to project another image of the Arab hostility in the Israeli public eye.

Since there is a high level of consensus among Israelis and Palestinians around the plausibility of a 'two-state solution,' the main area of concern remains the fear of terror and reprisals. In this context of lack of personal security to the individuals of both sides, the advocacy of non-violence in the Palestinian struggle for independence, even if not accompanied by support to the Oslo process, could be a tremendous contribution to setting up the conditions for more positive interactions.

Separately, we have analyzed the limitation of the 'people-to-people' work mostly as positive, but introverted, activities that lack clear political objectives, and therefore remain at best a constructive tool for interactions amongst a part of civil society. Such activities indeed build trust, affect attitudes, and reduce stereotypes among the participants in hundreds of programs. Yet there are two additional elements that have not been developed. One of the two missing dimensions is a deliberate attempt to affect the attitudes of policy makers. Sporadic interactions between peace-oriented Palestinians and pro-government Israeli parliamentarians have shown that there is a powerful tool for moderating the views of some. This has not been pursued by the Israelis in 'people-to-people' networks. Sometimes this kind of action can be conducted diagonally from one civil society to the leadership of the other or by jointly trying to affect the leadership of both. Wide publicity about such activities can also affect public attitudes.

The second dimension precisely focuses on efforts to address public opinion and grassroots attitudes. Little has been done to utilize the mass media, such as television, radio talk shows, and daily newspapers. Again, joint appearances (if possible the Israeli/Palestinian team speaking the language of each audience), co-authored op-eds, successful coverage of 'people-to-people' programs, documenting emotional movements are all appropriate methods. Needless to say, the multiplying effect of a deliberate effort to stimulate a better atmosphere is one of the most powerful tools - particularly at the time of electoral campaigns. It can also contribute to the adoption of confidence building measures such as the decrease of human rights violations, and amnesties for released political prisoners.

One would hope that a realistic and charismatic leadership could radiate confidence not only to its own people but also to the other nation. If such an atmosphere would simultaneously exist on both sides, then we could bring the Peace Process to completion. Even then we would submit that a handshake is not enough, and the human fragility of such equation has been seen in the tragic assassinations of President Sadat and Prime Minister Rabin. Such processes need to be accompanied by an active involvement of the peace forces at all stages of negotiation. Surely, when the time of reconciliation comes after the agreements, the public dimension of the process will require the groups and prominent individuals within civil society to play an exemplary role. What makes it more troublesome is that we do not find such statesmen available, even from one of the two governments. At this time the challenges of peace-building are formidable and the odds against the extremist forces -now backed also by one government- are not good. This has characterized the late period in our Process and only a more creative, professional, interactive and devoted peace movement on both sides can generate the dynamics that will trigger a real change of minds and hearts among their brethren.

We would like to express our gratitude to our research assistant Heather Coppley who was so instrumental in transforming our ideas into this article.

References
Issues related to the subject of this article have been treated by both of us jointly and separately in several publications, and among them:
Democracy, Peace and the Israeli-Palestinian Conflict, Edy Kaufman, Shukri Abed and Robert Rothstein, Boulder, Lynne Rienner Publishers, 1993.
See articles of E. Kaufman, 'The Effect of War and Occupation on Israeli Society' (pages 85-134) and M. Hassassian 'The Democratization Process in the PLO: Ideology, Structure, and Strategy' (pages 257-285)

Part 1 Israeli-Palestinian Peacebuilding: Lessons Learnt

The Role of the Israeli and Palestinian Civil Societies in the Peace Process, M. Hassassian and E. Kaufman. In: Is Oslo Alive, M, Maoz and S. Nusseibeh (eds.). Jerusalem, The Adenauer Foundation, 1998

'Israeli-Palestinian Co-authoring: A New Development Towards Peace?' E. Kaufman. Journal of Palestine Studies (Vol. XXII, 88, No 4, Summer 1993) pages 32-44

The Role of Palestinian NGOs in Peace Building, M. Hassassian. In: Academics and the Israel-Palestinian Peace Process: Past, Present and Future Roles, E. Kaufman and M.Hassassian (forthcoming).

*Edward (Edy) Kaufman, *(Ph.D. from the University of Paris -Sorbonne), Senior Researcher and Executive Director of the Harry S. Truman Research Institute for the Advancement of Peace, Hebrew University in Jerusalem. He has been involved in human rights NGOs at the international and national level, currently chairing the Board of B'tselem, the Israel Information Center for Human Rights in the Occupied Territories. He is also a Senior Researcher (and former Director) of the Center for International Development and Conflict Management of the University of Maryland-College Park and for the past five years has been team teaching a course on 'Conflict Resolution: the Israeli/Palestinian Experiment' concurrently with Prof. Hassassian.*

*Manuel Hassassian *(Ph.D. from University of Toledo, Ohio) taught Political Science at Bethlehem University, later becoming Dean of Students, Dean of Arts and is now its Executive Vice-president. He is also currently the Chair of the Palestinian Council of Higher Education. In his voluntary work he has been involved in Palestinian NGOs focusing on democracy and peace, and electoral monitoring. He received an Honorary Doctorate from the University of Reims, France.*

10 Reflections on Peace building

By Paul van Tongeren *

The following section of this book tells 35 inspiring stories describing peace-building initiatives from around the world. Here we focus on some of the lessons that can be learned from these and other examples. Naturally, these lessons draw on the work of the many experts who have reflected on this subject on earlier occasions.

U ndoubtedly one of the most important documents relating to these issues is the outline of guidelines and principles based on the accumulated experience and wisdom of the Institute for MultiTrack Diplomacy. Also included are elements of the 'Agenda for Peace and Justice for the 21st century' currently being drafted by the Hague Appeal for Peace, as well as the Strategic Plan developed by the Coexistence Initiative of State of the World Forum (see annexes).

1. Involve as many people and sectors as possible in peace-building
It is an obvious point but one which is, nevertheless, frequently overlooked: it is essential that as many sectors of society as possible be included in any peace-building process. Many of the following stories illustrate how individuals and groups take responsibility for the society they live in, and how they can make a real difference.

2. Strengthen local capacities for peace
If efforts to prevent, resolve and transform violent conflict are to be effective in the long-term, they must be based on the active participation of local civil groups committed to building peace. Strengthening such 'local capacities for peace' may take many forms, including education and training, nurturing the volunteer spirit in society and highlighting the work of local peacemakers in the media. Granting basic human rights such as freedom of speech and press and freedom to organise oneself are prerequisites for including the different civil organisations in the peace process.

3. Conceive peace building and reconciliation as a process
Peace is not an abstract goal but a process; it must be built-up over a long period of time. Building peace must be an organic process, growing at all

levels of society. Peace cannot be built just through exclusive conclaves of the leaders of the conflicting parties. The idea of 'historic agreements as a stepping stone to peace' has proven to be wrong on too many occasions. Longterm strategic relationships should be built which reach across the dividing lines of conflict in society.

4. Change and transform the conflict pattern: create hope

A common feature of many of the following examples is that they succeeded in breaking the logic of war. Successful initiatives create hope and stimulate people to disengage themselves from war, as is shown by the peace zones in Columbia and the struggle to preserve the multicultural character of the city of Tuzla in Bosnia. Although people could not prevent an escalation of the surrounding violence, they succeeded in creating local alternatives. By inspiring others these initiatives have an extremely important spin-off effect.

5. Create dialogue

Stimulate a feeling of interdependence, emphasise common identities and help people to understand the other side's position. Private peacemaking should focus on 'humanising the enemy'. The most effective dialogue often occurs when each side forcefully advocates its position and then listens to its opponent. It should be recognised that people can communicate with each other, but may not be ready for a dialogue. Much creativity is needed to bring the parties together for a first round of talks. In many situations -like in Somalia, Mali, Northern Ireland, Guatemala, and Sri Lanka- the importance of such an approach has been proven.

6. Promote education and enhance professionalisation

Educational programmes should stimulate the universal awareness of coexistence, tolerance and reconciliation. Those involved in the peace-building process must be thoroughly prepared and trained. Professionalisation of peace building can enhance its effectiveness.

7. Exchange experiences

Promote international exchanges between peacemakers from conflict regions. Learning from each other's experiences inspires innovative approaches as the examples of Sri Lanka, South Africa and Northern Ireland clearly show.

8. Include local authorities

The decentralised approach of grassroots and community-based organisations has resulted in many successes. Examples of these successes include the EU Peace Fund in Northern Ireland, the city approach of the World Council of Churches, as well as the creation of the over 200 local peace commissions in Kenya.

Private peacemaking should focus on 'humanising the enemy'

PHOTO HENNY VAN DER GRAAF

9. Strengthen coalition building between civil organisations
The effectiveness of civil activity is often hampered by a lack of coordination between groups operating in similar fields. As a result, scarce resources are wasted through duplication of tasks and failure to achieve synergy. There is a great need to create civil networks and/or platforms that promote coalition and constituency building. Global networks are needed to further strengthen individuals' and communities' capacity for peace building. Many of the following case-studies are an illustration of this need. Through networking they succeeded in multiplying their strength.

10. Institution-building
To sustain peace-building and reconciliation, institution-building should be stimulated at all levels of society and at the international level. In an increasingly globalized international system, the need to work at global institutions, actors and processes to create the climate for conflict resolution, prevention, peace-building and reconciliation, should be emphasised.

11. Make 'Conflict Impact Assessment' a requirement
In order to maximise the benefits of development aid, dispensing bodies - governmental, intergovernmental and private- should be required to assess

and report on the likely impact of their development-aid policies in terms of whether they will heighten or reduce the risks of violent conflicts.

12. Role of the corporate sector
The potential role of the corporate sector in peace-building is still not widely recognised. However, just as business can exacerbate tensions and fuel conflict, so it can contribute to building peace and security, as the examples of South Africa and Northern Ireland, described later in this publication, have shown.

13. Role of donors
As the Abraham Fund and the EU Peace Fund for Northern Ireland illustrate, the role of donors can extend beyond the simple provision of financial support for projects. Donors can provide an extra impulse in the peace-building process by stimulating conferences, agenda setting, and developing directories such as The Abraham Fund's 'Handbook of Interethnic Coexistence'.

14. Prioritise Early Warning and Early Response
That prevention is better than cure is a truth which needs to be better observed in practice. Civil society organisations, governments and intergovernmental bodies should dedicate much more attention and resources to prevention, as opposed to reacting to violent conflict. In particular, mere political should be generated for early responses to potential conflict situations, both present and future.

15. Promote an integrative approach to peace building and reconciliation by using a combination of approaches
In her contribution on Northern Ireland to this volume, Mari Fitzduff stresses the need for a variety of approaches to peace building. The experience of Mali provides a clear example of the importance of her message. The construction of a stable peace in the northern part of the country was not the result of any single action. It followed from a complex of efforts to rebuild trust, to address legitimate grievances, to reward combatants who chose to give up the fight, and to build incentives into the peace process that would assure the continued commitment of people on both sides of the conflict.
An integrated framework towards peace building should include
- a coherent and comprehensive approach by all actors;
- partnerships between, and the coordination of, the various members of the international community and the national government;
- a broad consensus on a strategy and related set of interventions;
- careful balancing of macro-economic and political objectives, and
- the necessary financial resources.

Twelve Principles of Multi-Track Diplomacy

1. **Relationship** - building strong interpersonal and inter-group relations throughout the fabric of society.
2. **Longterm commitment** - making an ongoing commitment to people and to processes that may take years to come to fruition.
3. **Cultural synergy** - respecting the cultural wisdom of all parties and welcoming the creative interaction of different cultural views.
4. **Partnership** - modelling a collaborative process by forming partnerships with local parties and with other institutions and coalitions.
5. **Multiple technologies** - utilising a variety of technologies, as appropriate, and creating new methods, as needed, to meet the unique requirements of each situation.
6. **Facilitation** - assisting parties to take responsibility for their own dreams and destiny.
7. **Empowerment** - helping people to become empowered agents of change and transformation within their societies.
8. **Action research** - learning from all that we do and sharing that learning with others.
9. **Invitation** - entering the system where invited or offered an open door.
10. **Trust** - building relationships of mutual trust and caring within the system.
11. **Engagement** - acknowledge that once we enter a system, we become a unique part of it, an engaged, caring, and accountable partner.
12. **Transformation** - catalysing changes at the deepest level of beliefs, assumptions, and values, as well as behaviours and structures.

© INSTITUTE FOR MULTI-TRACK DIPLOMACY

16. Mainstream Multi-Track diplomacy

Peace processes should combine Track One and Track Two approaches. Track Two diplomacy is usually most effective when it is linked to official processes and channels. For this, contacts as well as the exchange of information and experiences between both approaches should be frequent and structural. The history of the peace process in Cyprus provides one among many examples of the importance of linking both tracks. In making these links, the strengths, resources, and limitations of each approach should be taken into account.

* Paul van Tongeren *played a key role in the establishment of the European Platform for Conflict Prevention and Transformation. This NGO-Network evolved after the European Conference on Conflict Prevention in 1997, which was organised amongst others, by him and brought together over 1,200 persons from around the world. He has been involved in numerous Dutch NGOs in the field of development aid, peace and the environment. For more than twenty years, Van Tongeren worked as programme manager for the Dutch National Committee for International Cooperation and Sustainable Development (NCDO). Presently he is the executive director of the European Centre for Conflict Prevention, based in the Netherlands. This centre functions as the secretariat of the European Platform and aims to stimulate collaboration and synergy among participating organisations through information exchange, education and lobbying activities. Paul van Tongeren is the initiator and co-ordinator of this publication.*

** I would like to thank Hizkias Assefa, Ambassador John McDonald, Lewis Rasmussen, Lisa Schirch, David Smock, Johan Galtung, Mohammed AbuNimer, Juliette Verhoeven and Hans van de Veen for their valuable input.

References

Peaceworks - Private Peacemaking, David Smock (ed.). USIP-Assisted Peacemaking Projects of Nonprofit Organizations, United States Institute of Peace, 1998.

Preventing Deadly Conflict Final Report of the Carnegie Commission on Preventing Deadly Conflict, Carnegie Corporation of New York, New York, 1997

Do no Harm - Supporting Local Capacities for Peace, Mary Andersson. Collaborative for Development Action, 1996

From Civil War to Civil Society, Report of The World Bank and the Carter Center, 1995.

Part II
Cases

I

Track One: Governments

Introduction
Power for Peace

Track One diplomacy is about men in suits posing before squads of photographers before they disappear behind closed doors for discrete talks. It is also about encoded telexes and email-messages sent back and forth between embassies and government headquarters, evoking a world ruled by formal gentlemen-like codes, imperturbably exposed at press conferences and cocktail parties ♦ BY JOS HAVERMANS

T rack One diplomacy is the realm of traditional international politics as practised by foreign offices, ambassadors, special envoys and other officials representing governments. More than any other track, traditional diplomacy can play a decisive role in matters of war and peace.

The culture of Track One diplomacy, the traditional form of international politics, is clearly alien to the world of most Non Governmental Organisations and adherents of alternative political ways. However, proponents of unconventional diplomacy do not consider Track One to be inimical to less conventional approaches. All tracks that can lead to peace should be valued, they say, and the world of traditional diplomacy is no exception.

This point of view fits well with the non governmental peace builders' penchant for harmony and togetherness. It is also born out of pragmatic reasoning. Non-official actors in international politics are as aware as anyone else that the world of Track One diplomacy can exert enormous influence because, generally speaking, it has armies, guns and money at its disposal. Track One, in this sense, is synonymous with power.

Track One diplomacy is indeed suspiciously closely connected to warfare, because, as history books tell us, the same politicians who carry out delicate diplomatic manoeuvres can decide to use force should they prefer to pursue their political goals by other means. But its weight and resources can, of course, also make a difference if used on the side of promoting peace and reconciliation. It is exactly its ability to mobilize vast material resources that constitutes the major potential of Track One diplomacy over other tracks when it comes to going the difficult but rewarding path of conflict prevention, peace building and reconciliation. If politicians of conflicting camps are sincere in their determination to make peace, there will be peace.

The surplus value of Track One over Track Two diplomacy, therefore, is its ability to coerce on the parties in a conflict by directly or indirectly threatening to mobilize its military and financial-economic means. Track One can build up enormous pressure on conflicting parties to pursue a process of negotiation. A prerequisite for this scenario is that Track One actors are willing to intervene as a third party in a foreign conflict in the first place. There are signs that the world of Track One is increasingly receptive to unconventional approaches and collaboration with NGOs, as will be discussed later.

Another advantage of Track One over other tracks is that its actors have direct access to the most important players in a conflict when it comes to forging political agreements. A telling example of what Track One actors can contribute to reconciliation and peace building is the initiative of the Norwegian diplomat Johan Jorgen Holst. Holst discretely contacted Israeli and Palestinian diplomats and hosted secret negotiations in Oslo leading to a breakthrough in the Israeli-Palestinian conflict and the signing of the Oslo agreements in 1996.

The impact of Track One diplomacy can be enhanced enormously when its efforts coincide with complementary initiatives taken by Track Two or other non-official tracks of diplomacy. The signing of the ban on landmines in 1998, for instance, is the result of a successful campaign by international NGOs, but the involvement of Track One was obviously indispensable to anchor the agreement and supervise its implementation.

Scope of action

A major difference between Track One and Track Two diplomacy is that the former, although more powerful and affluent, is in many ways more restricted in the scope of its actions than the latter. This is because a conciliatory move by an official governmental actor is intrinsically connected to other national interests. For instance, if a mediatory intervention in a foreign conflict is interpreted as being partisan by one of the relevant parties in a conflict, this could lead to economic boycotts or lack of support in international fora for the intervening country concerned. NGOs could also suffer a backlash as a result of intervening in a conflict, but generally speaking they can damage nothing but themselves on the mediating side. An official diplomat or institution, on the other hand, represents an entire nation and its interests and is putting these interests at stake in any intervention.

In democracies, Track One Diplomacy's scope of action may be further limited due considerations of accountability and restrictive regulations of the legislature. Actors in other tracks usually have more freedom to act swiftly and try new approaches.

Track One diplomacy does have its weaknesses. The world of diplomats is said to have insufficient awareness of relevant expertise about international relations, peace and conflict resolution that resides outside the diplomatic community. Another peculiar characteristic of Track One is that commitment to a process of negotiation is often seen as a sign of weakness by political leaders. One of the most striking flaws of the official diplomatic world, however, is its lack of professional negotiation skills. In many countries, most formal negotiators are known to be still operating without training other than their own experience and intuition. As negotiations are becoming increasingly complex, in an increasingly interdependent and multipolar world, professional negotiation training would be a sensible attribute for all diplomats, McDonald and other advocates of multi-track diplomacy say.

In spite of its weaknesses, Track One actors have become more receptive to peace building, conflict prevention, early warning and similar concepts. In a remarkable move for actors who tend to base their behaviour on the traditional considerations of power politics, an increasing number of national governments has become susceptible to the ideas of conflict prevention and peace building. Belief in the feasibility of alternative approaches is also gaining ground among international organisations and local governments, two other categories that are classified in the Track One category.

In this respect Canada is at the forefront among national governments. Ottawa declared in 1996 that it wanted to set an example to the leadership of the international community by increasing its investment in peace building. It announced a comprehensive peace building strategy, consisting of support to non governmental peace organisations and plans to prepare government agencies, including the armed forces, for tasks in the field of peace building, conflict management, mediation and the like. In September 1997 the Canadian Peace building Program was set up within the Department of Foreign Affairs, giving the new approach a solid place in Canada's Track One diplomacy.

Great Britain's Conservative government decided in 1996 to embrace alternatives to traditional diplomacy, including conflict prevention. London sent its entire foreign aid staff to conflict awareness courses and allocated 1 million pounds to pilot projects in conflict resolution. The present Labour government is continuing on this road.

The left-leaning social democrat administration in Germany, which took office in 1998, has also expressed its commitment to conflict prevention and peace building. Other countries that have already begun to invest significantly in peace building include The Netherlands, Sweden and Norway.

National governments' commitment to peace building is often implemented indirectly, through support to organisations specializing in Track Two approaches. This form of collaboration and coordination between official foreign affairs and non governmental actors is warmly welcomed by most 'alternative' negotiators and peace builders. Complementarity comes into play here. Mutual additionality of Track One and Track Two diplomacy is considered to be of crucial importance to create synergy between the two.

In some cases of Track One contributions to peace making, governments can build on domestic conciliatory traditions. For instance, the initiatives taken by the government of Mali to defuse the deep rooted tension between nomads and sedentary groups in the 1990s -a case which is discussed later in this volume- is in many ways an example of such an approach. On March 27, 1996, President Konaré, Ghanaian President Jerry Rawlings, and leaders of the Mali rebel movements and a large delegation of international observers gathered in Timbuktu for the highly symbolic destruction of all the surrendered armaments in what was called a 'Flame of Peace', to celebrate a peace process initiated by Konaré and hailed as 'visionary'. Here, the Mali government succeeded in motivating local leaders and communities to get a national peace process going.

The growing consensus on the feasibility of peace building and conflict prevention is also visible in multinational organisations. The United Nations, for whom peacemaking is its major mandate, has spent most of the 1990s redefining its mission to include coping with internal conflicts. The Agenda for Peace, published in 1992, was the starting point for this adjustment and notwithstanding its numerous failures to stem violence, the UN is still working to improve its peacemaking abilities. Its early warning capacity, a prerequisite for any timely action to control an upcoming conflict, is said to have definitively improved. In theory, the UN has huge peace building capacities because it has the potential to bundle the resources and expertise of powerful member states. In practice, the organisation's abilities are, sometimes fatally, limited by disagreement or the member states' lack of political will of member states, especially the permanent members of the Security Council.

Regional organisations
In Africa, the consensus about conflict management since the early 1990s was captured in the institutional framework of the OAU's Mechanism on Conflict Prevention Management Resolution. This Mechanism is mandated to develop an approach to peace building for both internal and intrastate crises. So far, however, the OAU's new Mechanism has played a limited role. The OAU was still overtaken by violent events in the 1990s, a failure that can be attributed to its limited resources and staffing. But the OAU did send special envoys to several hotbeds to make attempts at mediation. In Congo-Brazzaville, this helped bring about an accord that temporarily stopped the use of violence in that country. In Burundi the UN representative forged a political agreement in 1994, which at that time defused tensions in the country. The OAU also deployed a monitory mission in Burundi, but this intervention is widely regarded as being of limited effect.

The Organisation of American States (OAS) has shown a much more modest commitment to the field of peace building and conflict management. It declared a form of interest in the field however with the establishment of the so-called 'Santiago Mechanism', an agreement on taking swift collective action in case of coup-attempts in any of of the member countries.

The Organisation for Security and Cooperation in Europe (OSCE) has developed one of the most effective structures of conflict management. A large portion of its early warning, early action and mediation capacity has been put in the hands of one individual, the High Commissioner on National Minorities. This official, whose function is to detect of ethnic tension in Eastern Europe, has been allowed a large amount of personal initiative. The silent but persistent interventions of the first OSCE High Commissioner, Max van der Stoel, a soft spoken Dutch diplomat, are highlighted in this section of this volume. He scored several successes in defusing upcoming ethnic conflict in countries such as Estonia and Rumania.

The personal peace-making qualities of Van der Stoel are matched outside Europe by former US president Jimmy Carter. Formally working as a non-official mediator, Carter's intervention on government level could be dubbed One-and-a-half Track Diplomacy. He managed to get peace processes going on a governmental level on several occasions. The Carter Center's intervention in Korea, described later in this book, taught the former president once again that Track One's confrontational tendency in dealing with political crises is often counter productive. Carter observed that the tendency towards imposing sanctions in international crises cuts off openings to communication. 'Nations rarely achieve their goals this way,' he commented flatly. Meanwhile, Carter's ability to change politicians' attitude also illustrates that Track One diplomacy is susceptible to arguments from outside of its own realm.

Openness to innovation and unconventional approaches are also breaking ground in the most modest section of Track One diplomacy: local government. New forms of international cooperation between local governments are emerging. These activities, especially those sustained by long-term ties between cities in different parts of the world, can also contribute to enhancing peace and reconciliation. While the flaws of local governments' actions are being taken into consideration (amateurs in the international realm could do a lot of damage), the potential of local authorities in the quest for peace increasingly gain recognition. The peace process in Tuzla furnishes some compelling examples of what local governments can accomplish. Personal commitment and colleague-to-colleague contacts are key factors in the success of peace building and municipal international cooperation has extensive experience with this strategy.

Some of the cases that are presented below may not fit in the Track One category in every detail. Given that, reality can never be completely made to conform with a schematic straitjacket, the editors took the freedom to take a pragmatic approach. Jimmy Carter is not a government official, but his reconciliatory efforts are exclusively aimed at the highest governmental circles and his stature as a mediator is to a large part derived from his personal experience as president of the United States, the world's top Track One position. The Mali peace process has been an undiluted governmental initiative, despite the fact that its implementation unfolded partly through actions by local communities. The Tuzla peace initiative also shows the sign of a mixture of actors but is nevertheless interpreted as having its centre of gravity in local governmental circles. The OSCE and UNESCO reconciliation activities are Track One in its purest form.

Selected Bibliography

Conflict Prevention & Post-Conflict Reconstruction - Perspectives and Prospects. The World Bank, Post-Conflict Unit, Social Development Department, August 1998
Guidelines for Newcomers to Track Two Diplomacy, John W. McDonald. Occasional Paper no. 2, Institute for Multi-Track Diplomacy, Washington, D.C., November 1993
Inter-governmental Organizations and Preventing Conflicts - Political Practice Since the End of the Cold War, Klaas van Walraven. In: K. van Walraven (ed.), Early Warning and Conflict Prevention: Limitations and Possibilities, Kluwer Law International, The Netherlands, 1998.
Preventing Deadly Conflict - Final report of the Carnegy Commission on Preventing Deadly Conflict. Carnegy Corporation of New York, 1997
The General Principles of Multi-Track Diplomacy, Kumar Rupesinghe. ACCORD, South Africa, 1997

The Early Warnings of the OSCE's High Commissioner on National Minorities

Europe's Trip-Wire

Throughout most of the nineties, Mr. Max van der Stoel has ploughed with sustained vigour through the minorities minefield that is Central and Eastern Europe and the former Soviet Union. Nearly once a week, unmindful of the vagaries of the weather, undaunted by scepticism and even mistrust, the OSCE's High Commissioner on National Minorities has moved from Kyrgyzstan to Kazakhstan, into Albania, through Romania and Macedonia, listening with care to the various sides, asking questions, making suggestions, offering assistance.

T he High Commissioner's office, established in 1992 by the CSCE, precursor to the OSCE - Organization for Security and Co-operation in Europe - is akin to a trip-wire. His job is to alert the OSCE before tensions develop into fullblown crises. So the former Dutch Minister of Foreign Affairs, who has worked out of the Hague with an 11-person staff since January 1993, functions as an Early Warning and Conflict Prevention mechanism for the international community. Or, in the appropriate official jargon, he's 'an instrument of conflict prevention at the earliest possible stage'.

Ethnic conflict is recognised as one of the main sources of large-scale violence in today's Europe. Minority issues simmer or have exploded in many OSCE participating states - Albania, Croatia, Estonia, Hungary, Kazakhstan, Kyrgysztan, Latvia, Romania, Slovakia, the Former Yugoslav Republic of Macedonia and Ukraine.

There is no general agreement on what constitutes a (national) minority, either in the OSCE or elsewhere. Van der Stoel himself is not definitive. 'The existence of a minority is a question of fact and not of definition,' he says, quoting the Copenhagen Document of 1990: 'To belong to a national minority is a matter of a person's individual choice.'

He adds: 'I know a minority when I see one. First of all, a minority is a group with linguistic, ethnic or cultural characteristics, which distinguish it from the majority. Secondly, a minority is a group which usually not only seeks to maintain its identity but also tries to give stronger expression to that identity.'

Europe has no shortage of such groups. And the High Commissioner has accumulated a considerable portfolio based on interventions in a wide range of disputes between them and their governments.

His approach - conducting on-site missions, using preventive diplomacy at early stages of tensions, encouraging dialogue, and ensuring confidence and co-operation among parties - is possible because the position of High Commissioner is a comparatively independent one, the holder being free to decide when to intervene in a crisis, and the degree of such intervention.

Van der Stoel goes beyond the minorities' general complaints and the majorities' general justifications. His focus is on down-to-earth facts - the dull details that make all the difference. This approach is used as much in Albania (Greek minority concentrated in the southern region) as well as Croatia (displaced persons and refugees belonging to national minorities). It is used in the Baltic states of Estonia and Latvia where a great number of the population was not recognised as normal citizens when the countries regained their independence in 1991. If Russians have to pass an exam on Estonian or Latvian language, Van der Stoel wants to know, what sorts of questions are asked? (Extremely difficult ones.) If the governments insists on the non-Estonian residents being able to speak the language fluently, does it offer courses? If it takes so long to attend to a request for citizenship, why is that?

Intervening on behalf of ethnic Serb citizens of Croatia, who want to return home, he argues with care about definitions. Should they be called 'internal migrants' or 'displaced persons'? Then Van der Stoel reminds the government of Croatia of its pledge 'to create conditions for the voluntary, safe, dignified and speedy return of all displaced persons and refugees, regardless of their nationality and ethnic origin'. The Croatian constitution is also invoked. Article 15 states inter alia that 'Members of all nations and minorities have equal rights in the Republic of Croatia'.

That is the diplomat's hallmark - patience, reminding governments of their obligations to the rule of law, and holding them to their commitments.

When a row developed in the former Yugoslav Republic of Macedonia over the use of the Albanian flag by people of Albanian origin, he adopted a similar approach. (Twenty-three percent of the population of Macedonia is of Albanian origin.) Two people had died during disturbances related to the continued raising of the Albanian flags next to the flag of the Macedonia over two town halls run by Albanian mayors. After a visit (one of many to this country) and discussions, Van der Stoel urged 'all nationalities within the State to strive to find solutions for inter-ethnic problems by rejecting ethnic hatred and intolerance and by seeking constructive and continuous dialogue, with equal rights for all ethnic groups as the guiding principle.'

Intervening on behalf of the Slovak minority in Hungary, Van der Stoel focuses on the need for direct representation of the various national minorities in Hungary in the Hungarian parliament. And he takes a dim view of plans to cancel regional radio programmes in the Slovak language - lasting 90 minutes a day - on days that the Hungarian Parliament is in session, and replacing these reports with broadcasts of parliamentary debates. Likewise, he seeks to ascertain that the Hungarian minority in Slovakia and Romania is treated in accordance with the international standards.

Van der Stoel in Vukovar, Croatia   Photo Rob Hof

Ukraine's Crimean Tartars view themselves as indigenous peoples. After hearing there case, Van der Stoel suggests a legal framework within which this could be considered. While acknowledging that Ukraine is under no international obligation in this regard, the High Commissioner points to the general assumption that 'the right of persons belonging to national minorities as laid down in various international instruments also accrue to indigenous peoples.'

And he invokes Article 11 of the Constitution of Ukraine, which lays down some important principles regarding both indigenous peoples and national minorities by stating that the state will assist in the development of their ethnic, cultural, linguistic and religious identity.

So while the job of High Commissioner on National Minorities is framed by a set of good intentions reinforced by an exalted mandate, in reality its success has to be measured in terms of actual practice.

Van der Stoel himself says about his work: 'You should not expect miracles from this sort of work. You have to arm yourself against disappointments and against what you perceive as perfectly unreasonable criticism. I think I have to realize that I have achieved something when a situation does not destabilize any further or when a small step towards a solution is being made.'

No miracle worker, but a juggler perhaps. The varying interests and contending positions and perspectives held by minorities and political rulers of the states they occupy, must be balanced. Despite the impression conveyed by the name, this is not an Ombudsman for National Minorities, nor is Van der Stoel required to investigate individual human rights violations. This is the reason the job title is 'on National Minorities', rather than 'for National Minorities'.

Apathy is a big impediment. Van der Stoel, a diplomat experienced in today's harsh world realities, but patient and caring in his approach, is expected to cry wolf whenever a potential conflict looms. But what if no-one listens?

That was the case in Kosovo, where Van der Stoel acted until February 1998 as Personal Representative of the OSCE Presidency. In January 1999, while the international media focused on the 'crisis' there, Van der Stoel lamented another case of opportunity lost. 'I do not pretend that I have the magic formula,' he told a Dutch newspaper. 'But probably far too little has been done. I have the feeling that the international community has begun taking action too late.'

The assumption in the framework that established the post of High Commissioner is that protecting the rights of persons belonging to national minorities will contribute towards a country's ability to reduce the tensions that create a context for wider conflict.

The office has limited political clout, however. A fair amount of 'indirect' means can be used to press for recommendations, including a gentle reminder that an unfavourable report can have implications for the much-coveted relationships some of these nations seek with western nations and organisations.

'However, the role of these means should not be overestimated,' notes Stefan Vassilev, adviser to the OSCE High Commissioner on National Minorities. 'The events in Kosovo showed that international diplomatic pressure and dependence on foreign aid could not always serve the "carrot and stick" role.'

Further, the High Commissioner cannot handle individual cases concerning persons belonging to national minorities. His mandate does not permit the consideration of national minority issues in situations involving organized acts of terrorism or to communicate with or acknowledge communications from any person or organization that practices or publicly condones terrorism or violence.

'Early warning' must be followed by early action on the part of the world community. In that way, highly tense situations can be prevented from becoming full-blown conflicts.

To Van der Stoel's chagrin, in Kosovo such 'early warning' was unheeded until a point of no return was reached in that province of former Yugoslavia wrecked by fighting between secessionists and the Serbian national army.

Sometimes a softly approach is required - watching a case from the earliest stage possible, monitoring it carefully to see what changes occur. SICLOMON is the acronym used for this by the High Commissioner's staff - 'Situations to be closely monitored'. This is applicable when there are -still weak- signals of unfolding prerequisites for a trouble but it is too early for a full scale of international activities. Often too much international involvement could contribute to the development of the pre-conflict situation. To turn blind eyes or just wait and see is also not the proper response.

In this respect the High Commissioner can choose a 'passive' approach involving mere collection of data (as a follow-up to a signal obtained throughout the general routine monitoring process) through different means including sporadic contacts with some of the actors on the ground, contracts with other international organisations, and visit to a country. That can move to 'active' involvement, which entails visits, dialogue with the actors involved, the issuing of recommendations and taking some action.

'Inevitably, there is a "grey area" between the two categories,' notes Vassilev. 'There are also cases when development of a situation requires change of the High Commissioner's involvement from passive to active or the other way round. SICLOMON are also in this grey area.'

'Early warning' must be followed by early action on the part of the world community. In that way, highly tense situations can be prevented from becoming full-blown conflicts.

An important element of the High Commissioner's job is to build credibility and good working relationship with the various parties. 'The position of a close confidant with international leverage to all sides is the best option,' says Vassilev. 'Demonstrated preparedness to listen to and to understand each side's position and willingness to help each party in the process of finding mutually beneficial solutions is extremely helpful.'

The role must be carefully explained to all parties involved - the High Commissioner is not an international policeman but a facilitator or mediator. For example, normally none of the actors, is willing to make the first move in the form of inviting the other side to 'come to talk', which would be seen as a concession. The other side is also not willing to 'knock at the door of the adversary' or to 'come by foot' to it. Thus, establishing a mechanism or forum for dialogue through various types of round tables, consultations, seminars, and the like is of utmost importance, Vassilev suggests. An initiative by the High Commissioner, offering his auspices or hosting the event in a neutral site can sometimes be a face-saver.

Finding accord among the leaders is one thing; finding one that can be sold to the respective constituencies is another story.

'In other words, each party has to gain from the final deal more than it would lose in the eyes of the respective supporters. Very often this requires extra efforts by the High Commissioner to organize a package of "accompanying measures" (sweeteners) to the main agreement which make it attractive to both sides,' says Vassilev.

Sometimes reaching a partial solution is preferable to further escalation. After accord has been reached comes the hard part - implementation. In fact, 'effective implementation of the reached agreements is the most important part of the High Commissioner's involvement. Failure to carry the implementation through undermines not only the results of the whole process in question, but would also significantly reduce ... trust.'

The OSCE High Commissioner on National Minorities encourages and tries to facilitate larger and more active participation of minorities in the public and political life of the countries in which they live. He also adheres to the principle of integration vs. assimilation, in which efforts are made to overcome the fear (real or imaginary) that the majority of the population is seeking ways to assimilate a given minority, thus making it difficult to have real cooperation between them. Minorities are also encouraged to avoid self-isolation.

How the Touareg Rebellion Came to an End

Peacemaking by Consensus in Mali

'Let me repeat again today the pride that I feel to be at the head of a nation which has made tolerance and dialogue its cardinal virtues. As a modern state, Mali needs to add to its ancestral heritage of dialogue, a modern institutional infrastructure which demonstrates there is a real democratic process taking place.' (...) 'With this in mind, I shall ask my government to organize a series of regional Concertations in which every current of opinion will be able to express its views. Each participant will be invited to contribute to the debate, seeking to define solutions for tomorrow's problems. Our purpose will exclude systematic opposition to the ideas of others; nor will there be room for narrow sectoral demands. The government will bring to the discussion both its point of view and its proposals for change and together we shall seek the necessary consensus to achieve the transformations which we have started.' (President Alpha Oumar Konaré on 8th June 1994, the second anniversary of his inauguration as Mali's first democratic elected President)

The West African Republic of Mali ranks among the world's least developed and poorest countries, and in this vast and impoverished land, its northern regions are by far the least developed. With the exception of the 'interior delta' area of the Niger River and a few oases and mountainous areas, the entire zone is an infertile desert covering an area greater than France. Education, health care, water, communications, and transportation infrastructure are almost totally non-existent. In this area lives a ethnically diverse population numbering something less than one million inhabitants, of which the Songhoys and the Touaregs are the most numerous.

Like many of the nations of Africa, Mali has been governed for extended periods of its post-colonial history by non-democratic regimes. From 1968 until 1991, President Moussa Traoré presided over a repressive, corrupt, and incompetent one-party regime. Throughout the Traoré period, very little economic development took place, and that which did was largely restricted to the Bamako region and other regions of the south. The poverty of northern Mali was further aggravated by repeated periods of drought.

Traditionally, the Touaregs and Arabs have looked more to the north for trade relations than to the southern areas around Bamako, the capital of modern Mali. In the late fifties, northern peoples had pushed for the establishment of an independent central Saharan state, and in 1963, a revolt by Touareg supporters of this state was brutally suppressed. During the drought years, many young Touareg refugees ended up in Libya, where Libyan leader Muammar Gaddafy was both able and willing to exploit their alienation from Bamako. The Mouvement Populaire de Libération de l'Azawad (MPLA) was founded in Libya in 1988, by exiled Malian Touaregs who were serving as mercenaries in Libya's Arab Legion. When its leaders returned to Mali in 1990, they launched the rebellion of Mali's northern peoples against 28 years of repressive central government.

General-President Moussa Traoré reinforced his army in the north and launched a brutal and violent campaign to crush this rebellion. Many of the victims of the military's efforts to put down the rebellion were innocent civilians. The inevitable result of the military heavy-handedness was to turn previously uninvolved Touareg youths into rebels, and to antagonise other ethnic groups.

As the violence continued, the Touareg fighters issued a 21-point declaration which included various demands for improved economic development, better social conditions, reduced military presence, multi-party democracy, a greater political role, and amnesty for their rebel activities. The northern rebellion coincided with increasing civil unrest in Bamako and the south, as demands for multi-party democracy and an end to the Traoré regime grew louder. Traoré needed to bring troops back to the capital to prop up his tottering regime, and so, in January 1991, the government of Mali signed a peace agreement with the rebels.

It made little difference. In March, 1991, Traoré was arrested, and Mali began a transition process to multi-party democracy under the leadership of General Amadou Toumani Touré (known as A.T.T.) And in the north, despite the agreement, which was, in any case, viewed by many in the south as a 'capitulation', the violence continued. The MPLA, which had already split into separate Touareg and Arab factions, splintered further, and fighting among the factions was often as intense as battles between rebels and government forces. Military units carried out summary justice, in one case killing a group of rebel leaders who had been imprisoned in Timbuktu. Government officials could no longer safely travel outside of the northern towns. Traditional leaders, who were viewed by the rebel leaders as too closely allied with Bamako, were also perceived as enemies. Anarchy and banditry prevailed throughout the north.

'The experience shows that not only is peacemaking better than peace-keeping, but that it is much cheaper.'

There were continued efforts to put an end to the violence. Algeria, in particular, played a crucial role in promoting efforts to reach a negotiated settlement. The new regime also attempted to bring more northerners into the government. A Peace Agreement was signed in April 1992, a 'National Pact' which accorded a 'special status' to the north. The Pact also provided for the demobilisation of armed rebels and their integration into the Malian military or police forces or into civilian life, an exchange of prisoners, the return of refugees, economic development for the north (and commitments to seek international funding for that development), local responsibility for law enforcement, and, significantly, the

March 27, 1996: Attendants at the Flame of Peace ceremony in Timbuktu   Photo Henny van der Graaf

establishment of a commissioner for northern Mali, reporting directly to the President. This pact provided a framework for an end to the violence, but real peace would still prove elusive.

Conditions improved for short periods, but would then deteriorate. More than two hundred thousand people fled the fighting and banditry, taking refuge in neighbouring countries, or moving southwards. Acts of ethnically motivated violence were also reported in some of the larger cities and towns. As the elected civilian administration headed by President Alpha Oumar Konaré took office, the economy came under severe pressure from the combined effects of years of mismanagement and war. In May 1994, a new element was added to the already highly explosive mix - an armed movement known as Ganda Koy (Masters of the Land) was launched by sedentary peoples who were fed up with the violence and banditry.

Mali was on the verge of civil war.

That this did not occur is to the credit of President Konaré and his new Prime Minister, Ibrahim Boubacar Keita, who both understood that they could never impose a military solution on the rebels, as well as a large supporting cast of local and international actors who persisted in working with the warring parties to find a way to re-establish the rule of law.

The construction of a stable peace in Northern Mali did not come about as the result of any one single action, but as the result of a complex of efforts to rebuild trust, to address legitimate grievances, and to reward combatants who chose to give up the fight. Building incentives into the peace process that would assure the continued commitment of people on both sides of the conflict to peace.

Even while the violence continued, the government convened a series of meetings at the local level beginning in 1994. In convening these meetings, the government was embracing the African tradition (and following the pattern it had already used to effect the transition to democracy following the 1991 popular revolution) which goes beyond

Six essential aspects of the Malian peace process
1) Building civilian-military relations
2) Discreet mediation by national and international figures
3) Decentralisation of governance
4) Promotion of reconciliation through civil society
5) A process of disarmament and demobilisation
6) Investment in the re-integration of former rebel combatants

the traditional western democratic process where elections are the determining factor in shaping government. In the African tradition, decisions are taken at the village council, where elders preside over a discussion involving the entire community. Participants at the hundreds of meetings that took place from 1994 through 1996 included political parties, the administration, trade unions, religious groups, and NGOs, but subsequently, and more importantly, the local leaders, women's organisations, social organisations, economic co-operatives and associations, and other institutional representatives of civil society. All these meetings stressed the inseparable relationship between security and peace.

The administration also undertook to reform the military, improving conditions and training for soldiers, and improving communications both within the military and between the military and civil society. While both security and development were considered to be crucial to achieve stability in the north, the approach adopted by those involved in peacemaking efforts has been described as 'security first'. This followed from the logic that the armed civilian population would only give up its weapons if they believed that the security forces were capable of defending their families. Also the kind of development required to build trust and improve living standards in the north could only be achieved if donors felt confident that hostilities would not break out again and that development professionals could safely work in the former areas of conflict. Interestingly, one element of the overall peace plan was an attempt (with only limited success) to persuade development agencies to make modest contributions to the implementation of security projects.

As discussed above, Mali's northern peoples felt little connection to Bamako. Part of the wisdom of the reconciliation process pursued by the Konaré administration was to accept this reality and to work with it, by offering to extend more power to local authorities. Decentralisation has been a central plank of Konaré's vision of society. During the many meetings of civil society, one goal was to convince people to support locally elected authorities,

Beyond Symbols: Weapons for Development

In 'The Weapon Heritage of Mali', authors Van der Graaf and Poulton argue for a programme tying weapons collection to community development assistance. Instead of providing cash payments to individuals who hand in their weapons, development assistance is provided to communities for programmes like improved water systems, health care, and education. While a 'Flame of Peace' is in and of itself both practically and symbolically valuable, a development for weapons programme helps not only to reduce the number of weapons in circulation, but it also to bring communities together to provide for both security and development, and quite possibly to prevent those who hand in a weapon from simply going out and acquiring a new one.

consistent with one of the points agreed to in the National Pact, and this is now moving ahead with the establishment of a nearly 700 locally elected 'communes' throughout Mali. Robin-Edward Poulton, Senior Research Fellow at the United Nations Institute for Disarmament Research, who has worked on conflict resolution for many years in West Africa, describes the Konaré approach as 'ambitious' and 'visionary'. He observes that 'most of Africa's states will flourish in the 21st century only if they are able to reconcile the need for broader economic or monetary unions with the pressure from local groups to assume their cultural identities.' Poulton concludes that 'decentralisation is the new framework which will make people responsible for their own lives, for mobilising national resources and using them locally for productive investment.'

These activities certainly contributed to reduced tensions between the government, the northern non-combatants, and the rebel fighters. But peace could only be truly secured by a process of demobilisation and re-integration of the rebels into the fabric of Malian society. This was largely accomplished by setting up a programme which provided for the cantonment of former combatants, the turning in of weapons, the closing down of rebel bases, and the integration of some of the former fighters into either the armed forces or the civilian sector. Participants in the programme were paid $200 pocket money, free food and training, uniform and a small monthly payment during the duration of cantonment. Those who came in without a weapon received $100 and were accepted into a UNDP credit programme to help them establish themselves in civilian life. While fewer than 2000 of the ex-combatants were actually integrated into the police, the military, or civilian administration, between November 1995 and January 1996, another 9000 individuals benefitted from the civilian integration programme and nearly 3000 weapons were collected. The cycle of violence had been definitively broken.

> 'One of the most important lessons is that even small actions, undertaken at the right moment, can have enormous positive impact in restoring hope among struggling people.'
>
> KOFI ANNAN

On March 27, 1996, President Konaré, Ghanaian President Jerry Rawlings (chairman of the Ecowas at that time), leaders of the Mouvements et Fronts Unifiés de l'Azaouad (the MFUA, uniting the various rebel factions), Ganda Koy, and a large delegation of international observers gathered in Timbuktu for the highly symbolic destruction of all collected weapons in what was called a 'Flame of Peace'. The weapons were stacked into a giant pyramid, doused with fuel, and then ignited by the presidents of Mali and Ghana. The rival movements issued a joint declaration in which they affirmed the indivisibility of Mali, pledged their support to the Malian constitution, renounced the use of violence, exhorted their fellow African fighters across the continent to 'celebrate their own Flame of Peace', and finally, proclaimed the irrevocable dissolution of their respective organisations.

REFERENCES

The Weapon Heritage of Mali, Henny van der Graaf and Robin E. Poulton. Chapter in publication of the Bonn International Centre for Conversion: 'Weapons Collection and Disposal as an Element of Post-Settlement Peacebuilding.' 1998

A Peace of Timbuktu - Democratic Governance, Development and African Peacemaking, Robin E. Poulton and Ibrahim ag Youssouf. United Nations, New York and Geneva, 1998

Former President Eschews Lure of Golf Course to Reduce World Conflicts

Citizen Carter: The Statesman

What happens to Presidents after their term in office ends? Once voluntarily departed, or shoved out the door, do they spend long leisurely days by the leafy pond? Play endless rounds of golf? Covet high-profile memberships of corporate boards? Not so for former American president Jimmy Carter.

In June 1994 Carter could be found in Pyongyang holding intensive talks with Kim Il Sung, the North Korean dictator over a way out of a nuclear crisis with the United States. A few months later, Carter's name was back in the news. This time he was part of a three-member delegation trying to mediate the departure from office of Haiti's military rulers. By the end of the year, the former US president was trying to negotiate peace in Bosnia. As one American columnist described Carter, 'He goes everywhere, doing good.'

The visit to North Korea was made under a cloud of scepticism, and even some opposition, back in Carter's homeland. But there was more than grudging applause when the ex-President announced in a television interview a credible agreement with North Korea to 'freeze' the illegal nuclear programme, which President Bill Clinton had said publicly North Korea could not be allowed to pursue.

That deal effectively aborted a US campaign to press for international sanctions against North Korea. It also eased military tension between South and North Korea. In the same way - by talking, and attempting to find common threads for agreement - 'Citizen Carter, the statesman', as he has been described by the newspaper USA TODAY, pulled another rabbit out of the hat by brokering a deal that led to the United States calling off a planned invasion of Haiti.

The dramatic events in which Carter became involved in 1994 marked the culmination of an activist post-White House role the former President has carved out for himself since leaving office in 1981. Working through The Carter Center, a non-profit, privately run body based in Atlanta, which he set up with his wife, Rosalynn, in 1982, Carter has used the considerable weight of his office as former president to become one of the world's most effective peacemakers. In sometimes last-minute visits to disparate parts of the globe, the trademark charm and a reputation for caring, have opened doors closed to others.

Carter was president of the United States from 1976 to 1980. He was succeeded by Ronald Reagan. During his time in office, he was a central figure in the historic 1978 Camp David peace accords between Egypt and Israel. But the popular perception in the United States is that his presidency was marked by the Iran hostage crisis, an oil embargo, high inflation, and the like.

Run in partnership with Emory University, The Carter Center has set lofty goals which underpin some of the very ideals that were hallmarks of a Presidency which pursued a foreign policy based on human rights considerations. Already, the Center's work has erased some of the bitter memories of its founder's presidential years. Its Mission Statement include promoting peace and human rights, resolving conflict, fostering democracy and development, fighting poverty, hunger, and disease throughout the world.

Carter Center programmes are wide-ranging: eradication of Guinea worm disease in Africa, India, Pakistan and Yemen; working to promote democracy and human rights; increase farm yields in the developing world; child immunisation; the prevention of river blindness. In the United States, the Center runs projects to erase the stigma of mental illness and improve access to and quality of services and treatment for Americans who experience mental disorders. It runs various youth projects as well as in preventive health care programmes.

In addition, Carter Center monitoring teams have overseen multiparty elections in Haiti, Ghana, Panama, Paraguay, Guyana, Suriname, Zambia, Nicaragua and the Dominican Republic. The Atlanta-based centre has assisted the strengthening of the economic and institutional foundations of emerging democracies.

Carter personally, and members of the Center's International Negotiation Network (INN) -a 25-member conflict resolution body comprising Nobel Peace laureates, former heads of state, conflict resolution practitioners, representatives of international organisations, governments, and non-governmental organisations- have mediated many of the 30 major armed conflicts taking place somewhere in the world at any one time.

Described as an informal network of eminent persons, the INN is chaired by Carter, whose high personal profile tends to make less pronounced the contributions made by other INN members to activities undertaken by the Center's Conflict Resolution Program (CRP) in Sudan, Bosnia, the Great Lakes region, Liberia, Ethiopia, the Korean Peninsula and elsewhere. INN also ran a successful project in the Baltics which brought together Estonians, Russians living in Estonia and Russians from Moscow, to discuss integration of the Russian-speaking community into Estonian society.

In the words of The Carter Center, 'The CRP regularly monitors many of the world's armed conflicts in an attempt to better understand their histories, the primary actors involved, disputed issues, and efforts being made to resolve them. When a situation arises where President Carter has a unique role to play and specific conditions have been met, the CRP directly supports his intervention.'

INN member Kumar Rupesinghe says non-governmental organisations (NGOs) such as The Carter Center, being 'unofficial organisations', have the advantage of building trust and confidence between two sides and using their resources to work toward negotiation. 'With no strategic or political motivations, NGOs have greater flexibility... in responding to the needs of people,' says Rupesinghe.

But such is the profile given to The Carter Center by the man who founded it and who remains its driving force, that it is not likely to be perceived as just another NGO. In fact, at times the Atlanta-based body could be criticised for conducting a milder version of the Clinton administration foreign policy in North Korea and Haiti - supporting Washington's policy doves over the more hawkish elements. Before visiting North Korea, Carter obtained President Clinton's nod, although some officials in the State Department opposed to the trip. And while his initiatives in Haiti were undertaken in an unofficial capacity, the former President was thoroughly briefed beforehand and in turn reported on the outcome of his missions to Washington.

Others say by holding negotiations with Somalia's Mohamed Farah Aideed, North Korea's Kim Il Sung, Haitian military ruler Raoul Cedras, and Bosnian Serb leader Radovan Karadzic, the former President merely enhanced the reputations of despots. The more cynical view of Carter is that the ex-President is driven by a determination to erase the memory of a failed presidency, and restore his place in history, possibly by receiving the Nobel Prize for Peace.

'The former president has carved out a unique role as diplomat without portfolio, referee and preacher rolled into one.'

THE WASHINGTON POST

Not that such considerations matter to beneficiaries of the Center's varied programmes, who will no doubt argue that the ends are justified by Carter's high-profile and high-octane energy means. For it is the case that Carter's status and reputation -the sheer weight of the name- have opened doors and forced parties at loggerheads to explore the possibilities of reconciliation. Gritty diplomacy and refusal to take 'no' for an answer, have been Carter's hallmarks. And his approach have become so much an embodiment of the Center, there will doubtless be a big gap when he leaves.

'He's quite unusual,' notes Erwin Hargrove, a political scientist at Vanderbilt University. 'Most ex-presidents write their memoirs and retire. But Carter has a tremendous amount of energy and a desire to do good.'

Away from the fanfare, Carter and his team, including wife Rosalynn, used various other devices to bring warring parties around the negotiating table, or at least to consider that as a course. One year after that sequence of headline-generating ventures in North Korea, Bosnia and Haiti, Carter sponsored a major drive among Central African nations to secure the return of two million refugees displaced by the ethnic bloodletting in Rwanda. Meeting in Cairo, leaders of Zaire, Rwanda, Burundi, Tanzania and Uganda, agreed on various confidence-building and security measures in this regard. In the following year, the five leaders met again in Tunis, Tunisia to follow up their African initiative to promote peace, justice, reconciliation, stability and development in the Great Lakes region. In the Tunis Declaration on the Great Lakes Region, issued on March 18, 1996, the parties agreed on additional measures to meet commitments approved the previous year in Cairo.

Implementation of that initiative was subsequently overtaken by the pace of political events, including the overthrow of Zairian leader, Mobutu Sese Sekou, but focused world attention on the region, and galvanised involvement in efforts to deal with one of the major causes of instability. And the meetings secured, at the very least, a blueprint of commitments -pledges even- by Heads of State regarding improvement in the refugee situation, and reducing military conflict.

How does Jimmy Carter do it?

Writing in the New York Times in May 1995, Carter described the complexity of issues involved in the various conflicts raging across the globe and said they required 'innovative and varied approaches.'

Carter always recognised that there are usually cases in which one party -or both- want peace.

'However, most ruling parties resist any official intervention in their civil disputes. Without their approval, it is inappropriate for a foreign ambassador or the United Nations even to communicate with revolutionaries who are attempting to change or overthrow the government.'

All too frequently, Carter noted, the tendency was to impose sanctions rather than encourage communication. 'Nations rarely achieve their goals this way and either give trade advantages to their competitors or alienate their allies who advocate different approaches.'

Preparing for the 1995 Cairo summit, Carter visited Uganda, Zaire, Rwanda and Burundi for consultations with presidents, other political and military officers, diplomats, church officials and representatives of international organisations and NGOs. 'After some extremely difficult negotiations with sceptical leaders in Kigali and Bujumbura, they finally agreed to detailed agendas for our proposed conference,' Carter said in a report on the trip.

Interesting about the Cairo meeting was that it was closed to leaders from outside the region. An unpopular decision, but this resulted in what Carter described as 'totally unrestrained discussions of the most sensitive issues, old wounds were opened and mostly healed, and we all decided that a follow-up conference will be necessary, perhaps early in 1996, to include those who were excluded this time.'

They pledged in Cairo to prevent cross-border raids, remove intimidators from refugee camps detect and destroy the illicit and inflammatory radio transmitters; deliver persons indicated for genocide to the International Tribunal and urge others to do so.

Carter says he tries to convince participants in a conflict that he's not taking sides, keep goals in sight, and not allow himself to be side-tracked. 'I don't have a portfolio...' he told Washington Post while contemplating approaches to the Bosnian conflict in 1994.

That approach has led to Carter being branded an 'innocent abroad' disrupting efforts to toughen sanctions against countries considered hostile to the United States. But as the Atlanta Constitution notes, 'Carter's efforts seem to have contributed to easing some of the world's most difficult and intractable problems'.

Tuzla, City of Hope in War-Torn Bosnia

Partners at Work

At a time when 'ethnic cleansing' was normal practice elsewhere in Bosnia, in the city of Tuzla residents and local government succeeded in preserving much of their community's multicultural character. In explaining this extraordinary achievement Tuzla's mayor, Selim Beslagic, points to the city's tradition of mutual tolerance: 'We have always been a melting pot and have had the possibility to stay like that during the terrible war. That's why the nationalist forces could not manifest themselves here, though they have tried it.'

A nother prominent inhabitant of Tuzla, Vehid Sehic (President of the Forum of Tuzla Citizens) complements: 'During the ages Tuzla has always been an open city with a strong solidarity among its people. Being an industrial city Tuzla harboured some 27 nationalities.'

'Tuzla has always been different. It was the city that started first to resist the Ottoman occupation. Then Tuzla resisted the Austrian-Hungarian forces. After the first World War it started the first big labour protests and during Second World War it fought against the nazi's.'

Tuzla, the forth biggest city in Bosnia Herzegovina and the economic and cultural centre of north-east Bosnia, initially was spared during the war. But when the Yugoslavian People's Army withdrew from the city in 1992 Tuzla was shelled every day by the Serbs. On the 25th of May 1995 a grenade hit the central square killing 71 civilians and wounding more than hundred.

The Forum of Tuzla Citizen was founded in 1993 by a group of people that wanted to fight the 'nationalistic forces'. Despite threats thousands of people joined the organisation. Now it has members from many political and religious movements. The Forum backed Mayor Selim Beslagic in his striving for maintaining a multi-ethnic society.

Six years later, Forum-President Vehid Sehic looks at the effects of war: 'In Bosnia nothing is the same as before. Also in Tuzla nothing is the same any more. Tuzla is less multi-cultural as a result of the war. That's logical. But it is the city that succeeded best in preserving its character. Also Tuzla is the city that is most dedicated to the return of refugees and displaced persons.'

It was the hopeful conditions in Tuzla that inspired Dutch organisations and municipalities to create the Assistance to Bosnian Communities Foundation (ABC) in order to support the social and physical reconstruction of the region.

Teaching in the bathroom, Tuzla   Photo Linda Graham

Ralph Pans, former ABC-chair and mayor of the Dutch city of Almere, underlines the positive aspects of Tuzla. 'In Tuzla there still are mosques, Catholic churches and Serbian-orthodox churches. It is the only city that did not choose for one religion and one nationality while destroying the other.' At present it is the only municipality in Bosnia ruled by a coalition of non-nationalist political parties.

To support this 'struggle against nationalism and to give a chance to the processes of democratisation and reconciliation' two Dutch NGOs -the Network for Municipal Peace Policy (PGV) and the Inter Church Peace Council (IKV)- decided to set up the ABC-programme, which started in June 1996 in Tuzla. On the Dutch side, some 30 NGOs and schools, and nearly 20 municipalities are active in ABC. They cooperate with 25 partner-organisations in Tuzla.

ABC is unique because the partnership is formed by citizens organisations. The Dutch ABC-headquarters stresses that the programme 'is not a classical humanitarian aid-programme'. Along with the supply of the necessary aid goods and the transfer of knowledge, it is trying to create lasting relations between organisations and communities in Bosnia and the Netherlands. 'It is a real exchange of ideas among citizens,' comments Sehic.

The Dutch and Bosnian organisations work together in formulating, preparing, implementing and evaluating projects. Before activities can go ahead the mayor of Tuzla and local leaders of the 'sounding board' are consulted. According to Igor Rajner, formerly the local ABC-director, external assistance to local problems can only be effective if 'the decision making involves the community. And this is easier through decentralised cooperation, which, by its very nature, is closer to local power structures and civil society.'

Nevertheless the partnership does not imply complete equality between the teams. 'This is normal,' explains Sehic, 'Bosnia just came out of the war. That legacy is also reflected in the partnership. The Dutch have a stronger democracy and economy and have more knowledge, ideas and money.'

The ABC-programme covers a patchwork of small projects ranging from infrastructure, education, culture, child care, work with youth and the elderly, trauma treatment, medical support and help for displaced persons. In 1998 nearly US$ 1.5 million were invested. (The programme was made possible through a Dutch Government donation). Sehic: 'I think at the moment these smaller projects at the citizen level are better than economic aid or large projects. With smaller projects there is a larger trickle-down effect and they are easier to control, preventing mishandling of funds.'

One of the larger ABC-projects was the renovation of apartment buildings. About sixty percent of the inhabitants of Tuzla live in high-rise apartment blocks with 14 to 17 floors. Because of the war, water pipes, electricity, cables and elevators no longer functioned. Many inhabitants had to carry buckets of water upstairs. Sometimes rain water would trickle down the walls rendering those apartments which still had electricity extremely dangerous.

Three Dutch construction companies decided to contribute to the renovation of five buildings in Krecanska street, which had been selected for the project. The job was carried out mainly by the municipality of Tuzla and local constructors. During the renovation the elevators in the buildings were repaired, electricity was installed and new hydrofor pumps ensured that the water supply reached even the uppermost floors. The project not only provided comfortable apartments for 1,400 people, it also offered badly needed job opportunities to experienced

A Change in Ethnic Composition

Whereas Tuzla had a population of 130,000 before the war, by the time the war was over the number of inhabitants had dropped to 105,000. Some 25,000 people had fled abroad while 900 soldiers and 300 civilians from Tuzla had died in the fighting. In the meantime many refugees had sought safety in the shelter of the city. In 1998 it was home to 41,000 displaced people who had fled from other parts of the country, while another 4,000 refugees were living in camps in the vicinity.

Despite the efforts to preserve the 'multi-cultural character' of Tuzla the war has changed the ethnic composition of the city. Before the conflict 48 percent of the population were Bosnian, 16 percent Serb, 15 percent Croat and 21 percent were described as 'others'. In 1998 the Bosnians made up 63 percent of the population, Serbs 9 percent, 'others' 14 percent while only the percentage of Croats had remained the same.

construction workers. After the war, unemployment in Tuzla -which had previously been relatively affluent- reached eighty percent.

The ABC-programme also targeted other aspects of social life by addressing the tangible reminders of the war at the street level. In Simin Han, a village on the outskirts of Tuzla, many street lights were not functioning. In the morning and evening people had to rush to and from school and work in darkness. Bad visibility had already resulted in a number of accidents. With a donation of some US$ 4,000, electricity and streetlamps were provided. The community of Simin Han supplied the wooden poles.

'One of the most important things that happened to Tuzla was the international help we received. This broke our isolation: people from the normal world came to our world.'

'It's a small example of how collaboration can achieve quick results,' concluded United Nations agencies in the Atlas of Decentralised Cooperation for Human Development report. 'It is a project that literally 'sheds light' on the real meaning of cooperation.' ABC-coordinator Martin Aalders explained: 'We are involved in a partnership. And this doesn't mean importing ready-made solutions from abroad but stimulating the direct involvement of the institutions and the civil society of Tuzla.'

With the help of the Dutch partners other streets in Tuzla itself, such as Oktobarska street, were also illuminated, which not only helped prevent sprained ankles but also created a greater feeling of safety. Garbage collection became another priority. During the war garbage collecting vehicles broke down and refuse was often simply left on the streets. The Dutch municipality of Delft decided to donate a few hundreds of containers and some garbage collecting vehicles to Tuzla. This donation meant that large areas of the city could be cleaned-up.

The problems of Tuzla's thousands of refugees are also high on the list of priorities. Many of these refugees who had fled Srebrenica were housed in the nearby Mihatovici settlement. Here, a number of Dutch municipalities provided support for the construction of a day care centre for children. The Netherlands has a special relationship with the enclave that was supposed to have been protected by Dutch soldiers against Serbian aggression.

That the programme went beyond providing 'hardware' is illustrated by the cultural exchanges. When actress Baisa Baki from Tuzla visited the Netherlands she noticed: 'Theatre has another meaning for us. It is not a luxury any more, but a necessity. During the war it was the only way to give shape to our thoughts, our pain, the nightmare. That doesn't mean we only played tragedies. On the contrary, there was a great need for comedies. To be free from suffering for a moment. Now we are trying to reconstruct our identity by looking for plays by Bosnian dramatists. We will fill the holes in our culture.'

UNESCO's Culture of Peace

From 'divide and conquer' towards 'communicate and reconcile'

A world without wars? Cynics may find the idea unrealistic, even comical. But it is central to a programme launched in February 1994 by UNESCO and since adopted by other sections of the international community. The Culture of Peace seeks to take advantage of what the specialised agency of the United Nations terms 'a growing belief that the culture of war, which has characterised the dominant civilisations of the past, can now be replaced by a culture of peace.'

A lthough a cursory glance at the world map may give a different impression -ethnic tensions and conflicts in the Balkans, internecine wars in Africa, civil wars of varying intensity in Asia- UNESCO says the culture of peace concept is, in fact, taking hold. The idea underpinning it is likely to be boosted and more widely exposed in the year 2000, which has been designated by the United Nations as International Year for a Culture of Peace and Non-violence. 2001-2010 will be the International Decade for a Culture of Peace and Non-violence. Further, it is hoped to collect up to 100 million signatures by September 2000 on a Manifesto for a Culture of Peace and Non-violence drawn up by Nobel Peace Laureates that puts the obligation for peace on the individual as well as on the state.

UNESCO says the world has moved towards an order in which 'it is possible for the rule of international law and justice to replace reliance on military power.' In other words, a culture of peace can slip neatly into the vacuum left by the end of the Cold War.

At the conference in Yamoussoukro, Côte d'Ivoire, in July 1989, where the concept was articulated, participants urged a peace culture 'based on the universal values of respect for life, liberty, justice, solidarity, tolerance, human rights and equality between women and men.'

Three years later, the UNESCO executive Board and the body's general conference endorsed the Culture of Peace as part of the organisation's mandate to contribute to international peace and security. A fairly comprehensive set of objectives has since been developed.

UNESCO's director-general Federico Mayor says peace itself is being redefined. 'Instead of the absence of war, it is increasingly seen as a dynamic, participative, long-term process, based on universal values and everyday practice at all levels - the family, the school, the community, as well as the nation.'

That notion of peace is shared by the International Fellowship of Reconciliation (IFOR). Based in Alkmaar, the Netherlands, IFOR comprised people who have committed themselves to active non-violence as a way of life and means of achieving social, personal, economic and political transformation. IFOR secretary general Anke Kooke, and Interim Program Officer Jan Schaake, have linked the concept of A Culture of Non-violence to that of A Culture of Peace, with the latter embracing communication, democratic decision making and non-violent conflict resolution. 'It is the basis of freedom, security and equitable relationships and it encourages individual and group action for societal and structural change,' they state. 'A Culture of Non-violence embraces the non-violent understanding present in all spiritual practices.'

For there to be a transformation from a Root Causes of War toward a Culture of Peace and Non-violence, conflict resolution and societal changes should no longer be realised by violent means based on the isolation and destruction of the opponent, but by non-violent means, communication and democratic decision making. Courage and heroism are not based on the ability to use violence but on having the creativity to reach one's goal by non-violent means.

The overall transformation from a Root Causes of War towards a Culture of Peace and Non-violence is 'the transformation from exclusiveness and egocentredness towards sharing and community spirit; from 'divide and conquer' towards 'communicate and reconcile'. Just sharing not only involves other people dependent on the resources, but also future generations, animals and plants and taking the intrinsic value of natural resources into account.'

UNESCO considers itself well placed to carry the weight. The Paris-based body emerged from the shadow of war: formed just after the end of the Second World War, its constitution has echoes of the conflict. 'Since wars begin in the minds of men, it is in the minds of men that the defences of peace must be constructed,' states the section of the document frequently recited to underline the basis for the organisation's passionate endorsement of the Culture of Peace drive.

An intersectoral committee chaired by the director-general works with various other sectors and units of the organisation and has liaison with the United Nations in New York on the programme. In various countries, UNESCO National Culture of Peace Programmes keep the flame alight. Culture of Peace is integral to other UNESCO activities, including directly complementary ones like education.

The body's Associated Schools Project (ASP) has inaugurated an interregional pilot project called 'No to violence' in Brazil, Estonia, Haiti, Sri Lanka and Zaire. In 1995, Culture of Peace and ASP jointly sponsored several subregional peace festivals involving children between the ages of 11 and 13 in Cook Islands, Costa Rica, Greece, Grenada, Jordan, Thailand and Zimbabwe.

Joint approaches have been made on urban violence, attempting to link networks of schools in cities plagued by conflict. At various universities, UNESCO chairs have been established specifically devoted to the teaching of human rights and peace studies. UNESCO funds support independent media outlets in conflict-ridden nations like Rwanda, where the propaganda of Mille Collines radio station helped to foment the 1994 genocide.

Across the border, in Burundi, which has its own ethnic tensions, the organisation has helped sensitise journalists on the need for non-partisan and pluralistic information. Similarly in the republics of former Yugoslavia support given to independent media seeking to bridge ethnic divisions, have contributed to building up trust.

In various parts of the world, UNESCO field offices have been used as culture of peace dissemination points. Special projects have been undertaken in Africa, Latin America and the Caribbean; in Beijing, China, the UNESCO office has organised meetings with diplomats posted in the city to examine the implementation of peace programmes in multicultural contexts.

UNESCO clubs, some 4,800 of which are in existence, in over 100 countries, are also utilised to spread the idea. The fourth World Congress of the World Federation of UNESCO Clubs held in Romania in June 1995, decided to plan future activities around the theme 'Towards a World Charter of UNESCO Clubs for a Culture of Peace'.

El Salvador, Mozambique and Burundi have pioneered the application on a national scale of the Culture for Peace philosophy. Steps have also been taken towards setting up parallel programmes in Honduras, Nicaragua and Somalia. In El Salvador, the national Culture of Peace programmes coincided with the process of national reconciliation in 1993, based on the 1992 Chapultepec Peace Accords. Brokered by the United Nations, these agreements ended a long running armed conflict between the government and a guerrilla movement. So the UNESCO initiative was undertaken amid a broad programme to build peace after the conflict.

Courage and heroism are not based on the ability to use violence but on having the creativity to reach one's goal by non-violent means.

Following a Forum for Education and Culture of Peace held in San Salvador, in April 1993, under the co-sponsorship of UNESCO and the El Salvador Ministry of Education, the organisation helped mediate the process by which the government and civil society worked together in designing the strategic guidelines of the programme as well as its constituent projects.

In Burundi, the national programme was launched in December 1994, with the opening of a House of a Culture of Peace in the capital, Bujumbura. Staffed by a multi-ethnic team, the house provides both a symbolic expression of the national desire for peace and a material structure with the means and institutional power to put it into practice. 'It has become a centre for many individuals and groups working for peace,' says UNESCO. 'Despite the violence that has afflicted the city, work has continued on peace seminars for journalists, government administrators, educators and representatives from NGOs and the United Nations.'

One aspect of the Culture of Peace programme is a battle against on-screen violence. Here self-regulation is advocated, with the guidelines used by the British Broadcasting Corporation (BBC) considered appropriate. These require the consideration of questions such as whether the violence contained in a programme - be it fiction or non-fiction - is essential to the story. Can the violence be implied rather than shown? Are the brutal consequences of violence also apparent? Is violence being glorified?

'Faced with such questions,' says UNESCO, 'it is hoped that the media will begin to pay more attention to peaceful conflict resolution than it now does to violence.'

It's because of the momentum given the programme by such projects that director-general Mayor describes the culture of peace is 'a movement of movements in which everyone who is working for human rights, non-violence, democracy, social justice, sustainable development, women's equality, join together in a 'grand alliance' of social transformation.'

But how can violent conflict be ended?

In 'UNESCO and a Culture of Peace: Promoting a Global Movement', the organisation says there is no magic wand approach. The concept of creating a culture of peace will evolve and grow only through practice. 'As a movement, it is like a great river, fed from diverse streams from every tradition, culture, language, religion and political perspective.'

For UNESCO, the essence of the culture of peace idea is that it cannot be defined as the absence of conflict. 'In a diverse and complex world,' says the agency, 'conflict will always be part of life. Instead of fearing it, we must learn to appreciate and cultivate its positive non-violent aspects, which include creativity and the redress of injustice.'

What the programme's advocates seek to do is transform violent competition into co-operation for shared goods. Thus groups engaged in conflict would work together in the development process itself.

In managing these Culture of Peace programmes, UNESCO is entering new territory: there are few historical precedents.

Funding is also a problem. Although the Cold War is over, governments still spend large amounts on the military. Resources devoted to military expenditure are equivalent to the total income of half the world's population. As UNESCO itself acknowledges, 'the Culture of Peace is still not high on the list of global funding priorities'. Yet, it remains an obligation to support the process that ensues once combatants have ended their mistrust and committed themselves to building a new society.

'If we are to achieve a Culture of Peace, we must pay the price for it,' says the organisation. 'We cannot be successful without a global reordering of priorities in which the present emphasis on military peace-keeping is matched by a commitment at least as great to non-violent peace-building.'

The United Nations' initial emphasis (after the end of the Cold War) on peace-keeping operations, based on keeping peace between states, is increasingly being extended with a focus on peace-building, conflict prevention and the construction of a culture of peace. For peace-building is important not only for getting countries out of conflict, but as a device to shift them onto the path of sustainable development. 'Action for a culture of peace correspond more closely to the concept of peace-building than to peace-keeping,' says UNESCO.

Only time will tell if what UNESCO identifies as an 'emerging culture of peace' will eventually bring an end to the many conflicts that continue to take lives all across the globe.

2

Track Two:
Non-Governmental
Organisations

Introduction

Private Professionals for Peace

Track Two Diplomacy encompasses peace efforts embarked upon by unofficial, non-governmental organisations and individuals who specialise in conflict management. Private peacemakers try to generate non-governmental citizen interactions between parties in a conflict. Their aim is to help resolve conflicts by surpassing the logic of power politics and to encourage communication, understanding and collaboration between antagonistic communities ♦ By Jos Havermans

The former US diplomat John McDonald, who was among the first to provide Track Two with an underlying theoretical and analytical structure, believes that the strength of unofficial diplomacy lies in its ability to address the root causes of conflicts. More than any other approach, Track Two is able to reveal the underlying human needs that can fuel antagonism, he says. 'By allowing face-to-face communication, Track Two Diplomacy helps participants arrest the dehumanization process, overcome psychological barriers, focus on relationship building, and reframe the conflict as a shared problem that can be resolved collaboratively,' he believes.

Track Two differs from Track One Diplomacy in that it perceives its role as being part of a process of developing mutual understanding between larger groups of people, whereas Track One Diplomacy tends to limit its focus to the narrower world of the politician. Track Two tries to make its impact felt on the entirety of what it describes as identity groups: namely, communities that share a certain ethnic, regional, national, socio-economic or other identity. Rather than just trying to inspire politicians to make certain favourable decisions based on rational evaluation of options and interests, which is the Track One approach, Track Two seeks to help all the people involved change their way of thinking. McDonald: 'Track Two is transformational, positing a worldview in which power politics is superseded by mutual empowerment; identity groups at least join if not replace nation-states as the loci of power; basic human needs and not strategic interests set the agenda; collaboration and inclusivity replace competition and exclusivity; international relations are seen as ongoing relationships between all the people, not crisis or situational relationships between governments'.

Track Two Diplomacy is said to have become more relevant, because of a change in the nature of conflicts. Increasingly, conflicts are the outcome of internal strife in which the government is just one actor among several. In these circumstances, it makes less sense to make deals with governments because other actors, such as local leaders or rebel groups, may decide to continue fighting. In a context where other actors than the state play a crucial role in conflicts, proponents of Track Two Diplomacy envisage a larger role for their methods of alternative peace making. NGOs are perceived as being in a good position to act as Track Two peace workers. Since they are often rooted in, or deal with local communities, they are in a good position to fulfil a role in early warning and human rights monitoring. NGOs are also capable of helping to establish a well-knit local infrastructure across the levels of society that empowers the resources for reconciliation. NGO staff could even become engaged in negotiations on the local and sometimes national level.

Stalling manoeuvres

Landrum Bolling, who is an advisor to the Conflict Management Group and an expert on Track Two Diplomacy, states one of the advantages of private peacemaking: 'In dealing with troublesome problems it is often useful to find some mechanism by which new ideas can be tried out with minimum risk,' he says. 'Officialdom may be very inhibited about trying out ideas; even floating a balloon to an official of another country might seem to be sending more of a signal than is meant', Bolling continues. 'But if an idea is tried out with an unofficial person, then if it does not fly or if there are repercussions, the government can always disavow it. The person engaged in this informal communication naturally has to understand that he may be disavowed in this way and not have his ego invested in a particular message or point of view. He has to be totally vulnerable and willing to say, 'Yes, I made a fool of myself. That was wrong.' Just let it go.

'One of the possibilities of the informal approach is that it may offer a way of beginning a process of revising official policy with minimal risk and without loss of faith', Bolling concludes.

Bolling is well aware of the difficulties and challenges that actors in Track Two diplomacy face. 'Amateurs can cause damage', runs the one-liner that summarizes the number one concern of both adherents and opponents. People involved in informal citizen's diplomacy may be limited in their knowledge and background of a conflict. In that case, they could cause damage; especially if they do not acknowledge their limitations. Realizing one's flaws seems to be an essential first step to try to avoid the possible negative effects of interventions. Another weak spot of Track Two is that private peacemakers are more vulnerable to manipulation than their official counterparts. Some parties in a conflict feign a willingness to compromise and open talks with unofficial mediators in order to gain time to strengthen their military position. 'Track Two can be a waste of time as some Track Two diplomacy efforts are probably stalling manoeuvres', according to Bolling.

A major challenge for private peacemakers is to achieve and maintain balance and even-handedness and avoid acting as advocates for one of the parties in a conflict. Another, extremely difficult, aspect of Track Two work is dealing with the intense emotions of people directly engaged in a conflict. These emotions are connected to matters of life and death, which require insight on the part of peace workers. Private peacemakers should ideally be familiar with psychological issues such as victimhood, mourning, forgiveness and contrition.

Track Two diplomats must also deal with ethical issues. McDonald pointed out that intervening in conflicts carries innate moral concerns about power, ethnocentricity and the personal agendas of mediators.

Given these difficulties, it is no wonder that many projects in which Track Two Diplomacy was practised turned out to have only an indirect impact on a peace process. In many cases it is extremely difficult to determine to what extent, if any, Track Two Diplomacy has assisted a peace process. Most experts of the field, however, believe that as yet its potential has not been fully used. Compared to Track One Diplomacy, private peacemaking usually suffers from insufficient funding and limited human resources.

In general, Track Two Diplomacy can be most effective when linked to official peace processes at a governmental level. The proponents of Track Two also see opportunities to collaborate with adjacent non-governmental approaches. Since its inception in the 1980s, Track Two Diplomacy has seen the birth of a number of siblings, nephews and nieces who have been named Track Three, Four, Five, etc, diplomacy. These parallel tracks encompass peace efforts by actors such as the media, churches, schools and artists. The multiplicity and variety of actors involved in today's conflicts requires a similar multiplicity of partners to solve them.

Track Two remains the leading edge of this Multi-Track Diplomacy system. It is itself engaged in a continuous process of change. Theoreticians and field workers constantly seek to enlarge its impact and adjust Track Two Diplomacy to new international developments. The environment in which Track Two Diplomacy is developing seems to be encouraging. The well-heeled world of Track One Diplomacy is showing signs of becoming more susceptible to alternative diplomatic approaches. Some governments are actually willing to invest in alternatives to Track One policies. This implies that the ideas behind Track Two Diplomacy are gaining wider acceptance. It also means that the Track Two approach can count on receiving more resources. Peace-making by professional non-governmental organisations, therefore, has potential for further growth and development.

Unlike Track One officials, who are part of a single, formal bureaucratic political system, Track Two actors come from many different realms. Each player has his or her own culture and values. In most cases though, Track Two 'diplomats' have an academic background and are employed by action-oriented organisations that see it as their main mission to deal with conflict. This endows these actors with a considerable degree of professional credibility. And a professional, scholarly background is a welcome asset in Track Two Diplomacy, since experience has shown that private peacemakers need to be fully familiar with the history of the conflict and the range of issues it entails and should also be sensitive to the potential risk and threats to those invited to participate. This makes high demands on peace workers' competence.

The activities of Track Two peace workers vary from organizing problem-solving workshops, acting as messengers and go-betweens to help set up a dialogue between antagonistic communities, offering mediation courses to local leaders, organizing seminars and conferences and private one-on-one diplomacy behind the scenes.

As some of the cases presented below demonstrate, Track Two Diplomacy can make a difference. In Somaliland, for instance, the so-called Boroma process, which was supported by the Life & Peace Institute led to a landmark breakthrough. Starting locally among elders at the sub-clan level in 1992 and moving upwards through society to clan level and from there to a national level, the process, which was supported by the Life & Peace Institute, culminated in a meeting of elders of all clans of Somaliland who in a remarkable display of participatory democracy elected a government and a president.

In Colombia, to give another concrete example, the Dutch NGO, Pax Christi provides support to local village communities who have declared themselves neutral in the conflict between guerrilla and national army. Representatives of Pax Christi were stationed in the villages to support the peace initiative and provide the kind of protection that the presence of foreign neutrals brings with it in these circumstances. A similar example of Track Two activity can be found in the Philippines, where peace zones have been formed by the Coalition for Peace (CfP), an umbrella organisation for more than fifty organisations based in all the regions of the Philippines engaged in professional peace building.

In the Croatian town of Osijek, Track Two peace work took the form of educational and advisory programmes. There, local academics established the Center for Peace Nonviolence and Human Rights, which functions as a Track Two organisation. Members of the Center focus on long-term results in trying to help Croats and Serbs create mutual understanding and work toward reconciliation. 'Reconciliation is the beginning of spiritual renewal and is a prerequisite for building relationships which will preclude violence', the Center's founders say in a mission statement. Other successful examples of Track Two Diplomacy are taking place in Sri Lanka and Cyprus, where processes have been unfolding that are depicted later in this section of this book.

Selected Bibliography

    Conflict Resolution - Track Two Diplomacy, John W. McDonald and Diane B. Bendahmane (Eds.). Institute for Multi-Track Diplomacy, Washington, D.C., 1995

    Conflict Resolution Wisdom in Africa, Jannie Malan. African Centre for the Construction Resolution of Disputes (ACCORD), 1998

    Multi-Track Diplomacy - A Systems Approach to Peace, John W. McDonald and Louise Diamond. Kumarian Press, 1996

    Participating Approaches to Peacemaking Strategies, Ed Garcia. UN University, Tokyo, 1993

    Peace by Peaceful Means - Peace and Conflict, Development and Civilization, Johan Galtung. PRIO, Oslo, 1996

    Peaceworks - Private Peacemaking, David Smock (Ed.). USIP-Assisted Peacemaking Projects of Nonprofit Organizations, United States Institute of Peace, 1998

    Preventing Deadly Conflict - Final Report of the Carnegy Commission on Preventing Deadly Conflict, Carnegy Corporation of New York, New York, 1997

    Preventing Violent Conflicts, Michael Lund Endowment of the United States Institute of Peace, Washington DC, 1996

    Prevention and Management of Violent Conflict - An International Directory, European Platform for Conflict Prevention and Transformation. Utrecht, The Netherlands, 1998

Sri Lanka's National Peace Council Builds New Relationships

Waging Peace against War

On the surface, it seemed like an idea whose time had come. At the invitation of the National Peace Council (NPC), elected Sinhalese politicians from the Matara district in the extreme south of Sri Lanka had crossed a physical and psychological division by visiting Tamil counterparts from Batticaloa district in the east. What was meant as an exercise in encouraging reconciliation between distrustful communities, got off to a less than fortuitous start, with a testy early tone ironically triggered by words encouraging friendship.

'**W**e should live in peace', a Sinhalese politician had said. To which a young Tamil woman retorted: 'First let us enjoy our rights, and then we will talk about peace.'

But thereafter the initiative, promoted by the NPC and the German agency Frederick Ebert Stiftung (FES) shifted onto a smoother path, the two groups showing more willingness to listen than to allow old assumptions to dictate their positions.

The Tamil woman's intervention led to the Sinhalese delegates concluding their main role was not to talk, but to listen. By bringing them face to face with the realities of life in the east where there is a Tamil majority and a dominant military oversees retarded development, NPC had made another step in a laborious process of building relationships and planting the issue of conflict resolution among people either unfamiliar with the concept, or distrustful of its consequences.

Sri Lanka's name used to be a byword for paradise island; now it epitomises the intractability of ethnic conflict. A high-intensity military confrontation between government security forces and the Liberation Tigers of Tamil Eelam (LTTE) drags on without any sign of either side winning - or evidence of willingness to compromise. It is a brutal war, costly in human and economic terms. Thousands have died or been injured, hundreds of thousands displaced. In 1996, according to a study by the Marga Institute, losses attributed to the conflict chopped 21.3 percent of Sri Lanka's Gross Domestic Product (GDP).

Last year's discourse between Sinhalese and Tamils in Batticaloa was part of a series of measures launched by the National Peace Council to promote a peaceful solution to the conflict effectively waging peace against a bitter war. It was also a coming of age event for the bi-partisan body.

Before that, the NPC had invited 20 Members of Parliament (MP)to spend five days in the Greek island of Crete studying the degree to which the peace and reconciliation experience of South Africa could be applied to Sri Lanka. Beyond the lessons learned from that exercise, the residential nature of the programme - the fact that participants lived together and interacted for five days - forged personal relationships across the ethnic and political divide. The concept of conflict resolution and modern negotiating techniques and methods were introduced.

'We reject the logic of peace through war. Instead we say don't wage war on our behalf.' Then the NPC took 23 MPs from nine Sri Lankan political parties to Northern Ireland. They met leaders and representatives of all unionist and republican political parties and para military groups and the British and Irish governments. There the direct lessons were so sharp, a dramatic step was taken. The MPs, in instances deviating from the official lines of their respective parties, issue a joint statement calling for an all party consensus and the need for talks with the LTTE. Such a joint appeal had never previously been issued, and it caused quite a stir. Much intra-party debate resulted, but, in the end, some of the parties did use that discussion as a launching pad for changes in their approach to the peace process.

NPC-facilitated trips by MPs were then undertaken to Mindanao, the Philippines (to study a conflict that lasted for a quarter century, involving a battle for separation by the Muslim dominated Mindanao island) and to the Chittagong Hill Tracts in Bangladesh (where as Buddhist minority battled a Muslim dominated state for a similar period of time before entering into a peace agreement).

Three-day residential workshops organised by NPC in all 13 local government bodies in the southern district of Matara, drew Members of Parliament representing four political parties active in the area and elected to these bodies. Basic conflict resolution skills were taught. Failed peace moves were evaluated. Attempts were made to learn from the experiences of peace processes in other countries.

A high point was reached on January 4, 1998. Some 1700 delegates from communities in all 25 districts in the country, held a major convention and urged an immediate end to the war. About 1200 of the delegates were Sinhalese, 350 Tamil, and 150 Muslim. More than half were from areas of Sri Lanka affected by conflict - the north-east and bordering districts. Among the participants were 50 disabled soldiers who approved the resolution.

Extensive workshop discussions had preceded the convention. Held at district level over a five-month period, these gave impetus to a call by the national convention for radical restructuring of the state along lines that would permit a form of self-government for all 'nationalities and communities', within one country.

President Chandrika Kumaratunga, Opposition leader Ranil Wickremasinghe and the LTTE's International Secretariat in London all sent messages of goodwill. 'Any just and fair solution towards ushering in peace in the island' was welcome, the LTTE said in a message which came on the day after the convention ended. President Kumaratunga said the government pledged to do 'everything possible within our power to achieve a political solution with the co-operation of all sections of our society'. And Wickremasinghe said the country's war mentality had brought with it hatred and destruction. 'There can be no victors in war,' he said.

'Parliamentarians and local government representatives who had otherwise only known each other through the verbal battles they fought in Parliament and the political stage, found themselves compelled to interact with each other, building new personal relationships across party lines.'

Established in 1995 to build 'a peoples movement for peace', the NPC membership is carefully balanced so as not to give even the impression of bias. That is critical in a country where political and ethnic demarcation lines are so clearly drawn. The NPC was launched during peace talks between the government and the LTTE. Previous attempts to promote peace had concentrated at the level of the top leadership. These had collapsed. Agreements reached were reneged on. And the general population had remained 'unaware, suspicious and therefore rose up against or were easily manipulated by opposition orchestrated protest.'

When the 1995 peace talks that formed a backdrop to the setting up of the NPC broke down and hostilities resumed, the organisation set about 'creating an environment for resumed negotiations' between the government and the LTTE. The nature of the approach adopted was seen as critical to the success of this process - a complementary, supplementary and catalytic role, targeting the political elite, but also paying attention to middle level catalytic agents and grassroots. The aim: to build political will and consensus for a negotiated settlement while raising awareness among and giving public expression to popular desire for peace.

'A hallmark of attempts at conflict resolution have been the lack of bi partisan consensus among the two main Sinhala dominated parties in the South coupled with a unilateralist approach to the minorities,' notes the NPC's Tyrol Ferdinands in a background paper explaining the council's role and functions.

'Political will has often been channelled into unilateralist attempts rather than giving leadership for the formation of a national agenda,' he notes, 'while processes that were mediated in an attempt to build a southern consensus on the national issue became politicised and exploited for narrow political gain.'

The NPC felt it was imperative to stimulate political will and consensus for negotiations, and thus set about assisting in risk management among political elites by demonstrating that peaceful change through negotiations was both possible and preferable while being complementary if not helpful to their own political projects.

Getting people from different parties travelling, living and learning together had a strong impact. In turn, that led to discussions about the need for 'a new political culture of co-operation' that would overcome the current impasse brought about by confrontational politics. State level actors got the opportunity to interact with those from other conflict situations in a non-formal setting. Devoid of the protocol demanded by official programmes and the positions such responsibility entails, otherwise unthinkable options were considered and sometimes surprisingly adopted as the creative way forward.

The process is not always smooth. Sáma Yámaya (Time of Peace), the NPC newsletter, reports on a conflict resolution workshop held by the National Peace Council in the north-western Puttalam district for about 20 community leaders, at which several participants denied there was even an ethnic conflict in the country. They declared that they did not have problems with Tamil neighbours, who likewise had no problems with them and questioned the value of workshops for 'powerless' people like themselves, who could not change the macro-level politics where the 'real decisions' about war and peace are made.

Nonetheless, evaluations undertaken with participants revealed they felt the NPC programmes helped create a more informed political debate, enabled those involved to give a more realistic assessment of Sri Lanka's conflict and understand more clearly the dynamics of conflict and the price required to be paid for peace.

And how was a small civil society-based conflict resolution group able to sustain such a programme?

The composition of the NPC -ethnically and religiously diverse individuals, drawn from the various political shades- probably helped in gaining general acceptance and subsequent co-operation of political parties. Ferdinand: 'It is also probably the reason why no other civil society group has been able to conduct such a programme in Sri Lanka in the past and why many who have attempted to replicate the process since have not succeeded.'

NPC's own definition of itself helped. As a civil society based conflict resolution organisation, the body limited its role to complementary, supplementary and catalytic functions - as against being a protest movement. It facilitated a process of building the resource and capacity of politicians to deal with issues of conflict and resolution. Special care was taken not to give appearance of political bias.

For the Council, Sri Lanka's current conflict has its roots in the inability of a British Westminster style democracy to safeguard and respect the rights of minorities through effective power sharing. 'Discrimination in areas such as language, education, employment and land led to non violent protests by the minority Tamil community. When these protests were violently suppressed, Tamil youth commenced and intensified an armed struggle with the objective of creating a separate state in the Northeast of the island.'

Sinhalese politicians from Matara found the visit to Batticaloa an eye-opener. A report on the initiative published in the Sáma Yámaya, took note of how the separateness of the participants was brought home at the workshop which was one of the main activities on the programme. 'Conversations had to be translated back and forth, between Sinhala and Tamil,' the newsletter noted. One participant was led to comment: 'This looks and feels as if delegations from two different countries are meeting.'

The workshop functioned as a forum for sharing difficulties faced by local level elected politicians in exercising powers that are supposed to be vested in them by central government. How can local communities work towards realising the goal of a negotiated peace? Frustrations about 'the endless talk at the top' led to delegates identifying the need to build understanding and consensus at a community level while reinforcing the need for political leadership.

One Sinhalese politician, a beneficiary of the NPC's training in conflict resolution, said: 'We who constitute this delegation - PA and UNP (the ruling People's Alliance and the main opposition United National Party) - were like snake and mongoose a few months ago. Today we have travelled to the war zone together and are in dialogue with you. It's a process that can easily be extended to the LTTE as well.'

A simulated 'negotiation' was conducted by the two sides with respect to a political solution to the conflict. Tamil politicians presented their view of the powers that should be vested in the north-east region which would be Tamil dominated and is claimed as the Tamil Homeland. After scrutinising the list presented, the Sinhalese politicians objected. According to the list, they said, virtually nothing had been left for the central government. The Tamil politicians accepted this as a legitimate objection, and began revising their list. However the process was stymied: because the workshop had to end. The point had been made though. Sincerity, political will and dialogue can bring about a mutually acceptable compromise.

Returning to Matara, the Sinhalese politicians agreed that what they saw had confirmed the validity of lessons taught during the NPC workshops. Dialogue had engendered changes in hard positions. Could this micro-level change also be possible at the macro-level - between the government and the LTTE?

The Continuation of the People's Power Revolution in the Philippines

A Pearl of Great Price

One day the inhabitants of Hungduan in the Philippines did a brave thing. They succeeded in getting the guerrilla New People's Army to withdraw from the locality. The next thing the municipality did was to prevent the army from setting up a detachment in the town. From this experience, the Coalition for Peace developed the concept of Peace Zones. It would be established by local communities wanting to protect their residents from the violence and losses of armed conflict. Communities would declare those areas off-limits to armed operations by both sides of the conflict. The idea sparked a new impetus for peace-building in the country.

'It was the task of the citizens peace movement to pick up the pieces and continue and steer the peace process,' says Ging Quintos-Deles of the Gaston Z. Ortigas Peace Institute in the Philippines.

She is referring to the beginnings of the movement, its launching in 1986 with the people's power revolution.

When Cory Aquino came into power, she inherited a country racked in internal armed conflicts. There was the eighteen-year-old communist insurgency, a Muslim separatist movement in the south, and an oversized army conditioned to maintaining the power of the establishment and repressing civilians. Thus began a long lasting citizens movement aimed at peace and reconciliation, very closely interlinked with the movement for justice and democratisation.

The 1986/1987 peace talks broke down early. The peace movement therefore focused not only on communist insurgency, which had posed the most widespread armed opposition to government and with which the underground movement and broad segments of the social change forces have historic ties, but also on other internal strife.

And there were plenty of hostilities. One of Aquino's first steps was to call for peace talks with the communist insurgent forces. It was the first gathering of representatives from various people's movements to talk about the issue of peace. Her idea was that in a peace negotiation there should be space for the expression and participation of the vast majority of the people who bore no arms.

But the cease-fire was aborted and talks between the government and guerrillas broke down. It became clear that the peace talks on the communist insurgency could not succeed without the involvement of a third party.

'Thus,' explained Ging Quintos-Deles at an International Colloquium on Peacemaking in the Philippines, 'our intermediate objective has been the building of this third party from among our own people.'

Quintos-Deles is executive director of the Gaston Z. Ortigas Peace Institute, the secretariat of several major Philippine peace organisations, including the Coalition for Peace(CfP), an umbrella for more than fifty organisations based in all the regions of the Philippines, and the National Peace Conference (NPC).

Initially, when the CfP sought to keep the government and the NDA at the negotiation table it was rebuffed with the retort: 'Why? Who are you? How many are you?'

From then on, it reoriented itself. From primarily urging the peace process and promoting the peace agenda to the parties involved in the armed conflict, it shifted to building and making visible the national 'constituency for peace'. It saw the need to evolve local initiatives to end the conflict on the ground.

The CfP wanted to encourage new approaches to peace which could positively influence policy on military operations and thus relieve local communities of the burden of armed conflict. The strength of the Coalition has always been that it supports local communities and local groups to take up grassroots-based peace initiatives, while at the same time integrating itself with initiatives focused at peace processes at a national level. It began stimulating one of the most dramatic actions which local communities could take: the installation of peace zones.

In September that year, the idea was launched with the first of such geographical peace zones: the Zone of Peace, Freedom, and Neutrality (ZOPFAN) declared in Naga City by the Hearts of Peace (HOPE). This was followed in November by the declaration of a Peace Zone by the indigenous people of the municipality of Sagada. After that, many communities in several parts of the archipelago followed the idea.

The question is: how effective are these peace zones? It is not easy for a small community to make the armed parties recognise that their area is a peace zone. After all, the very notion of a peace zone negates all concepts of military movement.

'Whether the local group can sustain itself even when they are not recognised, and survive armed incursions, depends on if they had some structure already in place,' says Quintos-Deles. 'Such communities are either those of indigenous cultural peoples which have the basic indigenous structure still intact, or those, for example, where the church has done a lot of organising.'

A guerrilla force in the mountains Photo Henny van der Graaf

Thus, peace zone communities only have a chance to survive if they have a basic organisation. If not, the chance of failure remains large and the experience of militarisation can be very disempowering. 'The community that does not have indigenous internal structures cannot seem to do it,' says Quintos-Deles. 'And this should tell us a lot about where NGO organising should go on.'

Besides this, the peace movement needs to provide more cross-peace-zone experience for peace workers to broaden their view, says Quintos-Deles. After all, peace zones are very local experiences.

'You have here a pearl of great price, and make sure it's not stolen away from you,' said a participant to an international conference on peace in the Philippines ten years ago. The peace movement fears that there is always a chance that this might happen. For example, a national commission related to the government declared the peace zones as social development areas to be allocated 5 million pesos each. A former, similar experience in a peace zone had proved that the community became prone to patronage and corruption. Allocation of the money through the people themselves, and not through the local government, could avoid these practices, the representatives of the peace zones said. But, at the end, the Fidel Ramos government decided to donate the money through the local administration anyway.

Besides the CfP, there are a number of other groups who try to build peace from the grassroots. One of them is the National Peace Conference (NPC). Members are non-governmental and peoples' organisations. In 1990, after consultations with seventeen

The Non-violent People's Power Revolution of 1986

The murder of Ninoy Aquino in 1983 was the beginning of the end of the Marcos dictatorship. Although the assassination of the Philippines' foremost opposition leader was headline news around the world, it was almost unreported by the Marcos controlled media in the country itself. The media silence was accusation enough. Two million mourners attended the funeral ceremonies in the largest political demonstration to date in the history of the archipelago.

Something had snapped in the Filipinos' passive acceptance of the dictator's repression. The people wanted to reclaim their political freedom and dignity.

At the end of 1985, Marcos suddenly announced elections, to be held at the beginning of 1986. Aquino's widow, Corazon 'Cory' Aquino became the main opposition candidate for president. The elections turned out to be a farce. Aquino refused to concede defeat and called on her followers to rally the next day in Manila's Rizal Park. Close to a million supporters responded, to hear Cory outline a national campaign of civil disobedience. She called for a boycott of the businesses owned by Marcos' crony capitalists, and for a general strike to begin on February 25; the day of Marcos' inauguration.

A few days before the inauguration, two important politicians, Enrile and Ramos, announced at a news conference their withdrawal of support for Marcos due to the massive fraud he had committed at the snap elections. They called on the armed forces to join the rebellion and barricade themselves in Camp Aguinaldo. Marcos urged them to 'stop this stupidity'.

The archbishop of Manila called on all peace-loving Filipinos to bring food to the soldiers at Camp Aquinaldo, pray and keep vigil.

'They are our friends', he said.

The call was heeded. Assembling at the camp, people formed a human barricade to block an attack by forces loyal to Marcos. For once, the civilians were to protect the military.

The day after, a large marine force, led by tanks and armoured personnel carriers, headed for the camp. They were stopped a mile from their target by tens of thousands of people forming a human shield. The marine commander threatened to shoot. The people did not budge. They threw flowers and cigarettes at the soldiers in their tanks.

The soldiers had only learned to attack armed people. Helpless against this shower of affection from innocent people, they withdrew.

On February 25, almost two million people came out to protest on the EDSA, the Epifanio de los Santos Avenue, a main road named after the revolution. Nearly the entire Armed Forces had peacefully deserted Marcos in support of Cory Aquino. The EDSA revolution had been bloodless; the people formed the winning party.

sectors, a peace agenda was passed. 'The Basic Peace' agenda was going to be pushed by the people's movement both with the government and the National Democratic Front.

From 1990 on, more and more organisations became members of the peace movement. This demanded co-ordination. The Gaston Z. Ortigas Peace Institute came into existence as a base for the various volunteer citizens' groups.

'We are all practitioners,' says Quintos-Deles about the peace movement in the Philippines. 'We do not have time enough to study and reflect on what we do. We hope in trying to make things understandable to others, we will make things understandable to ourselves.'

The Catholic church has played an important role. More than three-quarters of the population is Catholic and the church has had a large influence. Before the revolution, it was a major power with some credibility among the people. The Catholic Bishops' Conference of the Philippines (CBCP) has a network of thousands of parish churches all over the country. Its pastoral letters had become more and more critical towards the dictatorship and urged non-violence and passive resistance. During the People's Power Revolution, the church was in the forefront, gathering the people, calling for non-violent resistance, and, at the same time, trying to avoid a bloodbath.

Citizens take the initiative in Urabá

Colombia: Zones of Peace in the Heart of a Bitter War

A series of communities of peace have been carved out recently in Colombia's Urabá province. Bearing the stamp of 'active neutrality', they press for adherence to provisions in the Geneva Convention on human rights that armed actors have an obligation to ensure protection of the civilian population. Largely forgotten and ignored, this principle provides a raison d'être for the Colombian peace communities. The aim is to break the logic of war.

In 1998, one of Colombia's various guerrilla movements, the FARC, shifted between 1,200 and 1,800 of its fighters from the south of the country into the north-west. Not long afterwards, on August 3, they launched a sustained offensive against a joint army-paramilitary base near Pavarandó, a town in the region of Urabá. The battle lasted 15 hours. The post was destroyed. After the guerrillas retreated, the army took over Pavarandó. It was rumoured that locals cooperated in the guerrilla offensive but when, at the end of August, the army withdrew, effectively abandoning the local population to the shadowy paramilitary who had already driven thousands of people from their land, there was no revengeful rampage.

The paras, by and large, left the civilians alone. With the help of the diocese, they had organised themselves and declared their 'active neutrality'.

Every conflict has its civilian toll: non-combatants killed and injured by crossfire; women, children, even the aged. Schools and health centres closed. Damaged infrastructure. Economic growth stalled; unemployment on the rise. In Colombia, where the national army and guerrillas share combat zones with freelance paramilitary death squads, civilian populations are like ham in a sandwich. Who to trust in this three-pronged civil war? On which side should allegiance be bestowed? With what consequence?

In Urabá, a province close to the Panamanian border in the country's north-west, choices can be deadly. The region has heavy guerrilla traffic. Fractured groups with trademark acronyms - ELN, FARC, EPL - fight a battle-fatigued army over territory. This cat-and-mouse game has gone on for two decades. Once the centre of the banana industry, Urabá has become a gigantic battlefield, its civilian population caught in an ever-tightening political pincer. Civilians may see themselves as victims caught in the middle; others see them as key to guerrilla prospects. A whole series of metaphor-laden truisms have been utilised to illustrate the relationship between fighters and civilian populations who provide succour. 'Guerrillas need the support of civilians like fish need water,' is one. This by way of explaining why the army and shadowy paramilitary groups operating in the countryside murder accused guerrilla helpers and force villagers out of their homes. Somewhat indelicately, they call this action, 'taking water from the fish'. Or, even more ominously, the 'scorched earth' strategy.

The concept of 'active neutrality' began taking root in Urabá in 1997. At San Jose de Apartadó, a village not far from the small provincial city of Apartadó, the principle got its first test, and reached its apogee. Violence between paramilitary and guerrillas had forced many residents to flee in 1996. Inhabitants from surrounding areas were concerned. On March 27, 1997, supported by the Apartadó diocese, a number of people from San Jose de Apartadó, joined 29 surrounding hamlets, in a public declaration of peace and neutrality. Before witnesses including a delegation from Pax Christi from The Netherlands, they proclaimed they would not cooperate with any of the parties involved in the civil war.

'What do you do when you are a mother and your son who has joined one of those armed groups comes to you with a request for food? What does an observer do if an unknown person comes along with a fatally sick baby who needs medicine?'

Pax Christi Netherlands has been actively present in Colombia for a good ten years; in the area of human rights and as mediator between parties involved in the conflict. This Catholic peace movement has organised several international delegations that visited Urabá. With its visit in March 1996, the international presence in Urabá was started.

Paramilitary groups and guerrilla have made an already difficult life for the civilian population in Urabá, into a veritable hell. Convinced the army could not combat the effective 'hit and run' strategy adopted by guerrillas, Urabá's most notorious paras, the Castano brothers, known by the acronym ACCU -Peasant self-defence of Cordoba and Urabá- centred their offensive on depriving the guerrillas of civilian support - 'scorching the earth'. In truth, the civilians were pawns for all combatants. Not only guerrillas, but also the army. Forced to provide information, food, medicine, and accommodation, they were left in no doubt as to what would result from failure to comply.

ACCU's 'scorched earth' approach was brutally effective. A group of paramilitia would enter a village and openly identify themselves as members of the ACCU. Then they would arbitrarily slaughter people. A farmer would be shot in public to back up a demand that all members of the community leave the area. And if intimidation failed, the army would bomb the village. Later, paramilitary units would return and murder accused guerrilla helpers.

Dutchman Wim Westerbaan has seen evidence of the civilian hardships. Travelling by foot and horseback, and sometimes using the river as a young observer for Pax Christi Netherlands, he has had extensive contacts with people in the region. In his written account of the Urabá Peace Community, Westerbaan recounts the story of a woman he met while on his way to La Union. She had lost her husband and fourteen-year-old daughter at the hands of the paras, killed in trademark fashion.

'First they tie them up and then beat them up,' she says, talking of the way paramilitaries treat their victims. 'After their death, they dress them in guerrilla uniforms and leave them lying on the ground.' (Dressing victims in the clothes of guerrillas is a frequently used tactic of the paras. Official reports then say the victims died in a fight.)

Whole villages went on the move. Hiking, sometimes for months, seeking refuge in a variety of places - kids, the sick and old. Thus was the 'water taken from the fish'.

When fighting first intensified in Urabá during 1996 and 1997, some 17,000 people were made homeless. More than 6,500 refugees fled towards Mutatá, a 'neutral' area. A similar number gathered in Pavarandó. In October of 1997, the diocese of Apartadó assisted them to form themselves into called peace community 'San Francisco de Assis', and to facilitate their safe return to their own land. Initial hesitancy over the repatriation, even by aid organisations concerned about armed activity in the areas, were overcome once it emerged there were cattle farmers, paramilitaries, or others, eager to snatch the property - after which return would be virtually impossible.

What interests triggered and sustained the conflict in this particular region? Was it a cover for drug smuggling? Or were the various offensives connected to plans for building a second Panama canal? Some thought people were being chased out of their homes to facilitate the exploitation of the region's rich forests by business interests linked to powerful politicians. Was 'scorched earth' - removing people - a prelude to removing trees and preparing for extensive cattle farming activities? In Urabá, such activity had serious implications for the black community, who have occupied the region for generations.

In the end, Pavarandó residents freely established a total of eight peace settlements. A series of repatriation exercises resulted in people eventually returning to the 49 settlements from which they originally came. A Pax Christi delegation that visited all eight settlements, travelling along the river by fast boat, encountered a more optimistic mood than that which prevailed the previous March. Uncertainty had been replaced by a general air of confidence in the future. What had changed?

'The concept of peace communities works,' says Eric Laan, of the Pax Christi Latin America department. 'Everyone was aware that without the methodology and adherence to the concept of 'active neutrality', they would never have the prospect of returning to their own land again. So many people who could have otherwise been murdered, or forced into the slums of big cities, where they would live in serious poverty, now had a new perspective of the future.

Peace commissions hold daily meetings. An outside person acts as supervisor, and offers advice. This role is critical to the process - the involvement of an international person offering protection, and being a guarantee of neutrality. That person engages in dialogue with various parties when conflicts arise. The role is more than advisory: ensuring rules of the peace community are kept by the displaced persons, is part of the mandate.

Colombia, October 19, 1998: first anniversary of the Peace Community of
San Francisco de Asis

PHOTO ERIC LAAN

While there is a positive feeling about the presence of representatives from Pax Christi, given the crucial role they play in the process, there is scepticism in some quarters about the methodology used in the peace communities, and the extent to which it dilutes influence over these communities, even by religious leaders. In fact, some have called for additional observers besides Pax Christi.

'Of course, the acceptance of neutrality has difficulties,' says Laan. 'What do you do when you are a mother and your son who has joined one of those armed groups comes to you with a request for food? What does an observer do if an unknown person comes along with a fatally sick baby who needs medicine? 'What does a peace committee do when an unknown person establishes himself in the village? The peace community is confronted by these sorts of dilemmas. It is therefore necessary to have permanent supervision and education.'

Lured by the aura of neutrality that hangs over the communities, a large number of international organisations have established a presence in Urabá. Mainly aid agencies and human rights bodies, they have joined national bodies and set up operations to provide help and support for initiatives underway to help the civilian population. Help has also been promised by the Colombian government, particularly after it was petitioned by the peace community of San Francisco Asis. However, much of the promised assistance has not materialised, leading to more dependence on overseas bodies like Oxfam. Government officials have also failed to establish and staff schools in each peace community and improve on provision of health services.

Organisers of the peace communities believe the areas should be, more or less, self-sufficient. In fact, the diocese wants to get refugee farmers returning to the land and working the soil, which is one reason the handing out of land titles is being encouraged. However, that process is being held up by violence: some government employees involved in the handing out of titles have been threatened.

Economic activity has also been impeded by the conflict. Important transportation links have been blocked, and the army has refused to allow some trading activity it considers likely to help the guerrillas. Considerable hardship has resulted from this, though peace communities have been less affected than other areas.

Generally, it is true that the various armed factions have left the peace communities alone, though, from time to time, violations of the neutrality of areas by paramilitary, military and guerrillas have brought the process into serious jeopardy. Paramilitary leader Carlos Gastano has promised to respect the peace community; the army also says it supports the process. Local guerrilla leaders have orally supported the existence of the zones, but in fact still create problems by continuously trying to remain present in the communities.

Yet they remain under heavy pressure. In the first peace community, San Jose de Apartadó, there have been 50 murders since the declaration was made in March 1997. Nonetheless, according to Westerbaan, the concept is slowly, but surely, taking root. On March 23, 1998, the first anniversary of the peace community of San Jose de Apartado, refugees who had come out of La Union returned to their homes and formed there a new peace community working together with the 'mother village' - San Jose. That was something unthinkable at the start of 1997.

In the previous month, February, the second return project had begun: 104 people were sent to the village of Clavellino, to be joined later by another 1,000. Clavellino was burnt out so first social facilities had to be provided. And the beginning of March, a preparatory group left for Domingodó, to prepare for the return of 800 people.

Members of the community have committed no politically motivated murders since they declared peace. The situation is complicated, however. Not every inhabitant is a member of the peace community. An unknown number of those murdered did not support the declaration. Many of these were picked up by paramilitaries.

With the offensive they launched on August 3, 1998, FARC wanted to strengthen its hand in bargaining with the government, and press demand for a strategic location in the potentially rich Urabá area which they traditionally control. Further, the guerrilla group has an eye on the rich cattle and banana farms in the region that now pay taxes to paramilitaries.

But after more than 20 years of guerrilla rule in Rio Susucio, talk of coexistence with the local population has an empty sound. Many of the local population scoff at talk about their alleged social programs. It is however acknowledged that the guerrilla presence is a foil against the paramilitaries.

In general, says Pax Christi, the concept of a peace community has had a positive effect. Armed factions, to a certain extent, have respected the areas, and agreed not to violate the territory, and to offer opportunity on the peace community to provide food in the proximity of those needed.

The international presence has facilitated a better feeling of protection for the peace community, although it has not totally stopped the fighting.

'The sending of observers to supervise the peace community is a crucial factor in the success of the process of returning refugees, and of the whole process in general,' says Pax Christi's Laan. 'In light of expected military tensions, after the guerrilla offensive, it will be good if the international community, for example, by way of European parliament, would express its support for the peace communities and ask armed factions to respect them.'

REFERENCE

Peace Communities in a War Zone - An Experiment. Experiences of an international observer in Urabá, Colombia, Wim Westerbaan. CMC/Pax Christi International, Utrecht, 1999

The Center for Peace, Nonviolence and Human Rights in Osijek, Croatia

Working to Establish Civil Society

Katarina Kruhonja, a mother and a doctor of nuclear medicine, remembers the sense of despair and inadequacy she and Kruno Sukic, a teacher of philosophy and literature, both felt as they tried to come to terms with the war between Serbia and Croatia which had turned their lives upside down. 'We accepted,' recalls Katarina Kruhonja, 'that we could not stop the war, that we could not influence what was going on, but we were responsible for the future, for our children and for the generations that were coming, and for a new State that was just beginning. We were disappointed in our parents and teachers who had not taught us adequately about the reality of war and its lessons, and also disappointed with ourselves because we had been so passive before.'*

When these two residents of the eastern Croatian city of Osijek first met in 1991, they had little in common except that feeling of despair and an almost desperate desire to do something positive to confront the violence - both explicit and implicit - that had permeated all aspects of life in Osijek. 'When the war started,' recalls Kruhonja, 'I was a witness [to] the hatred which, in a very tangible way, was visited upon us by shelling, by bombs falling directly on our town ... At the same time I was also the witness [to] the way this hatred was spreading quickly and damaging people much more than the bombs were damaging them.'

In the days that followed, 90 percent of the city's residents fled, and those who remained were often forced to shelter in basements. But a group of individuals, including Kruhonja and Sukic began to meet regularly, to discuss their feelings about the war and what concrete steps they could take to influence their society to move away from violence. From those discussions by candlelight in the shelters of Osijek emerged the Center for Peace, Nonviolence and Human Rights.

As the Federative Republic of Yugoslavia unravelled at the beginning of the 1990s and the former Yugoslav republics asserted their independence, the structures of a 'civil society' were sorely lacking. As Kruhonja writes, 'The tradition of NGOs as forms of democratic civil society was hardly known. All organisations dealing with different civil society issues were established, financed and/or controlled by the state.' During the 1980s however, a few feminist and environmental organisations had been established, and these became the

Principles
Members of the Center must accept a set of seven principles which define its philosophy and approach to conflict resolution:
- The organisation is non-governmental, non-partisan and non-profit
- The aim of the association is to protect human rights and freedom and to promote and apply creative, nonviolent methods of conflict resolution
- Human rights and freedom are an expression of basic human needs
- Peace is a dynamic process
- Work on behalf of human rights, freedom and peace takes the form of educational and advisory programmes affirming and effecting peaceful and creative means
- The Center's work focuses on long-term results and helps people to become more self-aware in order to create understanding and work toward reconciliation. Reconciliation is the beginning of spiritual renewal and is a prerequisite for building relationships which will preclude violence
- The work of the Center is public and open to all people of good will, regardless of ethnic background, national affiliation, religion or ideology.

nucleus from which various anti-war, human rights and peace organisations developed. Organising around peace and human rights issues was made especially difficult at a time when Croatian nationalism was ascendant and peace organisations were viewed as 'anti-patriotic' and were, in Kruhonja's words, 'marginalised'.

But beginning with six members meeting in each others' flats, the Center evolved into a multi-faceted organisation with programmes directly effecting the lives of thousands of people in Eastern Croatia.

The Center now carries out its work in four broad areas - psychosocial work on behalf of the victims of war, including displaced persons; human rights; peace education; and peace-building and community development. Some of its members draw their strength and commitment to peace organising from their religious faith, while others are motivated by political analysis and a personal philosophy which embraces the principles of nonviolence. In its work, the Center is assisted by a steady flow of volunteers from abroad, as well as financial support from international organisations.

'Our first activities,' recalls Katarina Kruhonja, 'were to support the population wounded by war with the idea that long-term support and healing would be necessary to achieve the momentum so that individuals and groups wounded by war could overcome the war trauma and become carriers of reconciliation and peace-building efforts.'

About 34,000 people from surrounding areas that had been occupied by Serb forces took up residence in Osijek. Beyond the hardships that these people endured, their presence has also put additional stress on a city already suffering from the economic and material effects of a devastating war. The Center organised one of the first workshops in Osijek (and perhaps anywhere in Croatia) for social workers, psychologists and volunteers who were working with displaced persons. It was followed up with another workshop for 60 people, including displaced persons and humanitarian assistance personnel, to help the displaced persons prepare to return home. 'In that time, when ... low grade military activities were going on, it was the very first voice coming from civil society in Croatia for a peaceful solution to the problem in our region,' says Kruhonja.

The Center has subsequently undertaken several other creative programmes to assist displaced persons in and around Osijek. In many cases, the driving forces behind these programmes are themselves displaced persons. One example is Petar Gazibara, a former teacher and elementary school headmaster. Gazibara, who was driven from his home in the village of Bilje, across the Drava River from Osijek, was instrumental in organising a photography programme for young displaced persons in the Cepin refugee camp, just outside of Osijek. He was also involved in organising sewing groups to train displaced women in sewing and tailoring on sewing machines provided by international donors. The programme has provided these women with a source of income, and has also served an important supportive function for women suffering from the psychological traumas of being forced from their homes.

Another initiative of the Center has been a gardening programme at the Cepin camp. A leading force in promoting this project has been Martin Kovacevic, another refugee from Bilje. The gardening programme has provided another source of income to jobless refugees, and like the sewing programme, it has had important therapeutic value as well.

Another important international initiative in which the Center participated, along with other groups, was the establishment of a 'Peace Bridge' in the town of Mohacs, Hungary. In the climate of mistrust and fear that has followed the end of the war, it was not always possible to return, even for visits, to areas that were abandoned during the war. But the 'Peace Bridge' programme brought people from both sides of the conflict together in a nearby town across the border in Hungary, where they were able to meet and to begin to engage in dialogue and to try to move towards reconciliation.

Human Rights Advocacy
The Center's principles prominently mention human rights, but there is little to suggest how support for human rights can be translated into concrete programmes. But early on, before the Center had even defined its human rights advocacy programmes, it was confronted with a challenge. A woman approached the Center, asking for assistance to resist pressures to force her from her home (see box). The Center intervened on her behalf, and the woman and her daughter were allowed to stay in their home. In succeeding months, the Center took up the cases of twelve more families. Though there is no way to measure the overall effect, it is quite possible that many other families were also able to remain in their homes because of the example set with this first intervention.

The advocacy also evolved into a more general campaign at the national level to end the practice of eviction based on ethnicity. 'Our effort was to make our government aware that this was not acceptable, even during the war,' says Kruhonja.

PHOTO ROB HOF

The Center now maintains human rights offices in five locations, including Osijek, with six lawyers working on behalf of individuals whose rights have been violated. Besides housing cases, the office also takes on many cases addressing citizenship rights, employment rights, pension rights, right of return and reconstruction, women's rights, and rights of conscientious objectors. These activities are on behalf of all members of the community - both Croats and Serbs. As of 1999, more than 5,000 individuals have received assistance from the Human Rights Office.

Peace Education
Peace education, which has been a third important element of the Center's programme, takes two forms - self-education, and education of others. During the first year of the Center's existence, the main efforts were towards self-education. Members of the Center were still looking for ways to deal with the emotional traumas that they had lived through. They were also trying to find ways to create an effective movement to work for peace and reconciliation in an environment where there were few examples from the pre-war, Communist era.

Between 1992 and 1995, the Center members participated in more than seventy-five seminars, workshops, and conferences. Many were held in Osijek, but members also travelled extensively abroad, where they established and solidified links with other peace activists. An important focus was on the development of interpersonal skills, including nonviolent communication, listening skills, mediation, and conflict resolution. Trainings in

Meeting the Challenge

'Tanja', the wife of a Yugoslav army officer, lived with her teenage daughter in a flat that had been assigned to the Yugoslav army before the break-up of the Yugoslav federation. Her husband had been taken prisoner at the beginning of the war. Armed men began to visit the flat at night, insisting that she would have to leave her home. She tried unsuccessfully to get support from local authorities so that she could remain in the flat, but they refused to intervene.

At one stage, her daughter was so frightened that she fled to a neighbour's flat. But that proved to be fortuitous, as the neighbour was outraged by the treatment 'Tanja' was receiving simply because of her family relationship to a military officer. She herself had similar status, and she also had a Serbian name, so that she might have received the same sort of treatment. The neighbour had heard about the Center for Peace, Nonviolence and Human Rights and suggested that 'Tanja' approach the Center to ask for help. With support from the Center, 'Tanja' was able to remain in her flat, and her daughter eventually completed her studies at the university. All three women became active in the Center as volunteers, helping others in similar cases of eviction, as well as other activities.

For Katarina Kruhonja, who acted as advocate on behalf of 'Tanja', it was a sort of trial by fire, in which she came to understand, among other things, the enormous pressures brought to bear on the local authorities to evict ethnic Serbs in order to accommodate Croatian refugees. But more importantly, she came to understand the need for both the victim and the advocate to take a firm stand - the victim claiming the rights he or she is entitled to, and the advocate taking responsibility for those whose rights are denied.

the history and practice of nonviolence were another important area of study. There were workshops for teachers and for Center members working with displaced persons. Educational programmes around human rights were also a major focus.

With a stronger foundation in nonviolence, conflict resolution, and the other areas related to Center work, the Center began to organise various outreach activities to provide a peace education element to the overall programme. Logically, one early area of activity was among teachers. After attending several peace education training sessions herself, Center member Ljerka Tonkovic initiated a series of 'Creative Workshops' for displaced teachers and children, where the emphasis was on the cultivation of non-judgemental approaches to interpersonal communication. Some 500 teachers have participated in Center programmes, and 45 have become trainers in peace education. An estimated 4500 students have benefited from these programmes.

Peace-building and community development

The Center is also working towards reconciliation through its 'Conflict Resolution Training for Religious People and Community Leaders' programme, sponsors youth activities to provide support for young people who have suffered emotional trauma as a result of the war, and organises programmes for women on alternatives to violence, dealing with trauma and conflict, communication skills, human rights, democracy and community development.

The Center's peace building programmes support the peace process in areas where citizens were forced to flee their homes during the war and are now returning. It emphasises the integration process of the Serbian population within Croatia, and the re-establishment of trust and a sense of common security in communities torn apart by the war. Its ongoing project 'Building Democratic Society Based on a Culture of Nonviolence', carried out in co-operation with the Life&Peace Institute of Uppsala, Sweden, is deeply involved in reconciliation work in five communities of Eastern Croatia. The aim is to help empower individuals to resolve their conflicts nonviolently, and to strengthen the structures of a democratic civil society. Elements of the multi-dimensional programme include such activities as workshops and trainings on identifying and solving community problems, community development activities, women's and youth empowerment programmes, peace-building through media and culture, educational work on democratic institutions, and legal assistance for returning refugees.

In Croatia's fractured post-war society, it is clearly too early to state definitively that a permanent peace has been established, or that civil society has firmly taken root. The tradition of civil society is too new, the pain and the hatred have penetrated too deeply into the hearts and minds of Croatia's citizens, and the healing process will be long and difficult. But that healing process begins by addressing the root causes of the schisms in society, in standing with those who have been and continue to be the victims of war and hatred, and in creatively working to bring enemies together to rebuild society. Osijek's Center for Peace, Nonviolence and Human Rights can serve as example, within Croatia and beyond its borders, of the sort of institution which can, through the commitment of concerned individuals and the application of creative energy, make a very real contribution to the difficult task of reconciliation.

* See *Jegen, Sr. Mary Evelyn, Sign of hope: The Center for Peace, Nonviolence and Human Rights in Osijek (Life and Peace Institute: Uppsala, 1996). This citation and much other material in this article is drawn from this publication. The author conducted extensive interviews with members of the Center for Peace, Nonviolence and Human Rights during a visit in 1995.*

Multi-Track Diplomacy in Cyprus

Planting Seeds

The flourishing of a multi-track peace process in Cyprus in the 1990's can be attributed to three main factors: intentionality, synergy, and synchronicity. In this article, Louise Diamond, President of the Institute for Multi-Track Diplomacy, examines the role of these three factors in the success -and the challenges- of social peace-building on the island.

Intentionality

Our work in Cyprus began in 1991. Although Ambassador John McDonald and I had not yet opened the Institute for Multi-Track Diplomacy (IMTD), we had already written the first book on the subject ('Multi-Track Diplomacy - A Systems Approach to Peace') and were eager to see how the theory played out in practice. The invitation to become a third party player in Cyprus gave us our first opportunity to test these ideas in action.

Our initial two years of intense work in Cyprus were about creating a firm foundation. First, we wanted to build on what had gone before: the seminal Track Two work of John Burton, Chris Mitchell, Herb Kelman, Leonard Doob and Ron Fisher, in particular. We did this through consultations with some of them and with many of the Turkish- and Greek-Cypriots they had worked with, asking the question how we might add to the work already done there and make the next contribution. The response we got, almost immediately, was not to run more problem-solving workshops, but to teach the skills of conflict resolution so that, in the words of one participant, 'We can have those tools in our own hands.'

In responding to that request, we determined that creating a firm foundation for a multi-track process required being sensitive to the need for organic growth of the work in the unique circumstances of Cyprus where, at that time, there was very little bi-communal contact and no general knowledge about the principles and practices of peace-building. Therefore, we spent two years generating a base of support separately in each community, by slowly introducing conflict resolution through workshops and public talks. These workshops, and the wide round of local consultations that accompanied them, served the dual purpose of creating confidence in the concepts and methods of conflict resolution and trust in us as a useful, reliable and impartial third party.

Two other effects emerged from this slow development process. First, we were able to inform and gradually engage the US Embassy team, which was to prove extremely significant later. Next, the step-by-step building process generated a solid core group in each community who, having tested each new round of concepts and skills within their own family, work and communal settings, were then eager to meet with their counterparts from the other side to explore the relevance of this work to the bi-communal relationship and to the Cyprus question.

Synergy

From the original consultations with previous third parties, our work in Cyprus was dedicated to modelling partnership and inclusivity. Our earliest and most consistent partners were the local peacebuilders themselves. All of our activities in those first years were organized by a growing group of Greek- and Turkish-Cypriots who became advocates and allies in the work. It was clear to all that we were there to serve them in their declared bid to be change agents in and between their two communities, promoting rapprochement, reconciliation and peace-building at all levels of society. Thus some of the earliest work in conflict resolution was applied in family life, in gender relations, in political parties and between political factions - all within the same community.

We saw this core group of committed peacebuilders as our primary partner, and so helped institutionalize that relationship by creating a Bi-Communal Steering Committee. This committee met several times in those early days, with and without our presence, to set goals, offer programs, coordinate conflict resolution activity and third party visits, and maintain good communication with the political leadership in both local communities and with the international presence on the island as well. While this group eventually faded out of the picture, due to the success of the bi-communal work, which ultimately overwhelmed the local capacity for coordination just by sheer numbers of people involved, its presence in the early years was a critical factor in assuring local ownership and legitimacy for the process, as well as in providing transparency and accountability.

Our work evolved through an organic and progressive process of partnering. While many individuals, organisations, agencies, governments and inter-governmental bodies were to become involved, I will highlight here only a few of the key partnerships whose synergistic interactions moved the process exponentially forward.

The first of these, and completely central to our work, was the US Fulbright Commission on Cyprus. Funded by the US government, and connected, therefore, to the US Embassy in Cyprus through its Board, the Fulbright Commission was nonetheless seen as the only 'local' organisation that had the credibility to sponsor and convene groups within and between the two communities. With offices on each side of the 'Green Line' staffed by local people (and eventually its own meeting centre located in the UN Buffer Zone to accommodate all the bi-communal activity), and a strong history of supporting educational opportunities for young people from each side, this organisation had a long reach into elite circles in each community, and was trusted for its fairness, integrity and sensitivity.

The Fulbright Commission, under the leadership of its Executive Director, Daniel Hadjitoffi, recognized early on the power of this multi-track approach, and seeing the alignment with its own goals of building rapprochement and friendship, became an early, consistent and essential supporter of this process. Beginning in 1994, with the cooperation of AmidEast, a

US-based organisation managing US money dedicated for Cyprus, they have hired a continuous march of Fulbright Scholars in residence on Cyprus, to facilitate the bi-communal process by introducing new skills, convening and supporting new bi-communal groups and managing several grant programs that brought us and other third parties in for special programs.

The international players whose engagement became equally as important were the US Embassy (and ultimately the US Government's Special Envoys) and the office of the UN Special Representative for Cyprus. Our work has now spanned the tenure of three separate teams in each of those offices, each of whom has, progressively, seen the power of a bi-communal multi- track peace movement as entirely relevant to its policy goals, and has supported the process accordingly. This support has been invaluable, for it has been a valuable link to the Track One process, most especially in providing access to and pressure on political leaders in delicate moments and in giving international significance, through UN Security Council reports, US statements and other venues, to the bi-communal process. It also provided the umbrella of credibility within which this work could flourish, and that attracted high level influential players.

The other significant partnership to mention, which has formed the heart of the work since 1994, is our Institute's joining with Conflict Management Group (and originally NTL Institute for Applied Behavioral Science) to form the Cyprus Consortium. This Consortium has been active to design and implement projects on and off of Cyprus, secure grants and donations, develop materials, engage in networking and outreach on Cyprus matters, and deliver a core set of programs that have formed the backbone of the Cyprus bi-communal citizens' peace-building movement.

Briefly, these programs consisted for several years of bi-communal training events in conflict resolution and related matters. Sponsored by the Fulbright Commission and AmidEast, paid for with US money, and publicly supported by the US and the UN, these programs brought together large numbers of Turkish- and Greek-Cypriots from all walks of life for intensive, often residential, sessions of skill-building, dialogue and action planning for peace-building. Though some programs were for the general public, we soon started specializing in specific tracks, thus focusing at various times on educators, journalists, business and political leaders and youth. We also trained 50 trainers over the years, and provided coaching and mentoring as they went on to convene and facilitate their own bi-communal projects, dialogues and initiatives. We took pains to

'Many signed up to become involved, ready, for the first time in decades, to meet with 'the other side.''

include the Fulbright Scholars on our training teams whenever possible, so that their day-to-day follow-up with these groups could insure seamlessness and harmony of approaches, thus guaranteeing that the participants would not experience third party dissonance or competition, and assuring a common vocabulary and set of experiences for all. The scholars, meanwhile, would help select participants for our programs, and we would all consult together on the evolution and progression of the work over time.

By late 1997, when all bi-communal contact was shut down by the Turkish-Cypriot authorities due to developments in the international political scene revolving around European Union issues, the bi-communal movement spawned by the activities described here was huge. It was engaging hundreds of people on a regular basis, and thousands for special events; there were special groups from various sectors (lawyers, psychologists, educators, musicians, business groups, political parties, college students, environmentalists, among others) meeting and working together on their own common interests; there were specialized programs for high level influentials looking at the dynamics of intractable conflicts in general and of Cyprus in particular. Indeed, many individuals trained in our programs hold high political and governmental offices, or wield influence in the decision-making and opinion-making institutions of their respective communities.

By then, other sponsors, funders, governments and agencies were running programs as well, some with us; some on their own. University researchers were writing about the Cyprus peace movement, and the local trainers were frequently being invited to conferences and special events around the world to share their experiences, activities, methodologies and views. Several Greek- and Turkish-Cypriots had enrolled in advanced degrees in the peace and conflict studies area, and many were teaching what they had learned in their own communities, in informal and formal settings.

Throughout this time, many of the people involved participated in television or radio shows, were interviewed in or wrote for newspapers and magazines, and appeared in public forums discussing both their bi-communal experiences and their views on the Cyprus matter. There is a self-published bi-communal magazine that contains stories, poems, art and think pieces about peace and rapprochement. There were special programs in the classrooms, linking children through letter-writing; there was an internet project linking adults via email and the web.

In short, until stopped by Track One authorities (though still existing on a less active scale), there was a flourishing multi-track peace-building movement in Cyprus engaged in creating a human infrastructure for peace in that troubled island. That movement was the result of an intentional, cooperative and synergistic set of organically evolving activities on the part of several entities and partnerships, both formal and informal.

It is impossible to quantify the changes in the hearts and minds of all these people, and those whose lives they've touched. The level of activity, however, can speak to the personal transformations that were occurring on a daily basis, as people came to have a direct experience of meeting 'the other' in a new way, developing an understanding of their perspective, and seeking the common good together.

Synchronicity
The peace-building process described here took advantage of a rare set of conditions that made its success possible. First, the people were ready. Although there had been some Track Two initiatives previously when we began, and some sector-specific meetings, there had not yet been any massive involvement in bi-communal meetings. When the first publicity hit the streets criticizing those who attended our initial bi-communal events, one of the unexpected

effects was to make public the information that such meetings could happen. With that knowledge, many signed up to become involved, ready, for the first time in decades, to meet with 'the other side.'

Second, we should note that Cyprus is a small island, with a relatively small educated elite. In a system of this size, it is easier to identify and involve the key players, and to manage a systems-level focus. Word gets around a small society quickly, so information became accessible to a wide range of people. People know each other as in a small town, so networking is a natural element in the process.

Thirdly, Cyprus was basically undiscovered in the third party agenda. With the exception of the Track Two efforts mentioned previously, when we began working there, and for a very long time afterwards, we (the Consortium-Fulbright axis) were basically 'the only show in town'. As the whole field of peace-building has progressed, and as the Cyprus situation has attracted the attention of that field, many more third parties are now involved, but for a time the field was spacious and uncomplicated.

Finally, the timing was propitious. We entered the system during a relative lull in the formal political scene (though negotiations were ongoing, the situation was basically calm), and were able to both take advantage of and contribute to a period of confidence building at the citizen level before the political and diplomatic storms broke on the European Union question in 1997.

Challenges
This success story is not without its significant challenges and stress points. The most obvious disappointment is that we have not, to date, been able to make any noticeable impact on the formal Track One negotiation process, either in substance or process. As this article goes to print, the situation in Cyprus remains deadlocked and volatile. While we had many Track One players involved in our programs from both the Greek- and Turkish-Cypriot groups, we have not yet seen much positive transfer of their new perspectives into official policies. Indeed, we have, sadly, seen some negative transfer, as some in high positions have used what they learned to strengthen political positioning.

We are also frustrated, of course, by the fact that the political authorities can so completely close down all bi-communal activity for so long, despite the pressures of various governments and the UN. In this matter, we are especially concerned for the morale of the local peace-builders, whose momentum and enthusiasm has been so drastically tested. These are societies where, for whatever reasons, a tradition of civil disobedience has not manifested, so there is little in the way of ardent public demand for the re-starting of bi-communal activity. Quieter, more subtle strategies are being attempted, though some peace-builders have simply stepped away, feeling helpless, stymied and demoralized. For all of its multi-track depth, this process is still circumscribed by the ups and downs of the Track One scene.

Our work was also tested by the particularly strong dynamics of the conflict-habituated system in Cyprus. Because the tensions and patterns have been in play for so long, the assumptions, beliefs and behaviours that keep the conflict going are deeply embedded in the formal and informal aspects of the culture. The media, the educational systems, the political rhetoric, the daily discourse all work together to form a very limited lens through which people can experience their own situation, and these limitations act as powerful default settings throughout the system. Thus, when an individual or a group would break through into a new way of trusting or understanding, that learning would often be hard to hold on to as people returned to their daily lives, away from the support of the new culture of friendship, communication and cooperation that was growing within the bi-communal movement. The extended lack of opportunity to meet face to face has exacerbated this phenomenon.

A major challenge to the process came from its own success. As the bi-communal movement grew so rapidly, the 'managers' of the process on the ground -Fulbright staff, the Bi-Communal Steering Committee, the trainers group- became inundated with too many people, meetings, relationships, logistics and goals to keep up-to-date with. As a result, each new group that was formed tended to focus on itself, and bridges between the groups were hard to facilitate and sustain. Thus, various sub-sets became isolated within the larger process, and no one body was able to manage the integration and coordination that would have taken this movement to another level.

The Consortium also faced follow-up problems that mostly were a reflection of the difficulties of funding. Cyprus is not a place in the world that gets much high-level attention (although that is now changing somewhat), and few foundations and virtually no private individual donors were much interested in the happenings there. Thus the Consortium had to sit on the sidelines from a distance, unable to go with the flow of the process as much as it would have liked. We missed many opportunities, thereby, by not being in the right place at the right time, or by not being able to provide the ongoing personal support needed by the courageous and much-overworked local peacebuilders who were sacrificing their time, their personal lives and, in some cases, their livelihoods and personal safety, to keep the bi-communal process alive.

The story of multi-track diplomacy in Cyprus, with all its intentionality, its synergy and its synchronicity, is still unfolding. Though at the formal level things are stalemated, and the long string of relative lack of violence between the two communities remains fragile, seeds for a better way have been planted. These seeds grew in a burst of sunlight for a while, and now are hibernating in the dark and the cold. Some have already sent their delicious fragrance into the air, or dropped their fruit on fertile ground. Some will never grow, but those of us who have seen the incredible creativity, tenacity and dedication of the peacebuilders in Cyprus know for sure that somehow, sometime, those seeds will come to full blossom, and the garden of peace that flourishes in Cyprus will be a gift of beauty and delight to all the world.

This article has been written by **Louise Diamond**.

Life and Peace Institute Supports Local Capacities for Peace in Somalia

'We Cannot Just Have Peace, We Also Have to Live'

Since 1992 the Life and Peace Institute, an international and ecumenical peace research institute, has supported locally based peace processes in Somalia, to begin with in a consultative role together with the UN. However, when UNOSOM left in 1995, the Institute had established an ongoing support and capacity building program all over Somalia, which later came to be extended also to Somaliland. LPI's Susanne Thurfjell explains the Institute's guiding principles and approach to peace-building.

Somalia ... to most people the very name conjures up images of war-lords, anarchy and destruction. In fact the expression 'failed state' was first heard in connection with Somalia. Seven years have elapsed since the civil war broke out. During these years, security has been fragile, and fighting has continued in many places. However, it has also been noticeable that in the areas where the local authorities have been strong, more or less functioning local governance has been established, fragile and threatened, but still securing a basis for work towards some form of normalcy. In the Republic of Somaliland, which declared itself independent in 1991, a peace and reconciliation process through the elders has resulted in a national government, which has yet to be internationally recognized.

The daunting challenge for the people of Somalia has been - and still is - to find a way to move from a state of fighting and anarchy to a peaceful society, although there is no central government, not even a general peace agreement, to serve them as a starting point.

An alternative way forward is indicated through this social movement that takes place within the Somali society. It starts locally in the communities where people are involving themselves, taking responsibility for security and rehabilitation of their own community. The elders process in Somaliland is one example, the recently formed regional administration of Puntland is another expression. In the central region, around Mogadishu and in the south, they are striving in similar directions.

One of the most interesting peace and reconciliation processes was the so-called Boroma process. It went on throughout 1992-93 in Somaliland, initiated and led by the elders of the

Somalia: Peace conference, December 1996

FOTO SUSANNE THURFJELL

conflicting clans, starting locally on sub-clan level and moving upwards through society to clan level and from there to a national level, culminating in the so-called Boroma conference, which was supported by the Life and Peace Institute. At that meeting all clans of Somaliland were represented through their elders, and in a remarkable Somali and participatory way they elected a government and a president. Both the government and the president have since been contested, but few Somalis, not even those who are unhappy with the outcome of the Boroma conference, would question the legitimacy and authority of the process that led to the outcome.

In Somalia the situation was more confusing. The elders' institution had become more corrupt during Barre's regime and their moral authority was often eroded. In 1994 LPI started to give technical administrative training to the members of the councils that were being rehabilitated in all the districts in the country, through a team of ten Somali trainers/teachers which had received training at the Eastern and Southern African Management Institute. For some time a training centre was established in Baidoa, but the occupation of Baidoa by General Aideed's troops made the situation too uncertain so instead the training team travelled over the country setting up regional workshops. Since 1994, more than 2,000 council members have received basic administrative and executive training. At the same time, the councils have been equipped with a basic kit for administration and a building has been rehabilitated for the council to be housed.

The assumption was that if the councils were equipped and the members were trained they would be able to perform their services to the communities and a strengthened basic structure for local governance would emerge. Out of this structure the regional and national authorities would then grow.

This was right in the way that when the councils were better equipped they had greater possibilities to meet the demands of their communities, and in some districts this worked. Above all, it has been quite noticeable that the training increased the awareness among the council members, and also in the communities in general, about the necessity to build representative and democratic structures in the communities. Many participants in our workshops have expressed hope and a renewed energy to tackle the problems in their areas.

It was wrong in the assumption that a sound and functioning administration would come automatically, once the 'tools' were provided through training and basic material resources. Experience showed that for the local authorities to function, there were many components that had to fall into place. There had to be a mutual relationship of trust and accountability between the people in the communities and their local leadership. Where this was not to be found, the councils remained passive or even disintegrated.

To broaden the approach and give a more comprehensive support to the capacity building programs for the councils, LPI, in 1997, added new components to the training curriculum. Topics such as conflict transformation, reconciliation and peace-building, democratic values and leadership, gender, human rights, development and resource management, small arms and conflict. The new curriculum evolved in cooperation with the trainees and it grew into a regular Civic Education Program. The over- riding questions in the training sessions are: How do these issues relate to the situation in Somalia, and how do they relate to an inclusive peace process? What can we ourselves do to bring peace?

'The guiding principle behind our activities is the bottom-up approach. Local communities's capacities are strengthened through carefully tailored intervention measures aimed at assisting them to use their indigenous knowledge, cultural and social resources and traditional structures. We call it A Community Based Building of Peace and Democracy.'

Other groups within civil society have requested LPI to provide similar training for them. In 1996 LPI widened the target groups in order to include groups of teachers, journalists and media personnel, police and law enforcement officials, artists, etc. In Somaliland the parliamentarians have requested a workshop on the Civic Education including also sessions on constitutional order, relationship between public and private spheres, and good governance. For each different target group the curriculum and the training is adapted to their special perspective and needs. During 1998 the work has continued and has included business people, elders, traditional birth attendants etc.

From the very start of LPI's involvement in Somalia, LPI has aimed at supporting and strengthening the women -

Components of the programme
The stated aim of LPI's Somalia/Somaliland Program was to identify and support broad-based, long-term participatory peace processes, based in the communities, initiated and owned by the people in those communities. Certain social groups stood out as strategically important, local authorities, elders councils and women, and they became the focus of the capacity building program, which evolved out of the situation on the ground. The four major components of the programme are:
1. Support to locally initiated elders' reconciliation conferences.
2. Capacity-building/Institutional Support programs for district, and village councils.
3. Capacity-building program for women.
4. Civic Education Program, which now constitutes a major component of all programs, whether for Institutional Support or the Women's Program.

To implement this vast training program LPI has grown considerably from being a research institute based in Uppsala, Sweden, to having a busy regional office in Nairobi, Kenya, with five zonal offices inside Somalia/Somaliland. A staff of 30 are involved in the training programs, coordinated by four senior staff at the regional office. In 1998 LPI also started a Civic Education Program in southern Sudan.

particularly on community level- in their work for peace, and in their efforts to participate as 'full members' in the Somali society. Women play a new and for them unaccustomed role in the new civil movement, to such an extent that they are often referred to as the 'social and economic back-bone of Somalia. They have also a natural inclination to be bridge builders between the clans. A woman belongs to her fathers clan, but through marriage close ties are created with the husband's clan, particularly since the children belong to the clan of the husband. This bridge-building capacity of the women has always been used to create bonds between the clans, also in traditional reconciliation processes.

In 1994, two women from each region were given training as LPI resource persons. They were then to help LPI to arrange training sessions in each region for women in the districts. Since then 960 women have participated in 24 workshops in many different places in Somalia. The women are active on community level, they come from all clans and all areas of Somalia, and attend the workshops in order to discuss how they can work together for peace. They discuss how to organize themselves, strengthen and support each other and find ways of working together with the men for a future for their families and people. Selection criteria guarantee that participants have an active interest to work for their communities and that they are respected in their communities.

Since tensions and suspicions between clans can be intense, these workshops have provided a possibility for the women to come together and build bridges across clan-lines. Later interregional workshops provided that bridge-building space across regional boundaries. Workshops for business women and political women were also held. New resource persons have been trained and are now to be found in all regions in Somalia and Somaliland.

It is true that the women have had more than their share in the gruesome suffering caused by the war. Much of the advancement that women had gained during Barre's time suffered a set back during the war. It is equally true, however, that the war has opened new venues for the women in Somalia. Before the war only educated women in the capital and main towns made advancements. The war has provided new opportunities, particularly in the trade and commerce sector for women.

Conclusion

The central element to LPI's approach to peace-building is to empower local actors. The approach starts at the community level, eventually aiming to lay the foundations for regional and national reconciliation. All through its involvement in the Horn of Africa, LPI has had as a guiding principle that the process has to be based on and firmly rooted in the local communities. The strategic actors are representatives, men and women, of local communities, enjoying trust and confidence in their communities. From there it can grow and gradually transform the entire society into a society and culture of peace.

It is partly through the women on the ground that LPI fully came to realize the need for a more holistic approach to peace work. Peace is not abstract, it has to make a difference in the lives of people. As one woman expressed it in a workshop: 'We cannot just have peace, we also need life!' Peace has to take the form of a peaceful and non-violent society with respect for all people irrespective of age, sex, religion, ethnicity or clan belonging. Peace has to translate itself into security, food, health, education for the children and possibilities to make a decent living for ourselves and our families. It is not something we can sit and wait passively for others to give us, but we ourselves can, and indeed have to, keep working at it continuously.

This article is an abridged version of Susanne Thurfjell's essay: 'Community Based Building of Peace and Democracy in the Horn of Africa - Life and Peace Institute working to support local capacities for peace.'

REFERENCE

Building the Peace - Experiences of Collaborative Peace-building in Somalia, 1993-1996, Wolfgang Heinrich. Life and Peace Institute, 1997

3

Churches

Introduction

Religion - The strongest power

In this era of economic liberalism and unquestioning belief in the power of market forces there is a tendency to think of every individual as a 'homo economicus', a person wholly engaged in the rational pursuit of self-interest. But looking after number one is just a part of human nature: equally important are such seemingly outmoded qualities as altruism and faith ♦ BY JOHAN VAN WORKUM

As history shows, religious faith or belief can often prove to be a much stronger force than considerations of pure self-interest. In some circumstances people will even sacrifice their life for their faith. Irrespective of whether this powerful force works for the good or bad of mankind, it would be a great mistake to think that the globalisation and economisation of thought has diminished religion's importance. Religion continues to act as one of the major well-springs of human behaviour. Man is incurably religious although the form and object of his religious feelings may change over time.

The role of religion in respect to peace-building and conflict can often be ambiguous. As the following pages show, religious institutions such as churches are frequently to be found at the heart of conflict prevention and peace-building activities. However, there are also examples of religious institutions failing to promote peace and even fanning the flames of conflict.

In the last decade of the 20th century people slaughtered each other in Rwanda and Burundi, apparently for political and/or ethnic reasons. However, most of the slaughterers were Christians, and many were of the same, Roman Catholic, denomination. As such they acted against their religious convictions. Subsequently the Church had major problems reconciling itself with events. How was it possible that the Church and religion generally had so signally failed to prevent the bloodshed? How was it possible that Church-goers and even priests could have participated in the slaughter? Several missionaries from abroad left the country in disillusion, others failed to return to their posts while an African Roman Catholic priest who emigrated to Belgium, is suspected of involvement in the slaughter and is said to be receiving the protection of church authorities in his new country. The major international Christian denominations are now discredited and seem to be losing ground to local churches and sects.

Historically it seems that religion has more often acted to fuel conflicts between peoples and nations than to appease them. In itself this is strange, because in their spirit and their fundamental principles almost all religions aim at peace and co-operation between all human beings. However, wanting the best for mankind clearly does not prevent the devout from turning to religion for help in their worldly struggles, nor does it prevent religious leaders blessing armies and their weapons before they go into battle.

Because Christianity and Islam are the major world religions it is useful to review the place of peace and conflict in their respective histories. In Europe, it is clear that the Reformation has been the source of many violent conflicts. The Peace of Augsburg in 1555 -stating that the religion of the prince shall be the religion in his principality- could not prevent the outbreak of the Thirty Years War half a century later. When the weapons were finally laid down following the Treaty of Westphalia, in 1648, large parts of German speaking Europe had been depopulated on a scale comparable with an outbreak of plague, while the political map of Europe changed beyond recognition. The medieval Roman Empire had ended and peoples, princes and other statesmen had seemingly come to accept the existence of religious differences both between and within countries. Some half a millennium earlier Pope Urbanus II called a crusade to free the Holy Land from Islam. Modern historians think one of his objectives was to put an end to the wars and violence within Europe by presenting his quarrelsome knights with an external enemy.

And yet the roots of Christianity are clearly non-political. In the sense that Jesus Christ taught that his Kingdom is not 'of this world', he was what we would call today a spiritual king, not a king with armies or 'King of Hosts': 'Don't you think my father would send me immediately over twelve legions of angels when I would ask Him?' However, this phase in Christianity lasted for only three centuries, until the Roman emperor Constantine adopted Christianity as the religion of the empire. This linkage of religion with politics was soon followed by a corresponding political intervention in religious matters. One of the main contemporary theological debates focused on the humanity of Christ: was Christ only man, or did he also have a second Divine nature? In 325, fearing that the debate would lead to divisions in his empire, Constantine instigated the Council of Nicea and began to exert pressure in favour of the majority view in favour of the dual natured Christ. Because Constantine and his successors later suppressed the minority, Arian, line, the modern 'Credo' presents Christ as both God and man, except in those areas which were beyond the political reach of the empire such as the Coptic churches of Ethiopia.

The Prophet
Violence and conflict also feature large in the history of Islam, which like Christianity has its roots in Judaism. Unlike Christianity, Islam was from the outset both a spiritual and a political movement. The Prophet was not only a religious leader and founder of a world religion, but also a political leader, conqueror and founder of the Arab-Islamic empire.

In most countries the principle of partition between church (the religious institutions) and state (the political institutions) developed during the last two centuries. It is a principle that fits well with the tenets of Christianity but is more alien to the old Islamic countries. The concept of Jihad -the holy war for promoting Islam- encompasses both the armed struggle and missionary work. It aims to spread and propagate Islam both as a spiritual and as a political force. At the same time, preaching other religions within Islamic society is forbidden and believers who renounced their faith were originally subject to capital punishment - like a deserter in war. Today, in many Islamic countries Sharia -the introduction of the (religious) Islamic laws into the state laws- is widely debated.

But even in Europe the partition of church and state is not complete in all countries. In Great Britain, for example, the Sovereign is both head of state and head of the Church of England. Thus, in 1995 the 50th anniversary of the end of World War II was frequently celebrated in cathedrals with a mixture of religious, national and military ceremonies. The Scandinavian countries also have (Lutheran) state churches. In Greece, where the Greek Christian orthodox religion is a national religion, proselytising by other Christian churches is an offence.

Religion is a powerful force and its power is undiminished. The names of most political revolutionaries live on in history, but the reputations of religious revolutionaries can endure for millennia: Confucius, Moses, Buddha, Christ, Paul, Mohammed. Linking religion and (political) power is an explosive mixture, even when the religion in question has its roots in doctrines of love and peace-building.

In practice religion, together with ethnicity, language, class and a common history, is a main element in building the collective identity of a people. Religion helps define and distinguish the 'in' group from the 'out' group, the 'we from the 'you': it is both inclusive and exclusive. Each of these elements can help catalyse social or political tensions into an open conflict and then subsequently act as a barrier, prolonging divisions even where the social or political tensions can easily be resolved.

In Israel and the Middle East, all five elements -religion, ethnicity, language, class and history- are active. In another hotbed of conflict, Northern Ireland, it is mainly religion and class; in Bosnia Herzegovina it is history and religion; in Kosovo and Chechnya, religion, history and language; in Rwanda, ethnicity and to a lesser degree, class and history; in Cyprus religion, ethnicity and also history; in East Java class and religion; in Ambon and Afghanistan, religion and ethnicity; in the Lake district of Africa and in Sierra Leone it seems to be mainly ethnic. In all these areas, social or purely political tensions are a condition for triggering conflict, but, as we have said, resolving those tensions does not automatically mean an end to the conflict.

But despite all its dangers, religion can also be a very strong force for peace-building and conflict resolution. Religion can provide a platform from which to tackle other causes of conflict such as social tensions, ethnicity, language, and history. Religion is a powerful agency of peace because virtually every world religion teaches the principles of peace, justice, love, humanity and co-operation. Some relatively young religions, such as the Baha'i and the Sufi movements, are even founded on the idea that in these fundamental principles, all religions have the same message.

Consequently, religion has several faces. In one respect it is a force for group identity, proselytising, 'holy' war and dictatorial fundamentalism, but it can also be a force working for a cosmopolitan humanity, peace, love and community. In its positive aspect, religion provides people with a common language of belief. However, to realise religion's potential for peace-

building, it is first necessary to remove it from the hands of the politicians. Only in this way it is possible to counteract its negative potential as the provider of an exclusive and divisive group identity in situations of conflict.

As a first step it is important to reverse the decision of Emperor Constantine. No one knows what would have become of Christianity had Constantine not made it the state religion of the Roman Empire. Today we have numerous practical examples of what happens when the roles of church and state are separated. Today, churches function mainly as elements of civil society. Freed from political powers the authentic spiritual message gets new credibility. The aims of that message remain political, but they are not the politics of self- or group-interest. Accordingly, the religiously motivated movement is less likely to be involved directly in the political system. In this chapter the reader will find several examples of the liberated power of religion at work. Most of them involve activities to try to bring reconciliation after a period of war, suppression or violence.

It is little wonder that United Nations agencies and non-governmental organisations are paying increasing attention to joint projects with religious institutions and networks. UNESCO has set up a programme examining the role of religion and is convinced of its value as a source of insight and ethical valour. In 1994, UNESCO organised a conference in Barcelona on religion's contribution 'to the culture of peace'. Its final declaration appeals 'for sincere acts of repentance and mutual forgiveness, both personally and collectively, to one another, to humanity in general, and to Earth and all living beings. Religious people have too often betrayed the high ideals they themselves have preached.' The conference called upon the different religious and cultural traditions to join hands 'in spreading the message of peace'.

In February 1994, the 7th World Religions Conference was held in New Delhi. In a declaration sent to the secretary general of the UN, the conference underlined the policy of 'preventive diplomacy' aimed at preventing the escalation of conflicts and violence. The participants offered their services as mediators, negotiators and facilitators of non-violent conflict prevention and reconciliation.

Established in 1948, the World Council of Churches (WCC) is an ecumenical movement of Christian churches which is concerned not only with matters of faith but increasingly with social concerns such as the promotion of justice and peace. Examples of its activities are to be found in the following chapters of this book.

Core business
The WCRP (World Conference on Religion and Peace) considers peace as its core 'business'. Originally an initiative of religious leaders from Japan, the United States and India, it held its first conference in 1970 in Kyoto, Japan. By forming groups on local levels it aims to bridge religious divides in different regions and communities. In the 1980s, the WCRP established local groups in the Punjab in India with Hindu, Muslim and Sikh memberships. In the 1990s it has been active in Sierra Leone, Kosovo and Indonesia - home of WCRP President, Dr. Abdurrahman Wahid. The Roman Catholic organisation Pax Christi is also active in the Caucasus and the Balkans.

Mention should also be made of the International Network of Engaged Buddhists (INEB), headed by Sulak Sivaraksa from Siam (Sulak prefers to speak of Siam rather than 'Thailand' because the latter name suggests that there is only one ethnic group in Siam). INEB has national and or regional groups in over thirty countries, including both the traditional Buddhist countries and the diaspora. This movement counters the oft-heard accusation that Buddhists are only concerned with their personal salvation and lack any wider social commitment. INEB condemns consumerism and selfishness - two main characteristics of contemporary Western culture.

The violent inner-city neighbourhoods in the United States provide a further challenge which has been met by religious initiatives. Here, community centres supported by local interfaith groups have helped to rebuild peaceful relations and end the poverty that feeds the violence. Also in America, the Chicago World Parliament of Religions (CWPR), inaugurated in 1893, commemorated its centennial with a 'Call to Guiding Institutions' - religious, governmental, corporate, educational, and media - to offer gifts of service which would make long term differences in the world.

The Fellowship of Reconciliation is an international interfaith organisation with local chapters which organises denominational fellowships - for example, the Buddhist Peace Fellowship, and the Jewish Peace Fellowship. It promotes programmes and activities centred on the themes of peace, disarmament and racial and economic justice.

Reconciliation is of course at the heart of the peace-building process but there exist some significant differences in the role given to the concept in different religions. In the Christian faith, for example, reconciliation is a central issue but it is embedded in a context of regret, asking forgiveness, forgiving, and repentance. In this way it can produce justice. But when church leaders take a neutral position during periods of repression and later start preaching reconciliation the chances of true reconciliation and real justice are remote. So too, when several parties are responsible for a conflict and one will not acknowledge its share of responsibility or show repentance, there is little chance of a successful one-sided 'reconciliation' being successful. South Africa's Truth and Reconciliation Commission provides a very interesting example in this respect.

The following pages present some examples of the power of religion as a force for peace. There is the example of the World Council of Churches, which in the 1990s launched several programmes in reaction to the upheaval and violence in that followed the collapse of the Soviet Union. In Cambodia, the Buddhist Dammayietra Centre in Phnom Penh trains monks, nuns and laypersons for annual interfaith pilgrimages to end violence. The 'pilgrimages of truth' were organised between 1992 and 1997, aimed at breaking the cycle of retaliation, hatred and revenge through non-violence and the Buddhist concept of compassion. In Kenya, the National Church Council launched a multi-faceted programme to press for peace and reconciliation among the rival groups in a reaction to the flare-up of ethnic violence. The final example describes the contribution of church workers to the still fragile democracy and peace in Guatemala.

SELECTED BIBLIOGRAPHY

Healing a Nation's Wounds - Reconciliation on the road to democracy, Walter Wink. Life and Peace Institute, 1997.

The Churches Role as Agents of Peace and Development (series), Life and Peace Institute (with issues on Costa Rica, Argentina, Zimbabwe, Brazil).

Power and Peace - Statements on peace and authority of the churches. Life and Peace Institute, 1998.

A History of the World Conference on Religion and Peace, Homer A. Jack. WCRP.

Risking Peace - Reconciliation at the heart of our mission. Publication for the Second European Ecumenical Assembly in Graz, 1997.

Global Responsibility - In search of a new world ethic, Hans Küng. Continuum Pub Group, 1993.

Role of Religion - Peace and Conflict Issues Series, UNESCO Publishing, 1996.

Religion and Development - Towards an integrated approach, Philip Quarles van Ufford, Matthew Schoffeleers (ed.). Free University Press, Amsterdam 1988.

Christian Peacemaking - From heritage to hope, Daniel L. Buttery. Judson Pr. 1994.

The God of Peace - Toward a theology of nonviolence, John Dear, Jim Douglass (designer). Orbis Books 1994.

The Art of Forgiveness - Theological Reflections on Healing and Reconciliation, Geiko Müller-Fahrenholz. WCC Publications, Geneva, 1996.

Church Council Bridges the Ethnic Divide

Voice of the Voiceless in Kenya

'Ethnic identification is a sensitive, emotional issue, one that is easily manipulated. Ethnicity can become part of the transition phenomena when people do not know how to relate swiftly and correctly to rapid political change. In such times of uncertainty, it is easy to politicise ethnicity and to build a support base from it.' (Sam Kobia, former general secretary of the National Council of Churches of Kenya (NCCK) in 'The Quest for Democracy in Africa', 1993)

The government's complicity in the violence in Kenya (see Box) is both deeply troubling, in that it reflects the absence of the rule of law within the Kenyan political system, but also just slightly hopeful, to the extent that it suggests that the violence was not triggered by such fundamental differences, bitter rivalries, or deep-rooted hatred between neighbouring ethnic groups that reconciliation between the parties can never be achieved.

Estimates vary, but it is generally agreed that, beyond the dead and perhaps 30,000 wounded, more than 300,000 people have been displaced due to ethnic violence. And naturally, with this enormous displacement, economic and social displacement have followed, with families divided, health and educational infrastructure disrupted, and food shortages occurring because of crop damage and the inability of farmers to work their fields.

To address this large scale refugee problem, and to try to work for reconciliation among the rival groups, the NCCK has launched a multi-faceted program called the NCCK Peace and Reconciliation Project. Financial support for the project has been provided by the Government of the Netherlands, at the outset (1992-1993) through the Dutch Ministry for Development Co-operation, and later on, via Dutch Interchurch Aid (DIA).

The NCCK, which dates back to 1908, is an umbrella organisation for Christian churches in Kenya. It has a long and consistent record of working to spur development at all levels - economic and political as well as spiritual. In campaigning for greater democracy and a more open society, and attempting to serve as the 'voice of the voiceless', it has clashed with the authorities on more than one occasion. The NCCK's own investigations into the causes of the communal violence of the early nineties led to the very same conclusions as those of outside observers: the violence was politically instigated.

The Peace and Reconciliation Project was primarily an emergency relief program during its first phase, at a time when the victims of ethnic violence required assistance. But the focus has gradually shifted from relief and rehabilitation to peace and reconciliation, with concerted efforts underway to 'prevent ethnic conflict, improve inter-ethnic relationships, reduce the suffering as a result of ethnic violence, and create awareness on issues causing conflicts.'

It was during phase II, from 1994 until 1996, that the first efforts were made to present an integrated approach in which relief and rehabilitation efforts were linked to reconciliation programs with a more social focus. Subsequently, beginning with phase III in August 1996, more extensive reconciliation programs were initiated to not only restore hope to the victims of violence and provide them with a means to earn a decent living, but also to assist them in re-integrating themselves into the communities they had fled.

The basic administrative unit of the Peace and Reconciliation Project is an 'Area Peace and Rehabilitation Committee' (APRC), which draws its membership from a cross section of local inhabitants including representatives of local leadership, churches, NGOs, youth, and women. In fact, the success of the program has been premised on the active participation of the local population.

'One cannot resolve conflicts and make peace unless the root causes of the conflicts have been identified and dealt with. This can only happen if the root causes can be identified by local communities themselves within a context they are familiar with.'

These APRCs organised hundreds of Good Neighbourliness Seminars, open to elders, local opinion leaders, local politicians, educators, community workers, government workers, and members of other important groups and organisations at the local level. At these seminars, the participants could discuss the causes of the local conflicts and analyse the effects that these conflicts had on their communities, and could examine potential strategies for successfully resolving the conflicts without resorting to violence.

In those meetings held for community leaders, the leaders own roles in promoting peace and reconciliation were a focus of the discussions. Meetings held exclusively for women gave women the chance to participate in ways that wouldn't have been possible in mixed seminars. In seminars focusing on youth, the participants were challenged to re-evaluate the values that resulted in them perceiving 'the other' as enemy, and encouraged not to allow others to manipulate them into acts of violence, but rather to channel their energies into more constructive activities. Intercultural sports and social activities were also encouraged.

Those seminars bringing together elders and traditional leaders were of particular importance, as traditional leaders are held in high regard and retain enormous influence in their communities. Their roles as peacemakers are crucial.
During these seminars, some 200 Village Peace Committees were established. Peace Committee members were drawn from both the displaced persons and those who had remained in their villages, and they were responsible for a wide variety of activities: to act as arbiters between the various interest groups within the community, to initiate efforts to

Inevitable Ethnic Violence?

In the ethnic patchwork that is Kenya, it is sometimes convenient to point to ethnic conflict as an inevitable element of the culture. And that has all too frequently seemed to be the case as Kikuyus and Kalenjins have battled and slaughtered each other over the past decade. Kenya is, after all, a nation of more than 40 distinct ethnic groups, where dozens of languages are spoken, with a set of borders imposed on it by an outside colonial power, a national government that asserts authority across those ethnic divides, and a system of government not entirely consistent with traditional Kenyan notions of authority or governance. And the ethnic divisions have clearly been a major factor in determining the political landscape of Kenya since before independence. But in fact, much of the ethnic violence that has recently plagued Kenya and claimed several thousand lives has its roots not in fundamental ethnic rivalries, but rather in politics.

Outside observers, from the United States government to independent human rights organisations like Amnesty International, Article 19 and Human Rights Watch have all concluded that the serious ethnic violence which flared up during the run-up to multi-party elections in 1992, and again prior to the elections in December 1997, was instigated by the government and the ruling party, the Kenyan African National Union (KANU). While it is true that these ethnic clashes took place primarily between the original Kalenjin inhabitants of the Rift Valley region, and other ethnic groups who had migrated to the region and settled there (and later, in the coastal regions as well), it is generally agreed that the violence was motivated by a desire of the KANU leadership to assure electoral victory by launching a campaign against members of those ethnic communities who affiliated with the opposition, so that they would be forced to flee or would not vote to oppose KANU candidates.

restore local amenities and set priorities, to serve as representatives of the local communities on the APRCs, and together with the APRCs, to function as a sort of 'early warning system' to detect and de-fuse ethnic tension before it erupted into violence.

Beyond the small scale seminars intended to bring people with similar social positions together, the project encouraged local officials to organise larger community meetings called 'barazas' to discuss issues related to peace, security, and resettlement with a broad cross-section of stakeholders within a community.

Key interest groups, such as legislators, religious leaders, and public administrators were invited to participate in specialised workshops designed to provide these individuals with information and experience that would help them to reduce ethnic tensions and overcome mistrust. For example, at workshops attended by legislators, the conflicts in Kenya were placed against the backdrop of ethnic conflicts in other African states, with an examination of the causes of these conflicts, and discussions on the ways to resolve disputes nonviolently. In considering strategies for peacemaking, it was suggested that 'conflict transformation' might be a better description of the process, where the essential ingredients for successful resolution demand that the parties to a conflict come to a basic understanding of the root causes of their dispute, and seek a solution that both sides view as fair, based on the premise that 'justice is a prerequisite of peace.'

The NCCK has been publishing a monthly magazine that reports on both reconciliation efforts and incidents of violence. It has also actively distributed peace and reconciliation posters in the affected regions, many produced by schoolchildren in the local communities. To encourage an exchange of ideas among the members of the APRCs, it has sponsored exchange visits, and has sponsored similar activities for youth groups and women's organisations. To assist the resettlement of the victims of violence, it has created a 'Central Clashes Rehabilitation Register' with data about land purchases, organised monthly meetings on resettlement issues, and provided material assistance to individuals and groups to help them make a new start.

At the outset, the NCCK conducted extensive interviews with a broad range of stakeholders so that it would come to a more complete understanding of the causes of conflict. And throughout the duration of the project, it has worked with these stakeholders, so that they have a sense of ownership. In evaluating the success of the project, M.E. Witte-Rang of the Dutch ecumenical development organisation OIKOS attributes much of the success of the project to this approach. 'When people own a project,' writes Witte-Rang, 'they feel responsible and will defend their own activities,' adding 'it is a matter of principal: local people know better than anyone else the causes of the conflict and the possible solutions to end it.' (Witte-Rang, M.E. A Way Out of the Conflict (OIKOS: Utrecht, 1998)

In its own description of its activities, the NCCK attributes much of the Peace and Reconciliation Project's success to its 'inclusive' approach. 'You cannot make peace on your own or with a few enlightened people ... all actors, no matter whether they are perceived as friend or enemy, good or bad, influential or [simply members of the] community, they all have to be involved in the process.' And while that is no guarantee of success, it has, in the view of the NCCK, helped to reduce the level of violence in the Rift Valley, and enhanced mutual understanding among ordinary people.

WCC's Peace to the City Programme

Cities Unite to Conquer Violence

In many of the large cities of the world both destructive and constructive forces are at play. The focus of the global 'Peace to the City' campaign of the World Council of Churches (part of its Programme to Overcome Violence) is on imaginative efforts to overcome violence through cross-community work; to build bridges between communities drawn into violent conflict, and to bring reconciliation.

A t first sight, Rio de Janeiro, Brazil, looks like a paradise. Beautiful beaches, the Copacabana, the annual carnival. But for years there has been tension between the haves and have nots. Burglary, kidnapping, drug abuse and other crimes are everyday occurrences. The police response is equally brutal. The violence came to a head in 1993, when a series of ruthless killings shocked citizens and spurred them to put an end to the violence. People formed an organisation which would help bring peace to the city of Rio de Janeiro: Viva Rio.

'It was fear, not compassion or charity, that inspired Viva Rio,' says its executive secretary in a documentary. 'Out of this feeling of fear came the idea that we had to do something, and we proposed a peace movement. Peace on its own can be a powerful argument against violence.'

Today, Viva Rio is a broad based civil society movement which works towards social integration. It is responsible for a range of projects that provide an alternative to violence, encourage community action, and promote public safety. The organisation has created a voluntary civil service, which gives thousands of young school dropouts a chance of education and job training in exchange for community action in their neighbourhood. It has a credit facility for people in the slums, who are not able to borrow money from the official banks. Viva Rio started with community sports groups and education for adults who had left their schooling unfinished.

A considerable part of Viva Rio's programmes is centred around youth. According to the organisation, it is the young people who create most of the violence and are at the heart of it. Often, the youth of the slums are jobless and do not attend school. They get bored and fall into criminality. The idea behind Viva Rio's activities is to guide these youth and others to become citizens again, says one of its voluntary workers. The projects are supposed to stimulate people to do something, either to play a basketball game, to work as a volunteer, or to follow an education. Also, a lot of the activities are aimed at getting to know each other better, so different groups won't rise against each other, but live together in peace.

The Rio the Janeiro success story has been the inspiration for the global 'Peace to the City' campaign, which was launched by the World Council of Churches (WCC) in Johannesburg in 1997. The Council is an international Christian organisation, built on the foundation of ecumenical collaboration. With 'Peace to the City' the WCC wanted to connect people and organisations who are actively committed to pursuing peace with justice. The Council selected seven cities where individuals and groups could share their ideas and current activities to overcome violence: Rio de Janeiro, Belfast (Northern Ireland), Boston (United States), Colombo (Sri Lanka), Durban (South Africa), Suva (Fiji) and Kingston (Jamaica).

Home-page of the Peace in the City programme

Take for example Suva, Fiji. Since 1987, there has been conflict between the Indian and ethnic Fijian population. An Indian political party had come into power, and the Fijian nationalists executed a coup to dislodge the new government. When violence increased, ordinary citizens began to question the dominant move of the nationalists. Church groups and people from other religions started to pray and work together in order to come to mutual understanding. Hindus and Sikhs went to church, Christians to temple. It created a new bond between the different ethnic groups. Nowadays, organisations set up workshops and other activities for bringing the groups together.

Most of the time, the Council works together with a local group, as in Colombo with the National Peace Council of Sri Lanka, a secular and politically non-partisan umbrella.

In the South African City of Durban, whose slogan is 'from capital of violence to model of peace', fourteen organisations take part in the campaign - from The African Centre for the Constructive Resolution of Disputes (Accord) to the KwaZulu-Natal Programme for Survivors of Violence. Since the early 1980s, the Durban region has been plagued by political violence, mainly related to disputes between the supporters of the African Congress (ANC) and the Inkatha Freedom Party (IFP).

Yet Durban has seen some brilliant ideas of peace building. An example is the 'Peace Monitors,' a kind of peace police. The provincial peace committee has taught ten members of each party the skills of reconciliation. The 'Peace Monitors' patrol the city to help establish and maintain the cease-fire. And they are successful.

In the city of Boston, the 'Ten Point Coalition' is a group of Churches working to mobilise the Christian community to help support black and Latino youth, especially those who are at risk of drug abuse, violence and other destructive behaviour. The Ten Point Coalition -named after the ten points that it represents -started a youth centre where violence is forbidden. The kids can feel themselves safe and secure. They are able to use their time constructively.

Initiatives like the Durban's 'Peace Monitors' and the youth centre in Boston are exactly what 'Peace to the City' is all about. The campaign highlights existing, creative initiatives for peace and community building during conflict situations. The goals are to make them visible and recognise the value of their approaches and methodologies. The seven cities and other cities and groups in the campaign form a network. They can learn from each other and exchange ideas. An important means for this is the internet, where anyone can swap ideas on the 'Peace to the City' web-page and read the latest news. The campaign is supposed to give others a reason to attempt something similar in their own context. The WCC's aspiration is to shape a broad and bold ecumenical movement to overcome violence.

The idea of using a 'city' in the campaign is not a coincidence. As centres of population, commerce, finance, political power and culture, cities form a metaphor for the modern world. Cities experience most forms of violence. They house the people and institutions that shape systems of globalisation and national military rivalries. Urbanisation takes its toll. People crowded into small spaces often creates severe stress on the environment as well as on human morals.

Yet people in cities also organise to reconstruct their communities, form new civic alliances to rebuild the potential for living with greater justice and peace. People bring about social change. Also, churches and other Christian and religious groups are in the cities. An initiative focused on the city gives new possibilities for partnership between those already involved in ecumenical networks and other faiths. To the Council, the city is the place where Christians can give 'dramatic, concrete and effective evidence' of their commitment to overcome violence.

Overall, the formula seems to succeed. The early results show a considerable willpower of the people in these cities to fight for change and participate in the campaign. According to the Council, 'a new peoples' movement is emerging'. This was affirmed at the WCC's Eight Assembly held in Harare in December 1998. There the delegates overwhelmingly approved the call for an eucumenical Decade To Overcome Violence for the years 2001-2010.

The Peace to the City campaign is part of the World Council of Churches' Programme to Overcome Violence (POV), launched in 1994. It was a reaction to the upheaval of violence in all parts of the world, even though the Cold War had come to an end and the Iron Curtain had come down. According to the churches, the current global 'culture of violence' should change into a 'culture of peace'. The POV can be regarded as a broad framework within which churches and groups can find their own place. There is room for many creative, interrelated initiatives.

With its origins forged in the midst of the Second World War, the World Council of Churches' engagement on issues of peace and justice did not begin with the Programme to overcome Violence. For fifty years now, the Council has been engaged in efforts to avoid war, minister to its victims, and to reconstruct societies destroyed by war.

After decades of experience in active programmes as well as theological reflection, a renewed emphasis on joining work for peace with engagement for justice came at a number of points in the 1990 Seoul Convocation on Justice, Peace and the Integrity of Creation. Soon after that, the Programme to Overcome Violence was established.

The churches are confident that the Programme can make a difference in many places of the world, although they know that it is one of the most ambitious initiatives undertaken by the WCC. After all, two decades ago Christians and their churches took a lead in building a popular movement against nuclear weapons, which brought millions into the streets of the cities. Broad citizen coalitions were formed linking churches and their members with others seeking to halt the nuclear arms race. To the Council, that 'hope-giving' and empowering movement showed that when people join hands and put faith into action, change for the better can happen.

'We affirm the full meaning of God's Peace. We are called to seek every possible means of establishing justice, achieving peace and solving conflicts by active non-violence.'

The World Council of Churches definitely has confidence in the vision and the power of the churches to work for peace with justice. In its early years, the WCC was dominated by Western countries, but, in the course of time, the churches of developing countries have gained more and more influence. The 330 member churches come from a wide range of social, cultural, economic and political backgrounds and represent nearly every Christian tradition. Although the Roman Catholic Church is not a member, staff of the Vatican co-operate in many different areas of work. WCC programme work is divided into teams, one of which is 'Justice, Peace and Creation.'

Apart from the Peace to the City Campaign, the WCC has developed other activities. It has created a data-base of church-based and church related peace groups which is now available for consultation. Groups can share their own experience or provide training or help.

The WCC has also organised consultations on non-violent approaches to conflict resolution and sponsors small inter-faith gatherings. It has designed training sessions on non-violent conflict resolution and produced education material. The Council is also initiating a survey of church initiatives that address the production, sale and use of small arms and light weapons.

In its battle against violence, the WCC gives special attention to the more vulnerable groups in society who are easily victimised and require support in their struggle for justice. Special attention is given to violence against women, and the WCC has just completed a Decade of the churches in solidarity with women. It helps ethnic minorities to find justice. Each year, prior to the UN meeting on Indigenous Peoples, the WCC hosts a weekend meeting. The Council supports the representatives financially, but, most important, is the provision of a 'safe place' where indigenous people can openly discuss and from which the governments must keep a distance.

Pilgrimages of Truth in Cambodia

Taking the First Step to Peace

Since 1992 an annual 'Dhammayietra' -literally, a 'pilgrimage of truth'- has been held in war-torn Cambodia. The hundreds of participants walked over long distances for peace and reconciliation, providing an example of a peaceful alternative to the norm of violence that has prevailed in Cambodia.

The tragedy that befell Cambodia when the Khmer Rouge seized power in 1975 is widely known. Up to 2 million people died from disease, hunger, torture, and executions. Vietnamese forces drove the Khmer Rouge from power three years later, but violence has continued to plague the country. Despite the signing of a formal Peace Treaty in 1991, and the presence during 1992 and 1993 of over 22,000 UN peace-keepers, many thousands of lives have been lost, many more thousands of Cambodian citizens have been wounded, and Cambodians continue to suffer severe economic hardships as a result of the continuing conflict. The rule of law does not exist. Human rights continue to be violated, and those parts of the country that have not been divided up among the various political factions are the domain of bandits and plunderers.

Peace-making in such a climate is a most difficult endeavour. Yet there are ordinary citizens, acting out of their belief in the power of non-violence and their hope for a more peaceful future, who refuse to give in to the climate of violence that has held sway in Cambodia for the last thirty years.

Perhaps the best known, inspiring, and successful of these efforts at non-violent organising has been the Dhammayietra. Each was both a spiritual pilgrimage and a physical pilgrimage through the Cambodian countryside. Cambodia is, of course, a predominantly Buddhist society, and the Dhammayietra walks are a very specific application of Buddhist teachings on the linkage between spiritual awareness and non-violent conflict resolution. Maha Ghosananda, one of Cambodia's most respected Buddhist monks, was instrumental in organising the first Dhammayietra, and served as the spiritual leader for that first walk and each succeeding walk.

Maha Ghosananda, who is often referred to as the 'Cambodian Gandhi', argues for a process of reconciliation derived from a deep-rooted sense of compassion.

'It is a law of the universe that retaliation, hatred, and revenge only continue the cycle and never stop it,' he has said. 'Reconciliation does not mean that we surrender rights and conditions, but rather that we use love. Our wisdom and our compassion must walk together.

Having one without the other is like walking on one foot; you will fall. Balancing the two, you will walk very well, step by step.'

All participants in the Dhammayietras prepared for their month-long walks by attending non-violence training programs at one of several locations in Cambodia. The first sessions at these training programmes were taken up with fundamentals: the philosophy of the walk, an introduction on meditation for peace, and an understanding of how basic Buddhist concepts can be applied to the difficulties of everyday life. Subsequent sessions provided examples of peacemaking, theory on non-violence, strategies for handling fear, and role-playing sessions to familiarise participants with potential situations they might encounter during the walk. Because of the serious risks of injury from unexploded mines, the training also included sessions on mine awareness, provided by non-governmental agencies.

> **Buddhist Prayer for Peace**
>
> The suffering of Cambodia has been deep.
> From this suffering comes Great Compassion.
> Great Compassion makes a Peaceful Heart.
> A Peaceful Heart makes a Peaceful Person.
> A Peaceful Person makes a Peaceful Family.
> A Peaceful Family makes a Peaceful Community.
> A Peaceful Community makes a Peaceful Nation.
> And a Peaceful Nation makes a Peaceful World.
> May all beings live in Happiness and Peace.
>
> *'Step by Step: Meditations on Wisdom and Compassion'*
> *by Maha Ghosananda*

Such training not only prepares the walkers for the Dhammayietra itself, but they create a large network of individuals trained in non-violent action and theory, capable of passing that knowledge on to other members of their own communities. From 1992 through 1997, thousands of people attended non-violence training sessions.

The central value that is the key to both the power and the success of the Dhammayietra is compassion, viewed from a Buddhist perspective as both the means and the end of personal and social liberation. Compassion is considered to be the one virtue which enables peacemakers to persist in non-violent action when confronted with violence and frustration. While members of the Dhammayietra movement recognise that the development of compassion is a long-term process, they offer several lessons from Buddhist practice as strategies that can be useful in cultivating it. Compassion serves as a defence against fear, which is seen as a precursor to violence.

As a corollary to the cultivation of compassion, the Dhammayietra philosophy advocates the cultivation of 'active mindfulness'. By this it is meant that when an individual is confronted with a difficult situation, he or she is capable of either quickly acting - or not acting, if that is more appropriate - with clarity of mind, based on one's own knowledge, experience, and understanding, rather than reacting to and being controlled by that situation.

If these two qualities are aspired to for the individual participants of a Dhammayietra, the quality that is essential to guarantee the integrity and credibility of the group process is non-partisanship. In Buddhist terminology, the Dhammayietra treads the 'Middle Path'. The

Dhammayietra is making a statement for peace and non-violence, and against policies, strategies, and actions that lead to violence, but that stance does not imply that it is opposing one side or another in a violent conflict. The position of the Dhammayietra is a clear expression of Gandhi's admonition to 'oppose the evil, not the evil doer.'

The Dhammayietra is an expression of commitment to non-violence, but it is also a complicated ongoing event, with somewhere between 400 and 700 participants, and it thus requires order, discipline, and logistical planning. Over the five years of the Cambodian Dhammayietras, an organisational structure has developed in response to difficulties encountered along the way.

In later years, overall co-ordination was placed in the hands of a committee of 17 people, all of them Cambodian monks, nuns, or lay people (in earlier years a smaller committee including expatriates co-ordinated the walks). The participants were divided into groups of about ten walkers, each with a group leader selected by the members. These leaders participated in meetings with the walk committee to assure a democratic decision-making process. Other members of the walk groups were designated to serve as assistants and representatives, with responsibilities for the distribution of essential supplies, food, water and information.

Perhaps the most important provision introduced in later years was a set of guidelines which constituted a framework within which the Dhammayietra could be expected to proceed smoothly. These stipulated that participants would attend the pre-walk non-violence training and refrain from riding in vehicles, using drugs, carrying weapons, wearing uniforms, or carrying flags.

Beginning with the fourth Dhammayietra in 1995, walk organisers incorporated a public education element. This included the distribution of pamphlets, dissemination of a 'Peace Health' message articulating the belief among health workers that war 'is the number 1 health problem in Cambodia', and public talks at villages along the route of the walk. At these talks, Maha Ghosananda would spread his message that Buddhism can serve as a basis for social reconciliation and compassion. Such events also provided opportunities for landmine awareness trainers to make presentations to local residents. Another focus, in 1996, was on the need to preserve Cambodia's forests, which are a crucial element of the Cambodian environment, and an important symbol of renewal in Buddhism. Unfortunately, serious damage has been done to Cambodia's rich timber resources, and one of the important sources of income for combatants in the Cambodian civil war has been the profits earned from exploiting those resources.

Although non-violent action is undertaken in the hope that a principled commitment to non-violence can provide a degree of protection for participants, non-violent action in a climate of violence remains a risky endeavour. This was vividly and tragically demonstrated during the Dhammayietras of 1993 and 1994. The first Dhammayietra in 1992 had succeeded beyond its organisers' expectations. Walkers had begun the Dhammayietra in refugee camps on the Thai side of the Thai-Cambodian border, and had walked to Phnom Penh. As a result of the walk, many refugees had been reunited with family members they had not seen since the

1970s, and the walk had succeeded - at least for a time - in breaking through the insidious climate of fear that pervaded the society. Several thousand ordinary Cambodians had spontaneously joined the walk, and tens of thousands demonstrated their support for the walkers as they passed through provincial seats along the way to the capital.

But at the beginning of the second Dhammayietra, from Siem Reap in the north of the country to Phnom Penh, several walkers were wounded when they were caught in a crossfire between government forces and Khmer Rouge fighters. Walkers also braved ongoing shelling which, though not directed at the walk, occurred on a daily basis along the first part of the route. The walk continued nonetheless, and by the time it reached the capital, the total number of participants had swelled to about 3,000.

The following year, with a fragile coalition between former combatants in place in Phnom Penh after UN-supervised elections, the organisers elected to walk from Battambang to Siem Reap - directly through a region of the country where the civil war still raged. Their hope was to maintain 'a zone of peace' around the walk. On the seventh day of the Dhammayietra, the walkers were accompanied by unarmed soldiers who were showing them a mine-free route, and as they walked, they encountered other armed soldiers conducting military patrols.

'Reconciliation does not mean that we surrender rights and conditions, but rather that we use love.'

'Suddenly,' wrote American participant Liz Bernstein, 'the walkers encountered a group of [Khmer Rouge] soldiers and a fire fight ensued. Bullets and rockets flew as the walkers lay on the ground.' The Dhammayietra had once again been caught in a crossfire, and this time three walkers were killed. Following this incident, there was considerable confusion about whether or not the walk would continue, and some organisers and participants left the walk, while others continued, by an alternative route, to the end.

After the sobering experience of 1994, organisers redoubled their efforts to provide adequate training to participants and to ensure that no soldiers would accompany the Dhammayietra. The walks in 1995 and 1996 proceeded without violence, with the focus in 1995 on the international campaign to ban landmines, and the focus in 1996 on deforestation (including the planting of thousands of trees along the route) and the ongoing civil war.

The risks and frustrations of the Dhammayietra are all too obvious - walkers have been killed and injured, and civil war and lawlessness still reign in Cambodia. What then can be said about the impact?

Canadian anthropologist, Monique Skidmore, observed the Dhammayietra was a 'new cultural ritual of remembering,' and that 'through the creation of new collective memories it will allow some Cambodians to emerge from the culture of violence created by the last 20 years of war'. Australian non-violence trainers, Robert Burrowes and George Lakey, both believe that the Dhammayietras build 'non-violent solidarity' between the participants who pass through zones of conflict and the local people who must endure the suffering caused by violence. Such solidarity, writes Yeshua Moser-Puangsuwan, of the Southeast Asia office of Non-violence International, 'further generates awareness of, and support for grassroots initiatives to halt the war. It also generates solidarity actions by grassroots activists in other parts of the world.' Moser-Puangsuwan believes that in this way the Dhammayietra can serve as a model for non-violent struggle in other parts of the world.

Awareness and solidarity may not, in and of themselves, be enough to end decades of violence, but, as one villager along the route of the walk said, 'It is the only thing that gives us hope. Every other day all we know is war.' It is in that fertile medium of hope that the seeds of an enduring peace can take root.

Working for Peace in Guatemala

Many Roles, One Goal

'To pardon doesn't mean to forget ... to pardon really means to create new attitudes, to provoke change inside people and between people, not just to palliate the violence and the hurt that remains.' (Juan Gerardi, Auxiliary Bishop, Guatemala City)

A s of early 1999, a tenuous peace has taken hold in Guatemala and an imperfect but functioning democracy is in place. Five years ago, this could only be a dream. How this Latin American country escaped from decades of war and terror is a long and complicated story. But it could not have happened without the brave involvement of people of faith - at many different levels, and in many different ways.

It can be said that the seeds of the war in Guatemala were planted centuries ago with the arrival of the Spanish. But its direct origins are in 1954, when a liberal democracy, headed by President Jacobo Arbenz, was overthrown in a military coup. Arbenz and his predecessor, Juan José Arévalo, had instituted reforms intended to extend power to the majority of poor Guatemalans.

The elite were almost exclusively 'ladinos' of Spanish origin, while over half the population was made up of indigenous people, many of whom did not speak Spanish and had little or no education. Till the late 1990s, two percent of the population controlled two-thirds of all arable land. Arbenz's proposals had included land reform.

With the coup, the reforms came to an end. Authoritarian military rule was installed and most forms of public dissent severely curtailed. This sparked another coup attempt, an unsuccessful one in the fall of 1960. After their failure, some coup leaders escaped to the east of the country and launched an insurgency. This ground on through the sixties and seventies. In the 1980s, government counterinsurgency efforts were intensified. Terror techniques were employed against both guerrillas and the civilian population. At least 440 villages were destroyed, one million Guatemalans fled their homes, and more than 100,000 people were killed or disappeared.

'Much peasant support for the guerrillas,' writes Paul Jeffrey*, a United Methodist Minister and frequent writer on Central American affairs, 'came from Catholics who found in armed struggle the only way to express the social concern they had received from the church.'

Throughout the long years of civil war, while some elements of the church establishment were satisfied with maintenance of the status quo, others campaigned for human rights and economic justice. Church workers helped the rural poor set up local co-operatives and other community organisations and began to identify and be identified with the insurgency. Along with leaders of these community organisations, they became frequent targets of the military.

Catholic priests and church workers frequently offered 'cover' to peasants and indigenous people when they took action in pursuit of justice. They supported peasants contesting illegal land seizures, farmworkers campaigning for fair pay and benefits, and refugees returning to their homes from Mexico and internal exile. Even more explicit were the actions of such faith-based groups as Witness for Peace, which placed delegations of foreigners in remote locations hoping their presence would shield local residents, including returned refugees, from violence perpetrated by the military.

Praying for peace in Guatemala

PHOTO PAUL JEFFREY

And, from the 1960s, writes Jeffrey, even when overt political activity was discouraged by the Vatican, Catholic bishops issued 'a series of pastoral letters and statements that progressively dealt more analytically with the root causes of the armed conflict.' In 1976, after a devastating earthquake, the Guatemalan Episcopal Conference (the council of bishops, the CEG) issued a letter stating that reconstruction should move beyond physical reconstruction to the restructuring of society to address social injustice.

In the 1980s, the CEG grew progressively bolder. 'Para construir la paz' ('In order to construct peace'), issued in 1984, described a vision of true democracy. In 1988, there was 'El clamor por la tierra' ('The clamor for land').
'The clamor for land,' the bishops stated, 'is without doubt the strongest, most dramatic and desperate cry heard in Guatemala.'

In 1986, the military leadership turned control of the government over to an elected civilian president, Vinicio Cerezo Arévalo. This presented the first opportunity to bring about a negotiated end to the violence. The 'Contadora Group', consisting of Colombia, Mexico, Panama, and Venezuela, issued a call for the establishment of a National Reconciliation Commission (CNR). This would include one representative each from the government, the political parties, and the Catholic bishops conference, along with one prominent citizen.

With the appointment of Rodolfo Quezada Toruño, the Catholic bishop of Zacapa, to represent the bishops, the Catholic church assumed a leading role in promoting dialogue and nurturing an environment conducive to peace and reconciliation. Meetings took place between members of the government, the military, and the unified forces of the guerrillas known as the Guatemalan National Revolutionary Unity (URNG).

But little real progress was evident.

Then Rev. Paul Wee got involved. A Lutheran pastor from the United States, Wee had been working in Guatemala since 1981 and had been deeply affected by the horrors endured by the indigenous Mayan peasants. In 1986, he began to pursue a dialogue with people on both sides of the conflict. By 1990, he had got leaders of the Guatemalan military and the URNG to attend private talks in Oslo, Norway. At the end, the parties signed the 'Oslo Accords', which stated that peace would be the product of a participatory and stable democracy.

The ice had been broken. The CNR began to act as an intermediary at meetings between the URNG and important sectors of Guatemalan society. These meetings gave the URNG a platform to advance its agenda away from the battlefield. In addition, they presented other groups not directly involved in the armed conflict with the opportunity to state their own goals and their own ideas about how peace could be achieved.

In 1991, the government, the military and the URNG agreed on an agenda for continuing negotiations which included the themes of democratisation, human rights, socio-economic issues, and agrarian issues. By 1993, they both accepted the principle that 'military interests should give way to the creation of a political environment in which social conflicts could be resolved.' They also recognised 'the importance of supporting national reconciliation through the broad participation of society in the peace process.'

International church groups -the Lutheran World Federation, the National Council of Christ Churches USA, the World Council of Churches, and the Latin American Council of Churches- stepped up their work in Guatemala. They brought the military, the URNG, the government, and powerful Guatemalan business interests together for a series of talks. This led to a 'Framework Agreement' in early 1994 which laid the ground rules for ongoing negotiations and the establishment of the 'Civil Society Assembly' (ASC). Headed by Bishop Quezada, this was a forum for less official discussions on issues related to the conflict. In early 1996, efforts to reach a final agreement were intensified. Finally, on December 29, 1996, four guerrilla leaders and four government officials signed a peace treaty in

Guatemala's National Palace before over 1,200 invited witnesses including representatives from the religious communities.

Meanwhile the Catholic bishops had not stopped issuing pastoral letters urging that true peace had to be based on social justice. In 1995, 'Urge la veradera paz!' ('True peace is urgent!'), had detailed the social, political, and economic causes of the war, proposed a framework for peace, and described the path to 'true reconciliation.'

'It's undeniable,' asserted the bishops, 'that one of the fundamental causes of the more than 34 years of armed conflict has been the unjust and inhuman marginalisation in which the majority of Guatemalans, especially the indigenous and peasants, is submerged.'

This letter laid out a vision of reconciliation deeply rooted in Christian thought, where reconciliation begins with 'the recognition of blame and the interior disposition both for the one who has offended to ask forgiveness, as well as for the person who has been offended to pardon.' A 1997 letter stated, 'Peace is constructed on justice,' and added, 'peace will be impossible if we try to cover with a veil of lies the painful economic reality of our people, the anguish accumulated in the heart of so many victims of the genocidal brutality and the accelerating impoverishment provoked by the war.'

'The church never said "join the guerrillas". But you learned about injustice and knew that fighting was the only way to change things.'

With the formidable task of reconstruction and reconciliation in the post-war period, the role of religious people has shifted. Much of the work has been directed at creating an accurate record of what really occurred during the years of war. Two important players have been the Conference of Religious Guatemala (Confregua), which has provided legal assistance to victims of oppression, and the Office of Human Rights of the Archdiocese of Guatemala (Odhag), which has worked to document past abuses and to be a watchdog monitoring continuing abuses. Both of these efforts are consistent with statements issued by the bishops declaring that true reconciliation will only occur when the truth is known, the oppressors accept responsibility for their abuses, and the victims extend forgiveness to their oppressors.

But the most important initiative of the churches in the post-war period has been the Inter-diocesan Project to Recover the Historic Memory (REMHI). This carried out an exhaustive effort to record the testimonies of all citizens who suffered from violence perpetrated by any party during the entire period of conflict.

While there was some opposition to this process by those who said that 'genuine pardon means forgetting,' Juan Gerardi, the auxiliary bishop of Guatemala City insisted that 'to pardon doesn't mean to forget ... to pardon really means to create new attitudes, to provoke change inside people and between people, not just to palliate the violence and the hurt that remains.'

In order to carry out the REMHI project, hundreds of church workers were trained in interviewing techniques, provided with tape recorders, and sent out throughout the country to interview citizens in their own languages. In quite a few cases, those responsible for violence, many of whom had suffered emotionally because of what they had done, repented their crimes. For many people, the REMHI interviews provided a first opportunity to talk about what had happened to their loved ones with any sense of security.

REMHI carried out a total of 6,000 interviews by mid-1997. The testimony it collected provided information on approximately 30,000 killings, including testimony on more than 600 massacres. This information was entered into a computerised database for analysis. The final report was called, Guatemala: Never Again!.

An optimistic title. The report was released on April 24, 1998. Two days later, its instigator, Bishop Juan Gerardi, was brutally murdered. Uruguayan writer, Eduardo Galeano, had said to the REMHI coordinators:

'Memory is bound by fear and it's very difficult to break the ligatures of fear. Some have suggested the mistaken idea that to remember is dangerous, because by remembering, history will repeat itself as a nightmare. Yet experience suggests that what happens is exactly the reverse. It is amnesia that makes history repeat itself, repeat itself as a nightmare. A good memory permits us to learn from the past, because the only reason to recover the past is so that it serve to transform our present life ... Amnesia implies impunity and impunity encourages crime, both in personal and communal terms.'

* See *Jeffrey, Paul, Recovering Memory: Guatemalan Churches and the Challenge of Peacemaking, (Life and Peace Institute: Uppsala, 1998). Much of the information presented here is based this extensive report.*

4

Women

Introduction
Women's Many Roles in Reconciliation

Women are in a unique position to effect reconciliation and to promote values which lead to the prevention of violent conflict. They are often the first to take the risks necessary to move towards reconciliation ♦ BY SHELLEY ANDERSON

Today, women in many parts of the world are already intimately involved in reconciliation processes, processes often first initiated and implemented by women collectively. This work can be very practical, such as the summer camps the IDP Women's Association of Georgia organize to bring Georgian, Abkhazian and Ossetian children together, or Rwandan women's groups building of model villages where Hutu and Tutsi live together.

It is frequently part of a more strategic attempt to improve relations and build a sustainable, long lasting peace. At the beginning of the nine-year long war in Bougainville, women planned a peace settlement between secessionists and the Papua New Guinea government, played a key mediating role in the 1994 Arawa Peace Conference, and organized a mass meeting where women from all sides of the conflict agreed to work together for peace. An island-wide programme on nonviolent conflict resolution was developed, leading to trained women walking alone into the jungle to seek out and persuade guerrillas to lay down their weapons.

In Kenya, women in the Wajir Peace Group successfully intervene in conflicts between ethnic groups, partially by keeping careful track of tensions in the market place and rumours. The Sudanese Women's Voice for Peace promotes dialogue and reconciliation among different ethnic groups and guerilla factions in Sudan, and has established underground links between women in North and South Sudan. In Northern Ireland two women, the Roman Catholic Mairead Maguire and the Protestant Betty Williams, reached across sectarian lines to establish the Peace People movement.

Women's strengths for this role in reconciliation are many. They include good listening and communication skills, the willingness and flexibility to compromise, extensive experience in practical problem solving, and caring for real people above abstract principles.

Angela King, Special Advisor on Gender Issues and Advancement of Women to the United Nations, pointed out some of these strengths in analysing the role of women in the UN Observer Mission in South Africa (UNOMSA), which she served as Chief of Mission. 'The presence of women seems to be a potent ingredient in fostering and maintaining confidence and trust among the local population. In performing their tasks with their male colleagues, women were perceived to be more compassionate, less threatening or insistent on status, less willing to opt for force or confrontation over conciliation, even it is said less egocentric, more willing to listen and learn -though not always- and to contribute to an environment of stability which fostered the peace process.' ('Success in South Africa', UN Chronicle, No. 3, 1997).

Such strengths frequently arise out of women's already existing roles, and are often practised and honed within the family and local community. In some cultures, women have traditionally had a role in resolving more public, organized conflicts. In the early 1990s, the White Scarf movement in Armenia tried to use the old custom of women breaking up fights between men by waving white scarves to intervene in the conflict between Armenia and Azerbaijan. Conflict resolution trainers often encourage the revival or spread of such indigenous traditional practices. This can be very problematic, as in many cases such practices give women no choice about their role in reconciliation, and in fact constitute serious abuses of women's human rights. One example out of many concerns Afghanistan, where the custom of 'badh' involves a murderer's family would send a female family member to join the murder victim's family, in order to prevent revenge killings which would involve whole clans.

Under-resourced
Yet another problematic issue is the fact that when such work for reconciliation and reconstruction is seen as a 'natural' extension of women's role in society, it is taken for granted. This means the work goes unrecognized and frequently under-resourced. It is stripped of its political meaning and rendered, like much of women's work, invisible. Women remain marginalized, their problems ignored, their experiences unanalysed, and their skills under-utilized.

The question that must be addressed is when does capitalizing on women's strengths in peacemaking become perpetuating traditional sex role stereotypes, stereotypes that rationalize domination and inequality, which are two roots of violent conflict. Aware of this contradiction, some activists explicitly reject traditional stereotypes of women, arguing that the values and attitudes that give rise to these stereotypes are inextricably linked to the values and attitudes that give rise to war itself.

Women in Black of Belgrade, which provided the only sustained, public opposition to the conflicts in former-Yugoslavia, has made a clear stand on this issue, with an explicit feminist analysis. 'Since the beginning of the war most members of pacifist organisations have been women. Women's participation in such organisations is taken for granted in the sense that activities such as caring for other, healing the wounded, giving shelter and consolation are considered their 'natural' role. Having realized that these feminine traits are misused in a militarist society such as ours and that even the democratic opposition and the peace movement repeat patriarchal models, we decided to make our resistance to war public - not as a part of our 'natural' role but as a conscious political choice.' (Women in Black, 1994 pamphlet 'We Are', Belgrade)

Part of their resistance to war includes building and maintaining contacts with women throughout former-Yugoslavia, such as project Open Heart, which aids Serbian women and children returning to live in Sarajevo. Women in Black's work with refugee women has inspired other initiatives, like the 'I Remember' project ('Sjecam Se' in Serbo-Croatian) which encouraged refugee women, through art and writings, to record earlier positive examples of good relations between the different ethnic groups. Such personal histories lay the ground work for reconciliation.

Other women are motivated to become involved in reconciliation work, or justify their involvement, precisely because of their traditional roles in society. One case in point would be that of the Association of the New Filipina (Kabapa) of the Coalition for Peace in the Philippines, where rural women asked for a temporary cease-fire between combatants so children could be vaccinated.

One crucial role for women in most societies is that of a mother. Women's peace activism finds expression in the many mothers movements for peace and justice. Many societies make a distinction between the private world of home and family, and the public world, where issues such as collective identity and security are defined and decided. Within this traditional framework, women are defined mainly as mothers and relegated to the private world. Their intervention into the public world as political leaders dealing with questions of war and peace is seen as undesirable, even detrimental. Yet the same traditional role which often precludes women from public political life has also provided a major entry point, and justification, into politics. There appear two primary motivating factors for these mothers movements. The first motivation is the desire to learn the fate of disappeared adult children (and in some cases, unborn grandchildren) or other family members.

The best known mothers movement is perhaps the Argentinean movement known as Las Madres, or the Mothers of the Plaza de Mayo. Las Madres helped inform the eventually successful opposition to Argentina's dictatorship, just as the January 4, 1957 silent march of mothers in Santiago, Cuba, hastened the end of the Batista regime. Las Madres has inspired similar women's movements in El Salvador and Guatemala. In Sri Lanka, women also organized publicly around their disappeared adult children. Currently in Turkey, the Saturday Mothers are bringing together Turkish from different political factions and some Kurdish parents to discover the truth about the fate of their imprisoned or disappeared children.

The second motivating factor for such mothers movements is the attempt to prevent their children from being conscripted or deployed to front lines. Such a movement flourished briefly in the former-Yugoslavia, where the Mothers for Peace organisation successfully demanded the demobilization of thousands of men. A longer lasting movement is the Committee of Russian Soldiers' Mothers (KSMR), formed during the brutal Russian war in Chechnya. The organisation CONAVIGUA (National Coordination of Guatemalan Widows) in Guatemala also continues to campaign 'against the conscription of young men, not only to protect them from socialization into army culture, but because the mothers are economically dependent on their sons.' (Sorensen, p. 11)

These mothers movements are often the first public opposition to a conflict. While the original intent may not have been to oppose the conflict, the issues they take on can lead them

Women's strengths include good listening and communication skills (LPI workshop, Somalia)

to a critical analysis of the conflict and an awareness of the need to reach out to the other side in order to end and prevent further violence. Indeed, some movements, such as KSMR, split over this deeper, more critical analysis, with some components remaining focused solely on the return of their sons, and others developing a wider agenda for social change.

In either case, the fact that they are primarily concerned about their children gives them social legitimacy, and common ground with women from different sides of the conflict. Their identity as mothers and as women sometimes, though not always, also offers some degree of protection against official repression. They commonly have a decentralized organisational structure and very democratic decision making processes, which allows great flexibility in reaching out to others in the 'enemy' community. If not co-opted or destroyed by powerful stakeholders in the conflict, these movements can develop sophisticated proposals and strategies for an end to hostilities and repairing trust and cooperation between conflictants. The KSMR, for example, has made contacts with and continues to work with Chechen and Ingush women's groups around the location and release of prisoners of wars, and the more longer term issue of reconciliation and peace between their peoples.

A common problem all these movements face, no matter how the women identify themselves or what framework they place their work within, is the crucial issue of increasing women's access to political power and political decision making. As women bring their experiences and skills in peacemaking out of the private domain and into the public political sphere, how can decision makers be encouraged to listen to women?

Some women's groups have had a certain amount of success in gaining the political will to implement their proposals for peace and reconciliation. These cases include the Northern Ireland Women's Coalition, and the Liberian Women's Initiative (whose 'Bridges to Peace' programme in Monrovia works to prevent conflicts). Others still struggle to be heard, such as the Sudanese Women's Voice for Peace, and Palestinian and Israeli women involved in the 'Engendering the Peace Process'.

To gain access to political decision making remains a major challenge, a challenge that many believe has two sides. For not only must women peacemakers gain political power, they must transform those same political structures and processes into more democratic and egalitarian forms. A few token women with political power does not automatically mean improvement overall in women's political, economic or social status. Such improvements are essential if women are to become a more effective force for peace. Such a change would lay a more solid foundation for democratic participation and respect for human rights, which are essential components in building sustainable peace.

This must be done in order to effect real change and to deal with the root causes of war. For real, long lasting reconciliation involves a shift in thinking, values and attitudes. Such a paradigm shift cannot occur without a gender perspective, just as any effective analysis of the resistance toward reconciliation processes, such as the fear of appearing weak, of losing 'face' or actual power, or the fear of appearing less than a man if female leadership towards peace is accepted, must incorporate an analysis of the power relationships between men and women.

Female violence
War, preparations for war, and the entire process of militarization, are very gendered activities. Ideas about masculinity and femininity are used to promote and sustain violence, including organized, socially-approved armed violence. Although women do contribute to war, researchers such as Elizabeth Ferris have pointed out that war is a male construct. While women can be violent, as seen in the genocide in Rwanda, female violence is far less frequent, and often in response to severe and long term violence directed against them. Female violence is seldom ritualized or institutionalized.

Women have many roles in reconciliation. The functions women have in reconciliation processes are complex, reflecting the multiple roles women have in society. Like women's lives, such functions must be viewed holistically. Women are peace educators inside the family, in schools, in women's and mixed organisations, and elsewhere. Their networks and knowledge of local affairs make them effective early warning monitors, alert for rumours, increasing tensions, a sudden influx of weapons and others sign of potential conflict. Their sometimes extensive kinship links, social expectations and training can make women highly effective mediators. Their status as outsiders, the perception that they are not primary stakeholders in conflict, also reveal a role as negotiators and originators of new approaches to peace.

For people interested in reconciliation, the challenge is to develop an integrated gender approach. A complete understanding of the root cases of violence, and hence the corresponding attempt to build a culture or cultures of peace, can never be complete without an analysis of the politics of gender, or the power relationship between men and women. 'Notions of "masculinity" are a powerful tool in this process of making men into soldiers,' wrote researcher Jacklyn Cock about the apartheid-conflict in South Africa. 'There is a connection between masculinity and militarism; the traditional notion of masculinity resonates with militarist ideas. The army is an institutional sphere for the cultivation of masculinity; war provides the social space for its validation.' (Cock, p. 58)

Such notions of masculinity and femininity are also reflected in the ways governments and politics are conceptualized and structured, and indeed permeate the attitudes of entire cultures so much so that male aggression is sometimes seen as natural and inevitable.

Armed conflict does not erupt out of a vacuum. Perhaps the most common form of physical violence is that of violence against girls and women. It is estimated that some 40-60 percent of women and girls in any given culture will experience rape, domestic abuse and/or incest at least once in their lives. The links between this 'private' violence and the 'public' violence of armed conflict must be examined. The attitudes and values that give rise to the former lay the ground work for the latter. Both are rooted in mind sets where domination, control and beliefs in certain group's superiority and others' inferiority are central. A mind set that permits and justifies the use of physical or psychological force by a 'superior' against an 'inferior' cannot be safely relegated to one corner of life, such as the home, or certain personal relationships. It will become a part of public life. It is time, as UNESCO's Culture of Peace Programme notes, that the traditional 'feminine' values of tolerance, listening and openness to dialogue, become accepted as values for both women and men. Such a paradigm shift will pave the way for lasting reconciliation.

Shelley Anderson is coordinator of the International Fellowship of Reconciliation's Women Peacemakers Program.

SELECTED BIBLIOGRAPHY
From the IFOR Women Peacemakers Program (WPP)
- The newsletter of the IFOR Women Peacemakers Program 'Cross the Lines' appears three times a year in English, French and Spanish.
- An annual May 24 International Women's Day for Peace and Disarmament pack, with profiles of women's peace groups, action suggestions and an international directory.
- Reports and videos of the WPP European regional consultation and the Asia consultation for women in conflict situations.

All Her Paths are Peace - Women Pioneers in Peacemaking, Michael Henderson, Kumarian Press, 1994
Arms to Fight-Arms to Protect - Women Speak Out About Conflict, Olivia Bennett, Jo Bexley, Kitty Warnock (eds.). Panos Publications Ltd, London, 1995
Common Grounds - Violence Against Women in War and Armed Conflict Situations, Indai Lourdes Sajor (ed.). Asia Center for Women's Human Rights, Philippines, 1998
Freedom from Violence - Women's Strategies from Around the World, Margaret Schuler (ed.). UNIFEM, New York, 1992

Girls and Warzones - Troubling Questions, Carolyn Nordstrom. Life and Peace Institute, Sweden, 1997

Mass Rape - The War Against Women in Bosnia-Herzegovina, Alexandra Stiglmayer (ed.). University of Nebraska Press, 1994

Mothers of the Revolution - The War Experiences of Thirty Zimbabwean Women, Irene Staunton (ed.). Baobab Books, Zimbabwe; Indiana University Press, U.S., and James Currey Ltd., London, 1990

School for Rape - The Burmese Military and Sexual Violence, Betsy Apple. Earthrights International, Thailand/USA, 1998

We Have to Sit Down - Women, war and peace in Southern Sudan, Mirjam Pol. Pax Christi Netherlands, 1998

What Women Do in Wartime - Gender and Conflict in Africa, Meredeth Turshen and Clotilde Twagiramariya (eds.). Zed Books Ltd, London/New York, 1998

Women in Black - Women for Peace. Belgrade, 1994

Women and Post-Conflict Reconstruction - Issues and Sources, Birgitte Sorensen. UNRISD, 1998

Women and War, Jeanne Vickers. Zed Books Ltd., London/New Jersey, 1993

Women and War in South Africa, Jacklyn Cock. Open Letters, London, 1992

Women, War and Peace - An issue paper, Elizabeth Ferris. Life and Peace Institute, Uppsala, 1992

IFOR's Women Peacemakers Program
'War is a Very Gendered Activity'

'Saying you are sorry is the beginning of justice, the beginning of the healing process. So many grievances have never been addressed. Immediately the atmosphere changes when someone says: I am sorry. I did not know that this hurt you.'

Maria Hadjipavlou-Trigeorgis, a Greek Cypriot, was speaking of her work to bridge the divide between the Greek and Turkish Cypriot communities on Cyprus. Together with Turkish Cypriot activists like Sevgul Uludag, several thousand Cypriots have been trained in conflict resolution skills during the past few years. 'We try in our workshops to begin with the development of empathy. You have a right to your story and I won't judge you. That is a very powerful experience for participants,' said Uludag. On an island where UN peacekeeping forces, stationed for the last 16 years, have been unable to stop periodic violence, such empathy is sorely needed.

Apology as a first step towards reconciliation was recognized, too, by Vesna Terselic of the Anti-War Campaign Croatia. 'Saying you are sorry is recovering a sense of dignity, of respect,' she said. 'When I think of presenting a concept like justice publicly, maybe using the idea of dignity is important. Nationalists teach people that so-and-so hasn't allowed us our dignity. What is at stake is not national identity, but dignity. The word peace is useless in my country, but people still react and listen when we use words like dignity, respect.'

The women were speaking at the first IFOR Women Peacemakers Program's consultation for women in conflict situations. The European consultation was the first in a series of three regional consultations, which will culminate in the year 2001 with a fourth intercontinental consultation. The programme receives core funding from the Dutch Ministry of Foreign Affairs.

Though some IFOR (the International Fellowship of Reconciliation) branches and groups were already working for women, the Women Peacemakers Program is IFOR's first systematic attempt to increase the nonviolent empowerment of women. Spurred on by the 1995 UN Fourth World Conference on Women and the Beijing Platform for Action's very concrete recommendations regarding women in conflict situations, the Women Peacemakers Program is bringing an awareness of gender into all of IFOR's work. Several branches, including the Fellowship of Reconciliation in Zimbabwe, have now established their own Women Peacemakers Programs.

The Women Peacemakers Program is an experiment in developing and integrating a gender perspective into peace and reconciliation work. The programme recognizes that women play multiple roles in conflict -as victims, occasionally as perpetrators- and most of all as leaders

The Asia Consultation

'We've struggled for 10 years for democracy,' said a representative from the Burmese Women's Union. 'The movement is at a deadlock. Participating in this consultation has given me ideas about possible ways forward.' She was speaking at the end evaluation of the WPP's Asia consultation, held in India in late 1998. Almost half of the participants in this consultation were refugees or working in exile. They came from Bangladesh, Bhutan, Burma, Cambodia, Kashmir, Nagaland, Nepal, South Korea, Sri Lanka and Tibet.

The participants worked in a variety of organisations. The Tamil and the Sinhalese participants worked with the Family Rehabilitation Center, counselling torture victims and their families. The Cambodians had joined the newly formed Forum for Peace Through Love and Compassion, in order to spread the principles of peaceful conflict resolution. 'Everything is politicized in Cambodia,' said one participant. 'It is dangerous to speak of peace, because different political parties see peace as threatening. But we link peace with traditional Buddhist values, which everyone respecs.' One special feature of the Asia consultation was the meal and cultural night organized for participants by members of the Tibetan exile community in Kochi.

with innovative ideas about peace-building. The challenge became how IFOR could systematically support and encourage women in such work; how women's perspectives and experiences of war, of reconstruction and reconciliation, could be mobilized and utilized; how women's solutions and ideas could be disseminated to a wider audience.

The WPP consultations offer 'enemy' women the chance for face-to-face dialogue. The European regional consultation took place in early 1998 in Budapest, Hungary, and brought together women from Armenia, Azerbaijan, Croatia, Cyprus, Ingushetia, Israel, Northern Ireland, Palestine and Serbia. Activists invited from Abkhazia, Bosnia, Kosovo, and North Ossetia were unable to attend because of being denied visas, or, in one case, because of shooting at the airport, illustrating some of the difficulties that face women working in conflict situations.

'The idea had been to get together women who had substantial experience, both of conflict and of working with it; women who would have a great deal to teach each other and to learn from each other; women who would value support; women who would also be able to pass on the benefits of this opportunity to a wider network of women,' said co-facilitator and former IFOR President Diana Francis. In order to pass on lessons learned from the consultation, at least one facilitator of the next regional consultation also participates.

The programme included presentations on conflict resolution, dialogue, justice and power issues, and the model of social analysis developed by IFOR Honorary Presidents Jean and Hildegard Goss-Mayr. The difficult - but essential to reconciliation - issues of identity, responsibility and guilt, were tackled by participants in small group work. They discussed organisational aims, strengths, weaknesses and needs, with funding being identified as a major need by most participants. There was a fundraising workshop and hands-on training in using video equipment. During the last sessions, participants worked in small groups, then came back into the larger group to reflect on what would be useful to initiate in the next few months in their organisations, and what steps could be taken to make these changes. In presentations of their small group analysis, many women identified the need to provide civic education for women, and to increase women's influence in political decision making.

'It is easy to speak with the women here. They understand what you are saying. We need solidarity, and I feel that here from these women,' said Leila Yunosova, who worked with the Azeri Ministry of Defence in hostage negotiations during the war between Armenia and Azerbaijan. Participants found this sense of trust and of being understood empowering, especially as many shared an experience of being considered traitors because of their work for peace. The consultation helped to break down a sense of isolation. This feeling, compounded by a sense of helplessness, blocks many from working for peace. 'We work so hard and long, only to have the government destroy all our work in a day,' said Alexandra Zikic of the Center for Nonviolent Conflict Resolution in Serbia. 'The kind of things we do never get press coverage, so we always feel we are failing,' said Yaala Cohen of the Israeli women's group Bat Shalom. 'We've learned to judge ourselves by the media.'

'Nationalists teach people that so-and-so hasn't allowed us our dignity. What is at stake is not national identity, but dignity. The word peace is useless in my country, but people still react and listen when we use words like dignity, respect.'

Another common experience was an increase in gender violence during conflict, especially domestic violence. 'Men bring home this macho, gun culture,' said Orla Moloney of Northern Ireland. Christine Acheson, from Northern Ireland's Protestant community, agreed. She also pointed out: 'Women have learned a great deal about domestic violence, and recovery from it, which can be used in the wider context.'

Acheson also pointed out the differences between more recent 'crisis' conflicts, such as those in the Caucasus region, and conflicts that may have a lower level of casualties but that have continued for generations, such as the Northern Ireland conflict. Gulnara Shaninian of Armenia's Democracy Union found the comparison important. 'My generation had personal relationships with Azeris, lived side by side as neighbours, had good friendships. This generation only knows enemy images and war. This will make it harder to build peace for the future,' she said. Both Yunosova, and Fatima Yandieva of Ingushetia, were very interested in learning from the Northern Irish participants about the effects of long-term conflict on children.

Conflicts have an impact on women and girls in very specific ways, ways which have too often been ignored or unrecognized: as primary caretakers of children and the elderly, as victims of war rape, as refugees, increasingly as armed combatants themselves. War is a very gendered activity, and activists dedicated to eliminating war must incorporate a gender perspective in their work.

Lively discussions at a Life and Peace workshop in Somalia Photo Susanne Thurfjell

The Women Peacemakers Program is an experiment in developing a gender perspective into peace work. The WPP recognizes that women play multiple roles in conflict -as victims, occasionally as perpetrators- and most of all as leaders with innovative ideas about peace-building. Incorporating a gender perspective -looking at the power relationships between men and women, and at how women and men may be affected differently by the same event- raises some very problematic issues. When should traditional sex role stereotyping or unequal power relationships be confronted, and when accepted? Can the definition of peace work be expanded to include development issues, such as income generation? During the last decade development agencies -and their funders- have realized the close links between development and peace, and the key role women play in both. Without peace, development is impossible. Without women, neither sustainable peace nor development can take place. Organizing an income generating project that brings women from different communities together can have many benefits, but does not fit in with a traditional peace or reconciliation framework.

> '*Women have learned a great deal about domestic violence, and recovery from it, which can be used in the wider context.*'

Another problematic issue is the definition of peace itself. What is the exact difference between 'peace time' and 'war time' to a woman being beaten by her male partner or a girl

WPP's objectives

1. Prevention of violence. This is being met through the Cross the Lines component: the regional consultations of women.
2. Education and training in active nonviolence. Such training helps grassroots women's organisations develop skills in nonviolent conflict resolution, mediation, and leadership. The first such training took place in the Chittagong Hill Tracts with 30 tribal women; other training are scheduled in Uganda, Nigeria, Chad and a special training for young women in Nepal.
3. Documentation and analysis of women's peace initiatives. This involves collecting and making available existing materials that explain the links between militarism as an obstacle to development and women's role in reconstructing societies broken by conflict, in building peace and reconciliation, and in strengthening civil society. Women's strategies and experiences are documented through videos and various publication. An annual May 24 International Women's Day for Peace and Disarmament action packet, produced in cooperation with the International Peace Bureau, has been published with networking information, profiles on women's peace groups, suggestions for actions, and contact addresses. In addition, the WPP publishes the newsletter 'Cross the Lines' (in French, Spanish and English) three times a year, with news of women's peace initiatives and discussions on strategies.
4. Support for the building of self-reliant and sustainable women's groups. Requests for help, from peace researchers, or groups who want to get on email or submit a grant proposal, are linked by the WPP with organisations that can provide technical and financial support.

being sold into prostitution? According to a study commissioned by the World Health Organization, some 40 to 60 percent of women and girls in any given culture will experience rape, domestic abuse and/or incest. How does this 'private' violence humanity differ from the 'public' violence of armed conflict?

Yet another issue is the crucial question of increasing women's access to political power and political decision making. Women are not just victims. Groups like the Liberian Women's Initiative and Sudanese Women's Voice for Peace; the experiences of female United Nations election monitors in South Africa; the role of church women in ending Bougainville's brutal war. These cases and more show that women are leaders in peace and reconciliation efforts. Yet without access to political decision making, women's solutions go ignored.

The challenge for women peacemakers is both to gain political power and to transform political structures and processes into more democratic and egalitarian forms.

The Women Peacemakers Program grapples with all these issues. While this four-year programme has only finished its first year, we have discovered that women's approaches to peace are myriad. Women see the links between human rights education and the need to build more democratic governments, especially the need to educate women about our human rights; the connection between violence in private life and public acceptance of war; and the need to build a sound economic base for sustainable peace. Most of all the Women Peacemakers Program has seen how, with support in the form of training, solidarity actions, and finances, women can lead the way to peace.

This article has been written by Shelley Anderson, Program Officer for the IFOR Women Peacemakers Program.

Women Take the Peace Lead in Pastoral Kenya
Back to the Future

In the early 1990s, a group of women were having a good time at a wedding in Wajir district, a remote and violent area in Kenya. 'We looked around,' recalls Fatuma Sheikh Abdulkadir, 'and realised that a cross-section of all the clans had attended the wedding and we were feeling good. But outside this small compound, the happiness and the mixing was not there. So we discussed at length - what is happening with our society?'

I n the remote regions of Africa over which they roam, the weather sets the pattern of the nomadic pastoralists' movement: rainfall dictates the pace of life. Movement is constant. Pasture must be sought.

Past conflicts have left a legacy of suspicion. The blocking of access to an animal water pan, or a problem between market vendors, can be like a match applied to dry leaves. Political interference by outsiders doesn't help.

In Wajir, the second largest district in Kenya, rainfall averages just 200 mm per year. Some 275,000 people occupy 56,600 square kilometres of largely barren landscape bordering Ethiopia and Somalia. This is a recipe for conflict. So too is the composition of the population. Three major clans - Ogaden, Ajuran and Degodia - and several smaller clans, battle to make a living. Eighty percent of them have a source of livelihood from herding camels, sheep and goats.

In 1992, there was yet another drought. Most of pastoralist families had little or no access to essential services. Childhood immunisation was 23 percent compared to 71 nationally in Kenya. There was inadequate healthcare. Low livestock immunisation. Seventy percent of cattle and thirty percent of camels were lost.

Violence became the order of the day. Deaths followed incidents between the Ogaden and Degodia clans over alleged land encroachment and violation of political space. In one, near Lagbogol, over 20 people lost their lives. Homes were destroyed and livestock taken. Members of the security forces were killed. Refugees and weapons were shifted across the border from conflict-ridden Ethiopia and Somalia. Thieves went on the rampage. There were hijackings, looting and arson, rape, murder.

But there were still normal things. Like weddings.

It was after a wedding that the Wajir Peace Group was born. One thing led to another.

Dekha Ibrahim Abdi

Discussions began, first at the workplace and in the homes of other women and men.

The violence continued. At Wagalla, a small trading centre outside Wajir town, two herders from the Degodia clan were killed. Women from that clan refused to sell or buy from women of the Ajuran clan, and would not allow them entry to the market. More fighting. More injury. More police in action. Heightened tension.

These incidents provided a major test for the nascent peace group.

When they encountered more police indifference, the women went to see the District Commissioner. They asked for his co-operation. The District Commissioner approved their plan to intervene and asked for feedback as to the outcome. Meetings were held with professional women from all the clans. They were informed about the problems and of the group's intention to bring the key women leaders together.

Contact was made with other women from different strata. Sixty people attended one of the meetings arising out of this overture. After a freeflowing discussion, they agreed to form a Joint Committee of the clans. This group would act as a kind of vigilante body, defusing tension and reporting incidents to the police.

'The formation of the committee helped a lot to put off the fire before it spread far,' says Dekha Ibrahim Abdi, one of the founders of the Peace Group.

In essence, the Wajir peace initiative has taken the region back to the future, by reviving basic methods of conflict resolution used in pre-colonial times to encourage the equitable sharing of the region's limited resources. Under the old Somali clan system, what appears on the surface to be a recipe for problems over access to land and water was regulated in a basic way, even during times of drought.

Within five years, the Peace Group has touched almost everyone in this remote region; its basic approach - community involvement, and the use of dialogue as a counterpoint to conflict. Participation was eventually widened to include young men working with NGOs, government departments and schoolboys. Elders were approached. Seventy of them attended a meeting on August 13, 1993. They agreed to the setting up of a standing committee of

Breakdown of the Pastoral System

During British colonial rule, and continuing into Kenyan independence, the pastoral lifestyle of Wajir's people -and the traditional system underpinning it- were undermined by setting of administrative boundaries leading to fresh conflict over access to natural and political resources. In the two world wars of this century, Somalis were pitted against Somalis, fighting on the sides of warring European powers. More bitterness and artificial rivalries were instilled. An attempt to secede from Kenya led to the Shifta War (1963-69). Negative feelings against the people of the Northeast were reinforced in 'down country' Kenya, and remain strong even today. Clan boundary disputes, inter-clan conflicts, and violence based on electoral politics wracked Wajir district during the post-independence period. A state of emergency was kept in place until 1992. The authorities used powers of arbitrary arrest to keep the Somalis in check. All ethnic Somalis were required to have special ID cards. Neighbourhood wars (Ethiopia-Somalia) and internal conflicts in the two countries spilled over into the region. Refugees, weapons and fighters realigned clan alliances and caused further instability.

fourty, with ten elders from each of the three major clans, and ten from minority groups. The decision of the fourty to agree to a peacemaking role marked a new stage for the initiative.

A further effort was made to deepen the peace and reconciliation process with the convening of talks between the Christian and Muslim religions. It was about that time that Unicef's compound in Wajir was attacked. The upshot: Wajir was declared an unsafe zone by the international community. Several NGOs moved out, though basic humanitarian services were maintained after intensive lobbying efforts by the women's peace group.

In the meantime, at the urging of Member of Parliament, Ahmed Khalif, all the Wajir elders who had joined the Wajir Peace Group attended a major conference in Wajir town. They agreed to form a 28-member committee comprising representatives of various clans. A declaration was issued, taking stock of the increasing intensity of inter clan fighting. Condemnation was made of the murder of the Unicef pilot and serious injury to a staff member. It was acknowledged that banditry and clan clashes posed a danger to the whole district.

Twenty-five leaders from the major clans and five from two other clans met to deliberate on the cause of the continuing internecine strife. A cessation was urged to the inter-clan fighting and stock theft. Agreement on a cease-fire, to take effect on September 29, 1993, was among a 14-point resolution passed by what has become known as the Al Fatah conference.

Thereafter, the peace initiative took on a brisk momentum. Infrastructure support was provided with help from the donor community. Public meetings and discussions involved a full range of community leaders. A new, more consultative atmosphere prevailed. Workshops delved into the roots of conflict, and how it related to the actual economic conditions facing the people of the region.

Referees' Rapid Response - An Example

In July 1998, while a continent away, in France, nations battled towards the final stages of the football World Cup in France, the north-eastern region of Kenya was wrapped in tension of a different kind. A fragile peace, painstakingly forged and monitored, was in danger of breaking down.

Quickly, the Wajir Peace and Development Committee sprang into action. Two clans were involved in the conflict that erupted on July 6 - Degodia Fai and Murrulle clan. The Committee activated its equivalent of a football referee to blow the whistle on the two groups and find a middle-ground. The Rapid Response Team comprised three elders, two women and two government representatives. Travelling 90 miles to the village where the dispute had developed over access to an animal water pan, they sat down, prayed and listened.

Those blocking access of the animals to the water - the Fai clan - said there was no 'clan problem', as such; the camels of the complainants were sick and could not be allowed access to a common animal pan. After talking to members of the nomadic family whose herd had been at the centre of the dispute, the team asked one of its members - a trained veterinarian - to investigate the condition of the camels. They were found to be healthy. A second opinion was sought from the secretary of the Wajir Peace and Development Committee, Mrs Nuria Abdullahi, also a qualified vet. She also found no signs of surra, the disease mentioned.

When that failed to satisfy the Fai clan, resolution strategies were activated. Each group was invited to sit separately, discuss the problem, and to find a solution. Out of this exercise came an initiative from the Murrulle family members themselves - that of moving their 'sick' animals out of the area within four days, with provision for family members to receive water during the period they were in-transit, and that they be protected from physical attacks as they depart.

This agreed, the Rapid Response Team members also suggested that, in the interest of future peace, a member of the minority Murrulle clan be added to the Water and Peace committee, thus making them feel part and parcel of the area, Ber Janai. Then details of the measures to resolve the conflict, and avoid the community scoring an own goal, were announced to the public.

By 1994, the atmosphere had healed sufficiently for discussions to move to a new stage. To ensure the peace was not a temporary affair, the Wajir Peace and Development Committee was established. It comprised Members of Parliament, religious leaders, businessmen, NGO workers, the security committee, women and clan elders. Its key instrument is the Rapid Response Team, made up of community leaders - elders, religious leaders, and security officers.

Charged with moving into any part of the district to diffuse tension and mediate in case of conflict or violence, the Rapid Response Team's fire-fighting role buttresses measures taken to go beyond just keeping the peace. In other words, economic and education deprivation are seen as part of the underlying reason for conflict.

Extensive research into ways of achieving permanent peace in the district led to another initiative. When elections approached, the peace group organised discussions involving elders, chiefs, parliamentarians and candidates, so as to reduce the tension normally associated with campaigning. Attention was paid to youth training schemes. Workshops were held. There were peace festivals. Peace Days. Preventive measures were instituted. At the core of the group's activities was an effort to improve the underlying causes of conflict, which were mainly economic, having to do with the sharing of resources.

Thus, by 1996, what had begun as an attempt to give form to throwaway comments, made at a wedding, had evolved to a new stage. Analysis of drought monitoring data concluded that the next one would be particularly severe in Wajir South and East. By September 1996, food was distributed to the affected area.

As Dekha puts it: 'Drought is one of the major contributors to poverty, and poverty is also one of the contributors to the escalation of conflict to violence. Anticipating the drought and early intervention has saved lives and also livelihood of the people affected.'

This story has largely been based on an article by Dekha Ibrahim Abdi: 'Citizen's Peace - Peacebuilding in Wajir, North Eastern Kenya'.

5

Media

Introduction

Better media, less conflict

Many advocates of conflict prevention are convinced that the media can play a critical role in defusing tensions and forging peace. But most media representatives are opposed to becoming actors in the developments they have to cover. Nevertheless, there are opportunities for them to be won over to the cause of conflict prevention ♦
By Hans van de Veen

Some ten years ago the Centre for Conflict Resolution and the Media Peace Centre in South Africa started the Mediation Project for Journalists, a series of workshops imparting conflict resolution skills to those in the journalistic trade. At first, one of the founders, Melissa Baumann remembers in a special issue of the Track Two magazine, 'many of the journalists we invited to attend declined, totally unconvinced that learning about managing conflict had anything to do with their profession. Their job was to "report the truth, the facts", they said. It wasn't the business of journalists to intervene.' This response was 'highly ironic', says Baumann given that at that time the media in South Africa was engaged in a general propaganda war, with different media representing different sides.

Now, in the late 1990s, the theory and practice surrounding the issue of 'media and conflict' has taken on a life of its own. 'The cynics persist, of course, in great number', Baumann says: there are still 'people working in the media who claim they must stay "objective" at all costs and that any sort of advocacy compromises the standards of journalism.' However, a growing number of professionals argue that the 'media and conflict' debate is not about taking sides in reporting conflict -except the side of peace and peace-building- but about journalists already being a third party in any conflict they are covering. Consequently, the argument that there is a moral imperative to use that access constructively is steadily gaining ground.

What role can the media play in helping prevent conflicts from escalating? Potentially a big one, agree both conflict mediators and journalists, but they disagree on how. Positive journalism is what we need, argues John Marks, president of the Washington-based NGO, Search for Common Ground.* 'Asking questions like: Where do you agree? Instead of focusing only on the disagreements.' Most journalists react to statements like these by pointing to the importance of responsible coverage of conflict situations: 'That's a big contribution already.' And journalists from the poorer parts of the world point to the fact that a lack of money and time prevents them from covering conflicts at all. 'Talking about media and conflict prevention is a luxury.'

Conflict sells; cooperation, or the process of resolving conflict, does not. It could be argued that, because of this assumption, the media tend to dramatise conflicts (either openly or tacitly) by focusing on irreconcilable differences between the parties, extreme positions and inflammatory statements, violent or threatening acts and win-or-lose outcomes. Furthermore, most news media ordinarily only turn their attention to conflicts at points of high public interest, such as dramatic escalation phases, unusually violent incidents, peace treaties, or other events considered especially newsworthy.

John Marks from the Search for Common Ground is one of a growing number of conflict mediators and humanitarians trying to convince journalists that, in situations of conflict, they can play an important role in helping to stop the escalation. The Australian NGO Conflict Resolution Network (CRN) even developed a 'Toolkit' consisting of practical suggestions for journalists on how to bring parties in a conflict closer to one another. 'Avoid simplistic representations of baddies and goodies', is one of the recommendations. 'Report areas of agreement as well as disagreement. This encourages the problem-solving process to continue', is another.

But most (Western) journalists are sceptical about this. Should they, for the sake of conflict resolution, downplay conflict, avert their eyes from the ugly facts of hatred and violence, or 'cry peace when there is no peace'? 'Of course not,' writes Joann Byrd, the Washington Post's ombudsman, 'but they should realize that conflict is not the whole story.' In covering conflict stories, Byrd suggests, journalists should add an 'S' for Solutions and a 'C' for Common Ground to the traditional 'five W's' formula (Who, What, When, Where, Why). She urges reporters to go beyond describing a conflict merely in terms of poles of opposition.

Courage
According to Mira Oklobzija, programme advisor at Press Now, a small NGO which supports independent media in Bosnia, good journalists already do these kind of things. She feels the negative image painted of the average journalist and editor is too much of a generalisation and singles out for special praise the role of independent, local journalists in conflict situations. 'It requires an enormous amount of courage and knowledge to keep one's independence in a situation like that,' she says. In a climate where the official press is frequently the mouthpiece of those in power, it's certainly not easy for a journalist to articulate critical opinions. Oklobzija also praises foreign correspondents who go looking for the news in conflict areas. Their information often plays a decisive role in preventing any further escalation of a conflict. But Oklobzija is very critical about editors who write on conflicts from behind their desks, using only the news files of the leading press agencies. 'At least,' she says, 'they should look for more, independent sources, especially from inside the country.'

'Editors seem to work from the premise that conflict is interesting and agreement is boring', Marks laments. 'A conflictual approach may attract listeners and sell newspapers, but it definitely has a negative impact on society as a whole.' To offer an alternative, ten years ago Marks started Common Ground Productions, with the aim of stimulating media productions which emphasise peaceful resolution of conflict, collaborative problem-solving and identification of common ground. He defines the central idea behind the initiative in the following terms: 'Conflict prevention is about heads, conflict is about hearts. So, with your activities you have to reach the hearts of people.'

'How do you reach huge numbers of people in conflict areas?' asks Marks rhetorically. Through the media, clearly. That's why his organisation supports projects for the printed media in Macedonia and the Middle East and has produced TV series in Russia, Macedonia, South Africa and Sri Lanka. The programmes concentrate on the most difficult issues in a society and are broadcast nation-wide. In Africa - where radio is the only medium that reaches a mass audience - Search tries to counteract the so-called hate-radio, the most horrendous example of which is Rwanda's Radio Mille Collines, which urged the country on to genocide. In Burundi, Search for Common Ground created Studio Ijambo, a production facility where a team of Hutu and Tutsi journalists produce programmes in the several languages of the country (see case-study).

Another example of the way NGOs can themselves step into the shoes of the media and produce their own television or radio programmes -or commission journalists or documentary-makers to do so- comes from the organisation Internews. In cooperation with the International Crisis Group and Human Rights Watch, Internews created mobile television crews equipped with satellite communications systems that can be deployed in volatile regions such as Kosovo or the Sudan. The crews provide coverage of 'pre-conflict' situations at below-market cost to news agencies around the world. 'We take the financial burden of covering pre-conflict situations off the broadcasters and agencies', Internews explains, 'because the economics of international news agencies do not support the coverage of impending conflict. It is simply too expensive.' (see case-study)

The Centre for Conflict Resolution in South Africa, Internews and Search for Common Ground are among a growing number of NGOs and mediators which are trying to convince journalists, in the western world and beyond, that it is not only conflict that can be sold to their reading, listening and viewing audiences, but that conflict resolution can be an equally marketable concept. Successful conflict resolution, they claim, can get good ratings.

While these organisations had great success in developing and broadcasting conflict prevention programming on local media within zones of conflict, they have however rarely been able to get that programming to viewers in Western Europe and the US. 'We see a real lack of information in the West about conflicts that have not yet turned violent but could in the near future', says Paul Greenberg, Internews' director of International Co-productions. 'We also see the international media regularly ignoring conflicts that have supposedly 'ended' but in fact have continued to fester because international assistance was too rapidly diverted. The constructive role that the international media could play in raising public awareness of impending-conflict and post-conflict situations is too often subverted by the economics of the media business. The blood and guts of an actual conflict bring rating points and profit whereas programming that focuses on preventing conflict is often too abstract to attract public attention.' NGOs, private foundations and media professionals, have to look for innovative projects that can begin to change the economics of electronic media in the West, says Greenberg.

Peace documentaries

The European Centre for Conflict Prevention is planning to enhance its media-activities on peace building. Information about existing documentaries dealing with conflict prevention/transformation and peace building will be collected, while at the same time the production of this kind of documentary will be stimulated world wide.

Conflict prevention and transformation have an enormous potential but much more support from all kinds of actors is needed to realise this potential, the European Centre feels. One of the ways to stimulate broader support for this approach is through the mass media. Many of the examples given in the present publication could be the topic of video documentaries, while many other, potentially inspiring stories, haven't been told at all. Information from readers about these kind of examples is widely appreciated, as well as information on existing documentaries or broadcast-reports in the field of conflict prevention, community- or peace-building and reconciliation.

For more information contact the European Centre for Conflict Prevention, PO Box 14069, 3508SC Utrecht, The Netherlands, Fax +31 (30) 253 7529, email euconflict@euconflict.org

Working with local media in areas of conflict, either through cooperation with existing media organisations or by setting up new media organisations with local journalists, has so far been the core business of 'preventive journalism'. In a majority of cases, this approach amounts to western organisations working with non-western counterparts, usually in poorer countries. It is considered as counter-acting the so-called CNN-effect, where governments feel compelled by television-generated public opinion to intervene in overseas conflicts, often creating more problems than opportunities.

NGOs agree that training local media, tailored to local needs, is one of the most valuable instruments to keep media organisations from contributing to the escalation of a conflict. There is also a strong case for recruiting and training local trainers who can, in the long-term, continue to build local media capacity adapted to the specific conditions. Another prerequisite for successful media projects is that they should be planned as long-term enterprises, which means that donors also have to remain financially committed for longer periods of time.

'It's nice to have training,' says a journalist working for Cameroon television, 'but we prefer to have the money to pay for the bus fares so we can reach the conflict area.' In her opinion, the lack of money and time to investigate the issues at stake are the main obstacles preventing African journalists from properly doing their job. 'It is this situation which makes journalists always vulnerable to the bribery of the government.'

Special, sophisticated programming increases the potential of generating constructive movements in a divided society. But in many cases, conflict prevention is already enhanced once a decent media organisation is established which follows the simple rules of good journalism. In areas where access to information is limited, providing any accurate, balanced

A Call for Stories about Peacemakers

Adventure Film Productions and the Peace History Society are pleased to announce the making of The Wounded Dove, a ten-hour documentary focusing on the great peacemakers of the 20th century. The ten episodes will be aired on various television networks worldwide, beginning January 2000.

We are looking for stories about individuals who performed dramatic acts of heroism in the interest of peace from 1900 to the present. Their stories will be presented in The Wounded Dove, the Quest for Peace in the Twentieth Century.

Adventure Film Productions
181 Bingham Ave.
Toronto M4E 3R2
Canada
Tel and Fax +1 (416) 694 9881
Email NeilLundy@compuserve.com

information already constitutes a huge step towards promoting peace. The better the media, the less the chance of an outbreak of violent conflict.

Opportunities for the courtship between media and organisations working for conflict prevention to turn into a stable relationship would undoubtedly improve if the rapprochement could be classified under the neutral motto of 'the quest for professional journalism' instead of ideals that are considered by media representatives to be beyond their scope.

For the time being the rapprochement is an experiment for both journalists and peacemakers. People active in this domain believe that evaluation of the current programmes should give directions as to what types of linkage between media and conflict prevention are best. This poses another challenge to the adherents of preventive action. Finding standards for impact assessment is difficult. Evaluating the preventive value of media may be nothing less than trying to measure the unmeasurable.

* This quote and other unrelated ones in this article are taken from the publication 'From Early Warning to Early Action' - A report on the European Conference on Conflict Prevention, February 27-28, 1997, Amsterdam, the Netherlands.

SELECTED BIBLIOGRAPHY

African Conflict and the Media, Abiodun Onadipe and David Lord. Discussion paper. Conciliation Resources, UK.

Journalism and Conflict Resolution, Johannes Botes. In: Media Development 4/1996.

Frameworks for Interpreting Conflict - A Handbook for Journalists. George Mason University, USA.

The Media, Humanitarian Crisis and Policy-making - A Report of an International Meeting. World Peace Foundation, Cambridge Massachusetts. 1995.

Late-breaking Foreign Policy - The News Media's Influence on Peace Operations, W. P. Strobel. Washington, D.C. US Institute of Peace Press, 1997.

Media - Peace-Building Through the Media, Part 3, G. Adam. Crosslines Global Report, December 30, 1997.

Spiral of Cynicism - The Press and the Public Good, J.N. Cappella. Oxford University Press, 1997.

The Media at War - Communication and Conflict in the 20th Century, S.L. Carruthers. London, 1998.

Understanding Global News, J. van Ginneken. London, 1997.

Professionalism in War Reporting - A Correspondent's View, T. Gjelten. Washington, DC: Carnegie Commission on Preventing Deadly Conflict. 1998.

Media Coverage - Help or Hindrance in Conflict Prevention, N. Gowing. Washington, D.C., Carnegie Commission on Preventing Deadly Conflict, 1997.

The Warrior's Honor - Ethnic War and the Modern Conscience, M. Ignatieff. New York, 1998.

The Media and the Military, P. Young and P. Jesser. London, 1997.

Media and Conflict. Special issue of the magazine Track Two, a publication of the Centre for Conflict Resolution and the Media Peace Centre, Rondebosch, South Africa. December 1998.

Internews Uses Media to Reduce Conflict

Beyond Talking Heads

Who can really tell the world about war? Politicians? Analysts? Peace negotiators? The 'talking heads' we see on the News? Or does the useful information really lie with ordinary people, those in the conflict zones who are trying to live their lives in the middle of it all? Surely their experience would help us to empathise and put pressure on our governments to end the conflict more than statistics about numbers killed and military hardware used?

These are questions raised by Internews, an international non-profit agency which works with local electronic media in conflict zones in order to go behind the headlines and find the people who are trying to survive them.

Take Ali Lahmar, for instance. This 38-year-old ticket collector daily traversed the deadliest rail route in one of the most dangerous countries on earth: Algeria, Northern Africa, where tens of thousands of people have died in civil war. Every day, Lahmar braved death on the Algiers-Oran route. One day, he faced it, and didn't survive to tell the tale.

But he had told his story just before that. In a 26-minute documentary titled 'Train of Hope', which focused on the personal and intimate side of life in Algeria. Part of a series of documentaries called, 'The Other Algeria', it gave viewers an overall impression, not of violence, but of hope.

'People say these terrible things are happening in our country,' says Nayla Abdo-hanna, one of the producers. 'But we have to hope and to go on with our lives.'

The series was made with production grants, technical and editorial support from Internews, which also sponsored 'Robert and Gasan: We Haven't Changed That Much'. This documentary is based on a video conference between two old friends, Robert Saakiantz and Gasan Ismailzade. Respectively Armenian and Azeri, the two men were both born in Baku, Azerbaijan and met in primary school. Their friendship continued even after Robert moved to Armenia, but, in 1988, ethnic conflict ruptured their personal links. Putting them in touch again for the first time in 13 years, Internews recorded the contact. During their three-hour exchange in August 1998, the two childhood friends discussed the conflict between their two countries.

Formed in 1982, and funded by public and private foundation grants, Internews tries to enhance tolerance and understanding by supporting independent media outlets in emerging democracies. It also promotes the use of the media to reduce conflict within and between countries. Projects in this area have been undertaken in the former Soviet Union, Eastern and Western Europe, the Middle East, and Africa.

Responding to the political changes in the former Soviet Union and elsewhere, Internews has assisted the formation of and helped to sustain the explosion of new media outlets in the former Soviet Union. As of the end of 1998, the agency produced 12 regular news and analysis programmes in the Commonwealth of Independent States (CIS). Some of these examined the role of the media or served educational purposes. Most were centred on depicting everyday lives - people long used to closed central government control.

'In the eight countries of the Commonwealth of Independent States where Internews currently supports non-governmental television, its innovative productions challenge both audiences and local journalists,' says a report in the organisation's newsletter.

Production efforts in the former Soviet Union began in 1993. The Moscow-based 'Local Time' brought together news stories from all over the former Soviet Union into a national television news magazine. Stations across the region each contributed a three-minute story. In return, they received a half-hour programme with news from other cities - unfiltered by state broadcasters.

A similar approach was adopted in other countries of the CIS, using programmes produced in local languages to enrich the media landscape. Viewer response was encouraging.

'What Internews strives to do is to create the programmes that each country's audience and stations need at any given time,' says Manana Aslamazian, Executive Director of Internews Russia.

That often means focusing on people, working with the people who are driven apart by war, local producers not correspondents. 'Kosov@: A View From Inside', is a series of four 13-minute episodes co-produced by Internews and Media Project, an Albanian production company. 'Our Daily Bread' was the result of a video-conference link in which Serb and Albanian bakers talked frankly about the political situation and hostilities in Kosovo, the former-Yugoslavia.

The following excerpt from the diary of Violeta Curcic, Project Director for Internews Belgrade, helps convey the difficulties involved in this kind of journalism.

> 'Pristina, May 1998
> Everyone is very nervous. It is the day of the link for 'Our Daily Bread.' This is a difficult one. Safet and Mica are bakers. Safet is Albanian, born in Belgrade, used to live in Kanjiza in Vojvodina, speaks Hungarian. By the end of the day he will sit down to talk via satellite with his counterpart, Mica, a Serb from Belgrade.
> Both of them have a lot to lose - Safet a bit more. He is concerned about the public reception of the link in his own community and what he is going to say or not say. At

the same time, he is afraid of the police. 'People are getting killed and beaten up very easily these days,' he says, 'and I have a family to support'. Later, Safet decides that the best way for him will be to speak in metaphors, in the traditional Albanian fashion.

People in Serbia and Kosovo have learned to understand eloquent silences, innuendoes, meaningful smiles and sighs. Afterwards, I realise that the real story of these two men is not only in what they said during the link, but in what they didn't say.'

Similar technology was utilised to good effect in a celebrated coup for Internews: the unprecedented live video dialogue between Americans and Iranians that occurred during the FIFA World Cup in 1998. A digital satellite link allowed soccer fans in New York and Tehran to have a face to face meeting. They discussed the widely anticipated World Cup game between Iran and the United States, sports in general, shared personal aspirations and touched on the political tensions between their countries. Video diaries were shared about their lives.

That video link was maintained during the course of the game. The audience reaction was filmed as developments unfolded on the field. There were strong images of Iranians cheering their team's goal, Americans showing their disappointment. (Iran won the game, 2-1) Producer Stephen Lawrence says over 30 television, radio and print news media across the globe covered the Internews link.

'While we have had great success in developing and broadcasting conflict prevention programming on local media within zones of conflict, we have rarely been able to get that programming to viewers in Western Europe and the US.'

Fewer participants were involved but there was no absence of passion in 'Vis a Vis: Blue and Black', a digital video link facilitated by Internews involving a black South African policeman, and his American counterpart. Sergeant Hendriek Mohale of the South African Police Service was based in Soweto; Sergeant David Van, a patrol officer in the predominantly black neighbourhood of Philadelphia, the 23rd District. Meeting via television monitors from their homes and workplaces, the two men discussed their lives and experiences, shared video diaries, and formed a friendship.

The programme was the second to be aired on the American Public Broadcasting Service. In the previous one, 'Vis a Vis: Beyond the Veil', broadcast August 27, 1998, an American and an Iranian English teacher, one in Washington DC, the other in Teheran, talked about the differences that had kept their two countries apart.

Both were pilot programmes. They were developed by Internews as part of an educational series on conflict for American Public Television and will serve as a model for other educational programmes.

But making programmes about conflict is one thing. Getting them on air, and having them viewed, is a different kettle of fish. Often the crucial role of the international media in raising public awareness of impending conflict and post-conflict situations is undermined by the short attention span of journalists and their editors. Hard economic facts of media life also play a part. Interest is sustained only as long as there are bodies to be counted and explosions to film. That ignores two crucial phases: the period before the conflict erupts, and its aftermath.

'The blood and guts of actual conflict bring rating points and profit whereas programming that focuses on preventing conflict is often too abstract to attract public attention,' says Paul Greenberg, Internews' Director of International Co-productions. 'We see a real lack of information in the West about conflicts that have not yet turned violent but could in the near future. We also see the international media regularly ignoring conflicts that have supposedly 'ended' but in fact have continued to fester because international assistance was too rapidly diverted.'

To overcome this problem, Internews has developed a project called Media Rapid Response, involving the creation of several mobile television crews equipped with flyaway satellite communications systems. These would be deployed to areas like Kosovo, where conflict is brewing, and footage provided to both Western broadcasters and local stations on both sides of the conflict.

Coverage of the 'pre-conflict' situation would be provided at below-market cost to news agencies around the world. Eventually Internews would work with channels in the west to develop 'early warning' sections of their broadcasts that could highlight the mechanics of emerging conflict in a clear and understandable fashion. Educational programmes will also be developed on the nature of local conflict, involving schools, universities and public television channels. In this way a constituency of viewers would be built up that could become more reactive to local conflict and exert more pressure on governments.

A third approach is Pre- and Post-Conflict programming for local channels. In addition to providing footage and programming to Western channels, programming would be developed on a local level that deals with local conflicts on site - as is currently being done in the former-Yugoslavia and the Caucasus.

The distribution of constructive radio or television programming, Internews staff believe, could help lower tensions in countries like Congo, Albania and Turkey, and in instances forestall eruption of full-scale war.

Radio Ijambo Bridges the Ethnic Divide in Burundi

Agnes and Adrian Won't Leave Home

Adrian Sindayigaya is a Hutu. Agnes Nindorera is Tutsi. Both are journalists in Burundi, Central Africa, where fear of becoming 'another Rwanda' pervades every aspect of life. Agnes and Adrian do assignments together, interviewing people from both ethnic groups to produce objective radio programmes for broadcast by Studio Ijambo.

Objectivity is risky in Burundi. Before 1994, the country's ethnic history had been bloodier than Rwanda's. Hard-liners from both sides influence the targeting of moderates.

'After a broadcast,' says Agnes, 'I often get a lot of reactions. People threaten me to my face or through the telephone.'

In 1993, 50,000 deaths resulted from conflict between Tutsis and Hutus; hundreds of thousands of lives were lost in the decades before. Many thousands fled their homes, seeking refuge in neighbouring lands. Rebels claiming to fight in the name of the majority Hutus are still at war with the Tutsi-led army and government. Each time there's a clash, tension rises. Fear is pervasive.

Adrian Sindayigaya and Agnes Nindorera are among the 30 multi-ethnic staff who work for Studio Ijambo. Ijambo means 'wise words' in the local Kirundi language. The outfit attempts to be a counterpoint to the use of the media of hate to forment ethnic violence. Eight paired Hutu-Tutsi reporting teams fan out across the country, gathering material for three weekly news programmes broadcast in French and Kirundi.

'The purpose of Radio Ijambo,' says Adrian, 'is to try to be as objective as possible - to find out the good things taking place in the country, talk about them, and let people know about them. To get politicians to talk about problems inside the studio.'

An estimated 85 percent of people in the area have access to radio broadcasts. Extremists have used this medium to foment conflicts between Hutus and Tutsis. Famously, Radio Mille Collines served this purpose in Rwanda. Anti-Tutsi passions have been stirred by a pirate radio station run by Hutus from within the Congo.

'Here in Burundi,' says Agnes, 'telling lies has become widespread. That is part of the reason for the current crisis. That is why people no longer trust one another. I think that by informing people and by telling the truth, we are helping Burundi find a path towards peace - a peace in which people are led by the facts, and not by the lies of the politicians.'

Based in the capital, Bujumbura, Studio Ijambo was set up in 1995 by Common Ground

October 21, 1993....
The first elected President of Burundi, Melchior Ndadaye, a Hutu, was assassinated in a coup attempt by the Tutsi-dominated military, triggering ethnic violence and military reprisals. He had been elected in June of that year. Ndadaye's successor, Cyprien Ntaryamira, died in April 1994, in the same plane crash as the president of Rwanda, Juvenal Habyarimana. Both leaders had been returning from a regional summit called to explore solutions to end violence in Rwanda and Burundi. In 1996, retired Tutsi military officer Pierre Buyoya seized the presidency in a bloodless coup.

Productions, part of the Washington-based group Search for Common Ground. With its range of programming, Studio Ijambo's 'wise words' are replacing diatribe; reconciliation is promoted as substitute for violence and distrust; balanced programmes instead of inflammatory words.

This is difficult when the journalists are themselves victims of the conflict. During the 1993 carnage, for instance, Hutu rebels killed 60 members of Nindorera's extended family. She faced a dilemma. Professional considerations or personal concerns? When she chose journalistic objectivity, she recalls, 'my brothers did not understand; my neighbours did not understand. They thought I had to stand for members of my family and be against the Hutus.'

Every day, now, she has to subjugate her personal feelings as she takes up her microphone and goes out on assignment for Studio Ijambo.

'I saw so many friends dying because of this crazy violence,' says her partner, Sindayigaya. 'I had many friends who died without any reason. You leave someone alive, strong, and then two months later they tell you he's been shot dead or he's been beheaded...'

Studio Ijambo was launched at a time when the Rwanda genocide led to fears about Burundi. Extensive consultations, involving NGOs and government counterparts, were followed by the opening of a Common Ground field office in Bujumbura. A radio production studio was one of several mechanisms to foster ethnic reconciliation. A scheme to involve women in the promotion of peace was also set up, along with an initiative to stimulate political dialogue.

Studio Ijambo's reputation was established with its first broadcasts in March 1995. Listeners liked the unbiased presentations; hard-liners were either sceptical or suspicious. Two biweekly cultural and social affairs magazines -Amasaganzira and Radio Express- were broadcast in Kirundi and French respectively, balanced by a popular soap opera, 'Our

Neighbours, Ourselves'. Launched in July 1997, in Kirundi, the soap focuses on neighbouring Hutu and Tutsi families in a rural district. The dramatisation of their lives is used to explore the complex relationship between the two ethnic groups. Themes of tolerance and reconciliation find echoes in the dialogue.

In September 1998, Studio Ijambo expanded its repertoire. Two new Kirundi language programmes -Sangwe and The Past and the Way Forward- were slotted in. On Sangwe, young people from different communities are encouraged to share ideas and express appreciation for music with an expert, who comments on the history of the particular genre chosen that week and sets the discussion within an analytical framework. The Past and the Way Forward, a weekly 10-minute programme, addresses human rights, peace and tolerance.

Studio Ijambo journalists operate in a country run through a tenuous power-sharing arrangement, where violence persists despite efforts at reconciliation. In November 1998, an Amnesty International report described the refugee crisis in Burundi as becoming more acute. Decades of violence and gross human rights abuses had caused massive population displacement, said the London-based rights group.

'In addition to the approximately 600,000 people who are now reported to be internally displaced, there are now 300,000 Burundian refugees in neighbouring countries in the Great Lakes region,' Amnesty International says.

Studio Ijambo's workers report on the refugees. Adrian Sindayigaya and Agnes Nindorera go to Kamenge to interview some who are returning home for the first time since the 1993 massacres.

Agnes is about to talk to a woman, when a tall, slim man suddenly appears and gently asks what she's doing. Dressed in civilian clothes, his sheepish expression is no mask for the authority he wields. He asks the journalists for identification; she, in turn, asks for his soldier's ID. Pulling a booklet from his breast pocket, he explains that he had approached her because she was acting suspiciously.

'Do you find all journalists suspicious?' she asks, smiling.

He eventually allows her to continue. By then, however, the woman she was preparing to interview has vanished, frightened off by the soldier - a reminder of what led to the original exodus, and the uncertainty of the returnees.

Close by, Adrian, her Hutu counterpart, has found his interview subject at the side of a road. Behind him, shells of abandoned homes set against green hills - a now-typical Burundi landscape. Adrian pushes the microphone close to the mouth of his subject.

'What ought peace to look like in Kamenge?' he asks.

'The most important thing is that the shooting should stop,' the man says promptly, arguing that ethnic difference is not the true cause of the violence. 'Hutus and Tutsis have lived together for a long time.' he says. 'If one became sick, we all helped one another. We shared everything.'

A group of teenagers look on, stabbing their toes into the ground, hands folded or held akimbo, listening. Adrian takes his microphone over to one of the boys. The boy looks away.

'We're a little shy,' he says.

He finally opens up a bit, to complain about not being able to go to school any more. He's 17. His friend expresses the hope that Hutus and Tutsis can live together. Then its the turn of Marguerite, 15, the only girl in the group.

'I spend the whole day at home, while other kids go to school. There's nothing for me to do... I believe there's a future in which we can all live together.'

Studio Ijambo

Back at Studio Ijambo's state-of-the-art facilities in Bujumbura, the programme is edited. It will be offered to Radio Burundi, which is government owned, or to overseas outlets - BBC, Voice of America, French radio. Occasionally, a programme is rejected by Radio Burundi because the management fears passions may be aroused by something that is said.

Nonetheless, Adrian injects a few polemics at the end of his report on Kamenge, asking whether the people of the suburb can really have any faith in the future if Burundian politicians 'won't sit around the same table and put an end to this civil war'.

Objectivity is not easy, he admits, but the determination to find a balance is strong.

'Sometimes I, myself, felt like surrendering,' he says. But I was in a dilemma. What if everybody wanted to leave the country? To whom should we leave it? It's my country, it's my home. Burundi is not hell. I was born in it; I have relatives here. I have to contribute to the building of the country.'

Agnes adds: 'I'm often depressed after going on an assignment. It can be so depressing. People threaten to kill me. But running away is the same as giving up.'

People are Calling for Peace

QUOTES FROM 'A PAZ E QUE O POCO CHAMA' ('PEOPLE ARE CALLING FOR PEACE')

'There are people without homes
Children abandoned on the streets
Peace cannot be delayed
Enough of this fierce war'

We Are The World. The South African Peace Song. These are titles of familiar songs of hope and unity. Based on their model, the Centre for Common Ground in Angola (CCG), the Luanda-based office of Search For Common Ground, brought together Angolan musicians from both sides of the conflict to create an Angolan peace song. In April 1997, 11 days after the formation of the Government of National Unity and Reconciliation in Angola, 35 of the most popular MPLA and UNITA musicians gathered in Lisbon to record A Paz E Que O Poco Chama, or The People Are Calling For Peace.

'Our people are running away in vain
And suffering more and more
For all the years fly by
Life is too short'

For three decades, Angola has been torn apart by conflict. First, the country struggled through a war of independence from Portugal. Immediately after gaining that independence, a civil war broke out between rival factions of the independence movement. After 30 years of warfare, violence has become an ingrained response to conflict. Despite hope that the Lusaka Protocol, the peace agreement signed in 1994 by representatives of the Angolan government and UNITA opposition rebels, would usher in a period of sustained peace and reconciliation, the atmosphere of war and violence persists.

'If we are to reveal ideas
Which express our joy
We must discuss with respect
What we are thinking'

The Centre for Common Ground in Angola is trying to change the ingrained response to conflict in Angola - to promote cooperation, joint problem solving, dialogue and other constructive, non-violent methods of dealing with conflict. Toward that end, CCG utilizes the media as a multiplier for its messages of reconciliation, peace and non-violent approaches to conflict. Its initiatives have included co-producing, with Ubuntu Productions, television and radio programmes about reconciliation. The Centre's latest media initiative is a twelve-part documentary series entitled Luzes Na Sombra (Lights in Shade) which focuses on individuals who have decided to make a difference in their community.

'Angola is women and flowers
It is the Mother the people love
End this suffering
People are calling for peace'

The centrepiece of CCG's media campaign, however, is the Angolan Peace Song. Music provides a way for CCG to approach Angolans where other, more orthodox methodologies have failed. Angolans have a deep affinity for music; it reaches beyond dialogue, beyond words, to their hearts and souls. Highly honoured in Angolan culture, musicians and their songs are effective tools for cutting through communication barriers. When a musician speaks out on an issue, Angolans listen. Musicians are therefore effective tools for peace.

'Old illnesses are returning
There are no more medicines
Wounds that no longer mend
The healing of peace is missing'

The Angolan Peace Song became an exercise in reconciliation and consensus building in itself. It took CCG a year of negotiations and mediated discussions to overcome the divisions between the musicians, and it took a leap of faith on the part of the musicians themselves to overcome their misgivings and make a joint stand for reconciliation. Famous Angolan musicians, Feilipe Zau, Bonga and Filipe Mukenga penned the song. Despite the differences, both stylistic and pedagogic, between the musicians, these three became the driving force behind its creation. As Filipe Zau stated, 'We can overtake ideological differences and musical antagonism, which exist but do not overtake this project.' In Lisbon, where 35 musicians, different in ideology and style, met to record A Paz E Que O Poco Chama, the music bridged the gap, and for three days they worked together to create a united call for peace in Angola. For Angolans, to witness musicians setting aside their differences and in one voice plea for peace proved that reconciliation was possible on all levels.

'Who does not want a different life
Whoever just wants to think about war
Does not want the well-being of the people
And has no love for his land'

CCG officially launched the Peace Song with a peace concert in Luanda on August 30, 1997. That evening, 1,600 people crowded into the Karl Marx stadium in Luanda and for four hours, they clapped, danced and sang for peace. Many of the musicians who helped record the song performed on stage. The concert was electrifying. To see MPLA and UNITA supporters, standing side by side, on stage and in the audience, it seemed that the Angolan conflict wasn't so intractable after all. Calls for hope and peace were shouted and sung with one voice.

'There is a hope in the air
That is the strength of us all
There is a song awakening
That hails from the time of our grandparents'

The Peace Song continues to do its work in Angolan society at all levels. CCG organized a second peace concert in May 1998 and a third will take place in Luanda, at the end of March 1999. With UNESCO funding, CCG distributed 10,000 cassettes of the song through schools, churches and community centers. Both the audio and visual forms of the song are aired on state-run television, as fillers during broadcasts of the National Assembly. In February of last year, a female parliamentarian ended her speech on the floor of the assembly with the closing words of the song, 'People are calling for peace.' Articles chronicling the development of the song and concert have appeared in the Journal de Angola.

'When the people are calling for peace
Give the peace the people want
Move your body, move your body
Dance very well this way'

As the latest series of hostilities threatens the search for a permanent peace in Angola, the Centre for Common Ground continues to use music as an outlet for the people's frustration, to offer hope and to demonstrate the possibility of the reconciliation to come. Music can be a form of protest, an expression of hope for those who no longer feel they can give voice to such emotions. As Paulo Flores, one of the participating musicians in the Angolan Peace Song said, '...music can signify more for peace than for war...when I compose I think of giving a voice to those who don't have [one]...' CCG continues to use the Angolan Peace Song as an anchor for our music and peace activities. Whether it is a large concert in Cabinda, or a small informal gathering under a tree, the Angolan Peace Song continues to wend its way through the nation, into people's minds and into their hearts.
'People are calling for peace.'

Most information as well as quotes in this article were taken from Dangerous Silence: Studio Ijambo Broadcasting Peace in Burundi, a video-documentary directed by Dutch film maker Rob Hof. The Box on the Angolan Peace Song has been written by Heather P. Kulp of the Angola Project of Search for Common Ground, USA.

6

Education

Introduction

Educating Critical Citizens

The 20th century has witnessed the most bloody and destructive wars ever known. The development of weapons of mass-destruction continues, as do conflicts between states and ethnic groups over scarce resources, racism is wide spread and there is a widening gap between rich and poor throughout the globalized economy. The need for peace education is greater than ever before, a recent international conference concluded. But how can peace education really be effective and how should complex and interwoven problems such as the above be tackled? ♦ By Maaike Miedema

'Education has to face up to the problem that people have a dizzying feeling of being torn between globalisation whose manifestations they can see and sometimes have to endure, and their search for roots, reference points and a sense of belonging', writes Jacques Delors, former Chairman of the EU-Commission, in 'Learning: The Treasure Within'. This Report to UNESCO of the International Commission on Education for the Twenty-first Century, describes the 'painful struggle' of the world society to be born. Education, argues the Commission, which is composed of fifteen internationally respected personalities, is 'at the heart of both personal and community development; its mission is to enable each of us, without exception, to develop all our talents to the full and to realise our creative potential, including responsibility for our own lives and achievement of our personal aims.'

Education, the Commission stresses, is an essential instrument in the search for a better and more just world. 'There is every reason to renew emphasis on the moral and cultural dimensions of education, enabling each person to grasp the individuality of other people and to understand the world's erratic progression towards a certain unity; but this process must begin with self-understanding through an inner voyage whose milestones are knowledge, meditation and the practice of self-criticism.'

More and more people feel that peace-building should start 'at home'. At a recently held preparatory conference for the Hague Appeal for Peace ('Building a Campaign for Peace Education', Geneva, November 1998) young people actively participating in the event stated: 'Many felt that before taking a wider global perspective, we needed to first find peace in our homes, schools, and communities. It was agreed that themes of justice, tolerance and peace had to be woven into the education of the children of the world, as they are the future leaders of the 21st century.'

This call for a new form of education is heard from many sides. The Delors-Commission sees 'a learning society' and 'learning throughout life' as keys to the 21st century. 'The far-reaching changes in the traditional patterns of life require of us a better understanding of people and the world at large; they demand mutual understanding, peaceful interchange and, indeed, harmony - the very things that are most lacking in our world today.'

Having adopted this position, the Commission further emphasises one of the four pillars that it describes as the foundations of education: Learning to Live Together. 'By developing an understanding of others and their history, traditions and spiritual values and, on this basis, creating a new spirit which, guided by recognition of our growing interdependence and a common analysis of the risks and challenges of the future, would induce people to implement common projects or to manage the inevitable conflicts in an intelligent and peaceful way.' (The other three pillars are Learning to Know, Learning to Do and Learning to Be).

Utopia? Maybe. But most people would agree on the desirability of reaching this Utopia. To move in this direction, developing skills for interpersonal contacts as well as the skills that enable independent thinking are seen as indispensable instruments.

PHOTOS CENTER FOR TOLERANCE EDUCATION

Student activities during the Values and Citizens programme of the Center for Tolerance Education in Jerusalem

'Teaching and learning never can be neutral', Marigold Bentley, educational advisor to the Quakers stresses. 'Education, through its place in any establishment, serves interests and power structures. We currently live in a world in which the system of nation states with national armies and national and regional defence systems are relied upon to keep the peace.

It is this system, and the set of assumptions which underpin this system, which dominate what is taught in schools.'

For this reason, 'critical citizenship education' is seen by many as necessary to allow young people to develop moral and political autonomy. In order for there to be civil society, young people must understand the underpinnings of that society. 'Critical thinking and thinking processes are at the heart of being able to understand, acknowledge and challenge what is identified as needing change', Bentley concludes.

Professor Chetkow-Yanoov of the Israeli Bar-Ilan University (see Box) agrees. In his opinion all citizens have to be taught how to use modern conflict-resolution technologies (like mediating, emphatic listening, negotiation and bargaining) at interpersonal and inter-group levels. 'That is why independent thinking skills have to be developed, not only to study the underpinning of the society, but also to analyze and understand their own behaviour. Because: peace begins with me.'

The Children Teaching Children programme in Israel (see case-study), one of the programmes initiated by the Jewish-Arab Center for Peace, could be seen as an example. The programme tries to establish a permanent dialogue between pupils of Jewish and of Palestinian descent. Over 50,000 children, young people and adults from Israel and abroad come to the Center each year to actively participate in seminars, workshops, courses, conferences and formal and informal educational programmes.

In modern society teaching information is not enough, researcher Edward De Bono states: 'Information is easy to teach. Information is easy to test. It is not surprising that so much of education is concerned with information. Thinking is no substitute for information but information may be a substitute for thinking.' De Bono claims that teaching thinking skills is most essential for the modern world.

A De Bono model of teaching thinking skills has for instance been used with children by the Education Advisory Programme of Quaker Peace & Service, and has been found particularly effective in dealing with playground violence. The students learn to look at a conflict situation from different points of view, with different 'thinking caps'. They are trained to look carefully at what they see around them, not just seeking facts and information, but also taking emotions, and new ideas seriously.

'Active learning (process and content) must be at the heart of peace education', Bentley argues. 'Evidence shows that through active learning methods, the young person understands issues more thoroughly and is more likely to take action as a result of that understanding. Active learning skills include valuing oneself and one another, understanding of other values and ideas, the ability to acquire and critically analyse information. These skills are a central part of peace education.'

One of the most effective places to start peace education with young people is with themselves, because peace in itself is an abstract and difficult concept, particularly for those

Peace Education through the Years

Early peace education before World War I came largely from the pacifist movement. Despite calls for an international centre to develop peace education, much of the work remained with small project and groups.

After the war the movement for peace education became international and was subsequently sponsored by the League of Nations. In 1925 a League General Assembly resolution established a committee of experts 'to consider the best methods of co-ordinating all official and non-official efforts designed to familiarise young people throughout the world with the principles and work of the League of Nations and to train the younger generation to regard international co-operation as the normal method of conducting world affairs.'

The same dilemma's which face much peace-work today, concludes educational advisor Marigold Bentley, 'were prevalent for peace educators in the 1920's and 1930's. The League of Nations, like the United Nations today, recognises the right of self defence and the right to go to war if deemed necessary. As a consequence, some peace education has been rejected if it adopts a pacifistic approach.'

So the dilemmas may have remained the same, but the focus of peace education has always changed and shifted, says Bentley, depending not only on current international affairs but also on the dominant ideas of the time. Movements such as moral disarmament, pacifism, nonviolence, international understanding, and intercultural exchange, have all contributed to peace education.

'The means through which peace education has been promoted has also chopped and changed this century. Whilst the bedrock of exploration and development of peace education has remained with small groups of people, there have been times when large congresses, international committees, and international legislation have been seen as paramount. The latter seem to have been far more influenced by the dominant political views of time.'

Over the last 25 years, much important work has been done in the field of peace education on the international level, in a host of different forums, concluded the participants at the conference 'Building Campaign for Peace Education': from the UN's educational organisation UNESCO's 1974 peace education policy Recommendations, to its 1994 Declaration on Peace, Human Rights and Democracy. This Declaration was signed by almost all governments in the world. 'However', the Geneva conference's Statement declares, 'while saluting the efforts of the pioneers, we are profoundly disappointed that worthy declarations and even formal commitments have in most countries not made a real impact on curricula, on teacher training, on classroom practice and on resource materials.'

who have no direct experience of war. In the UK anti-bullying programmes are part of peace education. Good programmes include workshop-style interactive- or participatory-learning lessons. Young people learn how to value themselves and the people they meet and they develop their communication skills.

Bentley: 'Through this work young people actively develop their problem-solving and thinking skills and are then equipped to take on responsibility for their own behaviour and, to a degree, the behaviour of the people around them. Long term work on these subjects is aimed at not only a short-term change of immediate behaviour, but attitude change over time.'

The anti-bullying programme is not only a good peace-keeping practice for children, teachers and parents. It also shows the problems of peace keeping in a nutshell. Bentley: 'The difficulty in dealing with bullying is that it can stem from the autocratic nature of the school itself.' When teachers don't listen to their students and abuse their power to discipline them, they lose their credibility in peace-keeping programmes.

'Needless to say, it is very difficult for any school to come to terms with institutional assumptions about the way things are done, particularly because it calls into question discipline, relationships and most of all, power structures', says Bentley. Truly dealing with conflict from a whole school perspective may demand changes throughout the institution. If we genuinely mean we want people to relate honestly to one another, a broad transformation of our social constructs and institutions is needed.'

Dealing with Conflict Today

Effective conflict resolution relies on close cooperation with education and healing professionals, argues Israeli professor B. Chetkow-Yanoov. 'When these three disciplines work together well, we become equipped to bring about system-wide transformation.'
- When conflict resolution efforts are supplemented to therapy, it can generate the individual and group healing which must precede mediation between bitter enemies;
- Conflict resolution, linked with education, makes theory-derived knowledge and skills available to various audiences;
- The linking of education and therapy enriches conflict resolution by equipping us to deal with value as well as behavioural changes. Skills such as buffering, mediating, arbitrating, and compassionate listening should be in the tool kits of all involved in conflict resolution.

All societies might well invest in formal educational services in order to prepare youngsters or newcomers for a future of peaceful coexistence, argues Chetkow-Yanoov. Such educational efforts might include the following:
1. help to unlearn/outgrow childish values, attitudes, and habits (for example: lessons at various curricular levels should teach that human beings can advance their careers on a basis of self-awareness, assertiveness, and actual accomplishments - not by rejecting or downgrading others);
2. teaching values (e.g. tolerance or respect for others) and practical ethics as part of the regular curriculum;
3. teaching children aspects of ethnic groups or cultures other than their own;

4. teaching all citizens how to use modern conflict-resolution technologies at inter-personal and inter-group levels;
5. making sophisticated healing and guidance services available to all persons or groups who have been exploited or abused;
6. reinforcing school-based lessons by parallel experiences in special summer camps, international youth seminars, organised tours to other countries, one year studies in schools/universities abroad, etc.;
7. updating the contents and experiences used to train student teachers (if coexistence values and technologies are to be taught in a wide range of school class rooms, teachers will have to be exposed to such topics, examine their own value commitments, and become convinced that such knowledge and involvement is indeed 'professional';
8. strengthen the impact of coexistence promotion at schools by enlisting the cooperation of parents and parent organisations;
9. recycling the teaching of peace-making knowledge, attitudes and skills several times during a persons's learning career;
10. making the mass media into partners in the resolution of conflicts ('if media people can be persuaded to report conflicts accurately rather than sensationally, they can contribute to conflict de-escalation');
11. promoting peace by offering appropriate courses and workshops on a wide range of topics.

'If we are taught to be afraid of snakes, wary of strangers, racist, or sexist, we can also be socialized to trust others, to cooperate, and to respect the law', concludes Chetkow-Yanoov. 'We can be taught how to negotiate, to compromise, and to bargain in situations of new or ongoing conflict.'

(Based on the book 'Social Work Approaches to Conflict Resolution', by B. Chetkow-Yanoov)

The statement from the Geneva Conference stresses this point too: 'We strongly promote the view that peace education should be a holistic process, extending far beyond the school's walls into community life, the mass media and popular culture and as such must incorporate perspectives from all disciplines.' At the same time, it is argued, peace education must be recognised as a fundamental part of the formal (and non-formal) system in all countries. 'If not, it will lack credibility, status and accountability.'

Teachers and students have tried to integrate peace education at all levels at the City Montessori School in Lucknow, India - the world's largest private school, with 22,000 students (see case-study). Here, peace education has become an integrated part of the school curriculum and parents, teachers and peers are involved in the education and upbringing of children aged 4-18. One of the founding principles of CMS Education is that a school is an extended family with the teacher acting as a role model and an example. Everyone involved in education must learn to consult, co-operate and participate for the benefit of the child.

The Center for Tolerance Education

The Center for Tolerance Education at the Van Leer Jerusalem Institute focuses on all segments of the educational system in Israel, to promote democracy and coexistence. The Center has two main activities. It functions as an umbrella organisation of all entities in Israel dealing with tolerance education. It enables exchanges of views and the adoption of Best practices. Furthermore, it aims to stimulate local authorities and schools to include tolerance education as a substantial part of their curriculum. 'In a global world with many conflicts and with increasing violence within educational institutions, a major educational effort for the youth must encourage, through inter-group dialogue and other educational initiatives, the growth of tolerance and mutual respect among peoples of various faith, ethnic groupings, cultures and value perspectives.'

The second activity is the Study Program Values and Citizens. The programme is conducted in 160 schools throughout the country -including state-religious and Arab- and uses current events as the point of departure for the study and discussion of fundamental issues on the public agenda. The students sum up their work on portable wall boards, that are taken from classroom to classroom to elicit discussions and are finally hung in the room in which the programme is to take place. The Center provides guidebooks, a video on running the programme, mobile poster boards for walls, and a year-long programme of conferences and in-service courses for the teacher-coordinator and student representatives.

Not only parents and teachers, also older students can help. In the Peer Mediation Project in the UK, older students learn how to intervene in conflicts between younger students. Older students can be trained to guide younger students in conflict resolving. In the school different 'generations' teach each other to be peace keepers.

The final declaration of the Geneva conference stresses the important roles other actors should play. 'We encourage publishers to promote peace education material and to ensure its effective distribution. Furthermore, development assistance agencies should promote elements of peace education as a component of their teacher training and materials production activities. Efforts of humanitarian agencies to introduce education for conflict resolution/transformation, reconciliation and peace to refugees and conflict-affected populations should be expanded. Above all, we demand that Education Ministries give peace education high priority and take systematic initiatives to implement it at local and national level.'

SELECTED BIBLIOGRAPHY

Three Decades of Peace Education Around the World, Robin J. Burns and Robert Aspeslagh (ed.). Garland Publishing, Inc., 1996

The International Peace Education Movement 1919-1939, E. Hermon. In: Peace Movements and political Cultures, Charles Charfield and Peter van den Dungen, Knoxville Press, 1988

Education for the Real World - Learning from the Real World Coalition, John Huckle. Development Education Journal 1997

Teach Your Child How to Think, Edward De Bono. Penguin, 1992

The Contribution of Education to Peacebuilding, Marigold Bentley. 1999

Social Work Approaches to Conflict Resolution, B. Chetkow-Yanoov. NY/London, The Haworth Press, 1997

Celebrating Diversity - Coexistence in a Multicultural Society, B. Chetkow-Yanoov. NY/London, The Haworth Press, 1999

Mediation Works! Conflict Resolution and Peer Mediation - Manual for Secondary Schools and Colleges, Mediation UK, 1998

Human Dignity - The Right to be Respected and the Obligation to Show Respect. The Centre for Tolerance Education, 1998

Root Causes of War/Culture of Peace, International Fellowship of Reconciliation, 1998.

Learning: The Treasure Within. Report to Unesco of the International Commission on Education for the Twenty-first Century. Unesco Publishing, 1996

Education for Global Citizenship - Examples of Good Practice in Global Education in Europe, North South Centre/Council of Europe, 1996

How Can We Learn to Live Together? A Handbook on Evolving Questions and Partial Answers around Coexistence and Community-Building. State of the World Forum Coexistence Initiative, 1997

India's City Montessori School Educates World Citizens

Gandhi's Visions Are Millennium Proof

The seeds of Mahatma Gandhi's visions are being nurtured in India, where a school that started in 1959 with five pupils has become the largest private school in the world with 23,000 students. Today the City Montessori School is a source of inspiration for schools all around the world. Dr. Sunita Gandhi, president of the Council for Global Education in Washington, believes this system of schooling is the way to educate socially-conscious citizens for the 21st century.

Sunita Gandhi was inspired by the ideas of her parents: Mr. Jagdish Gandhi and Mrs. Bharti Gandhi. In 1959 they founded the City Montessori School in Lucknow, the capital city of the Indian federal state Uttar Pradesh. 'Forty years ago, a young couple, my parents, had a vision of Mahatma Gandhi', says Sunita Gandhi. 'At their wedding they made a vow to serve humanity. They had a powerful vision, but no money. They borrowed ten dollars and started a school. They finally convinced a family to send their five children to the school. My father prayed and prayed that he would get students, and finally he got five.'

Over the years the number of pupils attending that school has grown from a hundred, to a thousand, to twenty-three thousand today. The City Montessori School provides an education for students in kindergarten through 12th grade that focuses on both academic excellence and emotional well-being. The vision of Mahatma Gandhi is incorporated in the education and is represented in the Four Building Blocks of CMS Education. Its curriculum focuses on defining values and learning about peace: students follow lessons in world citizenship, social responsibility, peace issues and religious values. Every CMS-event starts with a prayer for peace in the world.

'My parents are still energised by their vision. That vision is of Jai-Jagat', says Sunita Gandhi: 'Jai-Jagat was a slogan that Mahatma Gandhi adopted, and it stands for "glory be to the world, hail the world". This is the vision that has guided the school all these years. You can recognise the children that have been brought up in this system, they are compassionate human beings; they are world citizens.'

In 1992 the City Montessori School had an opportunity to prove that a value-orientated education and the promotion of peace could affect community life. On the 6th of December racial riots broke out between Hindus and Muslims. The centre of the conflict was the Babri mosque in the ancient city Ayodhya, in Uttar Pradesh, only 40 miles away from the capital city Lucknow. Earlier, in 1990 Hindu fanatics had already attempted to demolish the mosque thereby provoking severe religious clashes with many casualties. Two years later another atempt to destroy the mosque was more successful. More than 2,000 people died in the violence that followed.

The students of the City Montessori School tried to prevent further violence. They obtained a jeep with loudspeakers from which they played tapes of students singing unity songs. Behind the jeep walked 1,000 children and several thousand parents singing and carrying posters: 'We should live in unity.' 'The name of God is both Hindu and Muslim.' 'God is One, Mankind is One.' 'All Religions are One.'

The governor saw this as an opportunity to control the violence and animosity. He asked the City Montessori School to provide a meeting place for the heads of all the city's religions. Every day these leaders of the religious community held public meetings where the leaders and community were surrounded by models of a church, a temple, and a mosque and the children would sing about unity.

Lucknow indeed escaped the violence. Could the schoolchildren have made a difference?

According to John Huddleston, a senior official with the International Monetary Fund (IMF) they did. He visited Lucknow during the riots and reported in the magazine, *The Global Classroom:* 'My main impression is that this school system which has a track record of more than thirty years is making a significant contribution to the well-being of this city both in terms of quality and quantity. For instance, during the disturbance at Ayodhya [...] many towns in the area experienced civil unrest. Lucknow was an exception and many have attributed this to the moral impact of the school on the people of the city over a period of time.'

'Wars generate in the minds and hearts of people. It is therefore their consciousness that needs reform. Education defines human consciousness to a large measure. Therefore its role in creating peace in the world is paramount.'

According to Sunita Gandhi education can make a big contribution to achieving peace in the world. She says: 'I've lived in the USA for ten years, and feel that the problem of racism has the exact same symptoms or underlying causes as the problem of apartheid in South-Africa or the caste system in my home country India. When you divide children, when you put them into different camps, and when they do not coexist from the earliest stages of their lives, you sow the seeds for a lifetime of problems in coexistence. You can see this everywhere in the world. Children are not born prejudiced; it's we adults who introduce prejudice into their minds. There never was a war that was not inward, as Marianne Moore once said.'

Gandhi was educated at her parents' City Montessori School. She has been working at the World Bank in Washington for the past ten years on issues of education, women and

Building blocks

The education of the City Montessori School (CMS) is based on the Four Fundamental Building Blocks, as promoted by the Council for Global Education:

- Universal Values;
- Global Understanding;
- Excellence in All Things;
- Service to Humanity.

Taken together, these guiding principles promote the education of the whole child. To build virtues in children, teachers integrate an appreciation of value into the larger fabric of learning. Classroom activities centre around collaborative problem solving. When students write essays or participate in art, music or drama, they often focus their work on themes such as unity, peace, respect for the environment, or service. In addition, each day begins with a half-hour assembly run by students on similar topics. The striving for excellence is considered normal in the CMS. Parents and teachers are regarded as role models for the pupils. Both groups play an important role in the education of the children. That's why CMS actively includes parents in their training.

Parents are encouraged to be involved in the school curriculum as much as possible. They read books and articles the school provides to them with titles such as 'How Parents Should Behave with Their Children' and they are also encouraged to attend special seminars and meetings organised by the school.

Children are divided into small groups and assigned a mentor.

Sunita Gandhi: 'A teacher-guardian is a teacher who takes on the responsibility for the overall development, physical well-being and moral values. They strive for a relationship that makes the school an extension of the home.' Learning how to serve the world in theory is not enough. Students learn that they can make a positive contribution to their community by participating in projects in the city of Lucknow, like a trash collection project for example. Every year the children plant trees in collaboration with the Social Forestry Department. Students also adopt villages where they educate children and adults in literacy, hygiene and first aid.

participatory development. Now she has left the World Bank to concentrate on her work as President of the Council for Global Education, an international non-profit making educational institution dedicated to promoting the development of the whole child.

'Our goal is to promote a new vision of education for the 21st century', she explains. Gandhi believes schools are places where children learn to deal with each other, whatever religion, nationality or race. The three R's (reading, writing and arithmetic) are important skills, but the most important is that children acquire social skills and moral values.

'In my travels and work with the World Bank, I began to realise that education the world over needs major reform, that more of the same is not enough and that in fact, there was no point expanding an education that does not produce the results we seek from it. It is fine when children and adults are empowered by the learning of the 3 R's. However, when the same children go through the entire educational process, they emerge from it not quite so empowered and in most cases actually disabled by the education that is supposed to enable them.'

'The increase in crime world-wide, the despondency and hopelessness among youth, the decline in values everywhere, can all be traced directly or indirectly to a lack of a proper education and a failure to focus on values, both in the formal education system and in the home.'

'I have observed in the context of my own family's work, that education can be a highly empowering and positive experience for children. It can make them conscious citizens of the world focusing not only on their own needs but on becoming thinking, compassionate individuals able to contribute to the betterment of the world. Education world-wide seems to be following the same core derived from the 19th century industrial revolution in England. Children are divided by age and led into career streams. The focus is entirely material. This 19th century psychology is not adequate for the needs of the 21st century.
If we want a better world, a different world, we need to organize education differently.'

'A completely new focus in education is needed. Education needs reform at the core and not just some additions. This is why I left the World Bank and founded the Council. I knew that the Bank, which is more focused on expansion of education, would not be the best place to develop a model of education for the 21st century. Though once developed, it could be a good place for expanding it worldwide.'

Children Teaching Children in Israel

Investing in Future Decision Makers

'It's the most meaningful and dynamic project I've done in my 26 years of teaching,' says Miriam Chaim, one of the field co-ordinators of the Children Teaching Children project in Israel. 'We talk about the essentials of our existence, Jews and Palestinians in this country. What does it mean to be a member of a minority/majority group?

Miriam Chaim has been working for six years with the Children Teaching Children programme (CTC) in which Jewish and Arab girls and boys meet each other in school. CTC is a dialogue between people who live very separated lives in school and in their communities. The majority of Jews (approximately 80 perecnt of the population) hardly ever meets the minority of Palestinians, so how could they get to know each other? Their opinions are formed by their own collective narratives, myths, stereotypes, prejudices and media rather than by face to face contact.

Miriam Chaim: 'Our message to the children is not to take things for granted. Not to accept the situation as it is. We make both students and teachers think about reality in a different way. We use workshops and games. In highschool we play the parliament game. All children walk around in a class room with statements and opinions written on paper and hung on the walls. Statements about the flag, about the national institutions, about the division of resources... you name it. For example: at the present situation the flag is not representing the Arab community. On the wall are three statements regarding this matter: let's leave it as it is, let's add an Arab symbol to the Jewish flag, or: let's make a cosmopolitan flag where every citizen is represented.'

'Every child moves around the room and stops at the opinionboard where his or her idea is reflected. The children with similar ideas, both Jewish and Arab, find each other at this board and they are asked to form a party. Together they develop their own programme and propaganda. In the end all parties will debate. This way, the children learn that they can have common interests or disputes, and still express themselves openly. They can dialogue and confront over the controversies, and still act in the same framework.'

The Children Teaching Children programme has been running since 1987, and is one of the programmes initiated by the Jewish-Arab Center for Peace in Givat Haviva. This is a national education center, located in the Northern Sharon Valley in the centre of Israel. There are two directors, one Palestinian and one Jewish: Jalal Hassan and Shuli Dichter.

'Our mission is change the nature of citizenship in Israel from being focused on the Jews', says Jalal Hassan, 'to a citizenship that includes equally all the citizens of the state. We offer the teachers and the students a process of dialogue that will help them cope with the conflict between Jews and Palestinian in Israel and help them develop skills and abilities to change reality for the better.'

Over 50,000 children, young people and adults from Israel and abroad come to Givat Haviva each year to participate in seminars, workshops, courses, conferences and formal and informal educational programmes. The Encounter Program CTC is one of the activities of the center for teachers and pupils in junior high school. In 1996 more than 1,200 pupils and 80 teachers of 23 schools joined the programme, Jewish and Arabs in equal numbers.

Former premier Yitzhak Rabin congratulated Givat Haviva on their work: 'The peace process will only succeed if it takes hold at the grassroots level. The efforts of Givat Haviva are an important contribution to this urgent goal.'

After the election-victory of Netanyanu's Likud-party, the Ministry for Education made a massive cut in the Jewish-Arabic Encounter Programmes. Instead of the 25 per cent increase which was planned, Children Teaching Children had to reduce its activities by twenty percent. However, the center is not about to give in - the list of schools wanting to participate in their programme is longer than ever. The total budget of CTC is approximately 350,000 US dollar, of which 230,000 comes from fundraising. In comparison: a modern tank, such as used by the Israeli army, costs 12-15 million dollar.

Each CTC-project takes two years. Jewish and Arab schools, classes, teachers and pupils are paired into mixed teaching and learning groups which meet two to six times a year within the classroom setting in each community's home school on an alternating bases.

Over the course of the two years the Arab and Jewish teachers meet regularly, to evaluate and plan the next class. The teachers participate during this period in a on-going dialogue group where they can share their experiences. Ten field co-ordinators of the Givat Haviva's Jewish-Arab Center for Peace supervise the CTC-programme.

The character of the CTC-programme has changed over the years. The youngsters were supposed to teach each other their mother tongue. However, where most of the Arab children liked to improve their knowledge of Hebrew, many Jewish children were not prepared to learn Arabic. For a long time the encounters were mainly in Hebrew. 'Since we understand that language is a way of self-expression rather than just an instrument of communication, we try to encourage both sides to speak in their own language', says director Shuli Dichter. 'In the beginning the encounter was the focal point, later we discovered the importance of confronting the children with their own prejudices and anxieties. The encounter is now a tool to accelerate the educational process for each side to learn about itself and its attitudes towards the other side.'

The CTC is the only project in Israel of this kind permitted to function within the regular school programme on an on-going basis. It took a long time to bring Jews and Palestinians together on an educational programme that is a integral part of the school curriculum.

Shuli Dichter: 'When the state of Israel was established in 1948 suspicion and hostility between the Arabs and Jews dominated. At that time the Palestinians who stayed within the borders of the State (about 150,000) were given Israeli citizenship and were put under military rule. These Palestinian citizens were considered a potential threat. Education in relation to 'the other' was different for Jews and Arabs. In the Jewish students' curriculum the Palestinians were ignored. The few pioneering attempts to include the Palestinians in the Jewish picture were academic endeavours at studying the Palestinians from an anthropological perspective or in order to 'know the enemy'.

'For the Palestinians the language of instruction in schools is Arabic, but the Jewish-Israeli Ministry of Education dictated the curriculum. It included a massive body of knowledge, which was to ensure a deep acquaintance with the Jewish history, culture and heritage, including a justification for Zionism. In the first twenty years the Jews and Palestinians were not educated toward any kind of togetherness. In the few encounters between students, the initiative was always in the hands of the Jews, and the 'chosen' Palestinians were passive players.'

'When one is engaged in a dialogue, one must invest a great deal of emotional and intellectual energy. The outcome is never predictable, because in a true dialogue neither side's agenda takes precedence over the other's.'

In the 1970s and the 1980s educational concepts and methods were imported from the Western world. Those concepts, however, reflected the idea of a pluralistic civil society in a democratic context. Several potentially positive elements were brought into the encounters, such as the symmetric setting (half Jews, half Palestinians) in a workshop, and one Jewish and one Arabic facilitator. Nevertheless, the goals of the encounters were not achieved, due to the fact that the participants only met once, and then new participants were invited for the next encounter. This meant that the encounters were too short and lacking content and vision, necessary for an educational process of change.

Moreover the Jews and Palestinians represented two different nations, living in one state, each in conflict with the other. Neither of them are, or ever were, seeking to integrate or develop a shared identity. Bringing students together with the intention that contact in itself would change and improve the relations had the effect of further entrenching the traditional hegemonic relationship between the two sides.

Children Teaching Children was born as a result of the dissatisfaction with the existing methods of education towards coexistence in Israel at that time. CTC created the possibility to organise the encounters in a continuing process. Sharing responsibility for the programme, as well as it's undefined curriculum over a long period of time, created an atmosphere of openness.

Dialogue is never easy between Jews and Palestinians. 'On the Palestinian side decades of deprivation and the lack of legitimisation of their collective identity have been internalised. In a dialogue they find themselves obliged to teach the Jews about their experience, but are constantly torn between playing 'the good Arab' and authentically expressing their frustration and rage. The Jews, who's collective consciousness in Israel has been raised to view themselves as the masters of the land, legitimising this with the Jew's history of persecution and genocide, find themselves having to question their reality, which up until that point they had taken for granted.'

In a classroom six children are discussing the 50th anniversary of the Israeli state. What is for some a celebration is a disaster for others. The children, three Arabs and three Jews, are preparing a lesson for their schoolmates. 'I am a bit apprehensive about the anger of the Jewish schoolchildren,' admits Nadra (14), who comes from the Arab village Arara. Galit (15) who lives in the Jewish community of Tivon says: 'It's important to get the message to our schoolmates that they should avoid being offensive or provocative, but still to speak their minds.'

In spite of all the problems the participants of CTC have faced, the programme has been successful in some places. In Emek, Hefer, Baka, Nazareth, Tivon and Haifa students, like Galit and Nadra, have chosen to continue the programme for a third year, and have forced the organisation to develop a CTC continuation programme for high school students. CTC was also selected to be presented at the World Exposition 2000 in Hannover, Germany. It was one of the projects chosen in the category of Humankind and will represent an international model of dialogue between two conflicting communities.

In 1999 two programmes will be added: Dialogue Among Teachers and Dialogue Among School Principals. The two target groups are considered social change agents and community leaders and as such, both are expected to be a vehicle for a true dialogue between the two national communities in the state of Israel.

Director Jalal Hassan: 'We believe it is important to work with these leaders. These clubs or councils are made up of students who are elected by their peers, and possess a great deal of social awareness: they are leaders in their schools and have the potential to be key leaders in their communities or in the general public. Second, the students who join the programme will be volunteering their time during their after-school hours, signifying their dedication to the programme. Therefore, we believe we are investing in people who may later become decision makers.'

Maybe these decision makers will choose to invest in dialogue rather than tanks.

7

Arts

Introduction

Healing Divided Societies

Can art help build peace? Can the visual and performing arts be used to help bring about the processes of change and social development necessary for conflict management? The experiences of many people from around the world suggests that the answer should be a resounding `yes'. Apart from using works of art to support the creation of a just society, many of those working with the victims of conflict have discovered the value of techniques derived from the process of artistic creation ♦ By KEES EPSKAMP

'Successful tolerance education', says Haim Roet of The Center for Tolerance Education at the Van Leer Institute in Jerusalem, 'requires continuous active participation by people of different cultures and backgrounds at meetings and encounters in a natural, pleasant atmosphere. The more frequent the meetings, and the more people who participate in them, the more chances there are for success.'

Musical groups of all sorts, like choirs, dance troupes and orchestras, meet these requirements very well, feels Haim Roet, 'particularly as music touches almost every one, especially youngsters. Furthermore, through music, one can easily introduce those youngsters to different cultures in a natural atmosphere.'

The use of musical groups in tolerance education, requires relatively small financial resources, is mostly non-controversial and is usually attractive to sponsors. Consequently, a group of individuals from different backgrounds decided to set up the Tolerance Education through Music organisation in Israel. The main purpose of this NGO is to promote awareness of the potential of music as a tool in tolerance education. 'We will also bring together musicians and educators of different cultures and ethnic backgrounds', says Haim Roet, 'to prepare the necessary curriculum for youngsters of different ages, that are going to formal (schools) or informal institutes of learning (community centers).'

Tolerance Education through Music is just one out of many initiatives aimed at using the arts to address violent conflict. These include projects based on the performing arts (drama, music, dance), visual arts (posters, murals, comic books, pamphlets) and electronic media (radio, video, Internet). One of the options of such a culturally directed arts strategy is to address situations with a potential for violent conflict. In this context one might think of the 'early warning systems' developed by various agencies.

Cultural workers may, for instance, develop a dramatic performance with which they then tour a potentially volatile region. Another possibility for developing conflict-specific works of art is to be found in work with exiles and refugees. Still another option is to enter into a postconflict situation and join forces with local cultural workers to develop strategies of reconciliation. Such a strategy might include helping former combatants produce a video or comic book, with the proceeds going to restitutive actions.

During the 1990s, the arts played an important role in conflict resolution in many different countries, including South Africa, Namibia, Eritrea, El Salvador, Guatemala, Romania, Palestine, Cambodia, and among many indigenous people around the world.

In describing the role of the arts in processes of reconciliation after a period of violent struggle it is necessary to make some distinctions. Factors which need to be taken into consideration include an evaluation of the strength of the arts at community level with special attention being paid to opportunities for participation, or lack thereof, as in Central America; any national or international arts policies which have been designed to address pressing artistic capacity shortages (e.g. Cambodia). The assumptions on which such policies are based also need to be assessed. Also relevant are the approaches and instruments in training and education programmes that have been developed to operationalise the (inter)national policies concerning the arts and the administrative procedures to implement them.

In using the arts for purposes of reconciliation and rehabilitation, a distinction has to be made between using art as an end in itself and using art as a means to achieve an additional goal. Using art as an end in itself means that the artistic production, whether it be a piece of music, a wall painting or a sculpture, is meant to contribute symbolically to processes of reconciliation and rehabilitation. In this way, the work of art can bring together a culturally disparate audience and provide them with a means of celebrating their achievements in creating a new society.

When art is deployed as means to an end, it is more the 'process of making art' than the final result or end product which is important. In this case 'making art' is used as an educational or therapeutic instrument. Dramatic techniques are, for example, frequently used as supportive tools in assisting traumatised children in former war zones. Visual arts, such as wall painting and cloth weaving, are also known to be useful for these purposes. Within training sessions the dramatic arts are frequently used for purposes of simulation and role-playing. During these training sessions people can prepare themselves for problemsolving situations. Within the regular system of basic education, 'arts education' is often combined with themes related to violence, peacekeeping, prejudices, ethnic stereotyping, ethnocentrism and tolerance. Within the context of adult education these dramatic techniques and games are often used for developing conflict-management, leadership and community-building skills.

In most societies, drama, dance and music (the performing arts) are viewed as more sociable art forms than the paintings and sculptures and other typical products of the visual and plastic arts. The performing arts invite people to work together - to create collectively, to a much greater degree than the visual arts. Techniques related to the performing arts are regularly used to support people in their future development by means of training or

Romeo & Juliet on the West Bank

In 1994 two very talented theatre directors living and working in Palestine decided to join forces in order to stage a production of Shakespeare's Romeo and Juliet. The vendetta between the two opposing families the Montagues and the Capulets fed by hatred and passed from one generation to the next, was transposed to the situation in West Jerusalem. In the version staged by the Israeli director, Eran Baniel, and his Palestinian colleague, Fouad Awad Nimer, the Montagues become the Palestinians, and the Capulets the Israelis. The result is a fascinating adaption of Shakespeare's plot to the real historical situation of the Middle East. It was necessary to find sponsorship from abroad. Fortunately, the Lille Festival had chosen the theme of the 'New Middle East: Israel and Palestine' for its September 1994 edition and was consequently able to guarantee the financial support for this production. After its international debut the piece was taken on tour in and around Jerusalem.

education. Works of visual art, on the other hand, are more frequently used to commemorate and remind people of the efforts made to create a civil society and to fight for justice.

Figure 1 shows some of the primary uses of the visual and performing arts in (potential) situations of conflict. Examples referring to all four quadrants read as follows:

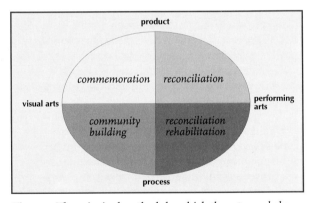

- the role of the visual arts in a processoriented approach is exemplified by the communitybuilding of the ghetto children in Washington who made a mural protesting against hand gun violence;
- the role of the performing arts in a productoriented approach can be illustrated by the performance of the South African anthem or the performance of Romeo and Juliet on the West Bank (see Box 1);

Figure 1: The principal methods by which the arts can help build a just society

- the role of the performing arts in a processoriented approach is illustrated by the use of music education as part of the therapy of wartraumatised children in Cambodia (see Box 2);
- finally, an example of the visual arts' role in a product approach is the erection of memorials and commemorative works of art.

In using stage performances to improve the mutual understanding between ethnic groups, a further specification of the relation between a product-oriented approach and the performing arts can be made, by distinguishing four forms of intercultural performing arts.

Cambodia: Music training for traumatised war children

The Music School Kampot forms part of the Khmer Cultural Development Institute, a Cambodian non-governmental organisation. It was created 5 years ago at the instigation of English ballet dancer, Catherine Geach. The school is unique in Cambodia and aims to promote the preservation and re-establishment of the traditional culture of the Khmer, the group in the Cambodian population. Much of their traditional music threatened to disappear as a result of the ongoing violence and long-running civil war. During the Pol Pot regime, the teaching and performance of traditional dance and music were forbidden. Today, only a few of the old artists are left in Cambodia. Most of them were killed by Pol Pot's regime.

The school provides an opportunity for children to be trained once more in these age-old cultural expressions. The school aims to reach children with a war trauma, abused children, orphans and handicapped children. Alongside the children who have been severely wounded and mutilated by some of the millions of land mines still hidden in the fields, there are many children who have been deformed for life by untreated illnesses such as polio. Music and dance may help these traumatised children to cope with their past.

- Representatives of minority groups -immigrants- tell their personal stories about the adjustments they have made to their new cultural context. For the audience, this kind of account provides an introduction to a different culture.
- Co-operation between artists from various cultural backgrounds; on stage a dialogue evolves between different cultures. The audience is confronted with different perceptions or even opinions from different cultural perspectives and introduced to distinct cultural differences. The stories and languages of different cultures become interwoven, cultural boundaries are traversed. Interculturalism becomes transcultural. Slowly a stage performance evolves which does not even touch upon the issue of cultural differences.
- Artists from different cultures perform together (are juxtaposed with each other) in a self-evident and self-explanatory way. The underlying cultural differences do not form the main theme of the performance. The artists and their cultural background are clearly recognisable; they keep their language and their accent. Sometimes this implies that the audience is not capable of following every syllable; this form changes fundamentally the means of conceptualising and making art. Performer and theatre director Eugenio Barba has experimented with this form.

Self-determination is central to any progress towards reconciliation. However, in any region that has been dominated by fear and suppression, self-determination is hard to achieve. One of the first problems confronting newly-formed governments in post-conflict situations is to replace the climate of fear and distrust among the population with a sense of cultural cohesion. In general this is done by articulating and working towards the goals of establishing equal rights and social justice for every citizen. Arts may play an important role during this process in terms of conflict prevention and intervention.

During the conflict	Post-conflict
society • experiment with alternative visions of a future society; • develop alternative and playful visions which outline the future nation and its organisation; • support the planning for alternative strategies to build up the nation as envisaged; • mediate between parties involved, especially beyond the medium of the spoken dialogue; • encourage the various (conflicting) parties involved not to close the door to an ongoing dialogue; • train people (by means of simulation) to gain control over their participation in political and socioeconomic systems.	• stimulate processes of democratisation and rehabilitation (e.g. drama performances to stimulate voters' behaviour); • increase understanding and appreciation of divergent world views; • articulate and work towards achieving equal rights and social justice (gender and ethnic specific items); • integrate art education into the national curriculum as a means of reconciliation and peace education in order to educate the next generation; • facilitate continuing dialogues at important moments, intercession and mediation.
community • inspire new visions based on trust and faith; • reach a working consensus within the community on fundamental issues; • create a sound organisational basis at local level; • develop strategies for 'future' community leaders.	• contribute to community development and community organisation; • improve community interaction and socialisation; • support in dismantling a climate of fear and distrust; • contribute to the creation of cultural cohesion; • use the arts to educate and train the adult population (collaborators, former freedom fighters, refugees in exile and community dwellers); • make people aware of their rights and also of their responsibilities.
individual • prepare the people for the post-conflict situation; • contribute to identity building; • take away ethnic stereotyping.	• contribute to conflict resolution; • empower ethnic groups; • address cognitive, affective and social needs; • strive for reconciliation through negotiating peace; • teach mutual respect and understanding; • support personal security and individual rights; • support therapeutic treatment of postwar traumatised adults and children.

Table 1: Using the arts: lessons learned during conflict and post-conflict situations

In general, the performing arts are the most sociable form of arts
PHOTO LINDA GRAHAM

In table 1 an attempt has been made to systematise the role played by the arts, showing their principal opportunities to support the struggle for a better society before and after the fighting, and the implications for the individual, the community and society at large. It is striking here that the support offered by using the arts is quite congruent with more general principles of conflict management.

Within this process it is important to encourage use of the arts as a means of helping a community to take control over its own development or prepare for good governance. In this context, artists acting as mediators shuttling between the opposing sides, particularly addressing the leaders of the conflict, are using their art as the vocalising point for ending the violence and seeking justice.

Lessons learned
- Never focus on images and stories or narrative sequences which emphasise disruption and conflict.
- Focus on a narrative or social context in which adults and children of both parties involved have an opportunity to intermingle.
- Focus on what the members of the targeted audience/communities share: family, love, emotions, games, their desire for peace, life, food, sleep, happiness and playfulness, and education.

- Avoid generalisations about ethnic differences.
- Include any details which help transform human beings into dramatic characters rather than stereotypes who can be used during games and dramatic play to show the full variety of persons living within the community.
- Do not forget to involve the subgroups living within each cultural group - for example, the country-dwellers who often have family living in town and vice versa; or people who have relatives living in exile or in refugee camps; be sure to include socioeconomic differences, education systems and differences in languages.

Most of these lessons are so obvious that their importance tends to be forgotten. Much reference has been made in this brief introduction to the performing arts. More elaborate case studies will be presented in the following pages. Helen Gould presents a case study on the use of drama in Northern Ireland, while John Ungerleider provides more insight into the use of music and poetry to build a bicommunal peace culture in Cyprus. A rather different example is provided by the controversial use of the arts by Italian fashion company Benetton whose campaigns centre on images intended to promote peace, tolerance, multiculturalism and to challenge stereotypes.

SELECTED BIBLIOGRAPHY
Aboriginal voices - Amerindian, Inuit and Sami Theater, P. Brask and W. Morgan (eds.). Baltimore, The John Hopkins University. 1992

Our Creative Diversity. Report of the World Comm. on Culture and Development. 1997

Popular music and redemocratization in Santiago, Chile 19731989, M. Mattern. Studies in Latin American popular culture, 16: 101113. 1997

Pedagogy of violence - Cardinal solutions to global survival through peace education, B.B. Oderinde. UnescoAfrica (Biannual of Unesco regional office, Dakar), 10/11 (September): 2745. 1995

Voice to the voiceless - The power of people's theatre. J. Scrampickal. New Delhi, Manohar Publishers. 1994

Palestinian theatre as a junction of cultures- The case of Samih alQasim's Qaraqash. R. Snir. Journal of Theatre and Drama (JTD; the University of Haifa), vol. 2: 101120. 1996

In writing this article, Kees Epskamp represents the foundation for Comparative Studies in Arts and Art Education in Global Perspective (CompArt).

The Arts' Contribution to Peace in Northern Ireland

Encouraging the Community to Have Fun

Back in the 1970s a group of young people in Belfast set out to alleviate their boredom and disaffection with the Troubles by establishing a live music club where musicians and audiences could mix, regardless of their cultural background. Punks, Rockers, Protestants and Catholics came together to promote 'what we deemed as the easiest bridge of communication between prods and taigs, music', says one of its founders, Petesy Burns, Chair of the Belfast Youth and Community Group.

This and other initiatives in drama, visual arts, literature, photography, community video and film which began to stir at the same time have inspired the evolution of more than 100 community-based arts groups in the city today. While the arts cannot claim credit for the historic Northern Ireland Peace Accord in 1998, it is entirely fair to say that they have played a supporting role in establishing a climate for coexistence, peace-building and reconciliation.

The key to this work is not necessarily just about throwing people together from different backgrounds and environments, and hoping that the arts will magic away the barriers and differences between them. It's about building up self-confidence in individuals and in their communities; about developing a strong sense of self-worth, so that relations are less strained by insecurities over identity and difference. In the context of Belfast, where the city has been divided by intimidating and isolating physical barricades between communities for the past two decades, the need to build up a sense of security in one's own back-yard is vital before one can feel secure being in anybody else's.

Achieving this has everything to do with participation and empowerment: the people of Northern Ireland have lived at the centre of a media circus for more than 25 years. Creative projects allow them, finally, to take control of the images and perceptions of their home, to offer their own commentaries on their communities, to share their opinions and create their own solutions, to have a sense of ownership in the wider process of development which is going on about them. In this context, the arts become participatory democracy in action.

One example of the transformation which can be wrought by creative activity is Belfast Carnival, a new project developed by a community arts organisation, The Beat Initiative, to encourage community-wide celebration and build a positive atmosphere and image of Belfast. a thousand people paraded when the carnival was first staged in 1995. Since then it

'If anger, hurt and despair need to be given a place within any effective, peace-building process, then so too must imagination play a role. If the aim is to remember and change then community arts offer a mechanism to enable people to remember, as well as encouraging communities to set out their aspirations and vision for changes. This process is clearly intrinsic to the task of seeking peace and reconciliation.'

has built from a one-person operation to an organisation which involves up to 30 artists and which works throughout the year with some of the most socially excluded groups in the city. David Boyd, its founder, was recently presented with an award recognising his role as a social entrepreneur. His local nominees for the award commented that: 'Amid bombs, bullets and sectarian mayhem he has consistently brought newness and alternative futures to the people of Belfast.'

There have been some ground-breaking community theatre initiatives which have enabled the people of Belfast to review their history from different perspectives. The Stone Chair, set in a Belfast graveyard, looked at the Troubles from the perspective of those who lay buried there. It inspired another group to investigate the history of their own predominantly Catholic area, Dock Ward, resulting in several productions which have made an enormous contribution to raising morale in the local community. One of the great, transformational experiences, it is said, is enabling Protestant people to play Catholics and vice versa.

Neighbourhood Open Workshop, one of the early pioneers of community artswork in Belfast, set up The Barricades Project with a group of teenage Protestant girls from one area making a video of an imagined encounter with a Catholic girl from a nearby housing estate. The second stage of the project brought the participants together with a group of girls from the neighbouring estate. Collectively they devised a play about their shared experiences.

A women's centre on the largely Protestant Cregagh Estate in Castlereagh, Greater Belfast has set up a writers group, The Spell Weavers, which runs weekly classes for women and has published collections of their work, which has had huge impacts on their self-esteem. 'Local people stopped the women in the street to talk to them about their work and friends, neighbours and family saw them in a new light.' The group also started running workshops in photography, drama, ceramics and craft. Each member of the group has contributed to a wall hanging on the issue of conflict which they see as the embodiment of their project and of coexistence: each woman created her own square and the designs, though discordant, come together to create a harmonious blend of colour and texture.

Northern Visions, a community media centre in central Belfast, has worked with a diverse range of community groups, including children, women, travellers (self-directed nomads) and the long-term unemployed, running training and workshops to enable them to make their own films, videos, documentaries and dramas. An important facet of their projects is handing over editorial control of the videos to their participants. A recent project brought

The Tale of His Shirt

Stretched across the board
The vast greenness spreads before me
Its aerial view
A series of fine lines and borders.
It's when I observe
It's then I am challenged
As I see the faded outlines
Where sweat and tears
Once soiled the landscape.
The power in my hand
I smooth a lifetime of
Creased Irish greenness
And under my own steam
Make a hole in the fog
Releasing the blur on my vision
And as I create the dividing lines
For arms that will carry arms
I tear away the labels
And trace seams it seems
Were hand made - man made
As I wander up and down
The front link past tinker and tailor
Finding myself
In the company of poor men
Wishing for beggar man or thief
Wishing for smoothness
A chance to hang
This Green Burden up.

Pat Turner of the Cregagh women's writers group, The Spell Weavers, wrote this poem after interviewing a Royal Ulster Constabulary wife. 'It struck me that if only we could iron out the problems of this green country as easily as that green shirt,' explains the poet. (Taken from the audio-tape 'I Know A Woman', published by The Spell Weavers)

together youngsters between the ages of 8 and 14 from different cultural backgrounds to record interviews within the community and create original film dramas and animations.

A small but thriving photographic studio and gallery in central Belfast is home to Belfast Exposed which holds a library of more than 100,000 images captured by participants from many different backgrounds during its community photography projects. The pictures tell a story not of a people overwhelmed by misery and violence, as the international media projects, but of a vibrant city. It is not that the Troubles are absent from the works, but whilst the menace of violence is ever-present, they project images of people living life despite the threat: children playing around the barricades, women enjoying the spirit of carnival; an old man playing a violin in a demolished suburb. Belfast Exposed has enabled people to go out and take the pictures which they feel are important and in so doing, changing our perceptions of Belfast.

In 1970s when the first public funds for community arts activity became available in Northern Ireland it seemed like more of a calculated risk. These days with well in excess of one million pound available for community art work -including peace and reconciliation funding from Europe- it is beginning to look like a serious investment.

David Grant, Director of the Lyric Theatre in Belfast studied the impact of community arts on community relations, and came to the conclusion that: 'One aspect of the Troubles which has influenced policy thinking in the arts has been the passage of time. In 1978, we were not as resigned to the prospect of their seeming interminability. The high-cost of long-term solutions seemed less attractive. The implications of this for community drama are that community projects are now perceived as less transitory and long-term development seems more desirable.'

But if any hard data was required to testify to the value of arts in community building in Northern Ireland, it emerged last year from a report by François Matarasso of the British research agency Comedia. The study showed that 93 percent of community arts participants in Belfast who participated in the survey felt more self-confident. The highest levels of learning were for communication skills and working with others. Nearly half said their involvement had changed their perceptions. 81 per cent said they felt less isolated. Almost two thirds said that they had visited new areas and developed a better appreciation of other's cultures.

Apart from anything else, the arts are enjoyable and inspiring and encourage the community to have fun, which has its own benefits when reality bites. In the NIVT Community Arts Awards Scheme review (1989) it is said that 'a community which celebrates together in harmony may find a greater inspiration to organise itself when it comes to some of the harsher issues of living.'

References
Playing the Wild Card - A survey of community drama and smaller scale theatre from a community relations perspective. David Grant/Community Relations Council. 1993
Playing Our Part - Arts and Community Development in Northern Ireland. Conference Report. Northern Ireland Voluntary Trust, 1990
Taking Risks for Peace. Northern Ireland Voluntary Trust, 1998

This article has been written by Helen Gould, coordinator of Creative Exchange, the forum for cultural rights and development, an international NGO dedicated to promoting the role of the arts in development, empowerment and rehabilitation.

Music and Poetry Build Bi-communal Peace Culture in Cyprus

'My Country is Cut in Two'

Cyprus is an island so small that it takes merely an hour to drive the narrow width from north to south coasts. Yet the Greek and Turkish Cypriot population have been completely segregated by ethnicity since 1974. Though they may live only hundreds of meters apart, children have grown to young adults over these twenty-five years and never seen someone from the other side. Yet if one were to watch folk dancers or hear Cypriot songs on either side, it is likely that the same tunes will fill the air. The popular folk tune 'Dillirga' is sung with Greek words in the south and with Turkish words in the north, but it is a song deeply linked to the identity of all Cypriots.

In growing numbers over the past years, when permitted, Greek and Turkish Cypriots have met together in the UN-administered buffer zone that bisects their island (the Turkish Cypriot authorities banned Turkish Cypriots from attending bicommunal meetings beginning on December 17th 1997; over a year later, the ban continues). They engaged in dialogue, build relationships and created an alternative to the mainstream cultures of nationalism and division that are highly militarized in both north and south. In the struggle to establish this alternative 'peace culture' in Cyprus, music and poetry play a significant role. From the Bi-communal Choir and mixed groups of rock musicians that perform at bi-communal events, to the songs citizens sing together when they want to express their desire for peace, music carries a powerful sense of liberation and reconnection for Cypriots from both sides, epitomized when they sing 'Dillirga' together, alternating Greek and Turkish verses.

Music and poetry has been used in Cyprus to transform conflict at conceptual, emotional and cultural levels - through mind, heart and body. Lyric music helps keep the vision of peace alive and deeply felt. It is a tool and impetus for communication, collaboration and celebration, cornerstones of a budding common culture, not Greek or Turkish, but Cypriot, non-divisive and hopeful - peace culture.

Since the 1960's, topical songs have raised consciousness about peace and justice worldwide. Home grown topical music has helped Cypriots to envision the potential for peace, reframe perspectives on the issues, and conceptualize imaginative strategies for conflict resolution. In the musical poem 'When Cyprus Becomes One', Greek Cypriot rap artist Hajimike crafts a hopeful image of conflict transformation with his wry vision of Cyprus' possible futures, the

dire or desirable scenarios which will emerge from an untenable status quo:
'Refugees in their home
missing persons reunited
weapons cast away
living life, having a say...
or is it such an impossibility
beyond the next century
a strange mystery, a fallacy
for Cyprus to be one?'

Informative songs promote greater understanding of the sources and dynamics of conflict, revealing the harm of stereotypes, and the need to build cooperative security as an alternative to living constantly on the brink of violence. An anti-war song promotes awareness and analysis about how conflicts can escalate or be mitigated through improved inter-group relations and non-violent approaches.

Greek Cypriot singer Katie Economidou performs the anti-war 'Kardashim Duymuz' ('My Brother') by famous Turkish singer/songwriter Zulfa Livaneli, a song that reframes conflict as a mutual problem, helping identify the common interests and fundamental human needs that are endangered by violence.

A good topical lyric stimulates thinking about problem solving, even creates a fantasy equation for resolving a conflict. Poetic imagery can enhance the ability to see both sides of an issue and common elements of transcultural identity, as in the poem by Neshe Yashin, 'Which Half':

'They say a person should
love their homeland
that's also what
my father often says.
My homeland
has been divided in two
which of the two pieces
should I love?'

The transformative impact of music reaches beneath the conceptual level, to the heart level, where it touches emotions and values, and energizes solidarity for action. Simple peace songs help teach peace as an essential value to children, helping adults reconnect with, and pass on, the feeling of peace. A visionary lyric reminds us about the critical importance of core human feelings such as hope and love, which can be empty platitudes when not grounded in as impactful a context as a good song, like John Lennon's 'Imagine' - still sung by Cypriot peacebuilders as a reminder of our common human potential.

The sonority of music itself helps process difficult emotions, catharting despair and denial, and validating repressed fears and hopes. It literally gives heart and hope, exemplified in performances of the song 'Umutzuz Olma Arkadash' ('Don't Be Hopeless My Friend'), based on a collaborative poem written by the student poetry group of prominent Turkish Cypriot poet Mehmet Kansu. The song, punctuated by handclap accents, essentially states that 'though there are tanks and guns around us' and 'though we can't touch each other's hands,' someday we will see 'peace and love together, like the rising sun.' Music encourages political action by supporting feelings of solidarity,

Bi-communal event

helping a political opposition develop group identity, lift morale in difficult times, and clarify its vision and values.

At the social and cultural level, music and poetry provide a forum for developing creative communication through collaborative projects, building common culture and celebrating together. Music facilitates intercultural communication by making possible listening across cultures through the universal languages of rhythm, melody and harmony. Lyric meaning and feeling are shared as artists improvise live or collaborate in recorded venues. Any collaboration deepens dialogue skills, such as listening and authentic expression, leading to a sense of mutual understanding. These skills form the foundation for collaborative problem solving and principled negotiation in general.

Working collaboratively in 1978 when there were no bi-communal meetings at all, Turkish Cypriot poet Neshe Yashin and Greek Cypriot musician Marios Tokas composed 'My Country is Cut In Two' ('Yurdum Ikiye Bolundu'). The Bi-communal Choir performs it in Turkish and Greek. It has been recorded by the famous Greek singer Yiorgos Dalaras who sings it in every concert, ironically often mixed with a nationalistic context and spirit. Katie Economidou recalls: 'I remember one night in Limassol where we were with Neshe in a concert by Dalaras and when he was singing this song everybody stood up and sang. A lot of them were crying and of course no one recognised Neshe in the crowds. I turned to her and said: you see what a gift you gave to these people?'

A poetry and visual art collaboration in 1995 produced the book 'Nicosia', with poems by Neshe Yashin and Michalis Hadjipieris set to paintings and murals of their common, divided city by Georgios Kepola. Poems and song lyrics are published along with articles in the bi-communal magazine Hade, begun in 1997.

Bands from either side, who had worked together to perform at bi-communal events, were in the early stages of meeting to produce and record a jointly written peace song to enter in the Eurovision contest when the bi-communal meeting ban froze all collaborative efforts. Ironically a story appeared in the Cyprus Mail, on April 1, 1998 stating that Cyprus' Eurovision song entry was disqualified since it was not bi-communally produced. This story turned out to be an April Fool's joke, but with poignant effect.

Peace culture takes root in songs that contain the spirit of peace in Cyprus and are known bi-communally. The best loved include famous Greek songwriter Mikis Theodorakis' 'Chrysoprasino Phylo' ('Golden Green Leaf'), referring to the shape and the colours of Cyprus in the Mediterranean, and Turkish Cypriot singer/songwriter Acar Akalin's hopeful 'Guzel Gunler' (Nice Days). Cultural self-identification is expanded by learning other peoples' songs. Katie Economidou recounts her daughter's favourite at bedtime is lullaby 'Durnam' sung in Turkish. In an atmosphere of multicultural cross fertilization and fusion, similarities and differences are appreciated.

The growing culture of 'world music' models a more international, global sense of cultural identity. The trusting relationships emerging from cross-cultural recognition promote reconciliation and forgiveness, as well as shared joy - a core element of peace culture. When Cypriots sing 'Dillirga' bi-communally, their common identity reveals itself as an exuberant memory with nascent cultural meanings.

Several large festivals in 1997 opened checkpoints into the UN Buffer Zone and thousands attended each time - a Peace Concert, a Bi-communal Fair, annual UN Day, and a Peace Festival organized by dozens of local groups from both sides. The Peace Concert was the second ever; in 1995 the first drew about 250 concert-goers from each side, at a time when there had been virtually no bi-communal contact to date.

Before the 1997 concert, the Turkish Cypriot news media published very threatening reports that made people afraid for their lives to attend and a Turkish pop singer had rocks thrown at his bus by the para-military nationalist Grey Wolves; after the show, Greek Cypriot young people were met by nationalist youth yelling and chasing them with stones. Still about 2,000 Turkish Cypriots and 400 Greek Cypriots attended. Young people speak of the lasting inspiration they still draw from the memory of that unified festive atmosphere.

At each large bi-communal event, music was the centrepiece of the day. Folk troupes and rock groups from Turkish and Greek Cypriot communities performed. Most significantly, joint performances, such as by Turkish Cypriot band Grup Net and Greek Cypriot group Klironomia, highlighted the shows with common Cypriot tunes sung in both Greek and Turkish. The communal feeling of celebration was held together by the music and dancing, once even in the pouring rain, a rarity in Cyprus. The same sense of undivided fun pervaded non-political disco dancing and sharing folk songs around the campfire at youth camps and conferences held off-island (such as in the US, Northern Ireland, Hungary) when contacts on Cyprus were not permitted.

This tangible spirit of unity is an undeniable shared reality, an unforgettable moment in time when distrust and hatred are overcome. Just as the bi-communal choir continues to rehearse separately, Cypriot melodies and musical memories sustain hope during difficult times such as these, a fertile seed to cultivate peace in a future when people can renew and expand their friendships across the Green Line.

DISCOGRAPHY

'When Cyprus Becomes One' by Hajimike, from Haki Mike on the Mike, Kebab Kulture, 1994.

'Kardashim Duymuz' by Zulfu Livaneli with Mikis Theodorakis from Together: Mazi/Birlikte, BMG, 1997.

'Krisoprassino Phylo' by Mikis Theodorakis on 14 Megales Epitixes, Lyra, 1996.

'Yurdum Ikiye Bolundu' on Haricten Gazel by Melike Demirag; and on Marios Tokas and George Dalaras, 1998.

'Guzel Gunler' by Acar Akalin and Ahmet Okan from Yediveren Dusleri.

'Dillirga' anon. Cypriot folk tune, various recordings.

REFERENCE

I Which Half in Nicosia, Nese Yashin. Cyprus. Thegona, 1995.

This article has been written by John Ungerleider, associate professor at the School for International Training, Vermont, USA

Benetton's Controversial Campaigns

The World of United Colours

With the desire for peace in the Middle East as its theme, 'Enemies' is a special issue magazine published by Benetton and 'Newsweek'. Its cover story features the 22-year old Bedouin, Musa Mazareb, and his 24-year old Israeli girlfriend, Enyar Lazarus. Their story is one of many accounts of relationships developed across the sectarian divide, such as the one of the friendship that grew up between a Jewish and a Palestinian mother after their babies were born in the same hospital.

'I t's so simple to be human beings, look at each other and smile at each other.' The Arab cameraman Nili Aslan (42) turns towards his Jewish colleague, Issa Freij (41). They carry heavy cameras and are wearing Benetton clothes. 'Meeting Issa has given me a bit of hope, especially lately, since everything has been so dramatic,' says Aslan. She replies: 'I like working with Nili, we look at things in the same way.'

Nili Aslan and Issa Freij (see photo p. 304) are the subjects of one of the photo-features in 'Enemies' published last year by Benetton and *Newsweek* and distributed in a print run of 6 million through the American weeklies and quality European broadsheets. Its 84 colourful pages document a reality which differs sharply from the familiar image of conflict between Palestinians and Israelis. In a form reminiscent of the family album, Benetton shows how ordinary Palestinians and Israelis -women, men and children- work and play together, laugh, make music, develop friendships and fall in love.

Although the 'models' in 'Enemies' wear Benetton clothes, the magazine gives no details of prices, fabrics or sizes. Instead the images are accompanied by quotes from their subjects explaining their relation to each other.

As such, 'Enemies' continues Benetton's now familiar tradition of campaigns centred on images intended to promote peace, tolerance, multiculturalism and to challenge stereotypes. Through posters, billboards, ads in the media and its own magazines, Benetton has tried to take its message to a global audience. At the same time, it has grown into Italy's fourth largest company with an annual turnover of nearly 2 billion dollars.

The series began in 1984 with the launch of the 'All the Colours of the World' campaign spotlighting groups of young people of different colour and race. The campaign sparked a heated racial debate in South Africa with sections of the 'white' media refusing to use Benetton images showing black and white children together. It wasn't to be the last time the company was to find itself at the centre of a storm of controversy.

The publication of a poster showing a black women breastfeeding a white baby led the black community in the US to accuse the company of perpetuating the racist stereotype of the black nanny and implicitly endorsing the subordination of black women. In its report, 'Benetton Advertising: A Story of Prizes and Controversy' the company responds: 'The true spirit of the photo -that equality goes beyond knee-jerk reactions and conventional perceptions- was however understood internationally'. In fact the photo went on to become 'the most-awarded image in Benetton's advertising history' the report adds.

A year later, in 1990, Benetton adopted the famous 'United Colours of Benetton' slogan which in combination with a series of symbolic 'black-and-white' images became the company's official trademark. These have remained a constant element in Benetton's promotional activities. As has an appetite for controversy. In 1996 the picture of two mating horses - one black, one white - once again led to expressions of outrage.

Unusually for a multinational, Benetton has not been afraid to address highly political themes. During the Cold War it ran a campaign with a photo of two black children kissing. One of them was wrapped in the Stars and Stripes, the other in the red flag of the Soviet Union. When the French president Mitterand met his Soviet counterpart Gorbachev in Paris, Benetton used the image to decorate the presidential route along the Champs-Elysées. A bemused Gorbachev is reputed to have asked, 'Who is this Benetton anyway?'

More shocking was the 1991 picture of a World War I cemetery in France which created 'unprecedented controversy'. Showing long rows of crosses symmetrically aligned, it served as a reminder, says company president Luciano Benetton, 'that in wartime nobody wins: beyond uniforms and races and religions, death is the only victory'. Three years later the enterprise launched its peace campaign with an equally controversial image of the blood-soaked clothes of a soldier killed during the war in former-Yugoslavia.

It might seem paradoxical that advertising campaigns intended to promote peace and tolerance should be the cause of such a public furore. In part the strong feelings aroused by Benetton campaigns can be explained by the suspicion that the company actively seeks to promote controversy in order to raise its own profile. Critics question Benetton's sincerity and accuse the company of exploiting suffering to boost its sales. However, this cannot alter the fact that Benetton produces 'controversials' -controversial commercials- that explore areas where other companies dare not go out of fear of losing their customers.

The creative force behind the Benetton images is photographer Oliviero Toscani, who began working for the company in 1982. According to Toscani his employer is actually a role model for other enterprises. 'They tell me that I have to do a piece of communication. I think that the company of the future, the one that is to survive in the future, is the company that will have a social-political responsibility,' he told *Scotland on Sunday*. In describing his relation with the clothes giant, Toscani likes to compare his situation to that of an artist such as Michelangelo who worked for the Roman Catholic Church. In fact he thinks that 'companies are the new churches. It is only through their input that problems can be solved. Most of them prefer to

Arab cameraman Nili Aslan and his Jewish colleague Issa Freij   PHOTO OLIVIERO TOSCANI

remain detached. But the economy is the key to progress in the modern world,' he said in an interview with the *Independent on Sunday*.

After a career spending photographing some of the world's most famous models, in his Benetton campaigns Toscani deliberately chose to work with ordinary people. In a typically trenchant interview with *The Guardian* he explained the philosophy behind this unusual approach: 'Somebody who buys a top model and uses them as a symbol is making a social political choice. It's actually more extreme and eccentric than mine. Hitler wanted Aryans. That's what they do with Claudia Schiffer, those fashion companies. That's what fashion magazines do. I call them the Fourth Reich publishers. You get all the rich and beautiful. All the alienated have to disappear. Style and culture magazines are like that, and so you are going to have a society that is intolerant.'

Toscani points out that it is not Benetton, but the media that present us with a distorted image of the world: 'We are getting further away from reality of the world. We have no point of view any more, because we read the paper, watch TV. Women have to be blond, tall and thin. Everything is based on the fact that we have to be accepted in society. Everybody needs consensus. Everything is getting flatter and flatter. People say that what I do is 'just a provocation'. It's not true.'

Instead of uniformity the Italian company aims to show the 'beauty of diversity'. One of the clearest examples of this approach are the posters published in 1998 to celebrate the fiftieth anniversary of the Universal Declaration of Human Rights. In the form of a play-bill, surrounded by portraits of young people from all over the world, the text of art.1 reads: 'All Human Beings Are Born Free and Equal in Dignity and Rights'.

Beyond its unique advertising campaigns, Benetton is also engaged in direct humanitarian action. Together with the French anti-racist association, SOS-Racisme, it has raised donations for some of the poorest African countries. Through the 'Italian Associazione per la Pace' it helps support war victims in Bosnia while in South Africa the company has organized a series of cultural workshops and seminars. In 1996 Benetton implemented 'The Colours of Peace', a project to supply 130,000 school children in Europe with books and posters to encourage them to be tolerant and to respect other cultures.

According to Benetton workers it is the press, religion and politics that are most to blame for creating a climate of intolerance. The press by showing negative images of conflicts, politicians for not resolving disputes and religion for frequently being the source of dispute.

'Here is the search for real people and real stories, here is the discovery of beauty without stereotypes.'

'If journalists would be artists, and if politicians would be artists, the world would be different,' Toscani told *Scotland on Sunday*. And in his introduction to 'Enemies' Luciano Benetton wrote: 'Conflicts aside, people want to live, buy and sell, fall in love. That which is divided by politics and religion, is united by the daily, normal qualities of life and relationships. There's a world where bombs scatter death among ordinary people; sometimes when they're running one of the most ordinary errands, like shopping; this is exactly where we've tried to record the deep longing for peace of two people divided by an endemic conflict.'

But others warn about the deceptive quality of images. Pictures may present a peaceful scene and create a positive atmosphere, but they don't necessarily disclose the real feelings of people. Abraham B. Yehoshua, an Israeli writer who is active in the Peace Now Movement, writes in his introduction to 'Enemies': 'But take care not to be misled. Notwithstanding the idealistic smiles and hugs in the pretty and colourful pictures, we have no way of knowing what lies deep down in the hearts of the people, Palestinians and Jews, photographed here in everyday situations. Do not be mistaken by believing that, just because they are talking to each other, laughing and patting each other on the back, they are not capable of hurting each other.'

Indeed, despite the cheerful images of friendship against the odds, some of the accompanying texts hint at deeper tensions. On the other hand Abraham Yehoshua acknowledges the value of the album when he explains the effect the pictures had on him. The most 'shocking thing' about looking at the photo's was when he discovered that often he could not distinguish the Arab from the Jew. 'And I find this so disturbing, because all my life I have been sure that it would be a simple matter for me to recognize a member of my own nation and race.' Yehoshua: 'Mistrust and suspicion can be dissolved and reduced by constantly breaking down stereotypes, not only of people, but also of relationships. And it is this which a book of photographs such as this one is aiming to achieve.'

Though 'Enemies' has a strong 'pacifist theme' it doesn't mean the catalogue paints a completely rosy picture of Jewish-Palestinian relationships. Many 'models' talk about their despair, pain, hatred and confusion. The Palestinian technician Muhammed Nabulsi (24) explains the meaning of his relationship with his girlfriend: 'Claire helps me put up with this rotten world, she's the solid proof that not all Jews are our persecutors. But it's not enough. I'm tired and frustrated at not being able to move around, at being at the mercy of any check point.'

Certainly one of the most surprising portraits is that of Zahira Kamal (52), a leader of the Intifadah, who is photographed with her Jewish friend and parliamentarian, Naomi Chazam (51). Maybe she best expresses Benetton's idea behind the catalogue: 'In order to create peace the involvement of each person is vital. Peace can't be delegated to politicians. That's why I'm in this photo, to communicate the need for peace, justice and solidarity to many people around the world.'

8

Sports

Introduction

The Pride of the Nation

The positive influence of sport on all aspects of human life - including its benefits for health, socialisation, self- confidence, leadership skills, and mutual understanding across divisions of race, culture and gender - means that its importance should never be ignored in any peace-building and reconciliation initiatives. The belated recognition of the true value of sport in promoting coexistence has, however, meant that sport development is a relatively new phenomenon ♦ By Elvis Ndubuisi Iruh and Marc Broere*

T hat sport can provide a useful channel for improving relations between nations with long-standing antipathies is clearly demonstrated by the ping-pong diplomacy which helped break the ice between the US and China in the 1970s, and, more recently, by the baseball match between a US professional team and the national team of Cuba. This resulted in one of the few suspensions of the ongoing boycott of the island by its big neighbour.

Another example of the bridge-building power of sport was the wrestling competition which ended over twenty years of hostility between the USA and Iran in 1998 (see case-study). Despite scepticism on both sides, the Takhti Cup International Wrestling Tournament went ahead in Teheran. American and Iranian wrestlers entered the ring to the cheers of an enthusiastic public and the contestants exchanged pleasantries after the competition.

Some time later America and Iran took a step further in their new-found relationship when they were drawn to play in the same group at the 1998 FIFA World cup finals in France. Again, media commentary prior to the encounter was apprehensive, with many articles predicting that the match would be marred by hostilities. Once again, however, the fears proved groundless with fans of both sides exchanging souvenirs including T-shirts in the national colours of America and Iran. Before kick-off the players presented each other with bouquets, posed for group photos, and even embraced. The match itself was one of the fairest in the entire tournament. The Iranians won 2-1, but the Americans were sportive in defeat.

Sport's role in nation-building is multi-faceted: a victory in a major international sporting event is of national importance. One of Africa's great statesmen, Dr. Kwame Nkrumah once said he had a dream of a 'united African country' where sport would play a vital role in forging the youth into one nation. According to Nkrumah, 'sporting success gives dignity and pride'. In 1960, when the Ghana national football team made a tour of Europe, Nkrumah instructed them to go and correct the Europeans' prejudices about Africa. He saw sport as the

first step towards building a formidable team which could contribute to the emancipation of Africa.
A clear exponent of Nkrumah's philosophy is Burkina Faso which has used sports to attract international attention and thus gain recognition for its various problems as one of the world's poorest nations. Despite its meagre resources, the country hosted the 1998 Nations cup finals, Africa's most prestigious tournament. During the competition, the slogan 'Sports for You, Sports for all' was to be seen everywhere. In 1984, the then leader of Burkina Faso, Captain Thomas Sankara introduced compulsory sport for the people under the slogan 'sport de masse'.

In South Africa, politics and football are intertwined. During the apartheid years, South Africa was excluded from international sports competitions. Although European cricket and rugby teams still toured South Africa in defiance of the international sporting boycott, they encountered a torrent of criticism. Left without international sports heroes of their own, black South Africans looked for alternatives abroad. In particular, Dutch football-player Ruud Gullit became incredible popular among black South Africans, not least because he dedicated his prize as European Footballer of the Year to Dr. Nelson Mandela, who at the time was still in prison.

Football established a base for the abolition of apartheid in the 1980s. Initially it had been organised according to the laws of apartheid: there were four football competitions, separated by race. But in 1978, footballers stuck their neck out and began a national competition in which mixed teams competed. Football was thus one of the first areas in which apartheid was abolished. Nelson Mandela has always been a passionate lover of sports. On the day he was elected president, he went to watch the South African national football team play.

Milestone
The South African team was allowed to resume international competition when, at a congress in July 1992, the country was readmitted into the World Football Federation (FIFA). The announcement was met with a standing ovation. The next milestone in South African football's rehabilitation was its appointment to organise the African Nations cup in 1996. Before the tournament few experts gave the 'Bafana Bafana', as the national football team is called, any chance of success. After all, three decades of exclusion from international football arena is not something from which you recover in just four years.

But South African rugby players and cricketers had already proved that it could be done. In an interview with the weekly 'Football International' immediately before the tournament, the South African national coach, Clive Barker referred to the importance of early success for his country. 'It is so unbelievably important for South Africa that we win this tournament. This is more than a game. In the awful days of apartheid the only thing the blacks proved they were better at was football'. At that time, football was a racial thing. Placards on the terraces proclaimed: 'In this we are better that the whites'. Barker says that any good performance in sport appeals to national pride and therefore when apartheid was abolished, sport took on a vital role. Nevertheless, the first successes were again booked by the whites: the cricketers became champions in 1993, and the rugby team followed two years later.

'That's why the African Nations cup must be the success of black South Africa. The will to win is no sporting requirement, it is a social duty', the coach explained to journalists before the competition commenced. Against all expectations, South Africa won the tournament. During the final match, Nelson Mandela sat in the stand next to then Vice-President, De Klerk and Inkatha leader, Buthelezi. These men have different views on political and ideological issues, but when it comes to sport, they are united. Who would have imagined this expression of unity ten years ago? A better example of reconciliation through football would be difficult to imagine.

The election of a democratic government in South Africa saw Britain and South Africa initiate a sports programme that would contribute to the process of rebuilding and reconciliation. In September 1994, the former British Prime Minister, John Major visited South Africa. As a result of the visit, the two governments drew up the 'South Africa and United Kingdom sports initiative programme.' The draft programme clearly showed how sport can work to realign social structures in areas of great political sensitivity. The aim of the agreement is to contribute to the normalisation of sport in the apartheid-free South Africa of today.

In his address to the South African parliament, Major said, 'sport has a huge part to play in the life of a healthy community. It is an outlet for the energies of young people. It develops individual character and teamwork. It gives enjoyment to people who, in many cases, have few facilities for recreation'. Since the agreement was signed, the British International Sports Development Aid Trust (BISDAT) has worked in collaboration with other organisations such as the UK Sport Council, Voluntary Service Overseas (VSO), the UK foreign and Commonwealth office, to ensure that the majority of South Africans get access to sporting facilities. They have since been working with local South African organisations to ensure sports reach the millions of people living in rural areas.

In Liberia, another country ravaged by civil war, sport has been the magic that has kept the people together, believes Liberian sports journalist, Emmanuel Williams. 'Every time the Liberian national team plays, the guns are silent. All warring factions put down their arms for a moment'. The journalist is lyrical about the role played by George Weah as a soccer ambassador for Liberia. 'He is the country's lone star that has singularly organised the national team during the war.' He is the best thing that has happened to Liberia since independence in 1847. He is a hero, a father, and an uncle. He is everything to the country', the journalist explained.

In an interview with 'International Football', Weah spoke of his role in the rebuilding of his country. 'Footballers are founders of peace, we are the pride of the nation, we do things that make people listen to us. It sounds like a slogan, but it is true: sport is a fantastic ambassador for peace. Football in particular unites people world-wide.' According to the prolific player, people mix with each other much more directly through sport than through any political manifesto. He describes sport as a form of popular culture, which is even more effective than pictures, books, poems, or music when it comes to bringing joy to a suffering people.

Sport is also gaining increasing recognition for its ability to help heal people - and especially children and youngsters- who have suffered from the effects of war. Professor W. Wolters from the Netherlands is only one of many experts who firmly believes that sports projects are excellent instruments to foster national reconciliation and help victims work through trauma. Moreover, he says, sports are relatively inexpensive, always an important consideration where resources are limited. His research into the treatment of trauma in many different countries, including Rwanda, has led him to conclude that 'sport is an important means of restoring people's psychological equilibrium.'

Politics and sport

Many victims of psychological trauma feel physically uncomfortable with themselves, explains Wolters. They feel that they are no longer in control of their own lives. Wolters believes that sport can help them recover that very basic sense of physical wellbeing. In addition, the social structure of sport is very important. Sport provides people with a social context where they can encounter other people in a non-threatening way and can get rid of harmful emotions. Rivalry and tension in sport are healthy elements, Wolters argues, they allow violent emotions to be vented in a rule-governed context. Furthermore, through sport, values such as respect for others and keeping to the rules are learned. 'That', he says 'is very important in Rwanda now'. (see case-study).

Politics and sport go hand in hand: sport can play a positive role in nation building and reconciliation but equally its power may be exploited for less welcome political ends. Thus the Nigerian dictator, General Sani Abacha, benefited enormously when his Olympic footballers came back from the US with the soccer gold from the Olympic games of 1996. Expressions of popular discontent with Abacha's harsh suppression of the opposition were for a while pushed into the background. In Cameroon, the failure of the national team threatened to destabilise the existing regime with President Paul Biya postponing an election after the disappointing performance of the country's football team in the 1994 World Cup. He was afraid that the people would blame him personally for the humiliating performance of a side which four years earlier had taken the World Cup finals in Italy by storm. Biya's fear was not altogether without justification, as he and his ministers had personally interfered with the selection of the national team.

Although the world of developmental co-operation has barely discovered sport's potential to contribute to the building of Africa, the few figures that have learned to appreciate its potential are passionate advocates of greater participation. Jan Pronk, the former Dutch minister for Development Cooperation says that African countries can gain self-confidence through success in sport. 'The building of nations is an important aspect of development. Hardly a single African country has a long history as a nation. They are often collections of a part of nations, with very many different languages and ethnic groups. In such a situation, everything which can stimulate national consciousness is positive.'

As an example of positive action in this field, Pronk points to the Sports Coaches Outreach (SCORE) project which -supported by Dutch development aid- aims to stimulate sport in schools in the townships of Soweto in South Africa. He also mentions the support for handicapped sport in South Africa, an area which has hitherto been completely neglected. There is a pressing need to develop special sports for the handicapped as part of the development of the society. We need to create options for various groups of the disabled, such as the deaf, the blind, the physical handicapped and the mentally handicapped. This need is recognised by the Norwegian Confederation of Sports which has started 'the sport for all project' in Zambia and Zimbabwe for children, women and the disabled.

While it is true that sport helps build bridges between nations and to unite people, the apparently straightforward discourse of sports development can hide some major problems.

For example, it is usually difficult for the majority of people to gain access to sports facilities. Mass mobility is frequently prevented by poor roads. Most sporting facilities in African countries are situated in urban areas while most of the population live in rural areas. These are the areas where donors or major players in the field can make a big contribution. For sports to be more effective, various governments especially from the developed countries must be ready to assist. Other organisations such as the International Olympic Committee (IOC), the Federation of International Football Association (FIFA), the Commonwealth Games organisation, sports manufacturing companies, private business corporations and successful individuals or philanthropists need to invest more in sports development in Africa. The governments and organisations could help to provide sporting facilities, provide equipment, help to recruit trainers, provide programmes for talent scouting, among other things.

SELECTED BIBLIOGRAPHY
Africa now - People, Policies & Institutions, Stephen Ellis (ed.), 1996
Voetbal in Afrika, Marc Broere & Roy van der Drift. 1996
Truth and Reconciliation - Obstacles & opportunities for human rights, Daan Bronkhorst. 1995
Football in Africa, Anver Versi, London, Collins. 1986

Marc Broere is the author of the book 'Voetbal in Afrika' (Football in Africa), Elvis Ndubuisi Iruh is a journalist from Nigeria.

Common Ground between the US and Iran

Wrestling a Route to Peace

On February 20, 1998, the United States flag was raised in the capital of Iran. There were no jeers. No boos. No shouts about The Great Satan. Instead, the atmosphere was friendly.

T he occasion was the opening of the Takhti Cup international wrestling tournament. Wrestling teams had flown into Iran from sixteen other countries, including the US, which had waged ideological war with this Islamic nation for nearly twenty years. Five American wrestlers comprised the first group of US citizens to set foot in the country since 1979.

'We had been told by Iranian friends that wrestling would be a good way to launch non-official exchanges between Iran and the US,' says John Marks, President of Search for Common Ground, an organisation that helped to arrange US participation in the Takhti Cup.

Those friends turned out to be right. The American team was met at Teheran airport by two hundred reporters. There were 13,000 cheering fans in the Azadi arena at the finals.

Ironically, the Takhti Cup, a free-style and Graeco-Roman competition, is held each February to commemorate Iran's 1979 revolution. It was that revolution which propelled the Middle Eastern country into a state of hostility with the US. Soon after, in a dramatic gesture of defiance against western power, 52 captive US diplomats were paraded through the streets of Teheran in a hostage crisis that lasted 444 days. The world held its breath as Islamic-Western tension was explosively launched.

It has taken almost twenty years for this hammer-hold of hostility to be broken - through ritual struggle. Wrestling, in other words.

The moment was auspicious. Overtures were also being made at the highest government levels. Iran's President Khatemi and US President Clinton had both, via the media, urged non-official, people-to-people exchanges. That helped smooth the arrangements and raised the profile of the visit. Wrestling came to be viewed as a metaphor for a possible new relationship, with fierce competition, but conducted within mutually accepted rules, in which differences would be accommodated within a framework of adherence to common humanity.

'Our Iranian friends felt that, because of the huge popularity of the sport in Iran, even hard-liners would not oppose the presence of American wrestlers,' says John Marks.

Hostility broken by ritual struggle

From its headquarters in Washington and Brussels, Search for Common Ground got in touch with Bruce Laingen, the most senior American official held hostage in 1979, who introduced them to the US Olympic Committee and USA Wrestling. Contacts were made between the governments of the USA, Iran and Switzerland. The latter government's officials now protect US interests in Teheran.

A European ambassador later commented that, by starting with wrestling, Common Ground had showed 'exquisite empathy' with Iranians. Traditional Persian samurai were wrestlers, not swordsmen.

'Our hope was, with Iran, that sports could once again provide an opening wedge in improving relations,' Marks explained.

Of the five wrestlers on the American team, one was a former Olympic Champion and two former World Champions. They 'wiped the mats with their hosts,' reported the Washington Post.

'The five Americans won nine of 12 head-to-head tussles with Iranians on the 500-member team that their country sent into the freestyle competition,' the newspaper cheered. But the Iranians got even in the end. They won two close matches, including the feature event of the tournament, and the final clash between 215-pound World Champion rivals, Melvin Douglas and Abbas Jadidi. This latter event had been a long-anticipated one. At the 1993 world championship in Toronto, Jadidi had defeated Douglas but was later disqualified for failing a drug test. At the Takhti Cup, he reasserted his supremacy.

But the true victor of the tournament was world peace.

At the end of their match, Jadidi and Douglas embraced while still on their knees, and walked off the mat with arms around each other. Former Olympic champion, Kevin Jackson, hugged his Iranian opponent after winning his match, and patted him on the back of the head. US wrestler, Zeke Jones, raised a small Iranian flag over his head from his corner of the arena at the end of his event, 'to show friendship between American wrestlers and the people of Iran... '

The Iranians were equally joyous.

'Their interest in Americans,' says Marks, 'mirrored what we experienced elsewhere in Tehran: namely, that Iranians seemed overwhelmingly pro-American. Obviously, hard-line radicals, who are jockeying for power with more moderate elements, do not share such sentiments. In fact, we heard that hard-liners, who represent a thin, but still very powerful slice of Iranian society, fear that pro-US sentiments might get out of hand.'

To avoid stirring up sentiments, no national flags were raised and no national anthem played at the closing ceremony of the tournament. Jadidi, however, received his award carrying a framed portrait of revolutionary leader, Ayatollah Ruhollah Khomeini, while his opponent, Douglas, carried one of Khomeini's successor, Ayatollah Ali Khamenei. The American said an Iranian official had asked him to hold the portrait of Iran's spiritual leader.

'By their actions and their words,' says Marks, 'the Iranian and American wrestlers demonstrated an alternative model for how their two countries could interact.'

And later, at the October 1998 presentation of the first Common Ground Awards to honour outstanding accomplishment in conflict resolution, Douglas and Jadidi won another award - for use of sports in conflict resolution and peace-making.

'As the stars of wrestling diplomacy between the US and Iran,' said the citation, 'they modelled behaviour for a new relationship between their two countries: competing fiercely, but within mutually accepted rules, they recognised their differences and allowed their common humanity to triumph.'

In taking a wrestling team to Iran, Search for Common Ground hoped to use sports as a means to break through a long-standing conflict - just as ping pong had been between the US and China in 1971, when the visit of an American team to China opened the door to more substantial links on the governmental level.

Common Ground believes rapid growth in non-official exchanges can make a major contribution to draining poison from US-Iranian relations, though, in the end, only governments can make peace. The organisation notes that it is also important to recognise the uniqueness of each country. Activities that are successful in one country do not necessarily work in another. Careful attention must be paid to cross-cultural design and adapting of programmes.

While in Tehran, Common Ground's Marks spoke to an ambassador for a European country, who explained the situation with regard to US-Iran relations in terms of differences in negotiating styles. Washington's approach is akin to the attacking strategy of a team playing American football, he said, while the Iranians behave like chess players. Thus one side wants to 'forget past results, march down the field, and make immediate scores', while the other shows a tendency to 'develop complex strategies, take nothing on face value, and play ahead a dozen moves.'

While the organisation believes that these differences in approaches can be overcome, to some extent, by confidence-building mechanisms, it also recognizes that there are profound differences between the US and Iran that call for top-level political attention. However, the

'It's About Feelings, About Human Emotions'

Not long after American wrestlers visited Iran in February 1998, five Iranian journalists spent two weeks in Boston and New York as guests of the New England Society of Newspaper Editors.

A few months later, in response to President Mohammad Khatami's pleas for people-to-people exchanges to break down 'the wall of mistrust', Search for Common Ground invited six Iranian actresses and female film directors to the US. This was a direct follow-up to the wrestling exchange, which had underlined the value of exchanges in areas in which the two countries excel.

Iran has emerged as one of the most important areas of artistic film-making in the world. More than 50 feature films are made in the country each year, including several which have won international awards. The Iranian women were able to screen their films at the Lincoln Centre and the Council on Foreign Relations in New York, and the film centre of the Arts Institute in Chicago. They also held a series of discussions with the US counterparts.

Iranian film producer, Fereshteh Taerpour, told the Lincoln Centre Film Society: 'We know there are some groups that are against any contact. What we're trying to show is that it's not dangerous to talk, and that the United States is not going to control our minds.'

During the visit, the six Iranian actresses, directors and producers, sought to portray another side of what is viewed by outsiders as severe restrictions on portrayal of Iranians women in film, since they have to wear head scarves even when depicted in home scenes, and cannot touch men unless related by blood or marriage. They told the Directors' Guild of America in New York that such curbs were actually conducive to creative expression.

Actresses used facial expressions, hand gestures and other devices to make up for the limitations, they explained, conveying through looks and words the emotions they felt, rather than by touching. Iranian movies have no violence or sex. They explore the complexities of human relationships.

'It's about feelings, about human understanding,' said Malak Djahan Khazai, an Iranian director.

organisation is convinced that non-governmental organisations like Common Ground can play a very important role in building bridges. To this end, Common Ground plans to work with other NGOs to carry out a series of exchanges between Iran and the US, including cross-cultural ties in areas such as the environment, women's issues, medicine, and refugees. Wrestling diplomacy provided an excellent example of how governmental and non-governmental processes can overleap and interact. When the US team returned home, President Clinton invited them -along with USA Wrestling and Search for Common Ground- to the Oval Office. This was seen as a positive signal to Teheran. White House spokesman, Mike McCurry, told reporters, 'it would be accurate to say that (the President is) drawing attention to an exchange that is maybe off the beaten path of diplomacy, but has something to say about the prospect and hope for more beneficial relations between peoples.'

Volleyball as Response to Rwanda's Trauma

'When One Is Active in Sports, One Does Not Commit Genocide'

With the Rwandan genocide of 1994 claiming over half a million lives, repairing the damage inflicted on Rwandan sport during this period might be expected to be low on the list of government priorities. Particularly since sport had previously been used to perpetuate violence and create hatred among people. Now, however, the new government feels sport could have a healing, therapeutic effect. A project to educate hundreds of volleyball coaches in the country should set an example.

'The genocide touched all parts of society and sport was no exception', says Member of Parliament Jean Mbanda in Kigali. 'The previous government built a stadium in each region, gathered in many footballers from neighbouring lands, but did absolutely nothing for sports at the grassroots. Rwanda only had one football competition in which the country's biggest teams competed. Nothing was done for youth and village sports. It was all a matter of short-term successes and propaganda', Mbanda explains. At the beginning of the 1990s, there was no longer even a Rwandan national team. 'The Hutu led government was not interested in the cultivation of the national feeling, which sports provided'.

Now, with a new government in place, a wind of change is blowing across the country's playing fields. According to the Minister of Sports, Dr. Jacques Bihozagara, 'the current Rwandan government believes sport can play an important part in rebuilding the country. Sports can contribute to reconciliation, to the cultivation of a feeling of national unity. Sports unites people'.

As a first step, the Ministry of Sport is creating a new national strucuture to encourage sport. As part of this programme, several hundreds sport instructors, sports leaders, trainers and referees are being educated and prepared to spread the message throughout the country. Sport has been assigned an important role in primary school education and village life. It is hoped that this will help young people traumatised by the events of 1994 once again find enjoyment in their lives and promote friendship amongst children. From primary school and village level, the plan will work upwards, with special attention being paid to traditional sports, sports for the over 35s, and for disabled people - a group whose numbers have been swollen by the genocide.

Among the Rwandan Government's advisors is professor W. Wolters of the Wilhelmina Hospital for Sick Children in Utrecht, The Netherlands. Wolters believes that sports projects are excellent instruments to foster national reconciliation and help victims work through

Training in Kigali   Photo Tim Kos

trauma. Moreover they are relatively inexpensive, always an important consideration where resources are limited. His research into the treatment of trauma in many different countries, including Rwanda, has led him to conclude that 'sport is an important means of restoring people's psychological equilibrium.'

Some of the activities intended to help Rwanda on its long path towards rebuilding and reconciliation are already underway. One of these is a volleyball project in Kigali run by former Dutch volleyball trainer Jaap Akkerhuis (62).
Akkerhuis's love for volleyball first brought him to Kigali in 1997. As a result of his experience there, the Dutch government decided to sponsor a volleyball-training project in Rwanda. The project's aim is to groom Rwandan youths to become volleyball coaches. In a country with 70 percent of its population between the ages of 15-30, the potential is clearly enormous.

Now Akkerhuis spends his days in the Amahoro stadium in Kigali working with groups of thirty men and women who are on average 25 years old. 'This is the first step towards developing the game of volleyball in this country', he says. The students are selected primarily on grounds of their affinity with children. 'It's nice if they already know how to play the game, but if not, I can teach them the rules. That's not the problem. It's more important that they get used to the disciplines of a team sport.'

At the end of the seven-year project, hundreds of Rwandan volleyball coaches will have been trained. They will then be expected to return to their own regions to impart their knowledge to the children at primary and secondary schools and in villages which as yet have no formal educational institutions. It is hoped that as a result of this 'missionary work' several hundred volleyball clubs will be created.

The Dutch government has taken the initiative through its Embassy in Kigali to ensure that the project gets all necessary equipment such as balls, nets, kits and teaching materials. During Akkerhuis's first visit there was only one ball for the whole group of students. Now, 1,200 balls are available.

Although volleyball is not a well known sport in Rwanda, people are getting used to the game. 'As I walk the streets of Kigali, children keep asking me questions about the game,' says Akkerhuis. 'Training sessions, are drawing big crowds and the would-be coaches who are in touch with their people at the grass-root levels are telling the same story'. The game also has the potential to reach out to children and adults that have been forced to spend long periods without employment in refugee camps.

The Chairman of the Rwanda Volleyball Association and a member of the Rwanda Olympic Committee (ROC), Robert Bayigamba speaks of a 'long-term vision'. Of course he dreams that a future national team will become volleyball champion of Africa. 'What we require is assistance to develop these talents at the grass roots'. But, Bayigamba says, 'for the moment this dream is of minor importance. The social structure of Rwanda has been demolished in recent years. This project can have a therapeutic, healing effect. It is a start, an important start.'

Jaap Akkerhuis is more cautious: 'reconciliation is not something I can create' he says. 'I train coaches so that they can train their own people, they are expected to organise competitions where the people can participate.' But of course the experienced volleyball coach hopes that with people from different groups playing together on a regular basis, his beloved game will help them reconcile their differences. Hopefully too, the social structures - like schools - that suffered so much during the genocide will be rebuilt in time and children will again be able to get a regular education and have the opportunity to take part in sporting activities as a matter of course.

Christine Mukamurangira, one of Akkerhuis' pupils, agrees wholeheartedly with her coach. She used to be a teacher but opted to take part in the volleyball project because she hopes it will help her forget 'the events' of 1994. She has a simple message: 'When one is active in sports, one does not commit genocide.'

Most of the quoted material in this article originates in the publication 'Afrika voetbalt' by Marc Broere and Roy van der Drift. KIT, Amsterdam/The Hague/Brussels, 1997, and an article in Dutch newspaper De Volkskrant, January 11, 1999.

9

Corporate Sector

Introduction

The Partnership Model

The corporate sector is today facing an unprecedented challenge on two fronts. Driven by international competition to expand into new markets and develop untapped resources, it is increasingly finding itself moving into countries where violence and chronic instability are the norm. Simultaneously, it is operating in a commercial environment in which consumers are demanding more and more accountability in the way companies pursue their operations ♦ By JORDANA FRIEDMAN AND NICK KILLICK*

U nfortunately, these two phenomena do not lie easily together. The free market may be the prevailing philosophy of our time but it is frequently coming into conflict with our collective sense of what is right and wrong, what is acceptable and what is not. The corporate sector is just beginning to wake up to this fundamental tension and is finding, to its surprise, that it is caught right in the middle.

How to reconcile these two apparently conflicting trends is a question many multinational companies (MNCs) are beginning to ask themselves with ever greater urgency. There is little doubt that instability is bad for business. Companies operating in unstable countries or regions may well see their assets seized or destroyed, their staff threatened or killed, their markets collapse and their profits slashed. Their mere presence can exacerbate tensions, fuelling the violence and providing a target for disaffected groups. In such circumstances, their actions and behaviour become a focus of international attention, prompting ever-closer scrutiny of their role in the conflict and potentially causing serious damage to their world-wide reputation.

The familiar examples of Royal Dutch/Shell in Nigeria, Freeport McMoran-Rio Tinto in Indonesia and BP in Colombia, amongst others, have served to highlight this complex interaction between business and conflict. In circumstances where access to wealth and resources is a driving force in a conflict, businesses of all kinds, but particularly MNCs, can become the targets of violence. This may either be because of specific actions on their part or simply because of their mere presence in an unstable country, or indeed both. The most obvious examples of the former come in situations where companies and communities clash over the exploitation of delicate but resource-rich environments. More often than not, the sources of the conflict lie firstly in the environmental damage visited upon lands owned and occupied by indigenous peoples, secondly in the failure of the companies, usually extractive and logging industries, to offer adequate compensation for the damage, and, thirdly, in the

Conflict is bad for business   PHOTO LINDA GRAHAM

aggressive tactics pursued by the companies in response to the inevitable and legitimate protests which follow.

In other cases, the conflicts may have little to do with the companies at all, at least in the first instance. The very presence in a poor or volatile region of a player of such economic influence can exacerbate or create the potential for violent conflict, even if the conflict seems to have more to do with ethnicity or political protest than economics. In other words, although there may not obviously be a strong resource dimension to a conflict, there is always room for people to challenge the economic status quo as a way of furthering other ends.

In such situations, however, companies are far from being helpless. Just as they can exacerbate tensions and fuel conflict, so they can contribute to building peace and security. Unfortunately, business has traditionally resisted involvement in activities that do not reflect its core competencies. But as companies continue to expand their influence economically and socially as well as geographically, they will increasingly have cause to address issues such as human rights, social justice and sustainable development. This is not simply because it is necessary or 'right' but because it is in their interests to do so.

The challenges facing MNCs should certainly not be under-estimated. Conflicts are complex processes. It is not always obviously apparent when and from where they are likely to erupt. Each one is essentially unique even if some appear to share many of the same traits. It is for

Recommandations

Partnership
- Consult frequently with local academic and political experts on community needs and expectations, political and economic challenges, etc.;
- Consult with all relevant parties in an area where business operations will take place (local communities, local and regional authorities, governments, etc.);
- Negotiate terms to satisfaction of all relevant parties before initiating projects;
- Design community development and environmental protection projects with multilateral and bilateral development agencies such as The World Bank and the United Nations Development Programme or humanitarian organisations which have core competencies in this area;
- Identify and support local, national and regional development and conflict resolution initiatives by other parties such as NGOs, churches and local communities.

Core Practice
- Incorporate a statement illuminating the intent to minimise conflict in a corporate code of conduct;
- Publicly commit to respected human rights standards such as Amnesty International's Human Rights Guidelines for Companies, the UN Declaration on Human Rights and The International Covenants on Civil and Political Rights and on Economic and Social Rights;
- Support either internal or external research to identify general, region-specific and industry-specific conflict risks and conflict impacts;
- On the basis of such research, identify policies and practices that would minimise both the threat of conflict to the company (risk) and the possibility of conflict occurring as a result of company action (impacts);
- Work with other companies in a region or industry to establish like-minded policies upholding environmental and human rights standards;
- Develop and implement mechanisms for internal and external verification and monitoring of company policies dealing with conflict mitigation (including codes of conduct, corporate statements, audits, impact assessments, etc.);
- Pursue inclusive employment practices that provide enhanced opportunities for indigenous or local populations;
- Set targets for percentage of workforce that is indigenous/local, percentage of senior management that is indigenous/local;
- Support trade union or alternative collective bargaining processes for workers;
- Support education and training of indigenous and/or local employees;
- Screen all members of security forces for prior human rights abuses or criminal activities;
- Participate in human rights training and non-violence for security forces, police and armed forces.

Social Investment and Philanthropy
- In consultation with local organisations and others, contribute to: traditional development initiatives such as infrastructure development (building roads, establishing telecommunications systems, building wells, irrigation systems and water sanitation facilities; constructing hospitals, schools and homes; supporting agricultural activities) community empowerment (funding doctors and teachers; providing technical training and educational materials, etc.). and post-conflict activities (retraining of former combatants, gun buy-back programmes, land mine clearance, land mine victim assistance and destruction of weapons;
- Support elections, democracy organisations, independent newspapers and other activities promoting a transition to democracy (providing ballot boxes, funding voter education programmes);
- Provide facilities, transport, office equipment, accommodation and other necessary resources to parties involved in negotiations;
- Offer business skills to support the peace process (public relations, facilitation/ mediation, language and technical expertise);
- Contribute resources to post-conflict reconstruction through development and investment partnerships with bilateral and multi-lateral development agencies, humanitarian organisations and other companies.

Policy Dialogue
- Lobby or advise outside governments whose policies (such as sanctions) may be contributing to conflict in the region;
- Influence the actions and policies of instrumental third parties such as the World Bank, the UN etc;
- Facilitate peace talks by acting as mediators or negotiators;
- Publicise and promote the 'peace dividend';
- Lobby for social justice legislation and campaign for human rights.

this reason that they need to be afforded special consideration. Basic standards of corporate social responsibility may be sufficient in developed countries but fall well short in situations where more is required than social philanthropy and simple good practice. This is an important distinction to stress because in less stable societies company strategies need to be focused rather than universal, holistic rather than piecemeal.

It is important also to make the distinction between situations where companies are the problem and where they become part of the problem. Both demand a combined and comprehensive approach but perhaps the former is in many ways more pernicious and yet easier to avoid. When a company becomes entangled in an existing conflict, it must look more widely for support and incorporate its strategies into those pursued by other bodies, including regional and international organisations. This is particularly true in countries where there may be no legitimate government and companies are essentially operating within a power vacuum.

The recommendations discussed here (see Box) address both these possibilities. They are designed to help minimise a company's negative impact on a society and maximise its positive contribution. They are divided into four categories: partnership, core business practice, social investment and policy dialogue. They are offered as practical tools which can assist companies to think more strategically about their operations and provide them with the necessary mechanisms to prevent or better manage conflict situations.

Conclusion

Gradually, the business community's traditionally narrow outlook is beginning to widen, spurred on by the recognition that under-development, instability and outright conflict are damaging not only to the affected societies but also to its own profitability.

We have researched the difficult interaction between business and conflict and highlighted many of the costs incurred by companies operating in unstable countries. But we have also found examples of businesses that are starting to explore new ways of coping with the complex problems underlying conflict. It is unfortunate, if understandable, that those in the vanguard of this new approach have had to be prompted by their own bad experiences. Nevertheless, how they choose to approach similar situations in the future will carry a significance beyond their own operations. The pressure on companies to act is growing and is coming not only from disadvantaged communities but from a coalition of individuals, organisations and institutions, state and non-state.

* This article is based on the paper 'Business and Conflict. A Research Study', published by International Alert, The Prince of Wales Business Leaders' Forum and the Council on Economic Priorities. April 1999. For further enquiries, or to order copies of the paper, contact Nick Killick, International Alert, 1 Glyn Street, London SE11 5HT, UK - Tel +44 171 793 8383 - e mail nkillick@international-alert.org

SELECTED BIBLIOGRAPHY

No Hiding Place - Business and the politics of pressure. Control Risks Group. London, 1997.

Multi-track Diplomacy - A systems approach to peace, Louise Diamond and John McDonald. West Hartford, 1996.

Companies in a World of Conflict, John Mitchell. London, 1998.

Human Rights Guidelines for Companies. Amnesty International UK Business Group. London, 1998.

Multinational Enterprise and Human Rights, A Report of the Dutch Sections of Amnesty International and Pax Christi International, 1998.

Local Business Pushing for Peace in Northern Ireland

'We Made it Less Easy for the Parties to Simply Walk Away'

Apart from its devastating human toll the sectarian conflict in Northern Ireland has had a major economic impact on the Province. The local business community recognised this in the early 1990s, and decided to actively push for peace. The business community has acted as a policy think-tank and a lobbying group, and recently it has also issued anti-sectarian guidelines. These initiatives have not only helped to reduce tension, they have also proved to be profitable.

It is hard to evaluate the exact economic impact of the Troubles -as the Northern Ireland conflict is known- but without doubt it has been immense. Loss of life, destruction of plant and premises, high security costs and a brain drain from Northern Ireland are among the most obvious consequences. But the violence has also kept out investments and tourists. To give some examples: while tourism contributed 7 percent to GDP in the Irish Republic in 1994, it amounted to only 1.5 percent in Northern Ireland. In the same year, almost one billion pounds were spent on law, order and security services.

The hidden costs of the Troubles are also considerable. There is a tradition in Northern Ireland of labelling businesses along sectarian lines. Sometimes these lines are real, sometimes they are imaginary, but the effect is the same: employees, customers and suppliers from 'the other side' are deterred.

Companies looking for a supplier or a candidate for a job openly or unconsciously ask themselves 'is he/she one of us?' instead of 'is he/she the best for us?'. Sometimes people cannot buy what they want, or do not have the job they would like, because they are afraid to enter certain areas. Other hidden costs include loss of motivation, absenteeism and disloyalty of workers because of harassment, bullying and unfairness in the workplace.

In the early 1990s, the Northern Ireland business community recognised the link between the Troubles and the slow economic growth of the region, and decided it was time to act. The Northern Ireland branch of the Confederation of Business and Industry (CBI) took the lead. In 1994, the CBI published the document 'Peace - A challenging new era', which became widely known as the 'Peace Dividend paper'. The message of the document was that peace would help spur economic growth and that economic growth would help consolidate peace. If violence ceased, according to the CBI, huge amounts of money that were currently absorbed by the Troubles, could be reinvested in education and infrastructure, which would be of great benefit for the economy.

The August 1994 cease-fire soon provided the evidence to back up the CBI theory:
* tourism jumped 20 percent within the space of a year;
* unemployment dropped to 11,5 percent, the lowest level in 14 years;
* over 30 million pounds in new investment ventures were announced.

Some time later the CBI launched another initiative. Together with six other trade and business organisations it created the Group of 7. This group included the Northern Ireland Chamber of Commerce and Industry, the Institute of Directors, and the Northern Ireland Committee of the Irish Congress of Trade Unions. In October 1996, it brought together representatives of all the political parties involved in the peace talks. During a meeting in Belfast, the Group of 7 presented its economic rationale for peace. The media and politicians at that time had begun to adopt the term 'peace dividend', although some -Unionists in particular- openly declared that business should stick to its own business, which is, in their view, doing business.

'A business cannot afford to be contaminated by a sectarian agenda.'

The Group of 7 organized five further meetings with political parties (collective rather than individual meetings are preferred under the Group's strategy of co-operation and impartiality). It also played an important role in the 1998 Drumcree stand-off, mediating between the Orange Order (a Unionist group that was not allowed to parade down Garvaghy Road, located in a Catholic neighbourhood) and the Garvaghy Road residents, which helped lessen the tensions. Other Group of 7 initiatives have included media statements strongly condemning all forms of violence and appeals to business colleagues to help build up corporate and grassroots support for peace.

The message of the Group of 7 is that Northern Ireland faces a choice between 'peace, progress and prosperity' and a future as 'one of the world's most irredeemable trouble spots'. The Group admits that business alone cannot build peace. But chairman Sir George Quigley claimed in the summer of 1998 that the efforts of the Group 'made it less easy for the parties to simply walk away'. A clear result of the contribution business life made to a more peaceful Northern Ireland was the visit, in June 1998, of a delegation of 17 business leaders led by US secretary of commerce William Daley. Daley openly stated he had come to Northern Ireland to 'support the peace process by facilitating business relationships between the US and the private sectors of Northern Ireland and Ireland'.

In the spring of 1998, together with several other leading business organisations, the CBI published a set of anti-sectarian guidelines for employers and managers. The guidelines, called 'Doing business in a divided society', were the product of a two-year process of debate between the organisations in partnership with the Community Relations Council (CRC), an independent charity that seeks to promote better community relations in Northern Ireland.

'Doing business in a divided society' builds on the work of Counteract, the anti-intimidation unit of the Irish Congress of Trade Unions (ICTU). Counteract organizes anti-sectarian training for unions and community groups and undertakes research into the incidence of intimidation in the workplace.

The guidelines go beyond existing laws that require employers to ensure that the workplace is free from discrimination and harassment. Instead of emphasizing the negative impact of sectarianism, they stress that managing diversity is good management practice. Companies with a good reputation are likely to obtain the best potential workforce and to retain it. They create a sense of satisfaction within the workforce which leads to more commitment and better performance. And because people are the most important resource in any business, such a policy creates competitive advantages.

Guidelines

To help companies screen themselves, the project Doing Business in a Divided Society developed checklists. This is the one for working with the community.

Has your business...
1. A thorough knowledge of how it is perceived in both main communities in Northern Ireland?
2. Evaluated the business costs/benefits of this image?
3. Decided whether this image is one it should have in order to be most profitable?
4. Considered to what extent the business and its staff are actively involved in the community at present, formally and informally, e.g. in schools, community organisations, charities?
5. Ensured that the appropriate balance of active involvement in the two communities is maintained?
6. Planned its future community involvement to ensure that it creates the image in local communities which it wishes to have?
7. Made an unequivocal commitment to being anti-sectarian in its community involvement?
8. Clearly communicated its anti-sectarianism to all staff?
9. Senior staff who consistently model good anti-sectarian practice in their work-related community involvement?

'Allowing political/religious considerations to prevent the retention and development of the best people does not make sound business sense,' the guideline points out.

The same goes for suppliers. By providing the resources of the company, they determine in great part the quality of its goods and services. 'The maxim "quality in, quality out" or conversely "garbage in, garbage out" applies,' according to the guidelines. 'Businesses need good suppliers as well as good customers. A business cannot afford to be contaminated by a sectarian agenda.'

Contaminated companies get less support from the community, the guidelines stress. This makes them vulnerable to crime and vandalism and limits their potential customer-base. Being actively involved in the community also helps a company to comply with quality and environmental standards, which have proven bottom-line benefits.

Despite the fact that the Northern Irish business community's peace efforts have received relatively little publicity they have nevertheless been enthusiastically received by experts.

'The Northern Ireland case shows that, even given deep-rooted animosity, politicians can still reach peace - especially if they focus on their common economic interests,' Jordana Friedman of the Council on Economic Priorities states in her research study 'The Corporate Sector and Conflict Prevention'. She adds: 'Like Northern Ireland, other countries should start applying the logic of economics to peace negotiations. No one talks about the "Bosnian peace dividend" or the "Middle Eastern peace dividend", despite the fact that both regions would benefit economically from a permanent end to violence.'

South African Business and the Transition to Peace and Democracy

From Honest Broker to Constructive Partner

The business community has played -and is still playing- an important role in the South African transition from violence to peace and from apartheid to democracy. Now, the South African nation -including the business community- faces the task of socio-economic development and economic growth. Without this, the best negotiated settlement and constitution in the world is, in the long term, doomed to failure.

The political transition: helping to make peace

Already in the turbulent eighties, some business groupings put pressure on the apartheid government to change its policies (e.g. the Federated Chamber of Industries and the Urban Foundation, which was formed by senior business leaders after the 1976 Soweto uprising). A small group of South African business leaders (mostly from Anglo American Corporation) went to Lusaka in 1985 to meet with a delegation of the banned ANC. And a number of business people were also part of the Dakar meeting with the ANC in July 1987.

During the same period, a small group of senior business leaders decided to take action and form an organisation to interact with the different political parties in the hope to assist a peaceful and negotiated settlement. They called it the Consultative Business Movement (CBM). It started by consulting with political leaders across the political spectrum, including the banned or restricted organisations. This led to the business leaders better understanding the political dynamics, and built relationships between business leaders, political leaders and activists. This credibility and these relationships enabled CBM to make a successful intervention in the peace process of the early nineties.

While the ANC was unbanned in February 1990, and several bilateral agreements with the South African Government were reached in the next 12 months, the country was no nearer to peace or constitutional negotiations by March 1991. When then President FW de Klerk unilaterally called a peace conference, the ANC reacted angrily and publicly, stating that they were not consulted and would not be part of the conference. This threatened the agreements reached and understanding built so far, and also forced the (mostly) black churches and trade unions into the ANC corner and the (mostly) white churches and business into the Government corner - a classic recipe for conflict.

A joint intervention by the South African Council of Churches and CBM, averted conflict. This intervention resulted in business, churches (black and white) and organised labour, as well as all the major political parties, jointly working on a peace process that led to the signing of the National Peace Accord in September 1991.

Once all the political parties had signed this accord, it was necessary to put the agreements into workable structures to have impact and lasting significance. This was done with the help of civil society, specifically businesses at local level, and with full participation and cooperation of political parties. This ensured that the Peace Accord had impact (and often prevented bloodshed) at the local level.

Although the Peace Accord did not end violence (it actually increased during the subsequent negotiations), it provided the foundation for the multi-party negotiations and an outlet for tension, by providing local structures with mechanisms to resolve conflict through negotiation and mediation. This role continued and peaked during the democratic elections of April 1994, with the active support of business.

The credibility and success of the peace intervention caused CBM to be asked by the political parties to assist the CODESA process (the Convention for a Democratic South Africa). In this, CBM was credible enough to be the second choice of both the Government and the ANC, after they did not want to accept each other's first choice. The support provided by CBM was mainly of an administrative, organisational and secretarial nature (e.g. meeting documentation), but took these important issues out of the domain of party politics.

The CODESA process deadlocked for political reasons in mid 1992. Late in 1992, while the parties were still formally deadlocked, CBM intervened to encourage further convergence on the regional issue. With 'passive approval' from the majority parties, it linked local academics with foreign counterparts to frame suggested principles regulating the powers of regions and central government. Many of the local participants were advisers to, or had close links with, the majority parties. Many of these advisers later served on the Technical Committee for constitutional issues at the multi-party negotiations. The team's final report, 'Regions in South Africa', debated options without firmly choosing between them. One of the participants noted that it was a 'highly political document presented as a technical document'. The CBM-report, as it was called, played a role in shaping ANC thinking and brokered consensus out of the public eye which formed for (at least) the ANC and NP the framework for a deal. It 'proved decisive at Kempton Park, where the ultimate agreement closely mirrored its report.' (Friedman & Atkinson).

When the MPNP (CODESA's successor) started in March 1993, the CBM was again requested to play a supportive role, but this time as administrater of the whole process. The underlying (and expanded) mandate from (especially) the two main parties was to monitor the process and communicate any stumbling blocks at an early stage. CBM contracted individuals acceptable to all the parties to assist with some of the work, but managed the administration itself. While some of the resources of the CBM were tied up in the MPNP, others were monitoring the negotiating process and encouraged the parties to push through to a peaceful and negotiated settlement.

The socio-economic transition: helping to make the country work

South African business has realised some time ago that the success of the political transition (including a model constitution) must soon be followed by a successful socio-economic transition. If not, the positive effects of the first will be lost and South Africa catapulted back into conflict. South African business has therefore, at different points in the transition, taken steps to ensure that it plays its part in this socio-economic transition. In that sense, it is also playing a crucial role in helping to make South Africa maintain peace.

President Nelson Mandela launched the National Business Initiative (NBI) in March 1995. At the time, it was seen as business' collective response to the Government's Reconstruction and Development Programme (RDP). In time, it became much more. The NBI was formed out of the CBM and the Urban Foundation, after widespread consultation with business, government, community and labour leaders.

The mission of the NBI is 'enhancing the business contribution to South Africa's success', focusing largely on socio-economic development. Its present operating areas are education and training, local government capacity building, housing delivery facilitation and local economic development.

The NBI works at two levels: on the first level it looks at problems in South African society from a strategic and innovative point of view, identifying blockages in the socio-economic delivery systems. It will then look at the policies that should be adopted and the institutional changes that are necessary to 'make the system work'. In cooperation with Government and other stakeholders it will then develop frameworks which, if implemented correctly and on a large scale, would address the problem. In all this, it not only relies on good policy analysis, but also bringing business principles into the management of public issues.

The second level of the NBI's work, which has emerged fairly recently, is the expansion of the frameworks and programmes that it has developed in consultation with other stakeholders. For this, it relies heavily on the involvement of its 160 member companies, through aligning their own corporate social investment programmes with the national frameworks developed. In addition, the NBI makes use of NGOs and consultants in implementing its frameworks on scale.

The education area is one example of business' impact in the last few years. The NBI has been working with the National Department of Education as well as the provincial departments of the three biggest provinces on the problem of the quality of education. Access to schools is not a problem in South Africa anymore, as more than ninety per cent of children of school going age are in school. The problem is that the quality of education in the majority of schools is very low. In looking at this systemic problem, the NBI devised a framework that would be applicable in every one of South Africa's 27,000 schools. The Education Quality Improvement Programme (EQUIP) is a whole school development framework, in which the governing body of a school (including teachers, parents and pupils) draws up a development plan ('business plan') for the school, identifying priorities for the next five years. Often, the expertise of local

The Business Trust for Job Creation and Human Capacity Development

The Business Trust was formally launched in early 1999 and its mission is to 'accelerate the creation of jobs and the development of human capacity in South Africa, while building productive relationships between business and government and demonstrating the business commitment to South Africa's success'. The Trust is composed of senior business leaders and senior government officials. The Trust will mobilise R1 billion (about $165 million) over five years, asking listed companies to contribute 0,15 per cent of market capitalization and non-listed companies two per cent of after tax profits of one year.

To achieve its objectives, the Trust chose two very specific areas: tourism and schooling. Tourism was chosen because it is projected to be the fastest growing creator of jobs in South Africa. In addition, the knock-on effects of increased tourism will be felt throughout the economy. Schooling was chosen because it forms the foundation of South Africa's human resource development system. Without good quality schooling, further education and training, tertiary education and on-the-job skill development will constantly have to compensate for the inadequacies of the basic education system and remain inefficient.

The Trust will operate according to strict business principles. It was decided to target project areas and identify a limited number of partner organisations with which it would contract (after reaching agreement on the targets set) to do the job. These 'wholesale' partners will then use 'retail' service providers to get the job done on time. For instance, in the marketing of the country as a tourist destination, the Trust will contract SATOUR, a public private partnership organisation, to market South Africa better. For this, SATOUR will subcontract various service providers (e.g. public relations companies). In return, the Trust will invest considerable funding in the marketing project.

The partnership between business and government will not only be at the level of shared responsibility in directing the Trust, but also at the operational level - especially where government agencies and departments must be involved (e.g. at the school level).

companies is utilised to assist in this process. Once this plan is completed, an EQUIP Board, consisting of senior provincial government officials and senior business leaders, accepts the plan and awards the school a grant of about R20,000 ($3,500) to start the implementation of the plan. This money can come from business or government or both. In this way, the governing body (and specifically the parents) takes responsibility for 'their school' and quality improvement can be sustainable. With the help of some of its member companies and NGOs, the NBI is now implementing the EQUIP framework in 250 schools across South Africa.

In Conclusion

Business has a moral obligation to be a constructive and loyal part of civil society, as well as the broader national framework. This calls for partnerships with government. On the other hand, as business needs a stable environment in which to operate, it is clearly in its own long-term interest to ensure that this environment is created and/or maintained. To do this, business has a 'vested interest' to play its role in broader society, including conflict resolution and other transitionary issues. Business' role in the South African transition was made possible by its resources and ability

to manage complex issues efficiently (e.g. logistics, management, organisation and information technology). Because it is not subject to understandably arduous public sector procedures, business can often cut the time for action and delivery. Business could also - especially in the highly politically sensitive and charged negotiation processes- stay neutral or at least objective.

To play this role effectively, business has to organise itself collectively, in addition to ordinary organised business bodies such as chambers of commerce. It was and is easier for collective bodies such as CBM or NBI to be more pragmatic, rise above short term business interests, and take specific steps to build credibility with the different parties.

In situations of conflict where the parties did not even talk, South African business (in its above mentioned collective form) played the role of an 'honest broker'. When small business delegations with trusted and credible people could carry indirect messages to and fro between the parties - to get some form of communication started, business acted as informal honest brokers. A slightly different situation was when business leaders played the role of 'shuttle diplomats' and helped to bring the Inkatha Freedom Party into the 1994 elections.

The managerial and organisational capacity of business opened the doors for it to play a 'secretariat' or organisational role in the 1991 peace process. This was also carried to a formal role for business (and the rest of civil society) in the implementing of the Peace Accord.

An unusual role for (even South African) business was when CBM played a facilitating role to bring constitutional experts into a non-threatening situation to consider and explore possibilities around the powers of regions and the national government. These possibilities were presented to the parties separately and played a decisive role in the eventual consensus.

It is clear that the South African business has played and is playing a significant and important role in the country's transition. This role is not played out yet. The challenge to effect socio-economic transition (including economic growth, economic empowerment and socio-economic development) will be central to South Africa maintaining the peace that has been achieved by the successful political transition.

REFERENCES

Bargaining for Peace - South Africa and the National Peace Accord, Peter Gastrow. United States Institute of Peace Press, Washington, 1995

The Small Miracle - South Africa's negotiated settlement. Steven Friedman and Doreen Atkinson (eds.). South African Review no 7, Ravan, Johannesburg, 1994

Business Initiative on Job Creation and Human Capacity Development, National Business Initiative. Unpublished prospectus, Johannesburg, 1998

This article has been written by Theuns Eloff, Chief Executive of the National Business Initiative, South Africa.

10

Donors

Introduction

The Financial Battery

Donors can make an important contribution to promoting co-existence and peace-building by providing the financial support which enables individuals or groups from different racial, religious and ethnic groups to participate in shared projects. Without funding, it is likely that these efforts would be significantly diminished ♦ By Hans van de Veen

'The financial battery of the system', is how John McDonald and Louise Diamond describe the funding world in their ground-breaking publication, 'Multi-Track Diplomacy'. Without it, they say, many of the peace-building activities in the world could not take place. The funding world occupies 'a place of great power in the system because of its essential role and because it is the agenda setter and gatekeeper for who does what in the field'.

The two case-studies which follow this introductory text, both provide excellent illustrations of the potential role of the donor community. They also illustrate the two main segments of society from which funding originates: the private sector (the dominant strand in the USA), and governments (more common in Europe). The multilateral world -dominated by the United Nations, IMF/World Bank as well as regional organisations- could be seen as a third wing of the funding world. Of course, funding by governments or international organisations overlaps to an extent with other traditional Track One initiatives, and can thus be considered a regular element of their peace-building activities.

Some governments, like in Norway, Sweden, Canada, the United Kingdom and the Netherlands, play an imporant role in supporting peace-building activities. The Dutch government, for instance, supports no less than a dozen of the 35 organisations/projects which are described in this publication. Norway supports the 'People to People' programme, bridging the gap between official peace agreements and the needed dialogue and communication between people (see Box).

The Abraham Fund (see case-study) works on both national and international levels, due in large part to many American Jews' interest in Israel. Fundraising is centred in the U.S. with supervision of the projects being carried out in Israel. Both offices share the task of soliciting, assessing, and distributing grants. This is a model that the Abraham Fund's founder, Alan B. Slifka, feels can be used for coexistence programmes in other nations with a large diaspora such as Ireland/Northern Ireland, or for nations such as South Africa that have aroused interest in other parts of the world. Slifka: 'There are numerous opportunities around the world for organisations modelled after The Abraham Fund.'

A typical governmental initiative -albeit unique in size and extent- is the European Union's Special Support Programme for Peace and Reconciliation in Northern Ireland and the Border Counties of Ireland (see case-study). The programme is one of the most important initiatives to grow out of the 1994 halt in the sectarian violence in Northern Ireland. The EU Peace Fund runs from 1995 until the end of 1999, and entails a total expenditure of some $750 million. It aims 'to reinforce progress towards a peaceful and stable society and to promote reconciliation by increasing economic development and employment, promoting urban and rural regeneration, developing cross-border co-operation and extending social inclusion.'

Many feel that the EU's swift action in order to 'maintain the momentum for peace' may have been an important factor in changing the psychology in Northern Ireland. An important motivating factor behind the entire programme was to encourage all of the people of Northern Ireland, and particularly those most marginalised, to make an investment in their common futures. Basically, the programme presumed that people with a financial stake in their future would be far less likely to risk their prosperity through a renewal of sectarian violence than those who had little to lose. It was therefore essential, the EU believed, to exploit the opportunities for economic and social reconstruction that peace presented.

Foundations
In looking at the role the funding community can play, McDonald and Diamond focus almost exclusively on the charity foundations that dominate the funding landscape in the USA. 'The assumption on which the work of this community is based is that those with wealth have a responsibility and an opportunity to make a positive contribution to the world through the judicious use of that money to sponsor worthwhile projects. Also underlying much of the philanthropy is the belief that the projects funded will explore critical issues, provide needed action, and contribute to the growth and evolution of humanity as it seeks a more peaceful world.'

Funding activity in the US is dominated by such large, mainstream foundations as the Ford Foundation, Pew Charitable Trust, MacArthur Foundation, Carnegie, Mott, and others. These foundations primarily fund major academic and research institutions whose interests lean toward area studies, security, and public policy issues. According to McDonald and Diamond, there are several smaller, more progressive organisations which appear to be more interested in grassroots-action projects, and are more likely to give to environmental, justice, anti-nuclear, and citizen empowerment programmes. Some of these are the Tides Foundation, Treshold, and Plowshares.

Then there are what McDonald and Diamond call 'quasi-governmental' organisations, such as the U.S. Institute of Peace, and the National Endowment for Democracy, which also provide funds for a variety of peace-building activities. NGOs in many Western countries working in the fields of human rights, development cooperation or humanitarian assistance, channel a growing amount of their funds into activities that are aimed at preventing the escalation of conflicts, transforming violent conflicts, or encouraging post-conflict reconciliation. Often, their funding comes from a mixture of sources: from governments to the public, and -in growing amounts- the corporate sector.

People to People

In 1996, due partly to the discrete but powerful initiatives of the Norwegian government, secret negotiations led to a breakthrough in the Israeli-Palestinian conflict and the signing of the Oslo agreements. Contained within the Interim Agreement between the governments was the concept of a People-to-People Program. The aim of this programme was to 'enhance dialogue and relations between their peoples (Israel and Palestine), based on equality and reciprocity, as well as in gaining a wider exposure of the two publics to the peace process, its current situation and predicted results.'

Uniquely this official Israeli-Palestinian programme is being implemented by NGOs. On the Israeli side, the CRB Foundation is charged with planning and funding the Israeli part of the programme. On the Palestinian side, the Palestinian Centre for Peace is vested with the implementing authority. Norway has commissioned the Norwegian research institute Fafo to set up and direct the Norwegian secretariat.

In 1996 the programme decided on a policy of funding projects implemented by non-governmental or grassroots organisations on both sides. A call for proposals was placed in Israeli and Palestinian newspapers, resulting in 120 applications for support from approximately 200 NGOs. All in all, by the end of 1997, the programme had considered more than 180 proposals and had funded 48 projects to the value of approximately USD 850,000. More projects were funded in 1998 and the programme has continued into 1999.

Projects eligible for support under the programme should:
- aim at enhancing dialogue and relations between Palestinians and Israelis;
- be implemented jointly by Israeli and Palestinian organisations;
- foster wider exposure of the two publics to the peace process through education and encourage public discussion and involvement in the peace process;
- increase people-to-people exchange and have the potential to bridge between large audiences on both sides;
- should take place in the region.

The programme is also ready to support larger projects as soon as the two parties are ready to engage in wider activities, such as, for instance, exchanges between public and private schools on both sides, as well as between educational institutions including the Israeli and Palestinian ministries.

While concluding that there will always be a greater demand for money than the funding community will ever be able to meet, McDonald and Diamond argue that 'new sources of funding, through the business community, funding networks, and international sources, will simply have to be found to keep up with this fast-growing field.'

SELECTED BIBLIOGRAPHY

The Handbook of Interethnic Coexistence, Eugene Weiner (Ed.). An Abraham Fund Publication, Continuum, New York, 1998.
Multi-Track Diplomacy - A Systems Approach to Peace, Louise Diamond and John McDonald.

The Abraham Fund Is Bringing Jewish and Arab Citizens Together in Israel

Supporting Grassroots Coexistence

In 1989, Alan B. Slifka, an American businessman and philanthropist, joined with Dr. Eugene Weiner, a rabbi and professor of sociology at the University of Haifa, to create a new organisation dedicated to strengthening relations between the Jewish and Arab citizens of Israel.

Nearly 20 percent of Israel's population -some one million citizens- are of Arab descent. With the exception of a small group of people who live in mixed cities, the majority of Israel's Arab and Jewish citizens live in separate communities, attend different schools, and grow up behind a veil of misunderstanding and prejudice. Slifka and Weiner recognized that the ability of Israel's citizens to coexist in harmony would be critical to Israel's future.

The Abraham Fund is the only not-for-profit fundraising and educational organisation dedicated solely to enhancing coexistence between Israel's Jewish and Arab citizens. Named for Abraham, the revered ancestor of both Arabs and Jews, The Abraham Fund is a non-partisan organisation that supports grassroots coexistence projects to bring Jewish and Arab citizens together to learn about one another and break down destructive stereotypes.

Today, The Abraham Fund is incorporated in the U.S., with 3,400 contributors in the U.S., Israel, Canada and Europe. Since the advent of its grant-making efforts in 1993, The Abraham Fund has distributed more than $5 million to more than 350 different coexistence projects across Israel.

The Abraham Fund has developed a strategy that remains true to its original vision, but which has changed and evolved over the last ten years as the Fund has learned more about the challenges of funding coexistence in Israel.

The Abraham Fund's first project, begun in 1989 and completed in 1992, was to compile a comprehensive directory of 383 Israeli institutions, all of which had coexistence projects and programmes. The Directory demonstrated the depth and breadth of coexistence programming, and proved to be a valuable compendium of information for the agencies and the public.

The organisation's strategy now consists of the following:
1. To financially support grassroots coexistence programmes in Israel through the grant-

The Abraham Fund - and its donors - are bringing coexistence to the forefront of public awareness in Israel.

making process. Each year, the Fund solicits applications from NGOs which have developed Arab-Jewish coexistence projects. These applications are carefully screened by a panel of evaluators (comprised of Jewish and Arab Israelis and Americans) who recommend programmes for funding. All projects supported by The Abraham Fund fall into one of three broad categories: advancing the professionalization of educators and leaders in coexistence, education for coexistence in the community and education in the formal school system. Abraham Fund-supported projects take place in a variety of different settings, from kindergartens to high schools, community centres and social service agencies, hospital and clinics, after-school theatre workshops and photography classes, and more. In addition to awarding grants, The Abraham Fund's office in Israel is active year-round as a resource for project directors, helps organisations develop new programmes, and provides advice and assistance in running programmes.

2. To raise funds from donors (primarily in the U.S. but with a new fundraising campaign in Israel) in order to fund existing projects and encourage organisations to initiate new programmes.

3. To use a variety of tools and techniques to reach out to Israeli leadership and society in order to inform and educate people about coexistence as an issue. This includes publishing brochures, newsletters, and other information (both in the U.S. and Israel), maintaining a website and implementing a public information campaign about its activities.

4. To educate the public about The Abraham Fund, its work, and the issue of coexistence by organizing educational outreach programmes in the U.S. and in Israel, which includes speaking in various settings (e.g. churches and synagogues, forums at non-profit foundations and Jewish organisations, the State of the World Forum). In 1998, the organisation published with the Continuum Publishing Group The Handbook of Interethnic Coexistence, the first single volume bringing together multi-disciplinary thinking on the issue of coexistence in Israel and around the world. To launch The Handbook, The Abraham Fund initiated a series of educational conferences about coexistence at major U.S. universities, including Brandeis University, American University, and the John Jay College of Criminal Justice. Future conferences are planned at the University of Haifa and University of Michigan, Ann Arbor.

5. To encourage Israeli leadership to recognize coexistence as a matter of national importance. To this end, The Abraham Fund has created an advisory group, The Israel Public Council, which includes 70 prominent members of Israeli society. Some of these members include former Yitzhak Navon, former President of Israel, Professor Moshe Many, former President of Tel Aviv University and Judge Abd-El Rahman Zu'bi, Israel's first Arab member of the Supreme Court.

In 1998, The Abraham Fund's Board of Directors voted to begin the development of two major new initiatives outside of its usual grant-making and educational activities. First, The Abraham Fund will develop large-scale 'signature' coexistence projects which will have an impact on a national level. The signature projects are expected to focus on various aspects of education and training, in keeping with The Abraham Fund's emphasis on coexistence education and on the professionalization of the field. The new projects will be differentiated from other Abraham Fund-supported programmes by both their size and their scope.

Second, the organisation is working to establish a National Coexistence Institute which can develop policy, advocacy, and practical teaching materials and methodologies for schools and universities.

Since 1993, The Abraham Fund has granted more than $5 million to more than 350 different grassroots coexistence projects in villages, towns, and cities throughout Israel. The organisation's grants range from $5,000 - $25,000, and results show that The Abraham Fund is making a difference.

Bijschrift

Nearly 30,000 children have learned about coexistence through educational programmes and after-school activities.

More than 2,500 teachers across Israel have received coexistence training and used coexistence curricula and materials developed by Abraham Fund-supported projects. These efforts have a 'geometric' effect, as teachers have then taught lessons of coexistence to their students.

More than 17,400 Arab and Jewish adults have been brought together to work on improving their neighbourhoods, thanks to The Abraham Fund's support of community-based projects.

Grants from The Abraham Fund have directly assisted more than 6,000 Arab and Jewish women through health, advocacy, and social service programmes.

Donor dollars have helped raise additional monies from foundations and government agencies in Israel and the U.S., leading to greater project support.

The Abraham Fund - and its donors - are bringing coexistence to the forefront of public awareness in Israel, and beginning to change the agenda of policy makers and public officials as they begin to realize the importance of Arab-Jewish coexistence and consider funding coexistence education on a national level. The organisation is helping to shape the field of coexistence in two key ways. First, by developing its grant guidelines to reflect the importance the organisation places on coexistence education, The Abraham Fund encourages NGOs to increase their programming in this arena. Second, The Abraham Fund has published a variety of educational materials such as booklets and brochures that outline coexistence theory and illustrate how NGOs are putting theory into practice. The Fund also publishes materials to raise awareness among American Jewish organisations and help donors understand the importance of coexistence funding.

Private funding is critical to support new and existing coexistence projects; to train new coexistence professionals and encourage organisations to hire these professionals; to educate teachers, case workers and other professionals to incorporate coexistence into their classrooms and social service projects; and to continue to enhance awareness of coexistence so that government funding for coexistence will increase.

This article has been written by Alan B. Slifka.

The EU's Special Programme for Peace and Reconciliation in Northern Ireland

A Major Investment in Peace

'The EU Peace Programme has made a crucial contribution to reinforcing progress towards a peaceful and stable society in Northern Ireland and to promoting reconciliation,' declares the UK's Secretary of State for Northern Ireland, Dr. Marjorie 'Mo' Mowlam. She and others feel that the programme may serve as a useful model for other trouble spots, where deep divisions in society have persisted and development has stagnated as a result of both the conflict and the resulting lack of those cohesive structures which would, ordinarily, take the lead in investing for future prosperity.

With the signing of the Good Friday Agreement in the spring of 1998, the people of Northern Ireland took a significant step towards ending nearly three decades of violence. Of course, political violence has affected the social fabric of Ireland for far longer, dating back some four hundred years. The conflict has, in many ways, fed on itself over all those years, with division, exclusion, misunderstanding, poverty, resentment, nationalism, and fear all feeding the oft-repeated cycles of violence.

During the 29 years of what have been rather euphemistically referred to as 'The Troubles', more than 3,500 people have died - primarily in Northern Ireland but occasionally elsewhere - and 20,000 have been seriously injured.

'The EU Peace Programme's twin objectives of promoting social inclusion and, at the same time, making the most of new opportunities to boost economic growth and advance social and economic regeneration have been central to its success.'

This most recent and most hopeful peace initiative was painstakingly brought to its successful conclusion following twenty-two months of difficult negotiations under the chairmanship of former United States Senator George Mitchell. Those negotiations began some two years after paramilitary organisations first issued cease-fire declarations in 1994. Though those cease-fires were subsequently suspended during 1996 and 1997, they had important effects at the time, in stimulating hope among the weary people of Northern Ireland, and spurring parties outside of Northern Ireland to take concrete actions to secure what was then a very fragile peace.

Among the significant actions from outside that grew out of the 1994 halt in the sectarian violence was the European Union's Special Support Programme for Peace and Reconciliation in Northern Ireland and the Border Counties of Ireland (1995-1999), which entailed a total expenditure of 691 million ECU (about $750 million). It aimed 'to reinforce progress towards a peaceful and stable society and to promote reconciliation by increasing economic development and employment, promoting urban and rural regeneration, developing cross-border co-operation and extending social inclusion.' About seventy-three percent of the funding over the five-year period of the programme was provided by the European Union, with most of the remainder coming from the governments of the United Kingdom and the Republic of Ireland. While the majority of the funding was earmarked for Northern Ireland, twenty percent of the funds were allocated to projects in the border counties within the Republic of Ireland. Programme guidelines also stipulated that a minimum of 15 percent of the funding should go to 'cross-border' activities.

That the EU was prepared to act quickly to 'maintain the momentum for peace' may have been an important factor in changing the psychology in Northern Ireland, for an important motivation behind the entire programme was to encourage all of the people of Northern Ireland, and particularly those most marginalised, to invest in their futures. Basically, the programme presumed that people with something to lose would be far less likely to risk their prosperity in a fight than those with little to lose, and that it was therefore essential to exploit the opportunities for economic and social reconstruction that peace presented.

With the inclusion of the most marginalised members of the community as one of the programme's highest priorities, it was essential to create an organisational model that would lend itself to the realisation of this goal.

'From the start,' notes European Commission member Monika Wulf-Mathies, 'it was clear that an innovative approach would be crucial to the Programme's success. The Commission operated on the belief that stability and prosperity are mutually reinforcing, but understood that creating this virtuous circle would require the widest consensus and participation of the local population.'

This meant, in essence, setting up a decentralised structure 'to operate as closely as possible to the ground and to encourage the involvement of local people and organisations in the direction and control of spending.' Significantly, funds were channelled to groups with little experience in administering large scale programmes or large amounts of money - a risk that was recognised and accepted.

Connecting to the gras roots has been achieved by channelling more than half of the programme's funds through organisations operating independently of the government. In Northern Ireland, for example, 26 District Partnerships were established, with oversight in the hands of a 22-member Northern Ireland Partnership Board whose members included representatives of political parties, trade unions, business and rural communities, and voluntary organisations. A conscious effort was made to assure balance in terms of religion, gender and political affiliation. At the local level, each District Partnership included elected officials, representatives of voluntary and community organisations, and the business, labour, and public administration sectors. Each District Partnership followed a six-stage process to develop a strategy for the use of the available funds ending with submission of an Action Plan to the Partnership Board. 16.6 percent of the 691 million euro was allocated to these District Partnerships. Across the border in the Irish Republic, six task forces at the county level fulfilled similar functions.

A variety of other administrative bodies were used to facilitate the effort to channel funds to the grassroots. Eight already existing organisations were designated as 'Intermediary Funding Bodies' with responsibility for selecting projects and disbursing funds to target groups. Nearly 30 percent of the programme's funds were passed through these Intermediary Funding Bodies. In addition, government agencies entered into contracts with five 'Sectoral Partners' to handle support for young children, women and adult education.

> *'Reconciliation leading to lasting peace would ... have to be founded in those communities which had been marginalised from mainstream society. This meant addressing the root causes of exclusion through social reconstruction in order to create a just and inclusive society in which everyone could participate.'*

Just what has $750 million dollars bought in terms of concrete programmes? Programmes have enhanced business and cultural links between Northern Ireland and the Irish Republic, provided technical and leadership training as well as childcare facilities to women wishing to enter the labour market, established pre-school playgroups and afterschool clubs for young children, offered retraining to individuals previously employed in the security sector, and provided development assistance for the tourist industry. In areas where communities suffered long-term, endemic poverty, comprehensive community development programmes have been launched, and community organisations have been established. Derelict parks have been refurbished to restore recreational facilities in areas where few alternatives existed. The priority given to adult education has been reflected in job counselling, guidance and training, especially for members of disadvantaged groups and the long-term unemployed.

With the recognition that poorly educated, underprivileged, alienated young people are prime candidates for membership in paramilitary organisations, various programmes have been set up to engage them more positively. For example, at a youth and technology centre in Londonderry called Powerhouse, young people have been given hands-on experience with high-tech equipment. In engaging these young people, issues such as drug and alcohol abuse are addressed, and the self-esteem and confidence of participants can be enhanced.

Although many of the projects funded under the Peace and Reconciliation Programme have been traditional 'reconciliation programmes', the great majority of the projects have had far more to do with strengthening the social and economic structures in the region. In so doing, the strategy of 'social inclusion' has functioned as a pathway to reconciliation.

Reintegrating ex-prisoners

When prisoners are released from jails, the risk is always great that they will be unable to adapt to life outside, and will return to prison. In the polarised environment of Northern Ireland, where paramilitary organisations retain important influence, ex-prisoners, whether they were members of a paramilitary organisation in the past or not, may be inclined to affiliate with these organisations. But numerous projects funded by the Special Support Programme have been designed specifically to address the needs of ex-prisoners, and to re-integrate them into their communities as productive members of society.

In Belfast projects which were assisted include those designed to help prisoners adapt to life outside. Belfast Self Build, for example, provides training in construction industry skills for former political prisoners. And LINC Resource Centre has received funding for two projects for ex-prisoners - one to provide training in computer skills, and one to provide ex-prisoners with a variety of social skills to assist in re-entry into life outside prison. 'If we're going to salvage anything out of this Peace Process,' says LINC Development Officer Billy Mitchell, 'it's the paramilitaries we have to work with ... and we have to stick at it to keep building confidence, building trust.' LINC has focused on building bridges and promoting dialogue at the community level.

The establishment of the District Partnerships helped to forge relationships across the political divide that had rarely existed in the past and may yield benefits extending far beyond the life of the programme. One close observer, Quintin Oliver, Director of the Northern Ireland Council for Voluntary Action, observes, 'The unique architecture of the partnerships is peculiar to the situation in Northern Ireland and was intended in itself to address conflict and encourage broad participation - based on principles of equality, where there was no 'lead' partner. All political and sectoral parties are still involved in District Partnerships and continue to develop the capacity to work together. The partnership members share views and use the expertise around the table in a constructive consensus building manner. People are becoming involved in positive decision making, many of whose previous experiences were based in opposition. The commitment shown by the individuals involved is an endorsement of the partnership approach. This process is part of the product of peace and reconciliation and should be valued.'

Northern Ireland's Members of the European Parliament (Dr. Paisley, mr. Hume and mr. Nicholson) said in a 1997 'mid-term report' on the Special Programme, 'There can be no doubt that the partnership element of the Special Programme has been a major success. The concept had been conceived of as an experiment, initially in the economic development context, later extended to other social spheres, with the objective of stimulating co-operation between communities and between different interest groups, including District Councils, at local level. It is an experiment which has worked. Indeed it is no exaggeration to say that the partnership concept is the element of the Special Programme which ... has made the most obvious contribution to the programme's basic objectives of Peace and Reconciliation.'

With an awareness that impatience and frustration have tended to undermine reconciliation efforts following the cessation of hostilities or civil conflicts, the European Commission, as well as the governments of the United Kingdom and Ireland all agreed that chances for success of the Special Support Programme would be significantly enhanced if the programme had an 'immediate and visible impact.' That has meant, quite understandably, that difficulties have been experienced in administering a programme where much of the infrastructure for implementation had to be created rapidly, but it has also had the desired effect. People have seen that peace yields concrete results.

Still, the EU has recognised that the Special Support Programme can't be a 'quick fix' but is, rather, simply the beginning of a long-term process, with important progress made 'in developing relationships at all levels and establishing new ways of working together.'

Monika Wulf-Mathies observes hopefully: 'The decentralised approach... may help inspire other regions wishing to adopt similar methods to strengthen local involvement in programmes [supported by the European Commission].' Naturally, the parties to a conflict have to first commit themselves to put aside their differences and work to rebuild society, but the example of the EU's Special Programme is both an incentive for them to do so, and proof that if they do, the tangible results will ensure greater security and prosperity.

This article is mainly based on the following two publications:
- *European Commission: Peace and Reconciliation - An imaginative approach to the European programme for Northern Ireland and the Border Counties of Ireland. Luxembourg, Office for Official Publications of the European Communities, 1998.*
- *Paisley, Hume, Nicholson: Special Support Programme for Peace and Reconciliation in Northern Ireland and the Border Counties of Ireland - Revisited. Report to Jacques Santer, President of the European Commission, 1997.*

All quotes have been taken from these publications.

II

Reconciliation

Introduction

Thoughts on Reconciliation and Reality

In the course of a public discussion on reconciliation held in South Africa, Reverend Mxolisi Mpambani told a story: Peter and John are friends. But Peter stole John's bicycle. Three weeks later Peter said to John, 'Let's talk about reconciliation.' John told him, 'We can't discuss reconciliation until you give my bicycle back.' Peter responded, 'Forget about the bicycle. Reconciliation is the important point.' John refused to have anything to do with him ♦ By COLLEEN SCOTT

Reverend Mpambani pointed out that returning something material was one form of the problem. But those who were murdered can not be returned: the survivors' aching emotional loss is something they must endure as long as they live. And the trauma of physical and emotional abuse, of torture and rape, cannot be erased in any material way.

In the same discussion, Heidi Grunebaum-Ralph, a doctoral student, noted that when speaking of reconciliation there is a danger of forgetting who was wronged and of encouraging a kind of amnesia which devalues the experience of those who have suffered.

Victims and survivors do not forget what has happened to them. If their experiences remain unaddressed and are allowed to fester they will have catastrophic consequences in the future. Attempts to evade the reality of those who have suffered hideously in the past set the stage for those memories to boil over in violent response to the immediate present; even worse, the memory of these grotesque realities are passed on to succeeding generations and become a mythology which will support equally hideous reaction in the future. Unless they are faced as a part of a complete reality, sooner or later memories are acted upon.

Archbishop Desmond Tutu, Nobel Laureate and Chairman of the South African Truth and Reconciliation Commission (TRC) has said: 'You can only be human in a human society. If you live with hate and revenge, you dehumanize not only yourself, but also your community. You must forgive to make your community whole.' But Simon Wiesenthal, a survivor of the Nazi concentration camps who is known for having tracked down more than 1000 Nazi war criminals, tells us that, 'Forgiveness is a personal matter, and I am not authorized to forgive on behalf of others.'

Thabo Mbeki, Deputy President of South Africa has observed that, 'Real reconciliation cannot be achieved without a thorough transformation and democratization process. True reconciliation can only take place if we succeed in our objective of social transformation.'

Charles Villa-Vicencio, former Research Director of the TRC, doesn't speak of reconciliation. He talks about achieving 'peaceful coexistence'.

The Archbishop is completely correct in his references to a dehumanized community, and Wiesenthal's point that forgiveness is a personal matter must persist alongside the truth the Archbishop makes clear. Certainly the ideal of reconciliation is easily -and frequently- misused, as Grunebaum-Ralph points out. When a nation adopts reconciliation as a focus it all too easily happens that victims and survivors are faced with an impatient demand that of course they must reconcile, and they must do so immediately.

Mbeki and Villa-Vicencio identify the central practical problem of reconciliation. Achieving reconciliation requires -and requires absolutely- some basic elements.

Reconciliation needs truth. People must know what happened, and why it happened to them. They need to know where their deceased lie; they must know if those who simply disappeared are alive somewhere, or are long dead. Truth is painful, but this pain must be endured if there is to be any hope of reconciliation.

Hasan Nuhanovic was an interpreter for the UN Military Observers and for the Dutchbat team guarding the demilitarized enclave of Srebrenica. She was an eyewitness of the events of mid-July 1995 when she lost her brother, father and mother. 'The Dutch, like the French, British and US governments, are trying to forget the Srebrenica massacre. They are doing nothing to help us, the families of the missing, to find out the truth about what happened to our loved ones.'

If there is to be any hope of reconciliation in the wake of the Srebrenica massacres, people like Hasan Nuhanovic must learn the truth of what happened to their loved ones.

Reconciliation requires that victims and survivors are heard. Their stories, their emotional and factual truths must be fully acknowledged. But the perpetrators must be heard too. Putting all these stories together creates a reality which is resistant to mass mythology constructed from the worn fabric of ancient grievances. An old Italian proverb tells us that noble vengeance is the daughter of deep silence. Avoiding that 'noble vengeance' is a matter of gently cultivating an openness to full reality when silence has been either harshly imposed, or is clung to.

In their creation, Truth Commissions focus on reconstructing memory. This requires that both the factual and the emotional truth is made clear. To quote the Guatemalan Accord for the United Nations sponsored Commission for Historical Clarification, it's purpose is 'To clarify with all objectivity, equity and impartiality the human rights violations that have caused the Guatemalan population to suffer, connected with the armed conflict.'

In her classic comparative study of fifteen Truth Commissions published by the Human Rights Quarterly in 1994, Priscilla B. Hayner notes that the El Salvadorian Truth Commission report had, in the end, confirmed what many people have long accepted as true.

But official acknowledgement of widespread abuses was important in itself. This observation applies to many of the Truth Commissions which have been convened in the last 25 years.

The question following the work of a Truth Commission is whether or not the parties running the government will build on the facts which have been uncovered. Governments and citizens may attempt to ignore what has been brought to light. But memory is almost impossible to wipe out.

Restitution and rehabilitation are essential to reconciliation: Mpambani's story is a simple explanation of one of the cardinal challenges facing those who would work for reconciliation. Restitution is another form of justice, and may well be a form which will much mean more to victims and survivors than will prison sentences for perpetrators.

Donald Shriver, author of 'An Ethic for Enemies' also notes: 'Apologies set the record straight; restitution sets out to make a new record...' But when large groups of people suffer intense and ongoing human rights violations, what is stolen is far more difficult to return than a bicycle. As one black South African put it when describing what had happened during apartheid: 'They stole the laughter of our children.'

Rehabilitation and restitution open the possibility of bringing the laughter back to the next generations.

Reconciliation is not a goal. It is a process. When thinking about reconciliation, we must remember the fact that today's perpetrators were yesterday's victims. Let us consider some common misconceptions and misunderstandings of what reconciliation is.

1   Equating forgiveness with reconciliation is an error. Both are effective in different ways, but they are very, very different actions. It simply may not be humanly possible for a person to forgive. But even when that's true, it's still possible for that person to choose to reconcile. A person may choose to follow the path of reconciliation for their own good, or for the greater (social) good, or for both reasons... and still not be able to forgive. And an individual may choose to forgive the perpetrator, but not what that perpetrator did, which will have consequences for the reconciliation process.

2   Acknowledgement can be almost as effective as apology, especially when forgiveness is not expected and reconciliation is sought. But equating acknowledgement with apology is a mistake. Simply admitting that you've done something that's caused great hurt or harm is a very different action from an apology on the basis of real remorse, especially with the intention to rectify the harm that's been done. It may be possible to reconcile when the truth is known. But forgiveness requires repentance which is also expressed by personal efforts to heal the damage and its consequences.

3   Another problem has to do with the assumption that there's one all encompassing truth which is humanly knowable. When a person has been tortured, or a loved one has been murdered, and the perpetrators of these acts disclose what they've done as fully as they are

able, their honesty may still not be the truth that the victims, or the survivors of atrocity desperately need to hear. There's an enormous gap between the factual truth, and the reality which encompasses both factual truth and the emotional truth. To re-create the reality which existed before, the factual truth must be known. But room must also be made for the emotional truth of the victims, the survivors, and the perpetrators. Reconciliation requires the painful acceptance of this reality, as imperfect as it will unquestionably be.

4 Unconsidered, unrealistic, unreasonable, and impossible expectations make reconciliation very, very difficult. If you commit atrocities, are a victim of atrocities, or are exposed to atrocity, it is not possible to return to a time before violations took place. The past can not be erased or changed. No one can be returned to a time of innocence before hideous acts are committed. Reconciliation can not restore the dead to life, or wipe out hideous memories. Neither can vengeance or revenge accomplish this - either of which will tend to perpetuate the cycle of action-reaction and cause and effect. Even punishment, as dictated by due process under rule of law, will not wipe away past suffering.

It is also true that a person may honestly believe that the act of telling their story will be enough, or that hearing a perpetrator's story will be enough, and that either or both together will create reconciliation. This may happen, and the presence of an outside agency which is devoted to the ideal of reconciliation will strengthen this possibility. But frequently a great deal more is needed.

5 There is also the problem of coping with atrocity. What is to be done with a person who confesses to having deliberately tortured and/or murdered thirty, forty, fifty people under orders from his superiors whose current 'wisdom' and long-range goals he believed in completely? In 'The Human Condition', Hannah Arendt argues that it is impossible to punish radical evil: '...men are unable to forgive what they cannot punish, and they are unable to punish what has turned out to be unforgivable. This is the true hallmark of those offenses which, since Kant, we call 'radical evil', and about whose nature so little is known, even to us who have been exposed [to them]...'

Youk Chang is a survivor and archivist of the Khmer Rouge atrocities in Cambodia. When reflecting on what should be done with the Khmer Rouge leaders now, he notes that it is impossible to truly punish them. 'How would they pay back two million lives? Should they die two million times? Live in hell for two million years?... The crimes they committed are so grave that I don't know what punishment would be fair.'

6 Lack of attention to the fruits of history and their relationship to individual and group motivation causes terrible problems. This is not a question of justification, but of comprehension which can lead to both the understanding, and the compassion needed - on both sides- for reconciliation to be realized. Jose Zalaquett is a Chilean activist and lawyer who served on his country's Commission on Truth and Reconciliation. He wrote, 'Memory is identity. Identities consisting of false or half memories easily commit atrocities.'
History is a chain of human action and reaction: the present, and the future, are

constructed in the past. No matter how hard we may try, what we can know about what has happened before -the history to which we react- is inescapably formed by what we are able to perceive. It is quite easy to say that there is no such thing as truth. It is much harder to admit that we all have limits of perception; that we all have false and incomplete memories.

7 Then there's the problem of scape-goating and community versus individual responsibility. It is tempting in the extreme to blame one's individual actions -or lack of action- on the ethos of the time. It's human to say to oneself: 'They did it. I didn't. I could never do anything like that. And I'd never support it, if I knew about it.'

But the problem is more complex than that. In 1946, when reflecting on German guilt for the atrocities of World War II, Karl Jaspers suggested that there are four levels of guilt, all of which must be addressed. First, there is criminal guilt, relating to the physical perpetrators of aggression. Next is political guilt, something that only active resisters were exempt from. Thirdly there is moral guilt, which involves anyone who closed their eyes to events, or who allowed themselves to be bought off by personal advantage, or by intoxication by events, or who obeyed from fear. Finally, there is metaphysical, or corporate guilt. This is a guilt we all share in by virtue of our common humanity. Jaspers tells us that only by recognizing the potential for evil in all humanity is it possible to create a new source of active life.

8 The belief that justice can only be defined as punishment of perpetrators of human rights violations creates a barrier to reconciliation. Donald Shriver observes that the development of thought from Plato and Aristotle to Kant and John Stuart Mill has been centred on the idea that justice is for the conferring of good, as well as the upholding of right. He writes that 'justice is a search, as well as a single event.'

In his introduction to 'Radical Evil on Trial', a first-hand analysis of developments in Argentina during the 1980s when an inhumanly brutal military dictatorship gave way to a democratic government, Carlos Santiago Nino observes that, '...it is questionable whether punishment of radical evil can effectively prevent such evil from recurring.' He later suggests that a preventionist theory of punishment may fare better. This must include the question of allocation of financial resources.
Shriver writes, 'Cherishing hope for revenge is one way sufferers of atrocity cope with their memories. But there is another way: facing still-raw past evils with regard for the truth of what actually happened; with resistance to the lures of revenge; with empathy -and no excusing- for all agents and sufferers of the evil; and with real intent on the part of the sufferers to resume life alongside the evildoers or their political successors...'

Justice must include some form of punishment of the guilty. But this is not the only definition of the word; and it may not even be the most crucial -or valuable- interpretation to use when seeking to promote the most fundamental social good in a country riven by war and oppression.

9   Time is a problem. Anyone who believes that a national focus on reconciliation can, or should, solve all problems quickly and simply is a fool. Reconciliation, and rebuilding a shattered society takes decades and generations of slow and steady work. As South African President Nelson Mandela points out, 'patterns of thought which have been there for more than three centuries can't be changed in four years.' The process of reconciliation very often takes more time than people may understand that they must be willing to give it.

Marie Smyth is the co-ordinator of an investigation on the experiences and effects of Northern Ireland's 'Troubles' on that population, and professor at Smith College in the United States. At a conference sponsored by INCORE (Initiative on Conflict Resolution & Ethnicity) on coping with transition, she said, 'From research done in other countries... one of the concepts they came across was that of Positive Revenge. Positive Revenge is when, recognizing the harm that has been done to you, you refuse to allow that harm to determine the rest of your life. You become determined to lead a positive life, to make a positive contribution, and not to let the perpetrator win... [Instead you] resist the damaging effects and triumph over them.' She goes on to note that some people who have had multiple bereavements or have themselves been terribly injured have managed to overcome their own situation and become active community workers for reconciliation.

What Ms. Smyth speaks of can indeed happen spontaneously and without any outside assistance, sometimes. But if we are serious about breaking the chains of cause and effect and inspiring reconciliation on a broad scale, then we must assist victims and survivors in their efforts to reach this point of personal reconciliation.

As was observed in a recent LatinoLink report on the publication of the Guatemalan Historical Clarification Commission Report, 'No one can today insure that the immense challenge of reconciliation through truth can be met with success. In order to do so, the historic facts must be recognized and assimilated in each individual consciousness and the collective consciousness. The country's future depends in great part on the response of the state and society to the tragedies suffered in flesh and blood by the immense majority of Guatemalan families.'

Or, and as the Final Report of the South African TRC points out, 'Reconciliation is a process which is never-ending, costly, and often painful. For the process to develop, it is imperative that democracy and a human rights culture be consolidated. Reconciliation is centred on the call for a more decent, more caring, and more just society. It is up to each individual to respond by committing ourselves to concrete ways of easing the burden of the oppressed and empowering the poor to play their rightful part in society.'

SELECTED BIBLIOGRAPHY

An Ethic for Enemies - Forgiveness in Politics, Donald Shriver. London/New York, Oxford University Press, 1995

Building Peace - Sustainable Reconciliation in Divided Societies, John Paul Lederach. United States of Peace Press, Washington DC, 1977

Country of My Skull, Antjie Krog. Johannesburg, Random House, 1998

Exploring Forgiveness, Robert D. Enright and Joanna North (eds.). Madison, University of Wisconsin Press, 1998

Past Imperfect - Dealing with the Past in Northern Ireland and Societies in Transition, Brandon Hamber (ed.). Derry/Londonderry, Initiative on Conflict Resolution and Ethnicity, United Nations University, 1998. Online copy available: www.incore.ulst.ac.uk/publications/research/dwtp/index.html

Peace by Peacefull Means - Peace and Conflict Development and Civilization, Johan Galtung. Prio Sage, London, 1996

Promoting Justice and Peace through Reconciliation and Coexistence Alternatives, Mohammed Abu Nimer (ed.), American University, Washington, forthcoming Truth and Reconciliation Commission Report, Volumes One through Five. Capetown, Juta, 1998.

The Forgiveness Factor - Stories of Hope in a World of Conflict, Michael Henderson. Grosvenor Books, Salem, 1996

Ways Out - The Book of Changes for Peace, Gene Knudsen-Hofmann (ed.). John Daniel & Company, Santa Barbara, 1988

The South African Truth and Reconciliation Commission

'Harrowing the Ground so that Others May Build'

The second time I went to South Africa to sit in on TRC hearings, Antjie Krog, a radio journalist with the South African Broadcasting System gave me a copy of a letter. The letter had been signed, first name only, and although the writer indicated what part of the country she was from, she wrote: 'I prefer to keep our address anonymous. We don't need any 'silencers'... an accident happens too easily.'

'After my husband had spent about three years with the Special Forces, our hell began. He became very quiet. Sometimes he would just press his face into his hands and shake uncontrollably... I never knew. Never realized what happened during 'the trips'. I had to be satisfied with 'what you don't know won't hurt you....'

'Today I know the answers to all my questions. I know where it began... The role of 'those at the top'... and 'our vultures' who had to carry out their bloody orders. The churches and community leaders. Of those who did everything to keep exclusive power. Today they all wash their hands in innocence and resist the realities of the TRC... I stand by my murderer who let me and the old White South Africa sleep peacefully... While those at the top were targeting the next 'permanent removal from society'.

'I have forgiven the freedom fighters for their bombs, mines and AK-47s they used so liberally. There were no angels... I would have done the same had I been denied everything... if I had to watch how White people became dissatisfied with the best, and still wanted better, and got it.'

'I envy and respect the people of the struggle. At least their leaders have the guts to stand by their vultures, to recognize their sacrifices... As long as the vultures were useful, tributes were dished out. Today, the same vultures are wasted and ask only recognition and support. They do not get it....'

'One night my wasted vulture told me: They can give me amnesty a thousand times but I have to live with this hell. The problem is in my head, my conscience. There's only one way to be free of it. Blow my own brains out. That's where my hell is.'

Deputy President Thabo Mbeki PHOTO GEORGE HALLET

Reconciliation after war and a hideously grotesque pattern of gross violations of human rights is a matter of creating peace in the present, and of sustaining peace in the future. Peace is not simply a matter of stopping physical violence. It is also a matter of helping people overcome what has been done to them... and of overcoming what they have done, so that a future might be built.

In and of itself, no Truth Commission can create reconciliation. Much less can a Truth Commission create peace. However, they do create conditions which make reconciliation and peaceful coexistence possible. They do this by uncovering the reality which embraces the factual truth of the past, and the emotional truth of both the past and of the present. No Truth Commission to date has done more to create such a full picture of reality than the South African TRC. The TRC has made it possible for the citizens of that country to begin to understand why people participated in such grotesque actions, and it has made clear what must be done to prevent such things from happening again.

This was accomplished in two ways. First, the TRC chose to work with a restitutive, rather than a retributive concept of justice. And second, they made the choice that all aspects of the Commission's work would be kept absolutely transparent. They emphatically encouraged the national -and international- public and media to be a part of this work.

Not all South African citizens are happy with the way in which the TRC functioned. In particular, some who survived torture, rape, abduction, and some whose loved ones were tortured and murdered in cold blood passionately desire that the perpetrators of atrocity be punished for their crimes. There's a strong undercurrent that justice has not been done; that the only thing that will assuage the bitterness of loss, of acid grief, of harrowing memory, and continuing painful present, is retribution.

A person who has not personally lived through such horrors is in no position to argue with this. Instead, let us consider how the TRC worked, and why it worked the way it did.

The TRC is the result of a negotiated settlement that ended the war in South Africa. No side won that war. If the negotiations had failed, there was a ghastly prospect that civil war would continue.

Archbishop Desmond Tutu PHOTO GEORGE HALLET

Military and security chiefs wanted a blanket amnesty, while some representatives of the liberation forces demanded trials. But some form of amnesty provision was essential to ending that war: without it the killing, the torture, the rapes and disappearances would have continued.

A compromise was eventually reached, and in May of 1995 President Mandela signed the Promotion of National Unity and Reconciliation Act (the Act) which lead to the creation of the TRC.

The TRC consisted of the Human Rights Violations Committee (HRV), the Reparation and Rehabilitation Committee (R&R), and the completely autonomous Amnesty Committee. Each of these committees was assisted in their work by the Investigation Unit, and by the Research Unit which was also responsible for the creation of the Final Report. The HRV Committee was at work for about 15 months. They received and investigated more than 21,000 statements from Apartheid's victims and survivors. They also oversaw hearings for various South African institutions, including media, business, the medical profession, and religious organisations.

The R&R Committee was responsible for developing a policy for reparations and rehabilitation for victims and survivors. They made recommendations on the basis of what was learned from the HRV hearings and submissions.

These recommendations were sent to the office of the President, and then to the Parliament. The TRC's Final Report recommends that over a six year period a little under three billion South African Rands should be paid out; however, this is being debated in Parliament at the time of this writing, and it is uncertain what the final decision will be.

The Act also included some specific elements which made it possible for the South African TRC to penetrate, to an unprecedented degree, the reality that had existed during apartheid.

One unusual element of the Act was that it granted the TRC power of subpoena. The TRC could and did legally compel persons to attend hearings and give evidence. If a subpoena was refused, legal penalties, including fines and jail terms were applied.

But the most important of these elements was the TRC Amnesty Provision. According to the Act, amnesty could be granted to individual persons who made full disclosure of all relevant facts relating to acts of violence associated with a political objective. The Act specified that employees of the state, including both Security Forces and the military, and members of the liberation forces, were eligible for amnesty for acts of political violence committed between March, 1960 and May, 1994.

Persons receiving amnesty from the TRC's Amnesty Committee are immune to prosecution in South Africa's civil or criminal courts. Conversely, those who applied but did not receive it, or those who did not apply at all, may face either or both criminal and civil charges, providing enough evidence can be found to write indictments. (97 percent of amnesty applications heard as of June, 1998, have been denied.)

The South African Truth and Reconciliation Commission created a direct linkage between amnesty granting and truth telling: amnesty for truth. If perpetrators had not voluntarily come forward much truth and much reality of that time would have been lost. Paper trails and evidence regarding perpetrators of gross violations of human rights do exist. But not a lot of it. And not enough to successfully prosecute all perpetrators of gross violations of human rights during apartheid.

'Our nation needs healing. Victims and survivors who bore the brunt of the apartheid system need healing. Perpetrators - those who tortured and killed - are, in their own way, victims of the apartheid system. They, too, need healing.'

The agonizing cascade of information coming out of the TRC hearings was challenged many times, particularly in courts of law. The TRC faced a barrage of litigation from perpetrators who didn't wish to be named in HRV hearings, and from political parties who had constitutional and bias problems with the process. Lawsuits were filed by survivors who did not require more information out of Amnesty proceedings because they knew what had happened to their loved ones and wished to see either criminal or civil cases mounted against alleged perpetrators in the hope that they would be found guilty and punished. Although only a few of these challenges had the specific intent of silencing the torrent of raw information pouring forth from the TRC in many cases, had they been successful, their effect would have been just that.

The truth that came out of these TRC hearings is about delivering justice, but not as in 'justice equals punishment of those proven guilty in a court of law'. For the TRC justice is about uncovering what really happened: it's about establishing reality in all it's conflicting perspectives. This essential form of justice would have not been found in the work of adversarial court cases. It required an amnesty process.

But justice is also a matter of the victims and survivors being able to tell their stories, to tell the reality of their experience and to make it public. There will always be a gap between the factual truth, and the reality which encompasses both factual truth and the emotional truth. To re-create the reality which existed before, the TRC has demonstrated that one must have the factual truth. But it has also clearly shown the urgent necessity of making room for the emotional truth of the victims, the survivors, and the perpetrators. All of these people must tell their stories: if the intention is to foster reconciliation, all of these people must be heard.

As was noted by the Constitutional Court of South Africa, the desire to see perpetrators of human rights violations vigorously prosecuted and then punished for their callous and inhuman conduct is legitimate. But they also wrote that: 'Much of what transpired in this shameful period [of apartheid] is shrouded in secrecy and not easily capable of objective demonstration and proof. Loved ones have disappeared, sometimes mysteriously, and most of them no longer survive to tell their tales...

'The Act seeks to address this massive problem by encouraging these survivors and dependents of the tortured and the wounded, the maimed and the dead to unburden their grief publicly... and, crucially, to help them to discover what did in truth happen to their loved ones, where and under what circumstances it did happen, and who was responsible. That truth, which the victims of repression seek so desperately to know is, in the circumstances, much more likely to be forthcoming if those responsible for such monstrous misdeeds are encouraged to disclose the whole truth with the incentive that they will not receive the punishment which they undoubtedly deserve if they do this. Without that incentive, there is nothing to encourage [perpetrators] to make the disclosures and to reveal the truth...'

To really understand the stunning accomplishment of the TRC, one need only turn to the five-volume Final Report. There were limits to the amount of truth the TRC could dredge up in its two and a half year life span, but within those limits, a picture of the whole is bitterly plain: it is impossible to create or sustain any mythology with regard to this civil war in the face of what the Final Report records.

The legacy of the TRC is eternal. Now, when we are still so close to it, we can only barely make out the meaning of the whole: each succeeding generation must build further on the reality the TRC has offered. There were flaws and omissions in the TRC's process and results. But the Commission did an extraordinary job of beginning.

This article has been written by Colleen Scott.

The Corrymeela oasis in Northern Ireland

A Sense of Community

Volunteers and participants in the Corrymeela Community's work are part of a unique experiment to create a common space within which all the various groups involved in one of the world's main trouble spots, can find an oasis of reconciliation.

I t is Friday night and Corrymeela Community member Lisa Bullick is recounting for a group of listeners, an incident that took place on August 15, 1998, in the centre of the town of Omagh, County Tyrone, Northern Ireland. A bombing in which 29 people were killed and many injured. There is silence as Lisa talks.

'I cannot describe to you the feeling of sadness,' she says. 'It's like a fog and cloud hanging over the whole town, and it will not lift.'

She was holidaying at a caravan site with her two young boys when a woman pedalling towards a telephone box shouted news that a bomb had gone off in the very centre of the provincial town in the midst of people doing their shopping. Lisa described her shocked reactions, and those of people she encountered. She told of going into the town on the Monday as a sign of solidarity.

Then she commented: 'I have to say that belonging to the Corrymeela Community has been one of the greatest comforts in the last month that I will ever know.' Her husband, Eric, also a member of Corrymeela, said he could not keep track of the numbers of people who had called to offer help, although the Bullicks did not lose any close relative in the bombing.

In the Oxford dictionary, definitions for the word 'community' are many and varied.
'All the people living in a specific locality'.
'A specific locality, including its inhabitants'.
'A body of people having a religion, a profession, etc. in common'.
In many conflict zones, including Northern Ireland since the Troubles, 'community' can even be a byword for factions - as in 'Catholic community' vs 'Protestant community', for example.
However, when applied to Corrymeela, 'community' refers to an all-embracing spirit (as in the Oxford Concise definition 'a feeling of belonging to a community expressed in mutual support').

Corrymeela is centred at a residential site near Ballycastle on the North coast of Northern Ireland. But it is not just a place. Describing it as a partnership involving a whole range of community groups, would be closer to the mark. A flexible programmeme allows full

At the Corrymeela centre

participation in a range of projects covering schools, Youth, Church, Community and Family groups.

It is a quest for reconciliation through sharing. Corrymeela is, at its essence, about facilitating personal contact as a way of reducing tension.

Ray Davey, who founded the Community in the sixties, explains the idea underpinning it thus: 'From the very start the idea of community has been very central in Corrymeela. No doubt, it was this that drew many people to it at the beginning and continues to do so. This search for togetherness is, indeed, very much part of everyone's inner life. The desire to belong, to be accepted and to be wanted are parts of being human.'

A YMCA Field worker during World War II, Davey was captured in North Africa and was a prisoner of war in camps in Italy and Germany. His experience of the community spirit engendered among soldiers held captive was counterbalanced by the evidence he observed of terrible inhumanity and injustice on the battlefields. As Presbyterian Chaplain at Queen's

University in Belfast, Davey sought new ways to deal constructively with conflict situations and to develop new relationships between 'traditional enemies'.

His emphasis on exploring and promoting a sense of 'community' occurred at a time of major changes in the world. In the sixties, Europe was enraptured in a mood of optimism. This spirit infected mainly young adults and students. 'The early Sixties,' Davey recalled, 'were times of listening and learning to discern the signs of the times and the later Sixties of commitment to the journey for peace.'

Drawing from similar experiences in Scotland (the Iona Community) and Northern Italy (the Agape Community), the Corrymeela Community was set up as '...a place where...the ideals of Christian Community' could be practised. Students, teachers, businessmen, ministers met and decided to obtain a building for use as a meeting place.

'We would not affiliate ourselves with any particular denominational structure, but were anxious not to fall into the old Protestant trap of forming a new splinter group,' recalls Bill Breakey, one of the founders. 'So, we resolved that we would all remain active in our own churches. We wanted to have, for ourselves, the richness of community experience and the power that a community can have; even to move mountains.'

That was in the mid-1960s. Today, the Corrymeela Community operates on several fronts. There is the residential centre located just outside the town of Ballycastle in County Antrim. In Belfast, the administrative office - Corrymeela House - serves as a base for field workers, meeting place for Corrymeela groups in the city, and a resource for many other groups who share some of the same aims but lack a meeting place.

A range of School, Youth, Adult and Church projects and open residential events for people from all traditions on social, cultural, political and religious themes is undertaken. It is considered important that issues of politics, religion, culture and social environment are discussed and explored. Broader perspectives are sought in such discussions. 'Encounters' involving young people meeting and sharing their experiences and listening to each other, form the basis of youth work. A programme like the Seed Group brings young people together to reflect on issues, experiences and influences that have shaped who they are. Such programmes, in which 18-25-year-olds participate, lead many to become more actively involved in reconciliation efforts in their own communities.

Through the Department of Education, Corrymeela Community has developed various intra and interschool encounter programmes which are supplemented by community relations projects. Support is also given to new projects in peace and reconciliation work, and training offered in fields of conflict, mediation, Christian education and the like. Victims and those under stress are provided with sanctuary and support.

At Ballycastle guests share in domestic chores as part of a living community with Corrymeela members, volunteers and centre staff. The place is a respite for families from different backgrounds and having a variety of affiliations. A similar, though smaller, 'hillside retreat' is

Paddy and William

Huge barriers separate the Catholic and Protestant areas of Belfast, Northern Ireland. Walls, rising as high as 18 feet, symbolic of both security and fear.

Corrymeela Community has used a novel method to encourage dialogue between families on both sides of the so-called Peace Wall. A 'feelings box' was opened. Anyone can place into the box a single word written on a piece of paper expressing what it was like to live in the shadow of the Peace Wall. Then the pieces of paper are taken out and read without giving away the identity of the writer. Those listening to the messages being read could add whatever they wished.

What emerged was that there were few differences between the ideas and feelings expressed by either side. Loss of loved ones evoked similar feelings from Catholics or Protestants contributors to the box. People on both sides shared common feelings about loss of loved ones, lost childhood, and other tragedies.

The 'feelings box' also burst with varied opinions on the word 'hatred'.

'I don't mean to say that I hate anyone,' one woman said. 'What I meant was that I don't wish to carry on knowing that I am hated, and that my children are hated.'

What did they understood by the word 'community'?

Both sides wanted peace, better amenities for their children, jobs. They wanted a community centre where both communities could continue to meet and support each other. Children have also been embraced in this attempt to get feelings out into the open, and encouraging a sharing of ideas. Two boys who usually throw bricks over the Peace Wall met at Corrymeela. Paddy is Catholic, William a Protestant.

Paddy was asked: 'What if you hit William?'

'Oh, I wouldn't.'

'How is that.'

'I'm a good shot. I wouldn't aim at William.'

'But sometimes you can't see who you will hit, the wall is too high.'

Paddy thought long and hard.

'Yeah, you're right. I'm going to have to climb up to the top of the derelict house where I can get a really good aim.'

'But Paddy, last weekend you could have injured William with a stone, because then you didn't know him. How would you feel about that now.'

'Bad!' said Paddy, and he and his friends decided to stop throwing stones over the Peace Wall.

located at Knocklayd. Opened in 1993, this is a smaller meeting space for groups and a quiet space for individuals. Its focus is on ecumenical spirituality.

During the summer family, youth and special interest groups visit that centre for a week in a programme adapted to suit the needs of each group.

Ballycastle, Knocklayd and Belfast are like resource centres for a dispersed Community of 200 people. In addition, there are 5,000 friends of Corrymeela spread throughout the community at large. In return for the assistance they receive from these centres, the friends and members feed their efforts into the development of the centres. These are, by and large, lay people: there is only a sprinkling of clergy. They span various social groups. There are members working full time in education, doing youth and community work, probation service, youth training and unemployment schemes, in health, industry, agriculture, the civil service, and the like. There are even politicians active among them.

It's a vital two-way process, key to keeping Corrymeela open, and challenging the community to be flexible to the real needs of members and to changes in the society. Members are encouraged to maintain links with local churches, neighbourhood and local communities. They are also urged to live out their commitment to family, at work or in local social and political situations, so as not to become isolated and sever their roots in the society.

As William Rutherford, an early member, explains, the origins of Corrymeela, 'belong to a very active form of Christianity, so in the beginning the burning question was 'What should we be doing?' Doing meant organising or running something. There was a fear that to meet just for the sake of meeting each other was very selfish. We were a Community dedicated to reconciliation, in a city and country crying out for reconciling acts.'

And John Morrow, who led Corrymeela Community from 1980-1993, wrote: 'The work of reconciliation can only be understood within the concrete context in which we live and work. It is essential to understand the kind of divided society which we have inherited, if the witness of Corrymeela is to make sense. There are an overlapping series of dimensions to the conflict which include cultural aspects like British or Irish identity, religious tradition (Protestant or Catholic), social or economic opportunity etc. It is not possible to limit our work even to those dimensions and any approach to the Christian understanding or reconciliation must take on board relationships between people of all ages, disabled and able-bodied, from both sexes, from different social classes, of conservative or liberal temperaments and the wider issues of race, other religious or no religion.'

It is a quest for reconciliation through sharing. Corrymeela is, at its essence, about facilitating personal contact as a way of reducing tension.

Morrow says the value of the Corrymeela Community is that it provides a centre owned by people from both traditions yet independent of the control of the official political or ecclesiastical establishments. At Ballycastle, three residential units serve guests. One of these is specially designed for youth and young adults. Learning through sharing of experiences is the focus. Dialogue and encounters are also tools.

Morrow notes: 'Work for reconciliation must allow people to begin from where they are. For example, our awareness of the way in which young adults in urban society from areas of social disadvantage have been easy fodder for paramilitary groups has led us to work in this sphere.'

Care has been taken to draw young people from a variety of backgrounds.

In the years since 1965, the community has more or less stuck to aims it set, including training Christian laymen/women to play a responsible part in society and the Church, providing opportunities for retreat, so that people under stress, or wishing to discover new meaning in their lives may find quietness for readjustment, enabling industrial and professional groups to meet for conference and study, and through work camps bringing together crafts people and voluntary workers in a realistic Christian fellowship.

But as Morrow points out, the highly stratified nature of the society and the educational system (Catholic and State) makes it important to provide opportunities for people to meet in 'lived' situations. In this way they will discover themselves as human beings.

He adds: 'The value of a centre jointly owned by people from both traditions, yet independent of the control of the official establishments either political or ecclesiastical, can only be understood in terms of the norms of Northern Irish society.'

This is a sentiment that found echo in the presentation of Lisa Bullick to the Community weekend, when after describing the horrors of the Omagh bombing and its aftermath, she spoke with warmth of the visit William Rutherford paid to the Bullick family the day after the memorial service. 'I felt that the Corrymeela Community was in my kitchen.'

Therapy and Reconstruction

Armies for Peace in Nicaragua

Not long ago they fought each other. Now they fight together. As Nicaragua's Peace Promoter Network, former soldiers from the Sandinista and Resistance armies are using their military skills to set examples of discipline, sacrifice and self-examination in the reconstruction of this central American nation.

A nd Nicaragua needs these qualities. The country is poor, structurally poor, lacking in the skills and infrastructure necessary to economic well being. There are no jobs. None that would guarantee a decent living at least, for former soldiers or anyone else.

Nicaragua is also run down. Years of civil war have ravaged roads, communication facilities, farms, water distribution networks... And human relationships and sensibilities.

'Violence occasions both visible and invisible damage,' notes Dr Alejandro Bendaña, President of the Managua-based Centro de Estudios Internacionales (CEI). 'It is not only infrastructures, but relationships and self-images which require rehabilitation. Formal peace settlements and elections may entail the formal end of hostilities, but bitterness and antagonism may remain alive in a society, along with access to weaponry, which can re-ignite latent rivalries.'

It is a familiar story. Post-War is not Post-Conflict. As UNESCO's Director-General, Federico Mayor, points out, 'countries in post-war situations frequently continue to be characterised by political instability, insecurity and everyday violence.'

Idle armies are a danger. They may take up warfare again as a means of protest, survival or delinquency, sometimes consituting powerful armed bands, both rural and urban.

'Demobilisation is not synonymous with reintegration any more than the absence of war is with peace,' notes Bendaña. 'More sacrifices are warranted in the post-war period, which is not a post-conflict one, but rather a stage characterised by complex and prolonged processes of social, economic and psychological reconstruction.'

Once held up as heroes or models for society, soldiers often find themselves now treated as troublesome reminders of a traumatic past. Sometimes, when they return to their families, they are humiliated and persecuted. They begin to see themselves as misused: the mechanical implementers of others' decisions.

In Nicaragua, however, ex-soldiers are seen as assets. The country's infrastructure needs rebuilding. Soldiers have useful skills.

'There are a number of traits associated with war which are also indispensible in peace-making,' notes CEI's Bendaña. 'Dedication, sacrifice, solidarity, discipline, teamwork, administration and organisation.'

Hence the former Sandinista and Resistance armies have been re-mobilised. Via the CEI's Education and Action for Peace Programme, they are being re-tooled in the arts of peace. The first of these is to value peace, to see it as something worth fighting for.

'Often there is the proclivity towards violence and contempt for life that may carry over into civilian life,' says Dr Bendaña. 'Training must emphasise the importance of a full life, organisation and coalition building. People must be able to see the importance of not fighting. Training in conflict resolution can play a positive role: more than resolve conflicts, training is geared to learning to handle conflicts creatively and, of course, non-violently.'

The Education and Action for Peace Program attempts to build on the positive traits the soldiers already possess using a participatory training methodology. Open learning packs are designed and explained.

'Human training (accompaniment, as opposed to counselling, based on empathy, including personal and collective psychological rehabilitation) is the groundwork for technical training,' says Bendaña. 'Too often governments and agencies neglect the role of reflection in training - or ascribe it to the religious sphere - when therapy and self-therapy should also be considered part of that training/human rehabilitation.'

Workshops aim at developing a mutually agreed action plan based on the needs the soldiers observe in their communities, as well as peace-building strategies. During implementation, the action plans are regularly reviewed and developed. Thus, as Bendaña puts it, training becomes the marriage of ethical and technical contents, of social and economic concerns.

'The experience of groups like the team of CEI, in training soldiers and ex-guerrillas to take on pacific civil roles, would be useful for those working with urban guerrillas in Euro-North America (sic).'

At the beginning, he notes, the trainee peace promoters may be 'committed to peace-building and may do many things in the short-term to achieve it, yet they may not have envisioned what a peaceful society might look like ten or fifteen years in the future. The CEI's work in the seminars to develop longterm vision and articulate what types of institutional structures are needed in the future helps the promoters to develop indicators that would reflect both a concrete expression of peace-building in the present and a way to identify the changes that have taken place or must take place to build peace.'

The Education and Action for Peace Programme began in 1991. Its first group of thirty graduates emerged in 1993. Since then, these Peace Promoters have received refresher seminars where they evaluate the skills they acquired in the original course and develop new skills. A permanent peace course has evolved. The aim is to support the ex-soldiers in becoming multiplier agents for peace in their regions.

The CEI calls this peace building from below.

'In and of themselves,' Bendaña argues, 'cease-fires, elections and political power-sharing will not produce democracy and development. The institutional arrangements in each country remain understandibly fragile, as negotiated agreements at the top can rapidly unravel or indeed fail to hold much consequence for those at the bottom. Herein lies the importance of promoting peace-building and development from below... Contrary to many assumptions in the North about outside 'neutral' mediators as the best reconciliators, we would look to resources within a people in order to arrive at a self-sustainable reconciliation and stabilisation process.'

The results are very encouraging.

'Few images can be more depolarising than that of joint enemies working and caring together,' observes Bendaña. 'Demobilised soldiers from all sides of the conflict are communicating, building relationships of trust, and beyond that tackling common problems in a unitary fashion. Not that they have been converted, reneged on their past or abandoned old political allegiances, but rather they have established new working frameworks of reconciliation in a framework of tolerance and mutual respect.'

Governments and agencies also think that 'neutral' mediators are the best reconciliators. Those who come from outside the conflict area. CEI sees it the other way around. Only those who need the peace will keep the peace, its staff believe. The aim is sustainable stability.

This article is largely based on 'Peace-building and Reconciliation in Post-War Settings - The Experience of Ex-combatants and an NGO in Nicaragua', by Dr. Alejandro Bendaña.

The Remarkable Initiatives of the Community of St. Egidio

Long Live Dialogue

'The Community of St. Egidio developed a technique which was different than those of the professional peace-makers, but which was complementary to theirs. The Community let her technique of informal discretion converge with the official work of governments and of intergovernmental organisations.' (Boutros Boutros-Ghali, former UN Secretary General)

In September 1994, during the eighth International Meeting of Prayer for Peace -which included leaders from most world religions- 'some Algerian Muslim friends', recalls Andrea Riccardi, the founder of St. Egidio, 'asked why Christians, who often create movements for the defense of human rights, remain immobile when a Muslim country is involved.' Ricardi continues, 'It sounded like a challenge which needed to be immediately accepted immediatly.'

That year St. Egidio had been devastated by the assassinations of two of its members, who had both worked in the diocesan library in the Casbah of Algier. The Community had maintained strong relations with Algeria for a long time, particularly with the Algerian church. Groups from St. Egidio had visited Algeria every year since the early 1980s within the framework of interreligious encounters and exchanges among young people on both shores of the Mediterranean.

'War is the mother of all poverty. War makes everybody poor, also the rich.'

Within two months after the Prayer for Peace meeting, St. Egidio organised a first colloquium on Algeria in its headquarters in Rome. Leading figures of the ferocious Algerian conflict, including the government, were invited. Many came. The government did not want to sit at a table with fundamentalists at first, but the Community persevered and talks continued. In the end, the participants asked for a further meeting to continue the talks. The 'Platform of Rome' had brought the fundamentalists back into the folds of legality, thus creating an environment which would lead to more democratic, stable and peaceful conditions. At that moment it seemed the first stones on the road to peace in Algeria had been laid.

Lay movement

The Community of St. Egidio began in 1968 when a group of students gathered in Rome to read the gospel together. In the slums outside the city, they came into contact with poor immigrants. The students got friendly with the immigrants and started helping their children to learn to read and write.

Thirty years later, this group of students has evolved into a lay movement of 15,000 people, two thirds of whom are in Italy, involved in voluntary and unpaid service for peace and reconciliation in cities of more than twenty countries all over the world. They share a certain spirituality and they measure themselves against the Gospel. Though the organisation now has a link with the Vatican, its heart is still the small church of St. Egidio in the Roman quarter, Trastevere, where every evening prayers for the Community are held.

In the last few years, the Community of St. Egidio has been discovered by the media due to its peace initiatives for Mozambique, Algeria, Guatemala and the Balkans. It also has close relations with groups from many other countries who have been suffering for years due to injustice and war - Lebanon, El Salvador, Armenia, Burundi and the Horn of Africa.

St. Egidio's development projects were the basis of the reconciliation process in Mozambique. Over a period of fourteen years, the Community had established solid relationships and contacts with both parties of the internal conflict, Frelimo and Renamo. This ultimately led to its assumption of a central third-party intermediary role in 1990. With these activities the Community won much praise (see Box). However, in an interview with the Washington Post, 'founding-father' Andrea Riccardi stated that the diplomatic activities of St. Egidio would be an exception in their work, and that their commitment to solidarity had never stopped.
'Our mainstay remains our work with the poor. But there is no contrast or difference between solidarity with the poor and solidarity with poor peoples. War is the mother of all poverty. War makes everybody poor, also the rich.'

The Community had also taken initiatives for peace on an international level. This was in Lebanon at the beginning of the eighties. After a meeting with the political key-figure Walid Jumblatt in St. Egidio, the Community succeeded in stopping the siege of a number of Lebanese villages in the Chouf mountains. At the same time, Christians were allowed to come back to the village.

In Guatemala, the Community facilitated the peace process by organising two encounters between the then president, Ramiro De Leon Carpio, and the leaders of the guerrillas.

'We have noticed that direct communication could conquer many obstacles during the negotiations,' observed Riccardi. St. Egidio also invited representatives of the Sudanese conflict for discussions, which, according to Riccardi, is one of the most difficult conflicts of this time. 'We think it is important to keep our doors open but without forcefully wanting to repeat the Mozambique model. We are of course no professional diplomats, but also no 'dilettantes', like a certain press has called us.'

In the last couple of years, the attention of the organisation has gone mainly to Burundi, Zaire and Eritrea. At the moment, it focuses primarily on Burundi. Along with former Tanzanian president, Julius Nyerere, and the U.S. special envoy Wolpe, it has helped to slow down the civil war. Thus, the peace process has two diplomatic 'tracks', one official and the other unofficial. The official diplomatic track, called the 'Arusha process', is facilitated by Nyerere. It brings together all Hutu and Tutsi parties to discuss major decisions.

The talks are co-ordinated with an unofficial 'second track' led by the Community of St. Egidio. It has attempted to arrange an agreement for suspension of hostilities between the Tutsi-led Burundian government and the principal armed rebel group, which is crucial, says U.S. envoy Wolpe, in order for a political dialogue to move forward in the official process. Government delegations and representatives of the guerrillas have visited the Community's headquarters.

Former-Yugoslavia is an area where the Community operates with great reserve. There are already many organisations working there, in several fields. The Community does not want to cause confusion which might lead to a delay in the peace process. Thus, it has chosen to restrict itself to a project for humanitarian aid for Serbs, Bosnian Muslims, Croats and Albanians in a certain region. It has also established contacts with the Serbian church. According to the Community, the rigid attitude of the Serbs is partly a result of their isolation.

'The major problem of peace is to convert warring people into political creatures. '

The peace initiatives between nations are probably the most well known aspects of the Community's work. But it also dedicates itself to reconciliation between different 'worlds' within society, such as the homeless, the elderly, migrants, gypsies, the sick, invalids - through its fight against poverty and exclusion.

The Community also organises an annual International meeting of Prayer for Peace. Various religious leaders take part in this. It was started in 1986, when the pope Johannes Paulus II held such a meeting. Every year, the prayers are accompanied by cultural initiatives for friendship and reconciliation between peoples. After roundtables, workshops, and prayers of different denominations, all the participants gather for a common ceremony, where they sign an appeal, light candles and observe a moment of silence. At the end, the religious leaders share a sign of peace.

Over the years, the number of participants in this event has increased. The dialogue has also become more refined: fundamental religious themes and concrete problems on peace and society are now debated, including the war in former Yugoslavia, Africa, and the arms trade.

In August 1995, the prayer meeting was held in Jerusalem. For the first time, Jewish, Christian and Muslim leaders gathered at the initiative of the Community. After two days of

Peace for Mozambique

Initial informal negotiations, by Mozambican church members and leaders of neighbouring governments, had got bogged down because the conflicting parties could not agree on the process and location for talks. Then the Community of St. Egidio hosted exploratory talks that subsequently turned into formal mediation. The four observers were asked to become intermediaries: Andrea Riccardi of St. Egidio; Don Matteo Zuppi, a parish priest who is also a member of the Community; Mario Raffaelli, an Italian parliamentarian, and Jaime Goncalves, the Archbishop of Beira.

The talks made significant progress due to the patience and persistence of the participants and the synergy resulting from diplomatic-juridical negotiations coupled with practical wisdom. After two years, observers from the United States, France, Great-Britain and Portugal were called in, as well as the UN - implementation of the peace agreement would need deployment of a UN peace-keeping force. A few months later, on October 4, 1992, at the headquarters of the Community in Rome, the Mozambique Peace Agreement was signed. The unlikely team of peace brokers had softened the hearts of people who had waged war for more than ten years. At the same time, it set up a technically complicated peace process which resulted in the holding of the first free elections in October 1994.

In the book 'Peace is Possible', St. Egidio leader, Andrea Riccardi tells journalists, J.D. Durand and R. Ladous, he was caught by surprise at the change in Mozambican people who had fought war for all those years.

'Why did they fight?' he said. 'In the first place because they saw no alternative. And at the end they got used to the war. But during the negotiations I witnessed the evolution of the guerrillas who slowly changed into politicians. For me this was a big miracle. Because although in principle nobody wants to have war, ways of mediation are not easy to find. For that, you have to cut loose from the logic of violence, which is anything but easy.'

In 1993, Boutros Boutros-Ghali, then Secretary General of the United Nations commented: 'For many years, the society worked with utmost discretion in Mozambique in order to bring both parties in contact with each other. It did not keep those contacts for itself. It was very effective when it came to involving others who could contribute to a solution. The Community let her technique of informal discretion converge with the official work of governments and of intergovernmental organisations. Since this experiment, the expression 'Italian formula' has been coined for this unique combination of government work and non-governmental peace efforts. Respect for both parties in conflict and for those who work in this area are indispensable for the success of similar initiatives.'

To the world, it was a miracle that a so-far unknown and relatively non-influential organisation had played such a big role in this very important peace process. But, according to Andrea Riccardi, the Community had not become some sort of a 'ministry of international relations'. 'Our moral power during the negotiations,' he said, 'was being the mouthpiece of the suffering insolvent populace, sometimes the only one.'

Together with local missionaries, the Community had collected letters and petitions for peace. Riccardi will never forget how the leader of the Renamo delegation had found a letter from his father amongst them. He had not seen him for more than ten years.

meetings, three olive-trees were planted in the old city. In 1998, the event was hosted in Bucharest, Rumania, co-organised by the Orthodox and Catholic communities. Muslim, Orthodox, Catholic, Protestant, Jewish and other religious groups attended the meeting. It was the first time in history that Catholic and Orthodox communities had worshipped together.

'We Christians are people of the word,' says Riccardi. 'We don't have a different weapon. I believe in the power of dialogue till the very last moment. It is not easy. Dialogue means a conversion towards the other person: you have to try understanding him, and at the same time help him to change his agenda.'

The Beacon of Neve Shalom/ Wahat Al-Salam

Harmony gets a Chance in Israel

'We are in a situation of total chaos, but this course has taught me a lot. I didn't know the Palestinians' world at all. I feel terribly upset.' (Israeli teacher)
'I don't know where all this is heading. We must act and not just talk. The situation is so bad.' (Palestinian teacher)

Two weeks before the encounter at which these voices were recorded, a bomb explosion in a Tel Aviv cafe and the resumption of building work at the Har Homa Jewish neighbourhood in disputed East Jerusalem, cast dark clouds over the peace accords between Israel and the Palestinians. Could teachers from the two sides still meet and discuss reconciliation? Or would external political developments poison the atmosphere?

In the event, although cancellation was briefly contemplated, the encounter took place. Part of a long-term course that brings together teachers from various schools in Israel and the Palestinian Autonomy, it was convened in the borderline Jerusalem Arab suburb of Ar-ram. Participants said the bombing and bulldozer activity had made them even more determined to proceed.

Thus while in the maelstrom that is the Middle East, words are usually shouted across a great divide, the above Palestinian and Israeli viewpoints were uttered by two teachers sitting in the same room. Their backgrounds no doubt influenced the perspectives they offered. But the fact that they could exchange views without having to raise their voices too high, was evidence of a revolution of sorts underway in Israel.

The Oslo Peace Process may be near rigor mortis; on the ground, ordinary Palestinians and Israelis are being encouraged to cross the ethnic, religious and political divide and explore reconciliation and dialogue in the face of the sometimes discouraging external political reality.

Neve Shalom/Wahat Al-Salam is widely regarded as a beacon in this regard. Located on a hilltop in the region of Latrun, between Tel Aviv and Jerusalem, the co-operative village was founded in 1972 by Catholic priest Father Bruno on the principle that the two peoples and three religions in the region had enough common values for their members to develop a community together.

Mistrust and Misunderstanding

Israel has fewer than six million people, more than 80 percent of whom are Jews, roughly 15 percent Muslim, 3 percent Christian and 2 percent Druze and other groups.

Israeli Arabs form a minority ethnic group within the pre-1967 borders of the State of Israel. Many see themselves as Palestinians. And that remains the prevailing perception of them because they are ethnically, nationally, and religiously distinct from the Jewish majority population. They have voting and other rights, but are not completely trusted in terms of loyalty. Thus they have the awkward status of being within the State of Israel - and also being part of the Arab people with whom the Israeli government has a tortuous relationship.

Israeli Jews form a majority ethnic group within the borders of the State of Israel but, in the wider Middle East, they feel themselves a beleaguered and isolated minority.

Despite this ethnic equation, notes Mitchell G. Bard, writing in The Handbook of Interethnic Coexistence, 'the level of hostility that exists between Jews and Palestinians from the territories does not pertain to relations with Arabs within the "Green Line" (i.e., those living inside the pre-1967 borders of the State).' However, 'mistrust and misunderstanding are characteristics of the relationship between Israeli Arabs and Jews.'

The village, or moshav, got its first permanent settlers in 1978-79 as part of a private grassroots initiative. It has since evolved into a member-owned and democratically-run independent small community, holding firmly to its objective of promoting peace with co-workers, neighbours, and individually. Jews and Arabs live together peacefully in Neve Shalom/Wahat Al-Salam (or NS/WAS for short). In the words of researcher Grace Feuerverger, 'Their goal is to create a social, cultural, and political framework of equality and mutual respect in which the residents maintain their own cultural heritage, language, and identity.'

Centrepiece of NS/WAS is a School for Peace which opened its doors to students in 1979 and has also functioned as training centre for teachers and group leaders. It is a bilingual, bicultural, binational elementary school co-ordinated jointly by a professional team of Jewish and Arab educators. Some are residents of the village, others come from the neighbourhood.

Decisions are take democratically. The School of Peace conducts bilingual workshops, in Hebrew and Arabic. Encounter groups are held, and consultation provided on the making of peace curricula. By 1985, the programmes of the School for Peace had reached 5,000 Jewish and Arab school children. Many teachers and student-teachers had been trained, and workshop weekends conducted to promote understanding and co-operation between Israeli Jews and Arabs.

Summer evening adult-education lecturers began in 1992. A year later, the School for Peace had managed, in the face of political resistance, to have nursery, kindergarten and primary school units established and recognised by the regional council of the Ministry of Education.

Children from neighbouring Arab and Jewish communities began to come to these institutions. By 1995, the waiting list of applicants wanting to living at NS/WAS numbered 150 (both Jewish and Arab). Neve Shalom/Wahat Al-Salam is thriving. A large olive orchard covers the hillside and its sheepfold is growing.

NS/WAS sets out to be nothing less than an 'alternative model for life in Israel based on co-operation and equality'. The School for Peace adopts the same principles. A vast array of outreach programmes exposes members of the community -and the many Israelis and Palestinians beyond the region who have an interest- to the possibilities of coexistence in a country where the word has particular resonance.

The coexistence activities are directed as much at promoting more harmonious relations between Israelis and Palestinians within the State of Israel, as those wider afield, in 'the territories'. Within the State of Israel itself, the need for coexistence is great.

With the Israeli government having endorsed education for coexistence as a priority, and established a special unit of the Ministry of Education specifically for this purpose, three different approaches have emerged for dealing with Arab-Jewish relations.

First, the encounter approach. Members of the two groups are brought together for short and intense encounters during which they are forced to confront prejudices and the issues at the root of conflict. The experiential approach has longer encounters which concentrate on joint activities of mutual interest. In teaching for democracy education is viewed as 'recognition of the equal right of all people to freedom.'

All three approaches are linked by common elements, including the recognition that language is at the base of one's national identity. Arabic is an official language in Israel; Hebrew is the dominant tongue. Palestinians are mostly bilingual, but Jews do not have a command of Arabic.

'Language is almost the only resource at an encounter that carries a real potential for conflict between the participants,' note Rabah Halabi, director of the School for Peace, and Michal Zak, the youth project co-ordinator.

'Since each group finds it more convenient to use its own language, and since it is possible to speak only one language at any given moment, fertile ground is created for real conflict over the choice of language to be spoken in the room', they write in the School for Peace Annual report for 1996-1997.

Theory and practice collide when the School for Peace has to deal with this issue. Although the policy is to allow both Hebrew and Arabic as legitimate languages for use at all times, Jews are ignorant of conversational Arabic, whereas Arabs have spent several years learning spoken Hebrew.

Irish, Cypriot, Palestinian and Israeli delegations in an international facilitators course that took place in the School for Peace

Thus, eventually, during encounters, language becomes a tool, used to 'score points'.

One female Arab participant in an encounter said: 'I won't speak Arabic because the Jews think we're primitive anyway, and I don't want to strengthen their opinion.' But another student said: 'As Arabs in Israel, our language is all we have left to our identity - and you want to give that up, too?'

On the other hand, one Jewish participant in an encounter said: 'I was annoyed when they spoke in Arabic because I suddenly felt that I had no control.'

At the NS/WAS primary school, a frontal approach has been made to deal with this problem by setting up a special trilingual language centre offering training in Hebrew, English and Arabic. A large room has been set aside in which pupils can independently choose language learning tasks well defined and explain so they can work with a minimum of guidance. The centre's role is supportive of the regular language courses.

Grace Feuerverger, who spent several years studying NS/WAS up close, says it is the quest for understanding between the two cultural/national groups and for awareness of the complexity of the Jewish-/Arab issue, that is at the heart of the peaceful coexistence between villagers.

In her report, titled 'Oasis of Peace: A Community of Moral Education in Israel', she notes: 'As a result of the constant social and political tensions that arise out of the Jewish-Palestinian conflict, moral negotiation in the village continues at all levels of discourse. I was struck by how the villagers were constantly negotiating the space between the tensions of competing national aspirations and their personal attempts at coexistence and goodwill.'

In another study of coexistence initiatives between Jews and Palestinian citizens of Israel, Haviva Bar and Elias Eady say those who have participated in encounter activities have acquired a 'more complex and realistic perception of the conflict' between Israel and the Palestinians.
'This is apparent in various areas: legitimisation of the other nation's existence and recognition of its national affinity; awareness that both groups cause hurt and suffer hurt; recognition by Jews that they, too, have a concrete, active part in the conflict. Another significant accomplishment of encounters is that they reduce the feeling of personal and group hatred that is attributed to the other nation...'

An Intergroup discussion between Jewish and Palestinian Arab adults, will typically use a model developed by the School for Peace to faithfully enact the characteristic patterns of contact between Jews and Palestinian Arabs in Israeli society. It is played out in the following way.

The majority group (Jews) shows a lack of recognition for the realities of oppression and discrimination felt by the minority group (Arabs) and for the legitimacy of a Palestinian national identity. In turn, the minority group uses various means to control or quash the expressions of nationalism from the Arab side. Newly empowered, the minority group uses its assertiveness to bring about change in the balance of power in the room. Thus from a situation of majority holding sway over a minority, the situation is shifted towards a dialogue of equals.

'Neve Shalom/Wahat al-Salam is a caring educational community ... dedicated to peaceful coexistence.'

Once each national group gives up its customary role, the dialogue can be advanced. The expression of power by the Palestinian group, and its acceptance by the Jewish group, changes the balance of power in the room. There is an equal dialogue. This opens the door to progress in negotiation.

Of course, the conflict that made the establishment of the village and its school so vital, is never far. In the middle of 1997, plans were made for a ground-breaking art encounter called 'Art as a Language of Communication'. It was supposed to involve a group of Israelis and Palestinians engaging in artistic experience and creativity.

Just days before the workshop, two Palestinian suicide bombers blew themselves up in the Jerusalem market, killing many people, and leading to the Israeli government closing off its territory to non-resident Palestinians, depriving thousands of their livelihood. After much agonising, the workshop went ahead. Five Palestinians and eight Israelis participated.

'I worked for many years in facilitating groups who live in conflict and in developing models for this work,' said one of the organisers, Diana Shalufi-Rizek. 'Still, I cannot remember such a touching event as I experienced in this workshop. Art is a magical, wonderful tool of communication, which facilitates cultural contract with a strong and positive human rough.'

And Palestinian participant Fadea said: 'The beautiful thing that happened is our meeting, as Palestinians and Israelis, in a place that made it possible to know the language and the love that is in our hearts.'

At the March 1997 encounter between Palestinian and Israeli autonomy teachers that was almost stymied by a bombing, there were 20 teachers from each side. The participants were aware that they were breaking ground: most Israelis and Palestinians still have little contact. It was the first time many of these participants were meeting on an equal basis. The juxtaposition was evident to most: while this encounter was taking place, relations between Israel and the Palestinians were deteriorating.

One participant took note of the dilemma.

'The talks outside had stopped. Should we conduct meetings in these conditions? As facilitators, we face many other dilemmas: How do we bridge between differences and motivation and in the expectations that each side brings to the meetings? The Palestinians want action; want to discuss future relations; want to change the situation. The Israelis want a process that will enable them to work on themselves.'

But in the end, despite all the difficulties, there was a willingness to continue dialogue and search for a note of optimism.

Appendices

Appendix 1
Organisations Involved in Peace-building

Below we provide details of some of the main organisations involved in peace-building. We have listed the organisations first by region, than by sector. As this is an ongoing project, the list does not pretend to be complete. We invite our readers to inform us of other organisations which should, in their opinion, be included in a subsequent edition.

Organisations by region

Global

Pax Christi International
Oude Graanmarkt 21
1000 Brussels
Belgium
tel +32 (2) 502 5550
fax +32 (2) 502 4626
email office@pci.knooppunt.be
http://www.pci.ngonet.be

Contact: Etienne De Jonghe, international secretary

International Peace Research Association
c/o COPRI
Fredericiagade 18
DK-1310 Copenhagen K.,
Denmark
tel +45 (3) 345 5050
fax +45 (3) 332 5060
email bmoeller@copri.dk
http://www.copri.dk/ipra/ipra.html

Contact: Björn Moeller, secretary general

EIRENE (International Christian Service for Peace)
Postfach 1322
56503 Neuwied

Germany
tel +49 (2631) 83790
fax +49 (2631) 31160
email eirene-int@eirene.org
http://www.eirene.org/eirene.org

Contact: Eckehard Fricke, secretary general

IFOR
Spoorstraat 38
1815 BK Alkmaar
The Netherlands
tel +31 (72) 512 3014
fax +31 (72) 515 1102
email ifor@ifor.org
http://www.ifor.org

Contact: David Grant, co-ordinator, Nonviolence Program

Peace Brigades International
5 Caledonian Road
London N1 9DX
United Kingdom
tel +44 (171) 713 0392
fax +44 (171) 837 2290
email pbiio@gn.apc.org
http://www.igc.apc.org/pbi/index

Contact: Helen Yuill, international coordinator

Africa

African Peacebuilding and Reconciliation Network
P.O. Box 63560
Nairobi
Kenya
tel +254 2 49324
fax +254 2 48208

Contact: Hizkias Assefa, director

All Africa Conference of Churches
P.O. Box 14205
Nairobi
Kenya
tel +254 (2) 441 483/441 338
fax +254 (2) 443 241
email aacc@maf.org

Contact: Daniel Mulunda-Nyanga, executive secretary

International Resource Group
P.O. Box 76621
Nairobi
Kenya
tel +254 (2) 574 092/6
email kilenem@africaonline.co.ke

Contact: Josephine Odera, programme manager

Nairobi Peace Initiative
P.O. Box 14894
Nairobi
Kenya
tel +254 (2) 441 444 or 440 098
fax +254 (2) 440 097 or 445 177
email npi@africaonline.co.ke

Contact: George Wachira, director

Waijir Peace and Development Committee
P.O. Box 346
Wajir
Kenya
tel +254 (136) 21175/21259
fax +254 (136) 21563

Contact: Dekha Ibrahim, trainer

Catholic Justice and Peace Commission
Ashmun Street (near corner Mechlin Street)
P.O. Box 10-3569
1000 Monrovia 10
Liberia
tel +231 227 657/225 930
fax +231 226 006/227 838

Contact: Samuel Kofi Woods, director

Pan-African Reconciliation Council
P.O. Box 9354
Marina, Lagos City
Nigeria
tel +234 (1) 835 004/843 578
fax +234 (1) 264 6082/4

Contact: Ebenezer Adeolu Adenekan

ACCORD
c/o University of Durban-Westville
Private Bag X54001
Durban 4000
South Africa
tel +27 (31) 204 4816/262 9340
fax +27 (31) 204 4815/262 9346
email info@accord.udw.ac.za
http://www.accord.org.za

Contact: Vasu Gounden, director

Centre for Conflict Resolution
University of Cape Town
Private Bag
7700 Rondebosch
South Africa

tel +27 (21) 222 512
fax +27 (21) 222 622
email mailbox@ccr.uct.ac.za

Contact: Laurie Nathan, executive director

Coalition for Peace in Africa
P.O. Box 53 687
2139 Troyeville
South Africa
tel +27 (11) 614 4141
fax +27 (11) 614 4114
email copa@iafrica.com

Contact: Brian Williams, director

Institute for Security Studies
67 Roeland Street
Drury Lane Gardens
Cape Town
8001 South Africa
tel +27 21 461 7211
fax +27 21 461 7213
email Issct@iss.co.za
http://www.iss.co.za

Contact: Peter Gastrow, director

Central and South America

The Arias Foundation for Peace and Human Progress
P.O. Box 86410-1000
Costa Rica
tel +506 255 2955 or 255 2885
fax +506 255 2244
email arias@arias.or.cr
http://www.arias.or.cr

Contact: Fernando Durán Ayanegui

Centro de Estudios Internacionales
P.O. Box 1747
Managua
Nicaragua
tel +505 (2) 785 413
fax +505 (2) 670 517
email cei@nicarao.org.ni
http://www.nicarao.ni/~cei (Spanish only)

Contact: Zoilamérica Ortega, executive director

North America

Canadian Peacebuilding Coordinating Committee
1, rue Nicholas Street
#510 Ottawa, Ontario K1N 7B7
Canada
 tel +1 (613) 241-3446
fax +1 (613) 241-5302
email cpcc@web.net
http://www.cpcc.ottawa.on.ca

Contact: Janet L. Durno, co-ordinator

The Abraham Fund
477 Madison Avenue/ 8th Floor
New York, NY 10022
USA
tel +1 (212) 303 9421
fax +1 (212) 935 1834
email abrahamfun@aol.com
http://www.coexistence.org

Contact: Alan B. Slifka, chairman

Carnegie Commission on Preventing Deadly Conflict
1779 Massachutes Ave., NW, Suite 715
Washington, DC 20036-2103' USA
tel +1 (202) 332 7900
fax +1 (202) 332 1919
email pdc@carnegy.org
http://www.ccpdc.org

Contact: Jane E. Holl, executive director

The Carter Center
One Copenhill
453 Freedom Parkway
Atlanta, Georgia 30307
USA
tel +1 (404) 420 5100
fax +1 (404) 420 5196
email carterweb@emory.edu
http://www.emory.edu/carter_center

Contact: Joyce Neu, associate director of CR program

CDR Associates
100 Arapahoe Avenue, Suite 12
Boulder, Colorado 80302
USA
tel +1 (303) 442 7367
fax +1 (303) 442 7442
email cdr@mediate.org
http://www.mediate.org

Contact: Susan Wildau, managing partner

Center for Global Peace
American University
4400 Massachusetts Avenue, NW
Washington, DC 20016-8071
USA
tel +1 202-885-5988
Fax +1 202-885-5989
email salima@american.edu
http://www.american.edu/academic.depts/a
cainst/cgp/

Conflict Management Group
20 University Road
Cambridge, Massachusetts 02138
USA
tel +1 (617) 354 5444
fax +1 (617) 354 8467
email info@cmgonline.org

Contact: Scott Brown, president

Institute for Multi-Track Diplomacy
1819 H Street, NW
Suite 1200
Washington, DC 20006
USA
tel +1 (202) 466 4605
fax +1 (202) 466 4607
email imtd@igc.apc.org
http://www.igc.apc.org/imtd

Contact: John McDonald, chairman

International Peace Academy
777 United Nations Plaza
New York City, NY 10017-3521
USA
tel +1 (212) 687 4300
fax +1 (212) 983 8246
email ipa@ipacademy.org

Contact: Chetan Kumar, associate

Local Capacities for Peace Project
Collaborative for Development Action
26 Walker Street
Cambridge, Massachusetts 02138
USA
tel + 1 (617) 661 6310
fax +1 (617) 661 3805
email mba@cdainc.com

Contact: Mary B. Anderson

National Peace Foundation
1819 H Street NW, Suite 1200
Washington DC 20006
USA
tel +1 (202) 223 1770
fax +1 (202) 223 1718
email ntlpeace@aol.com
http:// www.nationalpeace.org

Contact: Stephen P. Strickland, president

Search for Common Ground
1601 Connecticut Avenue, N.W.
Suite 200
Washington DC 20009
USA
tel +1 (202) 265 4300
fax +1 (202) 232 6718
email search@sfcg.org
http://www.sfcg.org

Contact: John Marks, president

TRANSCEND (A Peace and Development Network)
114 Conover Road
Robbinsville NJ 08691
USA
tel +1-914-773-3440 (office),
fax +1-609-799-2581
email 102464.1110@compuserve.co
http://www.transcend.org

Contact: Johan Galtung, director

Asia

Gaston Z. Ortigas Peace Institute
2nd Floor, Cardinal Hoeffner Building
Social Development Complex
Ateneo De Manila University
Loyola Heights
Quezon City 1108
Philippines
tel +63 (2) 924 4557 /6076/4601
fax +63 (2) 924 4557
email peace@codewan.com.ph

Contact: Teresita Quintos-Deles

National Peace Council
291/50 Havelock Gardens
Colombo 6
Sri Lanka
tel +94 (1) 502 522/594 378
fax +94 (1) 502 522/594 378

email peace2@sri.lanka.net
http://www.peace-srilanka.org

Contact: Tyrol Ferdinands, general secretary

Australia

Conflict Resolution Network
P.O. Box 1016
Chatswood NSW
2057 Australia
tel +61 (2) 9419 8500
fax +61 (2) 9413 1148
email crn@crnhq.org
http://www.crnhq.org

Contact: Stella and Helena Cornelius, directors

Europe

International Helsinki Federation for Human Rights
Rummelhardtgasse 2/18
1090 Vienna
Austria
tel +43 (1) 402 7387
fax + 43 (1) 408 7444
email helsinki@ping.at

Contact: Brigitte Dufour, legal council

European Centre for Common Ground
Avenue de Tervuren, 94
B-1040 Brussels
Belgium
tel +32 (2) 736 7262
fax +32 (2) 732 3033
email eccg@euronet.be
http://www.sfcg.org/eucen.htm

Contact: Sandra Melone, executive director

International Crisis Group
Miniemenstraat 26
1000 Brussels
Belgium
tel +32 (2) 502 9038
fax +32 (2) 502 5038
email intcrisis@compuserve.com
http://www.intl-crisis-group.org

Contact: Alain Destexhe, president

Helsinki Citizens' Assembly
Veletrzni 24
17000 Prague 7
Czech Republic
tel +420 2 2039 7301
fax +420 (2) 2039 7310
email hca@ecn.cz

*Contact: Thomas Krasauskas, executive
director*

**Berghof Research Center for Constructive
Conflict Management**
Altensteinstraße 48a
14195 Berlin
Germany
tel +49 (30) 831 8090
fax +49 (30) 831 5985
email n.n@berghof.b.shuttle.de
http://www.b.shuttle.de/berghof

Contact: Norbert Ropers, director

**German Platform for Peaceful Conflict
Management**
Hauptstrasse 35
D- 55491
Wahlenau
Germany
tel +49 (6543) 980 096
fax +49 (6543) 500 636
email Jetztisigu@aol.com

Contact: Barbara Müller, secretary general

Community of Sant'Egidio
Piazza Sant'Egidio 3/a
00153 Rome
Italy
tel +39 (6) 585 661
fax +39 (6) 580 0197

*Contact: Andrea Riccardi, founder and
president*

**European Platform for Conflict Prevention
and Transformation**
P.O. Box 14069
3508 SC Utrecht
The Netherlands
tel +31 (30) 253 7528
fax + 31 (30) 253 7529
email euconflict@euconflict.org
http://www.euconflict.org

Contact: Paul van Tongeren, executive director

**Centre for the Study and Management of
Conflict**
Leninsky Prospekt 32a
Moscow 117 334
Russia
tel +7 (95) 938 0043
fax +7 (95) 938 0043
email umara@eawarni.msk.su
http://www.eawarn.ru

Contact: Valery Tishkov, director

Gernika Gogoratuz Peace Research Institute
Artekale 1-1
Gernika (Bizkaia) 48300
Spain
tel +34 (4) 625 3558
fax +34 (4) 625 6765
email gernikag@saranet.es
http://www.sarenet.es/gerniakg

Contact: Juan Gutiérrez, director

Christian Council of Sweden
P.O. Box 1764
11187 Stockholm
Sweden
tel +46 (8) 453 6800
fax +46 (8) 453 6829
email skr@ekuc.se

Contact: Lennart Renöfält, director

Life and Peace Institute
P.O. Box 1520
751 454 Uppsala
Sweden
tel +46 (18) 169 500
fax +46 (18) 693 059
email info@life-peace.org
http://www.life-peace.org

Contact: Mark Salter, communications director

Transnational Foundation for Peace and Future Research
Vegagatan 25
224 57 Lund
Sweden
tel +46 (46) 145 909
fax +46 (46) 144 512
email tff@transnational .org
http://www.transnational.org

Contact: John Öberg, director

Conciliation Resources
Lancaster House
33 Islington High House
London N1 9LH
United Kingdom
tel +44 (171) 278 2588
fax +44 (171) 837 0337
email cr@conciliation.gn.apc.org
http://www.c-r.org/cr

Contact: Andy Carl, co-director

Corrymeela Community
8 Upper Crescent
Belfast BT7 1NT
Northern Ireland
United Kingdom
tel +44 (1232) 325 008
fax +44 (1232 315 385
email belfast@corrymeela.org.uk
http://www.corrymeela.org.uk

Contact: Trevor Williams, leader of the community

INCORE
Aberfoyle House
Northland Road
Londonderry BT48 7JA
Northern Ireland, United Kingdom
tel +44 (1504) 375 500
fax +44 (1504) 375 510
email INCORE@incore.ulst.ac.uk
http://www.incore.ulst.ac.uk

Contact: Mari Fitzduff, director

International Alert
1 Glyn Street
London SE11 5HT
United Kingdom
tel +44 (171) 793 8383
fax +44 (171) 793 7975
email general@international-alert.org
http://www.international.org

Contact: Kevin Clements, secretary general

St. Ethelburga's Centre for Peace & Reconciliation
The Old Deanery
Dean's Court London C4V 5AA
United Kingdom
tel +44 (171) 248 6233
fax +44 (1710 248 9721
email Ethelburga.appeal@dlondon.org.uk

contact: Martin Field, appeal director

The Mediation Network for Northern Ireland
128A Great Victoria Street
Belfast BT2 7BG
Northern Ireland, United Kingdom
tel +44 (1232) 438 614
fax +44 (1232) 314 430
email 100714.65@compuserve.com

Contact: Brendan McAllister, director

Oxfam
274 Banbury Road
Oxford OX2 7DZ, United Kingdom
tel +44 (1865) 311 311
fax +44 (1865) 312 380
email oxfam@oxfam.org.uk
http://www.oxfam.org.uk

Contact: Suzanne Williams, policy adviser on gender and human rights

Quaker Peace & Service
Friends House
173 Euston Road
London NW1 2BJ, United Kingdom
tel +44 (171) 663 1000
fax +44 (171) 663 1001
email qpsi@gn.apc.orgcdwq

Contact: Bob Neidhardt, Conciliation programme coordinator

Responding to Conflict
1046 Bristol Road
Selly Oak
Birmingham B29 6LJ, United Kingdom
tel +44 (121) 415 5641
fax +44 (121) 415 4119
email enquiries@respond.org

Contact: Simon Fisher, director
State of the World Forum
The Coexistence Initiative
1, Landsdow Close
Wimbledon

London, SW20 8AS, United Kingdom
tel +44 (181) 971 5060
fax + 44 (181) 879 0883
email coexistence@worldforum.org
http://www.worldforum.org
http://www.co-net.org

Contact: Kumar Rupesinghe, director

Middle East

The Abraham Fund
15 Arlozorov Street
Jerusalem 92181, Israel
tel +972 (2) 566 5133
or +972 (2) 566 5136
fax +972 (2) 566 5139
email tafjer@netvision.net.il
http://www.coexistence.org

Contact: Rachelle Schilo, executive Director

Harry S. Truman Research Institute for the Advancement of Peace
Hebrew University
Mount Scopus
Jerusalem 91905, Israel
tel +972 (2) 588 2300
fax +972 (2) 582 8076
email mstruman@mscc.huji.ac.il
http://atar.mscc.huji.ac.il/~truman

Contact: Edward Kaufman, executive director

International Peace Bureau (IPB)
41, Rue de Zurich
CH-12001 Geneva, Switzerland
tel +41 (22) 731 6420
fax +41 (22) 738 9419
email info@ipb.org
http://www.ipb.org

Contact: Colleen Archer

Organisations as described in the cases

Track One

Carter Center, USA. See list of organisations by region.

Interchurch Peace Council
Celebesstraat 60
2508 CN The Hague
The Netherlands
tel +31 (70) 350 7100
fax +31 (70) 354 2611
email HCA@antenna.nl

Contact: Mient-Jan Faber, general secretary

OSCE High Commissioner on National Minorities
Prinsessegracht 22
P.O. Box 20062
2500 EB The Hague
The Netherlands
tel +31 (70) 312 5500
fax +31 (70) 363 5910
email cscehcnm@euronet.nl
http://www.osce.org

Contact: Stefan Vassilev, advisor

OSCE Secretariat
Kaerntnerring 5-7, 4th Floor
1010 Vienna, Austria
tel +43 (1) 514 36 113
fax + 43 (1) 514 36 94
email pm@osce.org
http://www.osceprag.cz

Contact: Ján Kubis, director of Conflict Prevention Centre

UNESCO
7 place de Fontenoy
75352 Paris 07 SP, France
tel +33 (1) 4568 0877
fax +33 (1) 4568 5557
email cofpeace@unesco.org
http://www.unesco.org/cpp/

Contact: Leslie G. Atherley, director CPP

UNIDIR
Palais de Nations
1211 Geneva 10
Switzerland
tel +41 (22) 9173186/4263
fax +41 (22) 9170176
email plewis@unorg.ch
http://www.unorg.ch/UNIDIR/

Contact: Patricia Lewis, director

Track Two

Balayan (Community Development & Volunteer Fornationa Office)
University of St. La Salle
Bacelod City 6100
Philippines
tel +63 (34) 435 3857
fax +63 (34) 435 3857
email chvbalay@uls.edu

Contact: Cesar Villanueva, director

Centre for Peace, Nonviolence and Human Rights
O. Kersovanija 4
HR- 31000 Osijek
Croatia
tel +385 (31) 20 6886
fax +385 (31) 20 6889
email: czmos@zamir.net
http:// www.zamir.net/~czmos

Contact: Katarina Kruhonja, president

Community Relations Council, United
Kingdom. See list of organisations by
region.

Institute for Multi-Track Diplomacy, USA.
See list of organisations by region.

Life and Peace Institute, Sweden. See list of
organisations by region.

National Peace Council, Sri Lanka. See list of
organisations by region.

Search for Common Ground. See list of
organisations by region.

The Mediation Network for Northern
Ireland, United Kingdom. See list of
organisations by region.

Wajir Peace and Development Committee,
Kenya. See list of organisations by region.

Churches

Dhammayaietra Centre
P.O. Box 144
Phnom Penh, Cambodia
fax: +855 (23) 426 400 or +855 (23) 364 205
email cpr@forum.org.kh

International Network for Engaged Buddhist
3000 Soi 130 Latprao
Bangkapi 10240 Bangkok
Thailand
tel +66 (2) 374 1671
fax +66 (2) 374 1671
email yeshua@alpha.tu.ac.th

*Contact: Yeshua Moser-Puangsuwan, regional
coordinator*

International Peace Academy, USA. See list
of organisations by region.

The National Council of Churches, Kenya
Church House
MOI Avenue
P.O. Box 45009, Nairobi
Kenya
tel +254 (2) 338 211
fax +254 (2) 215 169

Contact: Rose Barmasai

St. Ethelburga's Centre, United Kingdom.
See list of organisations by region.

Life and Peace Institute, Sweden. See list of
organisations by region.

World Conference on Religion and Peace
International
777 United Nations Plaza
New York, NY 10017
USA
tel + 1 (212) 687 2163
fax +1 (212) 983 0566
email info@wcrp.org

Contact: William Vendley, secretary general

World Council of Churches
150, Route de Ferney
P.O. Box 2100
1211 Geneva 2, Switzerland
tel +41 (22) 791 6111
fax +41 (22) 791 6409
email sal@wcc-coe.org
http://www.wcc-coe.org

Contact: Salpy Eskidjian, co-ordinator

Women

IFOR, The Netherlands. See list of
organisations by region.

Life and Peace Institute, Sweden. See list of
organisations by region.

Pan African Women's Organisation
B.P. 765
Luanda
Angola
tel +244 (2) 390 779
fax +244 (2) 390 779

Contact: Assetou Koite, secretary general

WILPF
1 Rue de Varambé, C.P. 28
1211 Geneva 20
Switzerland
tel +41 (22) 733 6175
fax +41 (22) 740 1063
email womensleague@gn.apc.org

Contact: Barbara Lochbihler, secretary general

Media

**European Centre for Common Ground,
Belgium.** See list of organisations by region.

Internews Europe
14 rue d'Uzès
75002 Paris
France
tel +33 (1) 5300 9313
fax +33 (1) 409
email magda@calva.net
http://www.internews.org

Contact: Magda Zlotowska

Inter Press Service
Via Panisperna 207
00184 Rome
Italy
tel +39 (6) 487 1363
fax +39 (6) 481 7877
email ipstv@gn.apc.org
http://www.ips.org

Search for Common Ground. See list of organisations by region.

Education

Children Teaching Children
Jewish Arab Center for Peace
Givat Haviva
37850 D.N. Menashe
Israel
tel + 972 (6) 378 944/ 372 352
fax + 972 (6) 372 355
email: ctc@inter.net.il
http://www.inter.net.il/~givat_h

Contact: Jalal Hassan and Shuli Dichter, co-directors

City Montessori School Lucknow
12 Station Road
Lucknow, UP
India 226001
tel +91 (522) 215 483 /229 738
fax +91 (522) 212 888
email info@cmseducation.org
http://www.cmseducation.org

Contact: Bharti Gandhi, director

**International Peace Research Association,
Denmark.** See list of organisations by region.

The Council for Global Education
1270 New Hampshire Avenue NW
Washington DC 20036
USA
tel: +1 (202) 496 9780
fax +1 (202) 496 9781
email info@globaleducation.org
http://www.globaleducation.org

Contact: Sunita Gandhi, founder/director

The EMU Promoting School Project
University of Ulster
Magee College
Northland Road
Londonderry, BT48 7JL
Northern Ireland
United kingdom
tel +44 (1504) 375 225
fax + (1504) 375 550
email SL.Callen@ulst.ac.uk
http://cain.ulst.ac/emu

Van Leer Jerusalem Institute
The Center for Tolerance Education
43 Jabotinsky St.,
P.O. Box 4070
91040 Jerusalem
Israel
tel: +972 (2) 560 5231
fax +972 (2) 561 9293
email tolerance@netvision.net.il

Contact: Amira Perlov, director

Corporate sector

**Community Relations Information Centre,
United Kingdom.** See list of organisations by
region.

National Business Initiative
Metal Box Centre
25 Owl Street
Aukland Park 2092
Johannesburg
South Africa
tel: +27 (11) 482 5100
fax: +27 (11) 482 5507
email info@nbi.org.za
http://www.nbi.org.za

Contact: Theuns Eloff, executive director

**The Prince of Wales Business Leaders
Forum**
15-16 Cornwall Terrace
Regent's Park
London NW1 4QP
United Kingdom
tel +44 (171) 467 3656
fax +44 (171) 4673610
email info@pwblf.org.uk
http://www.oneworld.org/pwblf/

Contact: Jane Nelson director policy & research

Donors

Abraham Fund, Israel. See list of
organisations by region.

European Commission Peace Fund
Windsor House
9/15 Bedford Street
Belfast BT2 7EG
Northern Ireland
United Kingdom
tel +44 (1232) 240 708
fax +44 (1232) 248 241

Contact: Miles McSwiney

The People To People Program
The Norwegian Secretariat
c/o Fafo
P.O. Box 21751
Jerusalem
Israel
tel +972 (2) 656 3406
fax +972 (2) 656 3416
email fafo@netvision.net.il
http://www.people-to-people.org

Contact: Jan Hanssen-Bauer, director

Reconciliation

Agenda for Reconciliation
Roman House
Greencoat Place
London SW1P 1DX
United Kingdom
tel +44 (171) 828 6591
fax +44 (171) 828 7609
email afr@mra.org.uk
http://www.mra.org.uk

Contact: Peter Riddell, secretary

Community of Sant'Egidio, Italy. See list of organisations by region.

Corrymeela Community, United Kingdom. See list of organisations by region.

Glencree Centre for Reconciliation
Glencree
NR. Enniskerry
Co. Wicklow
Ireland
tel +353 (1) 282 9711
fax +353 (1) 2766085
email info@glencree-cfr.ie
http:// www.glencree-cfr.ie

Contact: Ian White, executive director

The School for Peace
Neve shalom/ Wahat al Salam
Doar- Na Shimshon 99761
Israel
tel: +972 (2) 991 6282
fax: +972 (2) 999 2697
email: nswassfp@trendline.co.il
http://www.ourworld.compuserve.com/homepages/nswas

Contact: Dan Bar-On, chairman

Appendix 2

People Building Peace through the Internet – A list of Websites

Resources available on the Internet have grown rapidly in recent years, and material relating to the fields of coexistence, peace-building and reconciliation is no exception. Below you will find a list of websites related to these topics which provide useful 'jumping-off points' for further research. These are principally a selection of the websites collected and consulted in the course of this project. The list does not pretend to be complete. Indeed, we invite readers to suggest additional sites.

Coexistence Network
The Coexistence Initiative is undertaken by the State of the World Forum. Its mission is to catalyse a global awareness of, and commitment to, creating a world safe for difference. The website includes information on State of the World Forum and its activities and also contains a coexistence handbook.
http://www.co-net.org/

European Platform for Conflict Prevention and Transformation
The European Platform for Conflict Prevention and Transformation is a network of European non-governmental organisations involved in the prevention and/or resolution of violent conflicts in the international arena. Its mission is to facilitate the exchange of information and experience among participating organisations, as well as to stimulate co-operation and synergy. The Platform's extensive website contains general information, a directory of some 500 organisations, conflict surveys and a news, reports and action section. The 'People building Peace' publication will also be available online.
http://www.euconflict.org

INCORE
INCORE, the Initiative on Conflict Resolution and Ethnicity, is a joint initiative of the University of Ulster and the United Nations University. The INCORE Internet Service is a central Internet resource for those in the area of conflict resolution and ethnic conflict. It is intended to serve not only academic researchers but also policy-makers and practitioners. INCORE has a Guide to Internet Sources on Truth & Reconciliation that provides Internet resources around the particular themes associated with conflict and ethnicity.
http://www.incore.ulst.ac.uk/cds/themes/truth.html

International Fellowship of Reconciliation (IFOR)
IFOR has branches and groups in over 40 countries. They all have regional and national priorities and activities and are active in at least one of the five IFOR international

programmes: Nonviolence Education & Training, Women Peacemakers, Youth
Empowerment & Children Rights, Disarmament & Peace Teams or Interreligious
Cooperation. Information on these programmes is available on their website. IFOR
publications, such as 'Cross the Lines', are also included.
http://www.ifor.org/

Life and Peace Institute (LPI)

LPI is an international and ecumenical centre for peace research and action. LPI aims to
further the causes of justice, peace and reconciliation through a combination of research,
seminars and publications. On the organisation's website information is available on their
conflict transformation programme, their research and publications. In addition, some
articles from their excellent quarterly publication 'New Routes' are available on-line. Links to
sites on research and action on conflict transformation are also included.
http://www.life-peace.org/

TRANSCEND

TRANSCEND INTERNATIONAL is a peace and development network of invited
scholars/practitioners working for peace and development by peaceful means such as action,
training, research, and dissemination, under the leadership of professor Johan Galtung. The
website provides many of his publications such as 'Conflict Transformation by Peaceful
Means: the TRANSCEND Method' and 'After Violence: 3R, Reconstruction, Reconciliation
and Resolution.
http://www.transcend.org/

Transnational Foundation for Peace and Future Research (TFF)

TFF is an independent, small and innovative force for peace. It believes that alternatives to
the main world trends are desirable and possible -indeed, necessary- if humankind is to
survive and live with dignity in a less violent future. The website provides general
information on activities and publications from TFF. It also runs interesting highlights (news
and background articles), special features (peace activities, books, actions and analyses) and
provides press info on international conflict management issues, particularly concerning
ex-Yugoslavia, Georgia and the UN.
http://www.transnational.org

Truth and Reconciliation Commission (TRC)

This is the website of the TRC and contains background material on the Commission, the
work of the different commissions and press releases. It also contains resources such as
documents and articles written by the Commissioners and staff, and provides links to South
African media sites, NGOs and to other relevant sites. It is also possible to download the 5
volume report of the Commission from this site.
http://www.truth.org.za/

UNESCO - Culture of Peace

This project aims to promote values, attitudes and behaviours in people so that they will seek
peaceful solutions to problems. In working with a wide range of partners, UNESCO aims to

advance a global movement for a Culture of Peace. The website contains information on this project, and news, documents, interesting sites and their on-line newsletter. Furthermore information on the 'Year 2000 - International Year for the Culture of Peace' is included.
http://www.unesco.org/cpp/uk/

United States Institute of Peace Library
The United States Institute of Peace is an independent, non-partisan federal institution created to strengthen the nation's capacity to promote the peaceful resolution of international conflict. The Institute has a virtual library that features a section on 'New Truth and Reconciliation Commissions' with background information and descriptions of the establishment, mandate, composition and reports of such bodies in 18 countries.
http://www.usip.org/library/truth.html

World Council of Churches (WCC)
WCC is an international Christian organisation built upon the foundation of ecumenical collaboration that serves the ecumenical movement by encouraging in its members a common commitment to follow the gospel. Working together with members and interested organisations, the churches promote reconciliation, theological dialogue, sharing of resources and the vision of a life in community, which is rooted in each particular cultural context. More specific information is available on their website.
http://www.wcc-coe.org/

Appendix 3

A Plan of Action for the 21st Century-Creating a World Safe for Difference

THE COEXISTENCE INITIATIVE OF THE STATE OF THE WORLD FORUM

The Mission
The mission of this initiative is to catalyse a global awareness of, and commitment to, creating a world safe for difference. The initiative on coexistence and peace building has as its goal to formulate and implement a strategic plan, which will bring coexistence into the mainstream consciousness of people around the world. How can coexistence become a compelling and enduring vision for humanity in the 21st century? How can we avoid the human tragedies, the genocides and ethnocides that have characterised the history of the 20th century? How can we build a world where there is tolerance for minorities and greater understanding between peoples? What are the medium- and long-term steps that need to be taken to create a world safe for difference? These were the questions posed in a series of meetings, roundtables and consultations that have been held by the State of the World Forum during the last two years.

Definition
Coexistence is an ideal without illusions. Its objective is not the seamless union of opposites, but a practical relationship of mutual respect among these opposites. Coexistence does not deny distinctiveness; in fact, it encourages it, respecting the rich diversity in an ethnically rich global society. Human civilisation has developed institutions and cultures for nurturing coexistence, such as regional autonomy, federalism and norms to protect and enhance diversity and pluralism.

Over the last century different civilisations and cultures have developed methodologies and resources to enhance coexistence. These methodologies include: dispute resolution practices, problem solving, organisational development, peace studies, civic leadership, labour relations, truth commissions, consensus building, search for common ground, conversion (transformation) tolerance, prejudice reduction, pluralism, coexistence education, etc. These rich and varied instruments drawn from different cultures need to be made available as a common resource for humanity.

The Vision
The challenge is to honour both diversity, as well as coexistence among that diversity; the longing in all of us to be part of the whole, and the equally powerful need to feel our uniqueness. This requires new standards to resolve conflict and prevent potential conflict through non-violence and tolerance methods that are global in scope, yet locally relevant. The

challenge remains to develop educational methods and systems that will synthesise new and existing models of coexistence into mainstream education and political discourse.

There are over 6,000 distinct cultures in the world today which, for the first time in history, are being drawn into the process of globalisation and are coming into contact with each other. This interaction between civilisations, ethnic groups and minorities will have profound consequences for the evolution of peace and stability in the next century. In some cases this contact will be positive, but in some cases it will have negative consequences. There is no higher priority than to develop a culture of peaceful and co-operative coexistence within which all groups can interact and coexist. There is no greater challenge than the task of setting an example for, and teaching our children about, the skills required for community building; living in harmonious and co-operative coexistence with those who are different, and settling conflicts without recourse to violence.

Next steps in the coexistence initiative
The Coexistence Initiative of the State of the World Forum will implement a strategic plan in order to create a world safe for difference. It will be based on the following six building blocks:

1. Coalition Building and Networking
2. Education
3. Legitimisation
4. Professionalization
5. Institution-building
6. Communication

The strategy will be implemented by enhancing, strengthening and connecting existing networks worldwide. The programme will, wherever possible, be a catalyst - linking and nurturing initiatives with other organisations.

1. Coalition Building and Networking

Objective
Encourage a global network and build capacity for coexistence between peoples and communities.

Action
- The programme will identify communities, individuals and institutions who have been working toward peace, reconciliation and coexistence between communities. Leaders of this movement will come from all walks of civil society.
- There will be a carefully designed series of regional and global meetings of coexistence leaders. These meetings will help to synthesise the experiences already gained in different multi-cultural settings and explore other innovative methods of reconciliation and forgiveness. As a beginning, several critical regions have been identified: The Middle East, The Caucasus region, South Asia, The Great Lakes region in Africa, and Europe.

The objectives of these meetings will be to:

a. Share experiences and synthesise the lessons already learned in community building.
b. Encourage the establishment of an organic network of trust and confidence building within each region.
c. Create space for dialogue among communities.
d. Encourage national institutions to increase their capacity for coexistence within their countries.

2. Education

Objective
- To promote an educational programme which will instil a universal awareness of coexistence, tolerance and reconciliation.

There are two billion children who will inherit the earth. Every child in the world should be given education and training in coexistence, community building, conflict prevention, mediation, and world citizenship. Education that builds a compassionate human being by teaching universal values, global understanding, and service to humanity.

The process of educating about coexistence should occur on every level of society: teacher's colleges, schools, universities, foundations, NGO's, community groups, governmental organisations, in the media and corporations, and in all informal networks of people such as families, celebrities, writers and poets.

Action
- Promote the development of coexistence skills within the classroom, through teacher training and the identification of relevant curricula, textbooks and videos to meet those training needs.
- Promote opportunities for people to meet in settings outside of the classroom.
- Encourage dissemination of coexistence materials to teachers and schools.
- Identify and work with organisations that are already focusing on coexistence education such as UNESCO, UNICEF, Save the Children and the Global Council for Education.
- Sustain and encourage in each country the creation of Centres of Coexistence and Tolerance, which can lobby the government, the Ministry of Education and Parents and Teachers Associations. These Centres will provide resources for state-of-the-art textbooks, videos, and other educational tools, which will be disseminated throughout the educational system.
- Convene a meeting of Ministers of Education to share ideas on how to promote coexistence education within the educational system and to encourage the establishment of an office for coexistence within each Ministry.

3. Legitimisation and Raising the Profile of Peace-building

Objective
Make coexistence a legitimate instrument of policy at all levels of society.

Whilst many peoples and communities are engaged in coexistence and community building, these initiatives are not always reflected at the policy level. Politicians, governments, and opinion leaders must accept that coexistence is a legitimate endeavour. Conflict needs to be recognised as an essential aspect of human behaviour. The fact that conflicting perspectives exist needs to be recognised and ways of living together must be found despite these differences.

Action
- Obtain the views of experts in initiating A Declaration of Tolerance, Coexistence and Peacebuilding for the 21st Century. This declaration will be submitted for adoption by the United Nations.
- Examine the UN declaration on the Rights of the Child and see how this declaration may be implemented.
- Develop a 'coexistence index' which measures and quantifies the performance of governments and encourages an annual report on best practices worldwide.
- Encourage the creation of a Council of Elders, which can provide wise counsel and guidance in evolving the programme.
- Build awareness and support among national leaders that coexistence is just as vital a national interest as is the nation's own sovereignty.
- Invite world leaders to speak about coexistence.

4. Professionalisation

Objective
- Promote the professionalisation of the discipline of coexistence.

The effectiveness of coexistence can be enhanced by encouraging steps to professionalise the work. The professional 'Coexistence Worker' must be trained.

Action
- Help synthesise and critically evaluate the body of knowledge in the field of coexistence.
- Create the training programmes necessary to educate professionals.
- Encourage rigorous evaluation research to determine the effects of intervention on the moderation of conflict.
- Produce a worldwide coexistence directory.
- Encourage universities and colleges to initiate coexistence studies.
- Design professional development training materials and evaluation methodologies, form partnerships, do research and development.
- Teach influential adults, such as school principles and teachers, about this work.

5. Institution Building

Objective
Facilitate the creation of sustainable institutions promoting coexistence and reconciliation. To sustain coexistence it is necessary to strengthen and create institutions, which can ensure and promote diversity. These institutions need to be encouraged at the political and the community level.

Towards a Charter for Coexistence
We stand for a world:
- safe for difference
- which celebrates human diversity as an affirmative good
- which protects children and minorities from the brutality of war
- which promotes education in coexistence and cooperative problem solving for every child on earth
- which encourages respect for minorities by the majority, and for the majority by the minority
- which provides mutually assured security
- which promotes institutions for reconciliation and forgiveness.

Action
- Identify and strengthen existing institutions and mechanisms in civil society.
- Identify and develop funding mechanisms to support coexistence initiatives.
- Co-operate with the UN and other multilateral organisations in improving their preventative diplomacy capacity.
- Encourage and co-operate in developing training programmes on coexistence education with the UNDP, UNICEF and UNESCO.
- Co-operate with the Human Rights Commission and its sub-commissions on the Prevention of Discrimination and Protection of Minorities, aimed at the peaceful and constructive ways of solving problems with minorities.
- Support efforts of the United Nations Declaration on the Right of Persons belonging to national, ethnic, religious or linguistic minorities.
- Support the work of the Committee on the Elimination of Racial Discrimination.

6. Communication

Objective
Create an effective communications strategy for the promotion of coexistence and tolerance. Communications is the means whereby greater understanding and accommodation can be reached between communities and peoples. In the process of rapid globalisation the media can play an effective role in promoting understanding and tolerance.

Action
- Explore a variety of ways in which to communicate the value of coexistence. Engage in dialogue with the electronic media on how best to communicate success stories of coexistence, and how to encourage and sustain programmes encouraging diversity.
- Encourage the creation of a publication on coexistence and peace-building.
- Establish an Internet website to provide a "clearinghouse" for coexistence information. The website will provide a resource for coexistence workers globally, and will include the following:
- A directory of coexistence workers around the world.

- Access to methodologies, tools, and approaches adopted by coexistence workers around the world.
- State of the art curricula, books, and videos available for education.
- Stories of coexistence, audio and video clips of coexistence in action.
- On-line chat areas for coexistence workers to link with one another.

The Coexistence Initiative from the State of the World Forum is a global initiative which is intended to create a network worldwide.

The Coexistence Initiative of the State of the World Forum
1, Landsdow Close
Wimbledon
London, SW20 8AS
tel +44 (181) 971 5060
fax +44 (181) 879 0883
email coexistence@worldforum.org
website http://www.co-net.org

Appendix 4

International Fellowship of Reconciliation (IFOR)

Since the end of the First World War, the International Fellowship of Reconciliation (IFOR) has been committed to active nonviolence as a way of life and as a means of change. Its activities for reconciliation, peace-building and conflict resolution range from the interpersonal to the international. The International Secretariat, currently based in the Netherlands, works through its branches and affiliates in over sixty countries. Most spiritual traditions are represented within IFOR.

The International Secretariat currently offers services in four programme areas: Nonviolence Education and Training; Women Peacemakers; Youth Empowerment and Culture of Nonviolence. Services within these programmes include: organising training courses in active nonviolence; producing and disseminating information and educational instruments; and facilitating the exchange of ideas and experiences. Within the framework of the UN Year for the Culture of Peace, 2000 and the UN's Decade for a Culture of Peace and Nonviolence for the Children of the World (2001-2010), the IFOR Culture of Nonviolence programme promotes the development of peace education curricula, economic justice, unarmed peace forces, zones of peace, and inter-religious dialogue.

In addition to the general IFOR programmes, IFOR members have their own programmes and activities such as: third party mediation; direct nonviolent protest actions; and empowerment through indigenous cultural arts.

The Coexistence Initiative of the State of the World Forum

The Coexistence Initiative seeks to catalyse a global awareness of, and commitment to, creating a world safe for difference. The goal of the Coexistence Initiative is to create and implement a strategic plan whereby the notion of coexistence is adopted by societies worldwide. The programme will identify communities, individuals and institutions who have been working toward peace, reconciliation and coexistence between communities. Leaders of this movement will come from all walks of life.

To achieve this goal The Initiative has adopted a six-prong approach.

1 Coalition Building & Networking: The Initiative will host a series of meetings among the leaders to synthesise the experiences already gained in different multicultural settings and explore innovative methods of reconciliation and forgiveness.
2 Education: Every child should be provided education and training in coexistence, community building, conflict prevention, mediation and world citizenship; education that builds a compassionate human being through the teaching of universal values, global understanding and service to humanity.
3 Legitimisation: While many people are engaged in coexistence and community building, these initiatives are not always reflected at the policy level. Politicians, governments and opinion leaders must accept that coexistence is a legitimate goal.
4 Professionalization: The effectiveness of coexistence can be enhanced by encouraging steps to professionalize the work. The professional 'Coexistence Worker' must be trained.
5 Institution Building: To sustain coexistence it is necessary to strengthen and create institutions which can ensure and promote diversity. These institutions need to be encouraged at the political and the community level.
6 Communication: Communications is the means whereby greater understanding and accommodation can be reached between communities and peoples. In the process of rapid globalisation the media can play an effective role in promoting understanding and tolerance.

The European Centre for Conflict Prevention

The European Centre for Conflict Prevention is a Dutch foundation hosting the Secretariat of the European Platform for Conflict Prevention and Transformation. It facilitates, initiates and co-ordinates activities of the Platform. This is a network of European non-governmental organisations (NGO's) involved in the prevention and/or resolution of violent conflicts in the international arena. Its mission is to facilitate the exchange of information and experience among participating organisations, as well as to stimulate co-operation and synergy.

In February 1997 the largest-ever-public gathering on conflict prevention was held in Amsterdam, the Netherlands: The European Conference on Conflict Prevention. The 'Amsterdam Appeal', an Action Plan for European leaders, was drawn up. It presented terms for an effective EU approach to preventing conflict, urging NGOs to make their work on this new field more effective by building coalitions and sharing information and experiences. At two subsequent meetings, proposals for the establishment of an effective coalition were developed: the outcome is the European Platform for Conflict Prevention and Transformation.

The Platform strives to be an open network of key organisations, national platforms and international networks, and aims to include participant organisations in all European countries. By organising bi-annual Platform meetings in the country holding the EU presidency, the Secretariat brings the participating organisations together to discuss relevant issues of the moment, from thematic issues to institutional questions.

Having, as its ultimate goal, the building of support for conflict prevention in general, and for relevant policy initiatives at EU level in particular, the Platform seeks to
- facilitate networking;
- support (the establishment of) national platforms/contacts;
- encourage co-operation and facilitate exchange of information as well as advocacy and lobbying activities among participating organisations;
- initiate catalysing and innovative activities;
- initiate educational activities;
- initiate media activities;
- enhance capacity and expertise in this field in Europe; and
- encourage transatlantic information exchange and co-operation.

To fulfil its proposed function as an information clearinghouse facilitating the sharing of knowledge and experience, the Platform has launched several projects.
- Prevention and Management of Violent Conflicts, An International Directory (1998). This publication offers an overview of organisations and institutions worldwide working in the field of conflict resolution. This is an update of the 1996 Directory and includes more than 450 organisations.
- Surveys on conflict prevention activities in European and African conflict areas, focusing especially on local and international key institutions. They also provide brief background analysis, guides to literature, experts and databases. In 1999 the surveys on African conflict areas, including a directory of African NGOs will be published. Later publications will include further regions, Europe including a directory of European and North American NGOs in 2000, Asia in 2001, and Latin America in 2002.
- Other sources of information are the quarterly Conflict Prevention Newsletter and the Platform's Website.

The European Centre coordinated this publication and will continue collecting inspiring stories of People Building Peace. The Centre plans to publish a second edition in 2000.